Listen to Me

Note to Readers

THIS REPRESENTS THE 13TH BOOK in my *Bringing History Alive* series, and I have chosen to explore a different biographical genre. Some may ask, why Buddy Holly? The answer is three-fold. Music has long played a prominent role in history; documentaries often feature popular background music from a given era. Secondly, it is important for historians and biographers to recognize and document innovation and achievement in different areas, including statesmanship, science, literature, and music. Lastly, our own personal histories are tied to music; many of us can remember exactly where we were and what we were doing when we first heard a song that captured our hearts and imaginations.

Even though he only lived for 22 years (1,169 weeks or 8,184 days), Holly's music has transcended generations. Buddy Holly was, without a doubt, an innovator and pioneer of rock and roll music.

As a cautionary note, Buddy's birth name was spelled Holley. After his first record contract misspelled it as *Holly*, he never corrected the mistake and performed under that last name. Therefore, both names, Holley and Holly, will appear at different points in the biographical timeline.

Additionally, Buddy's close friend and drummer for the Crickets, Jerry Ivan Allison, at some point, either before or after Holly's death, decided that he preferred to be addressed as J.I. rather than Jerry; when this occurred depends on the source. For the sake of continuity, in this book, when addressed by his first name, I have chosen to use J.I.

Buddy Holly lives whenever rock and roll is played.
Sonny Curtis (singer, song-writer, musician, and one-time Holly bandmate)

Prologue

NEARLY SIX DECADES HAVE PASSED since a small plane crashed in a snow-covered field in north-central Iowa, killing three popular rock and roll entertainers, Buddy Holly, Ritchie Valens, J.P. "the Big Bopper" Richardson, as well as their charter pilot, Roger Peterson. That tragic day, February 3, 1959, later immortalized in singer and song-writer Don McLean's unforgettable ballad, *American Pie*, is often remembered as "the day the music died."

Many music historians credit the origin of rock and roll to Bill Haley, a native of Chester, Pennsylvania. In 1954, Haley and his band, the Comets, recorded *Rock Around the Clock*, which was featured on the movie soundtrack for *The Blackboard Jungle*. The controversial film centered on the lives of teachers working in an inner-city, racially mixed high school. *Rock Around the Clock* was such a success that it remained Number One on *Billboard's* pop music hit chart for an incredible 22 weeks (it was also the first rock and roll record to top the *Billboard* chart), and catapulted Bill Haley and the Comets to stardom. In like fashion, many of those same historians regard the sudden, unexpected death of Buddy Holly as the beginning of the end for the first generation of rock and roll music.

While Elvis Presley is widely acknowledged as the "king of rock and roll," unlike Buddy Holly, he was neither an accomplished musician nor a prolific song-writer. In a professional career lasting just 18 months, Holly, either as a solo artist or in concert with his band, the Crickets, recorded 10 singles that ranked among *Billboard's* Top 100 popular music songs (seven made the Top 40, three were in the Top 10, and one, *That'll Be the Day*, reached Number One). Holly and the Crickets also cracked the American rhythm and blues chart on 11 occasions (four made the Top 100, four were in the Top 40, and three made it into the Top Three)—a significant accomplishment for white performers of that generation.

Of perhaps greater significance, 27 records cut by Buddy Holly or the Crickets were among the Top 100 most popular songs in the United Kingdom (25 made the Top 40, nine were in the Top 10, and two climbed all the way to Number One). The distinction between the singles released under the name of Buddy Holly and those credited to the Crickets is merely a legal formality, which will be later explained in greater detail. Regardless of the name of the artist or the record label, Holly is always the lead vocalist, and in most cases, the lead guitarist. Holly's singles' discography, both in the U.S. and U.K., is located just after the Epilogue.

Holly's influence on British music is indisputable, and his tour of the United Kingdom in 1958 profoundly shaped the careers of future rock and roll stars, like John Lennon, Paul McCartney, Keith Richards, Eric Clapton, and Elton John. It can be argued that the so-called "British Invasion" of the early 1960s might never have occurred, or at least would have been delayed, absent Buddy Holly's prior *American Invasion*.

It is not mere coincidence that the first record cut by John Lennon's pre-Beatles' band, the Quarrymen, was Holly's *That'll Be the Day*. In addition, the Rolling Stones' first American hit was the cover of a Holly song, *Not Fade Away*.

In less than two years, Holly not only demonstrated considerable gifts as a performer, but also was a prolific song-writer and budding record producer. Insisting upon creative control in the studio, Holly demonstrated remarkable facility with the now-primitive recording technology available in the late 1950s. He soon mastered the techniques of over-dubbing, echoing, and double-tracking. During stage performances, the Crickets' original line-up, featuring a lead guitarist, rhythm guitarist, bass player, and percussionist, became the standard model for subsequent rock and roll bands. Holly was also one of the first rock and roll artists to use the famed Fender Stratocaster guitar to produce the genre's now-familiar driving beat.

Holly was willing to employ instruments not considered part of mainstream rock and roll, such as the celesta and the organ. For the discerning listener, there are hidden gems in Holly's tunes; drummer J.I. Allison tapping the knees of his blue jeans as the sole means of percussion in *Everyday*, pounding an empty cardboard box instead of his drum set in *Not Fade Away*, and playing rhythmic paradiddles in *Peggy Sue*.

Near the end of his short life, Holly pushed the rock and roll envelope, performing with a symphony orchestra. The aptly-named "string session," produced unforgettable songs, including *It Doesn't Matter Anymore* and *True Love Ways*.

Buddy Holly's voice is unique and easily-recognizable, with alternating falsettos, distinctive hiccups, and mesmerizing stutters. Who else could expand the pronunciation of the name "Sue" or the word "well" into six unforgettable syllables? Holly also had the ability to shift the tone of his voice from high to low without loss of pitch.

Holly's songs include driving rock and roll, like *That'll Be the Day*, *Oh Boy*, *Peggy Sue*, *Not Fade Away*, and *Rave On*, as well as gentler, romantic tunes, including *Maybe Baby*, *Wishing*, and *Everyday*. Some of his songs, for example *Well All Right*, are simple in construct, using only a rhythm guitar, bass, and the repetitive tapping of a lone cymbal as instrumentation.

Holly's popular, yet easy-to-learn melodies, inspired a legion of followers, including John Lennon, Paul McCartney, Keith Richards, and Bob Dylan. In 1986, *Rolling Stone* magazine ranked Holly as Number 13 among its "100 Greatest Artists." That same year, he became a charter member of the Rock 'n' Roll Hall of Fame.

Lacking the flamboyance of Little Richard and Jerry Lee Lewis or the sexy, movie star charisma of Elvis Presley, Buddy Holly was akin to the boy next door. Nonetheless, Holly proved that a rock and roller wearing eyeglasses could generate a sound that made teenage girls swoon and inspired boys to hit the dance floor with their sweethearts. While Holly's bespectacled face never graced the covers of teen magazines or appeared on the big screen, his music will last forever.

Buddy Holly's musical career occurred at a time when many religious fundamentalists condemned rock and roll as crude, immoral, and even Satanic. Segregationists crudely characterized rock as "Nigger Music." These narrow-minded, misguided views were held by many citizens in Holly's hometown. Not until years after his death did Lubbock, Texas finally begin to acknowledge, much less fully appreciate, the musical genius of its most famous offspring.

The circumstances leading up to Holly's untimely death are both sad and bitter. Believing that a significant portion of his song-writing royalties were being sequestered by his secretive, likely unscrupulous manager, producer, and early benefactor, Norman Petty, Holly was in dire financial straits, and felt it necessary to join the ill-fated *Winter Dance Party* tour in early 1959, which culminated in his premature death.

What would the future have been like for Buddy Holly? He had plans to construct a studio to record promising young artists. He also wanted to establish his own record label and publishing company. Holly would have likely continued pressing the envelope of rock and roll and eventually explored alternative musical genres. These are among the great "what ifs" in music history.

LISTEN TO ME: The Brief Life and Enduring Legacy of Buddy Holly is a compelling story about a talented, innovative, and ambitious pioneer of rock and roll music.

CHAPTER 1

A Wintry Night in Iowa

AT 12:45 A.M., ON TUESDAY, February 3, 1959, snow was spitting from the sky as Carroll Anderson, manager of the Surf Ballroom in Clear Lake Iowa, parked his station wagon outside Dwyer's Flying Service at the Mason City Municipal Airport. Wedged inside the vehicle were the driver, his wife and son, and three members of the *Winter Dance Party* tour, 22-year-old Buddy Holly, 28-year-old J.P. Richardson (better known by his stage name, "the Big Bopper"), and 17-year-old Ritchie Valens. The cargo section of the station wagon was stuffed not only with luggage, but also the soiled laundry of an entire travelling musical ensemble.

Mason City, population 30,000, was named after the Free Masons who had founded the community. Just a mile or two east of Clear Lake, it was also home to the closest available airport.

The three rock and roll performers were delighted to avoid another restless overnight trip in a poorly-heated bus. Ritchie Valens and the Big Bopper had already contracted head colds, and Buddy Holly feared he was next in line. Once they landed in Fargo, North Dakota, the Big Bopper was hoping to head off the infection by finding a doctor to inject him with a dose of penicillin.

Holly was excited about the trip, itself—he loved flying and hoped to eventually obtain his pilot's license. Famed disc jockey, Alan Freed, later recalled Holly's impulsive nature and fearlessness about traversing the skies: "If you tied two orange crates together, put a wing on it, and said it would fly, he'd climb in and take off. He always had to get someplace ahead of others."

It was 350 miles to Fargo, North Dakota, but only three-and-one-half-hours by airplane, allowing Holly, Valens, and the Big Bopper to arrive several hours ahead of the remaining members of the *Winter Dance Party*. They would have enough time to launder the group's rank-smelling performing outfits (that had been worn every night for nearly two weeks), benefit from much-needed sleep in a warm hotel bed, and still have time to prepare for the upcoming show in Moorhead, Minnesota, just a short drive from Fargo.

The airport in Mason City was nothing spectacular—a tiny passenger terminal, several hangers, a single control tower, and the headquarters of Dwyer's Flying Service. The small airport was not even equipped with radar, forcing incoming aircraft to lock onto an omnidirectional beacon before landing.

Jerry Dwyer, proprietor of the on-site company, not only operated six charter aircraft, but also bought and sold airplanes. A veteran aviator, he proudly advertised his business as: "Your Friendly Cessna Dealer."

Earlier in the evening, 21-year-old Roger Peterson had learned that he was going to pilot three VIP guests to Fargo, when Carroll Anderson, at the request of Buddy Holly, had called to inquire about a late-night charter flight. Even though he had spent all day working on aircraft engines in Dwyer's hangar and would not have slept for 17 consecutive hours by take-off time, Peterson was energized; he loved rock and roll music, and particularly idolized Buddy Holly.

An experienced aviator, Peterson had earned his private pilot's license in 1955, at the age of 17. Three years later, he earned his commercial license. By February of 1959, Peterson had accumulated 710 flight hours (including 37 nighttime hours), without incurring a single mishap.

By habit and training, Peterson carefully prepared for the hastily-arranged excursion to Fargo. Even though he was not an instrument-rated pilot (having failed the practical portion of his certification test due to disorientation and inability to maintain the aircraft at the proper altitude), Peterson believed that he would have little trouble flying by sight from Mason City to Fargo.

At 9:30 p.m., Peterson had personally visited the Air Traffic Communications Station (ATCS), located in the flight control tower, to check the weather forecast. He specifically inquired about conditions at Mason City, Minneapolis, Redwood Falls, and Alexandria, Minnesota, as well as his ultimate destination, Fargo, North Dakota. The station informed Peterson that each location was reporting ceilings of 5,000 feet or greater and visibilities of no less than 10 miles. Climatologists in Fargo reported the possibility of snow showers after 2:00 a.m., followed by the passage of a cold front at around 4:00 a.m. Before he left the airport to spend time with his wife at home, Peterson was advised that an updated forecast for the Fargo area would be available at 11:00 p.m. At this point, Peterson remained comfortable with undertaking the late-night flight.

As an added precaution, Peterson telephoned the ATCS twice more from home, at 10:00 p.m. and at 11:20 p.m. The communicator reported that all stations along the flight route were reporting ceilings of 4,200 feet or greater and visibilities of 10 miles or more, indicating no significant deterioration in conditions from the previous report. The only major change came from Fargo, where forecasters now predicted that the cold front would pass through at 2:00 a.m., two hours earlier than previously thought. The conditions at Mason City had improved, with a 6,000-feet ceiling and visibility of 15 miles or greater. The temperature was 15 degrees Fahrenheit, with south winds gusting to 25 to 32 knots, and a barometric pressure of 29.96. Based on the updated forecast, Peterson judged that the flight could be turbulent, but otherwise safe.

At 11:55 p.m., both Peterson and his boss, Jerry Dwyer, personally visited the ATCS to obtain yet another updated weather forecast. No changes were reported along the flight route, but conditions in Mason

City were somewhat less favorable—a ceiling of 5,000 feet, light snow falling, and a barometric pressure reading that had dropped from 29.96 to 29.90.

Jerry Dwyer later testified to the Civil Aeronautics Board (CAB): "As far as weather for the whole trip was concerned, we both agreed that he (Peterson) might have to stay overnight at Fargo, due to the fact that they predicted a front to move into Fargo at approximately 3:00 a.m."

For reasons that remain unclear, Peterson and Dwyer either were not aware of or ignored two hazardous weather updates. At 11:35 p.m., a flash advisory was issued by the U.S. Weather Bureau in Minneapolis, reporting that a band of snow was moving through Peterson's proposed flight path between Mason City and Fargo, and that visibility would be "generally below two miles in the snow." At 12:25 a.m., the U.S. Weather Bureau in Kansas City, Missouri issued a separate flash advisory warning of "moderate to locally heavy icing areas of freezing drizzle and locally moderate icing in clouds below 10,000 feet over the eastern portions of Nebraska and Kansas, northwest Missouri, and most of Iowa." The Kansas City weather advisory was scheduled to remain in effect until 5:15 a.m.

After receiving an updated weather forecast, but failing to receive or disregarding the critical flash advisories, Peterson and Dwyer inspected the charter aircraft—a red and white colored, single-engine, propeller-driven Beechcraft Bonanza, Model 35, bearing the tail number N3794N. The aircraft, which had been in active use for 11 years and accumulated more than 1,200 hours of flight time, had been purchased by Dwyer in the summer of 1958. When Dwyer acquired the Bonanza, it had already passed through 10 different owners, and required significant renovations. "It was in pretty tough shape. I went through that son-of-a-gun. (I) overhauled the engine (and) rebuilt the landing gear. I had everything reupholstered. I had everything stripped out of that thing," Dwyer's chief mechanic, Charles McGlothen, recalled.

Since the overhaul, the airplane had performed admirably. Three days before, Duane Mayfield, a Cerro Gordo County Deputy Sheriff and amateur pilot, had piloted the aircraft and deemed it "fit." Just a day earlier, Roger Peterson had conducted two charter flights in the Bonanza—a daytime excursion to Des Moines and a nighttime trip to Minneapolis. Peterson's wife, DeAnn, had accompanied him to Minnesota and back, remembering that it had been "a beautiful night to fly." While most of Peterson's training had involved piloting a Cessna, he had flown most of his charter flights in the Bonanza.

Recognizable by its V-shaped tail, the Beechcraft Bonanza was a high-performance aircraft. First manufactured in 1947, the plane had earned *Fortune* magazine's 1959 award as "one of the 100 best designed mass production products." Weighing 1,559 pounds, with a weight capacity of 992 pounds, the four-seat airplane could reach a maximum velocity of 184-miles-per-hour.

The distinctive V-tail had been designed with only two exposed surfaces, one less than conventional, straight tail airplanes. With a reduced surface area, the V-tail lessened drag, as well buffeting produced by the wings and canopy. However, during turbulent flying conditions, inexperienced pilots had difficulty handling the Beechcraft Bonanza, earning it a morbid moniker—"the doctor and lawyer widow maker."

Satisfied with their inspection, Peterson and Dwyer rolled the aircraft from the hanger onto the tarmac. Peterson then started the plane's engine and warmed it up for approximately 10 minutes. Afterwards, Dwyer filled the Bonanza's twin fuel tanks with 80 Octane gasoline. Once more, Peterson started the aircraft and allowed the engine to idle for a few more minutes, before shutting it down at around 12:30 a.m.

As Carroll Anderson and his distinguished passengers exited the station wagon, they were greeted by 15-degree temperatures, snow flurries, and wind gusts up to 35-miles-per-hour. Bracing himself against the bitter wind chill, Anderson glanced toward the still-starry sky, and concluded that the flight was a go.

Jerry Dwyer and Roger Peterson greeted their charter customers in the company office. While Peterson was excited about meeting the performers, particularly Buddy Holly, Dwyer had to overcome his negative preconceptions of rock and rollers. "I thought all entertainers got drunk. But, they hadn't been drinking; they were just real nice kids," Dwyer recalled.

Inside Dwyer's office, each of the three passengers paid $36 for the one-way flight to Fargo. Warmly dressed in a yellow leather coat with a fur collar, Buddy Holly informed Dwyer that his brother was a pilot and talked about one day purchasing and flying his own Cessna. After Holly inquired about the distance from Mason City to Fargo, the three rock and roll stars used a pencil hanging from a wall map to calculate how far it was from Mason City to their respective hometowns. Holly determined that it was 900 miles to Lubbock Texas, while the Big Bopper learned that he was 1,000 miles from Beaumont, Texas. Valens was the most distant from home; it was nearly 2,000 miles to Los Angeles.

Before the pilot and his passengers boarded the Beechcraft Bonanza, Carroll Anderson helped load items into the luggage compartment, located near the middle portion of the aircraft's belly. The luggage and large pile of dirty laundry, 42-pounds total, made for a tight fit, and the Big Bopper, who had brought his guitar along for the flight, would have to stow the instrument within the narrow confines of the cabin.

A group of teenagers, who had followed Anderson's car from the Surf Ballroom, watched the performers as they were preparing to board the airplane. "Thanks for the show," they shouted over the howling wind. The rock and rollers waved back and mouthed, "Thank you."

At the last minute, Holly remembered he had left his briefcase in Anderson's station wagon. When he returned to the car, the teenagers applauded. Holly smiled and gratefully addressed his fans: "Who knows how long I'll be on top."

Dressed in a red-checkered flannel shirt and light blue pants, the Big Bopper wedged his bulky body into the backseat, directly behind the pilot. If he needed to self-medicate his head cold in route to Fargo, the Big Bopper had formulated his own elixir—a combination of whiskey and mouthwash.

Valens, wearing a new wool overcoat shipped from California by his mother, a day earlier, occupied the passenger's-side back seat. After settling in, he pulled the coat flaps over his aching ears, hoping to catch some sleep during the three-plus-hour-flight.

Holly, who rode shotgun, was ready to take-off. Since the only entrance to the cabin was on the passenger's side, an eager Holly was forced to briefly climb out to allow Roger Peterson access to the pilot's seat.

Anderson shook hands with each of the entertainers as they climbed aboard the Beechcraft Bonanza. "I wish you all the best," he said, bidding them farewell.

"Thanks," Holly replied to Anderson.

Holly closed the cabin door as Peterson started the plane's engine. While the aircraft taxied to the north end of runway number 17, Jerry Dwyer climbed the stairs to the observation area of the control tower. As the plane neared its point of departure, Peterson radioed the ATCS for an update on local and flight path weather conditions. The communicator reported no significant changes in route to Fargo, but indicated that conditions at Mason City had worsened—the precipitation ceiling was now only 3,000 feet with the "sky obscured," visibility was down to six miles, and the barometric pressure had dropped to 29.85 (indicative of an approaching cold front). Once again, Peterson was not advised of or cavalierly ignored the earlier hazardous weather flash bulletins.

Inside the tower, Dwyer asked the controller if Peterson had filed a flight plan. The controller answered no; Peterson had informed him that he would do so, once airborne. Dwyer was annoyed; his pilots had been instructed to never take off without first filing a flight plan.

For several minutes, the Bonanza remained immobile at the end of the runway. Was Peterson suddenly having second thoughts about flying into the weather that lay ahead? Was he in such awe of his passengers that he was too embarrassed to tell them that he was questioning his piloting skills, given the present atmospheric conditions? With his boss, Jerry Dwyer, looking down from the tower, did Peterson fear cancelling the flight and refunding the charter fares? Had he become acutely aware of his own fatigue, after not slept for 17 consecutive hours? Did Holly, Valens, and the Big Bopper, eager to arrive at their next destination, challenge him to go against his better judgment?

The latter possibility is not without foundation, as Buddy Holly's *Winter Dance Party* guitarist, Tommy Allsup, later explained: "I wouldn't be surprised if (Holly) didn't insist on that guy taking off that night, if there was any question or doubt. (Buddy would) probably say, 'Well let's go, we can make it. You don't have anything to worry about.'"

Any reservations Peterson had about making the flight eventually abated. A few minutes before 1:00 a.m., he throttled the six-cylinder Continental engine, sped down the runway, and lifted off into the dark sky.

The take-off was smooth and Peterson proceeded to an altitude of 800 feet, before executing a 180-degree turn and heading northwest toward Fargo. When Peterson failed to file the promised flight plan, Dwyer instructed the controller to radio the pilot. After transmitting the request several times, the controller was puzzled by Peterson's failure to answer.

Two minutes after the plane took off, Dwyer braved the frigid winds and stepped outside on the walkway encircling the tower. As he watched the white tail light on the Bonanza Beechcraft grow more distant, Dwyer was concerned that the aircraft appeared to be "drifting gradually downward." Unable to establish radio contact with Peterson, Dwyer tried to allay his sense of foreboding: "I thought, at the time, that probably it was an optical illusion due to the plane going away from us at an angle."

Dwyer's initial instincts proved correct; it was no illusion.

CHAPTER 2

Lubbock

IF ONE GIVES CREDENCE TO the nonsensical, but often used adage, "you can't get there from here," Lubbock, Texas falls into that geographical category. First settled in 1891 and named after Mexican-American war hero, Confederate Army Colonel, and founder of the Texas Rangers law enforcement agency, Thomas Saltus Lubbock, the town lies 323 miles west of Dallas, and just 90 miles from the New Mexico border. In 1936, the year that Buddy Holley was born, Lubbock was home to 25,000 residents, and the closest city of any size was Amarillo, 120 miles to the north.

Until Texas Technological College, now known as Texas Tech University, opened in 1923, job opportunities were mostly in blue-collar trade work, cotton farming, and cattle ranching. The pancake flat terrain was dotted with pasture land and farm fields, with very few trees to shelter the wind. The weather in Lubbock has never been for the faint of heart. Summers are scorching hot and often bone dry. Arctic fronts dip southward during the winter, bringing ice and snow storms. Winter days can be highly unpredictable; in February of 1953, the temperature dropped from 64 degrees at daybreak to 21 degrees by noontime. Fall winds can generate massive dust storms, while devastating tornadoes are a threat in the spring.

The prevailing philosophy of Lubbock residents in the early and middle part of the 20th century was political, social, and religious conservatism. Known as the "City of Churches," religious fundamentalism, led by the Baptists and Church of Christ, shaped the community's social mores. As late as 1972, no package stores were allowed within the city limits, and liquor could only be sold in private clubs or bars outside of town.

White rule dominated in west Texas, with African Americans sequestered in Lubbock's eastside "colored town." All the city's schools were strictly segregated. Racism during Buddy Holly's childhood and early adulthood was as virulent in west Texas as it was in Birmingham, Alabama and Jackson, Mississippi.

At 3:30 p.m., on Monday September 7, 1936, Labor Day, Charles Hardin Holley was born in a rented house located at 1911 6th Street in Lubbock. Weighing six-pounds and six-ounces, he was the son of Lawrence Odell ("L.O.") and Ella Pauline Drake Holley. The newborn was named in honor of his grandfathers, John Hardin Holley and Charles Wesley Drake. From the beginning, everyone called him Buddy; the way his mother had it figured, Buddy's Christian name was "too long for such a small boy."

On September 8th, Lubbock's *Evening Journal* newspaper ran a small article about Buddy's birth. The announcement was filled with mistakes, misidentifying the infant as a "daughter," inflating the birth weight by two pounds, reporting the place of birth as the Clark Key Clinic rather than the family home, and incorrectly listing the Holley's home address as *1913* 6th Street. This was just the beginning of the local press misrepresenting or ignoring Lubbock's later-to-become most famous citizen.

Buddy had three older siblings. Lawrence Odell, Jr, known as Larry, was born on October 7, 1925. Travis Don followed on July 10, 1927. The Holley's only daughter, Patricia Lou, was born on March 7, 1929.

Their father, L.O., had been born on November 4, 1901 on a farm in the northeastern Texas community of Honey Grove, near the Oklahoma border. As a young man, L.O. moved 200 miles west, to Vernon, Texas, where he worked as a short-order cook and met his wife-to-be, Ella Pauline Drake.

Ella had been born on August 29, 1902 in Bridgeport, Texas, not far from Fort Worth, before moving to Vernon. She was proud of her native-American heritage—Ella's grandmother was a full-blooded Cherokee Indian. Buddy and his siblings could rightfully claim to be one-eighth Cherokee.

L.O. and Ella married on June 8, 1923, and a year later, they moved to Lubbock, where there were thought to be more and better job opportunities associated with the newly-opened Texas Technological College.

Lubbock became the Holley family's permanent home, where L.O. worked at various jobs—cook, a $12-per-week salesman at Thomas Custom Tailors (a men's clothing store), and time-keeper for boxing matches, before finally settling into construction work. Even during the Great Depression, L.O. always seemed to find work, but supporting a growing family was often a struggle. In the first 13 years of Buddy's life, he lived in six different houses; all but one was rented. Two years after purchasing their first home, L.O. and Ella had to sell it, just to make ends meet.

In the leanest of times, the Holley family was forced to use oil-filled reading lamps and burn cow chips in their heater. "I guess we were poor, but of course, we didn't know that we were poor," Ella remembered.

Throughout the most difficult of times, a tenacious L.O. kept the family afloat. "There was never a worker like Daddy. If folks couldn't pay him, then he'd work for nothing," Larry Holley recalled.

Everyone in the Holley family, except for L.O., had musical talent. While L.O. considered himself the "designated listener," Travis was blunter in his assessment, recalling that his father "couldn't carry a tune in bag." Ella, her sister, and daughter all had good singing voices. Larry played the violin and guitar, while Travis mastered the accordion, piano, and guitar, the latter of which he purchased for $15, either from a pawn shop or a fellow soldier, while serving in the Marine Corps (both Travis and Larry enlisted in the Marine Corps during World War II; Travis was a fortunate survivor of the bloody siege of Iwo Jima in 1945).

In June of 1939, Larry and Travis sang and played together on a program aired by Lubbock's *KFYO* radio station. It seemed only natural, if not genetically programed, that Buddy would follow in the musical footsteps of his mother and older siblings. At age five, Buddy insisted on appearing in a talent show, alongside Travis and Larry. Unbeknownst to his baby brother, Larry had greased Buddy's violin strings, such that they were inaudible. Buddy's enthusiastic singing of *Have You Ever Been Sailing on the River of Memories*, however, helped propel the Holley brothers to victory and a five-dollar first prize.

At age 11, Buddy took piano lessons. Even though his teacher believed he had an aptitude for the instrument, Buddy quit after nine months, without offering an explanation. For the remainder of his life, he would occasionally play the piano, sometimes when writing songs, but never as a stage performer.

After watching a school classmate play a guitar, Buddy focused exclusively on stringed instruments. When his parents bought him a steel guitar, Buddy explained that he really wanted an acoustic instrument. "I want one like Travis has," he complained.

When Buddy was 12-years-old, L.O. and Ella purchased a used Harmony acoustic guitar for him at a pawn shop. From that point forward, Buddy was largely self-taught, eventually learning to play the guitar, mandolin, and banjo.

"I taught him a few basic chords—G, C, D, A, and E. And before long, he was telling me, 'No, Travis, you're playing it wrong; it should go like this,'" Buddy's older brother remembered.

"Buddy was very quick to learn. Mother used to say it was a shame that he wasn't so quick in applying himself to arithmetic and spelling," Travis added.

By the sixth grade, Buddy could play *Lovesick Blues*; a record made famous by his first music idol, Hank Williams. Holley admired William's mournful voice, which he learned to mimic. Not surprisingly, Lubbock-area radio stations played mostly country and western records, and Buddy was heavily influenced not only by Hank Williams, but also Jimmie Rodgers, Hank Snow, Bob Wills, and the Carter Family. He also listened to bluegrass musicians, like Bill Monroe, Lester Flatt and Earl

Scruggs, and Jim and Jesse. After learning to play the banjo and mandolin, bluegrass tunes joined country music as part of Buddy's musical repertoire.

Buddy was also drawn to gospel music—a genre that would interest him for the rest of his life. He particularly fancied Mahalia Jackson's *Move on Up a Little Higher*.

Throughout his life, Buddy was restless and impulsive. Buddy's first grade teacher at Roscoe Wilson Elementary School wrote on his report card: "Buddy bothers his neighbors in school." Though he was shy by nature, Buddy possessed a mischievous streak, and his laugh was described by another teacher as "infectious."

Holley's childhood was not unlike that of other lower to middle class children in Texas; he was a Cub Scout, a soap-box derby racer, and enjoyed playing baseball, fishing, and rabbit hunting. These activities, in addition to music, invariably took precedence over his school work.

While his family's means were modest, Holley was remarkably neat and fastidious in appearance. Throughout his life, Buddy would dress as sharply as his budget would allow.

In 1946, when his family moved outside the city limits of Lubbock, Buddy was forced to transfer to Roosevelt Elementary School, which entailed a lengthy daily bus commute. At his new school, Buddy was popular enough to be elected, along with a female classmate, Barbara Denning, as King and Queen of the Sixth Grade. During bus rides to and from school, he would entertain fellow students by playing his guitar and singing popular country and western songs.

At some point in 1949, when he was either 12 or 13-years-old, Buddy recorded Hank Snow's hit, *My Two Timin' Woman*, on a wire recorder that a friend, who worked at an electronics store, temporarily loaned him.

At age 13, Buddy began seventh grade at J.T. Hutchinson Junior High School. There, he met other aspiring musical entertainers, including singer and guitarist, Bob Montgomery, and Don Guess, a song-writer, bass-player, and steel guitarist, as well as Jerry Allison, who was developing into a skilled percussionist.

Born on May 12, 1937, in Lampasas, Texas, located 300 miles southeast of Lubbock, Bob Montgomery was the son of a construction worker. In 1949, the Montgomery family moved to Lubbock, and not long afterwards, Bob met Buddy Holly. With a shared passion for making music, the pair soon developed a lifelong friendship.

Buddy and Bob often practiced playing guitars and singing at their parents' homes. At one point, the boys managed to obtain a wire recorder, which preserved their versions of popular country and western (C & W) tunes they heard on the *Grand Ole Opry* (aired by Nashville's *WSM*), the *Louisiana Hayride* (presented by Shreveport, Louisiana's *KWKH*), and the *Big D Jamboree* in Dallas (hosted by radio station *KRLD*).

The duo eventually formed a band, with Bob playing guitar and singing lead vocals, while Buddy harmonized and played various stringed instruments. Montgomery explained the influence of bluegrass on their early performances: "When we started out, we were doing the Lester Flatt and Earl Scruggs songs, and Buddy played the banjo and mandolin for a while."

In 1950, Holley and Montgomery performed at parents' night at J.T. Hutchinson Junior High School, during which time they sang *Too Old to Cut the Mustard*, which was dedicated to the teachers in the crowd. In the resulting hullabaloo, Buddy's mother feared he might be expelled, but her youngest son apparently managed to avoid serious punishment.

In addition to their strident work ethic, the Holley family was intensely religious and regularly worshiped at the Tabernacle Baptist Church. L.O., Larry, and Travis served as deacons at the church, where members were expected to tithe 10 percent of their annual income. Tabernacle was home to a particularly conservative sect of Baptists who believed in a strict interpretation of the Bible and the literal existence of Heaven and Hell. The contrast between his religious upbringing and later involvement in rock and roll music would often create moral dilemmas for Buddy.

L.O. tended to be somewhat distant from his youngest son, perhaps a by-product of Buddy's stubborn and rebellious streak, and he consequently delegated most of the parenting responsibilities to Ella. Nonetheless, L.O. grumbled that Buddy was "tied to his mother" by "his umbilical cord."

Travis and Larry were both rugged and hard-working, like their father. Unlike Travis, who tended to be shy, Larry was more adventurous and fun-loving, which fostered a lasting bond with his youngest brother. Throughout his life, Buddy sought Larry's advice on matters, both practical and intensely private. "Buddy seemed to think I hung the moon, because I was an older brother and had been around a little," Larry remembered.

Larry eventually founded Lubbock Ceramic Tile, where both he and Travis worked. As he grew older, Buddy occasionally worked part-time for Larry.

In September of 1952, Holley matriculated to Tom S. Lubbock High School. At age 16, Buddy's appearance was anything but glamorous. A year earlier, when his vision was discovered to be severely impaired (20/800), Buddy had been fitted with eyeglasses. He was also afflicted with severe adolescent acne and crooked, discolored teeth; Buddy's absence of a pearly-white smile was a by-product of west Texas' over-fluoridated water supply.

"He was what we'd call a nerd. I don't think any of us took him seriously in those days," classmate, Jane Livermore recalled. Another female classmate remembered the future rock and roll star as shy and introverted: "Buddy looked like he was afraid that someone would talk to him." His freshman homeroom teacher saw a somewhat different side: "He was just a little fellow, very short. Buddy Holley was rather hyper—bubbly and vivacious. He didn't want to study. He bounced around in his seat, refusing to open a book. I worked with him gently, and after the first few days, he settled down."

At this impressionable age, Buddy was likely feeling somewhat ostracized and uncertain about his future. The less talented singers and musicians in the area envied and shunned him, which lessened his popularity. And, while Holley knew he was talented, he justifiably questioned whether his goal of becoming a professional entertainer was realistic.

During his sophomore year, Buddy hit a growth spurt and shot up to his adult height of five-feet, 11-inches. Even then, he remained a rail thin 145 pounds. The upsurge in stature, however, seemed to give him more confidence.

Continuing his habit from childhood, Buddy maintained a fastidious appearance, wearing starched shirts, creased blue jeans, and shined penny loafers. Because of his narrow waist, Buddy asked his mother to take in both legs of his jeans, thus tailoring them to be more firm-fitting.

While never a scholar, Buddy's report cards contained mostly A and B grades. English was his favorite subject, and Holley's handwriting was neat and legible. In 1953, Buddy was assigned an English essay, entitled "My Biography." Near the end of the paper, he revealed his ambitions, which were tempered by reality: "…I have many hobbies. Some of these are hunting, fishing, leatherwork, reading, painting, and playing western music. I have thought of making a career out of western music if I am good enough, but I will just have to wait and see how that turns out. I like drafting and have thought a lot about making it my life's work, but I guess everything will just have to wait and turn out for the best. Well, that's my life to the present date, and though it may seem awful and full of calamities, I'd sure be in bad shape without it."

Throughout high school, music never strayed far from Holley's mind, and he was active in two acapella choirs—the Choralaires and Westernaires. Once Buddy and his various bandmates began performing publicly and staying out late on school nights, he started skipping classes. On at least one occasion, he was expelled from geometry for failure to complete assignments.

By age 15, Buddy was dating the girl of his dreams. Buddy had first met Echo Elaine McGuire when they were both eight-year-old students at Roscoe Wilson Elementary School. Echo was a petite, attractive brunette with a radiant smile, and unlike Buddy, was a serious-minded, straight A student. Echo's father, O.W. "Mac" McGuire owned a dry-cleaning business, which placed her family on a higher economic and social level than Holley's. Nonetheless, Echo's mother and father grew fond of Buddy, who was brought up to be polite and well-mannered.

Buddy and Echo's first date was a high school football game, followed by a stop at Lubbock's adolescent gathering place, the HI-D-HO drive-in restaurant. Subsequent dates were simple affairs—roller skating, horseback riding, and playing ping pong at Echo's house, followed by a trip to the drug store to purchase a Coca-Cola. The relationship remained innocent and proper, as Echo later recalled: "Buddy didn't even kiss me until we'd been together for a year." The pair dated throughout high school and began talking about marriage.

Following the custom of the day, Echo wore Buddy's senior class ring on a chain around her neck. Utilizing his self-taught skills as a leather worker, Buddy hand-crafted his girlfriend a belt embroidered with her name.

The youthful romance, however, encountered what would eventually prove to be insurmountable obstacles—religion and music. The staunch conservatism of Buddy's Tabernacle Baptist paled in comparison to Echo's Church of Christ. "For some reason, Church of Christ kids have the idea that people who are not Church of Christ are not going to Heaven. That just infuriates Baptists," Buddy's brother, Larry, complained. Larry had previously dated and broken up with two girls who attended the Church of Christ: "Our two churches just don't see eyeball to eyeball on anything."

Of note, the Church of Christ did not permit music during their services. This, alone, was an anathema to Buddy, who lived for music.

Buddy tried to bridge the chasm, and often attended services at Echo's church. He even skipped the Lubbock High School Senior Prom, where Echo was forbidden to enjoy the music and participate in the dancing; instead, he escorted her to the Church of Christ banquet.

Even though Buddy would later use a portion of his first song-writing royalty check to purchase new pews for his home church, he could be mischievously irreverent. Echo remembered one such occasion, when she accompanied him to the Tabernacle Baptist Church: "The minister was asking for donations for missionary work and he looked at Buddy and said, 'How about you Buddy? Will you give ten dollars?' Buddy said, 'Do you think I'd be here if I had ten dollars?' I turned several shades of pink and almost crawled under the pew."

McGuire's parents forbid her from attending any of Buddy's musical performances. "I came from a very conservative background, and I didn't even dance. So, when Buddy would play for dances, I did not go. He accepted that as the way I was, but it was a separation between us," Echo later recalled.

When Buddy's musical interest shifted from country and western to rock and roll, it hastened the eventual demise of their teenage romance. Even though he was in love with Echo, his passion for music appeared greater. Niki Sullivan, who would later play guitar alongside Buddy, was certain that his fellow bandmate had no intention of abandoning his dreams. "If Buddy had a choice of going out on a date or playing his guitar, he'd play his guitar. Music was more important to him, though he and Echo did go steady," Sullivan remembered.

Having cut their musical teeth on traditional country and bluegrass tunes, Buddy and many of his teenage contemporaries were irresistibly drawn to what segregationists derisively labeled as "Nigger Music"—rhythm and blues (R & B), whose origin can be traced to the late 1930s. The music of R & B artists, like Antoine "Fats" Domino, the Drifters, Muddy Waters, Little Walter, Howlin' Wolf, Lightnin' Hopkins, Lonnie Johnson, Leadbelly, the Dominoes, and the Clovers, mesmerized Buddy and other young musicians. Buddy quickly fell in love with the up-tempo beat, rhythmic percussion, and unrestrained guitar riffs of R & B. Eventually, Holley supplemented his acoustic instrument with a Les Paul Gold Top electric guitar, which featured knobs to adjust the volume, allowing him to more closely mimic the R & B sound.

Disc jockeys in the segregated south were not allowed to play rhythm and blues records until late at night. In Lubbock, Buddy and other young R & B aficionados never expected their conservative fellow citizens to approve of, much less accept, this so-called "jungle music."

Not surprisingly, there were no rhythm and blues stations in west Texas. Consequently, anyone who wanted to hear R & B records had to wait until late night, after the local stations had signed off for the day, before tuning their radio dials to pick up distant programs.

Since direct current-powered radios were better able to pick up long-distance signals, Buddy and other R & B fans would sit in their cars and listen to programs like *Stan's Record Rack*, hosted by Shreveport record store owner, Frank "Gatemouth" Page, at radio station *KWKH*. Five-hundred-thirty-four-miles east of Lubbock, the radio program aired at 10:30 p.m. each night and featured R & B music. Buddy's friend and aspiring musician/songwriter, Sonny Curtis, would often spend the night at the Holley's house, so the two of them could listen to the distant radio broadcasts. Curtis remembered that those late-night programs were a prime source of Buddy's "blues influence." Lubbock disk jockey, Ben Hall, was also a frequent nighttime R & B listener: "You'd have to put the antennae right up. Even then, the signal often used to fade, and you'd have to turn the car around to make it louder. You'd keep turning the car this way and that through the number..."

Even though Buddy had been raised as a segregationist, his growing interest in R & B directly challenged prevailing social mores. This uncharacteristic racial enlightenment, which persisted for the remainder of Buddy's life, proved that music could trump bigotry. Buddy's adolescent revolt against Jim Crow was epitomized by the name he chose for his cat—*Booker T.* (in honor of Booker T. Washington, the educator, writer, and founder of Alabama's Tuskegee Institute).

In 1951, 15-year-old Buddy Holley began to transform his dreams of being a musical entertainer into reality. Jack Neal, a teenager who worked as a construction workers' assistant for Buddy's father, was also an aspiring performer. Born in Fort Worth, on March 3, 1934, Neal was a gifted guitarist and country music fan.

"At lunchtime, I'd get my guitar out of the car and sit and play out in the sun. One day, Mr. L.O. Holley saw me and said, 'My boy, Buddy, plays guitar, too. You all ought to get together,'" Neal recalled. That very night Buddy and Jack met for the first time, and immediately started playing and singing country and gospel songs. The duo harmonized well, and Buddy realized, with more practice time, they could perform on stage. Neal clearly recalled their first jam session: "I played rhythm and Buddy played lead."

Even though Jack was two years older than Buddy, the pair bonded from the start. Neal, whose kinfolk lived in Tahoka, some 100 miles south of Lubbock, often invited Buddy to go horseback riding, fishing, and hunting for ducks, coyotes, bobcats, and foxes.

Before long, they formed a two-man band, christened "Buddy and Jack," and participated in area talent shows, one of which was televised. While Jack sang lead vocals and played rhythm guitar, Buddy polished his skills as lead guitarist, while the pair performed traditional C & W tunes.

Away from the stage, Buddy and Jack maintained their close relationship. Among their limited extracurricular activities was "cruising" around Lubbock in Jack's 1948 Chevrolet Fleetline or L.O.'s flatbed Dodge truck.

When they were unable to perform on stage, Holley and Neal continued to practice, playing classic country tunes, and experimenting with musical composition, or as Buddy described it, "made up" songs. Neal would long remember Buddy's enthusiastic aspirations: "Jack, it's not that I want to be in the lamplight. It's not that I want to be rich. I just want the world to remember the name Buddy Holley."

Ambitious, impulsive, and impatient, an adolescent Buddy arrived unannounced at the radio station *KSEL*, requesting a face-to-face meeting with Ben Hall, a singer, song-writer, and afternoon disk jockey. Hall, impressed by Holley's bold initiative, arranged for Buddy and Jack to perform at a local sports arena.

Wearing a white cowboy hat, Buddy teamed with Jack and Weldon Myrick, an experienced steel guitar player, who had been invited to play with the duo. Their performance was well-received by the audience. Afterwards, Ben Hall, who was most impressed by Holley's talents, hired him as a studio background musician.

While Buddy was still in high school, two transformative figures emerged in his life. Born in 1913, David Pinkston, settled in Lubbock after attending Texas Technological College. He began his career in radio as a disk jockey at *KSEL*, where he created his on-air persona, "Pappy Dave Stone."

In September of 1953, Pappy Stone successfully petitioned the Federal Communications Commission to establish a new west Texas radio station. Located on the outskirts of Lubbock in a small building adjacent to a high-rise transmission tower, radio station *KDAV* went on the air in September of that same year, broadcasting only during daylight hours. Pappy later purchased three other radio stations—*KPEP* in San Angelo, *KZIP* in Amarillo, and *KPIK* in the state of Colorado. *KDAV* and *KPEP* became the first full-time country music stations in America, but occasionally expanded their format to include rockabilly records.

Pappy Stone recruited Hi Pockets Duncan, both as a disk jockey and *KDAV's* assistant manager. Born in 1914, in Haskell County, Texas, William Joseph Duncan was a World War II veteran, who had been wounded in action. Duncan began his career in radio as a disc jockey in Amarillo, where he developed his own show, "Hi Pockets Hank's Hillbilly Hop." From that point forward, he would be known as Hi Pockets Duncan. Pappy also recruited Ben Hall away from *KSEL*.

Beginning in 1953, Hi Pockets Duncan started his own weekly show—the *Sunday Dance Party*. Duncan, who also promoted and booked musical acts, had seen Holley perform, and was impressed by Buddy's talent and innate drive to succeed.

"I could see right away that Buddy had it—a lot of grit, a lot of determination—he just had more drive than the other youngsters there. He had a lot of talent, that's true. But then, everybody has talent of some sort or another. What Buddy had was the determination to develop that talent," Duncan emphasized.

Holley and Jack Neal were soon rewarded with a regular 15-minute segment on the *Sunday Dance Party* (later expanded to a half-hour), which became known as the *Buddy and Jack Show*. The program debuted on November 8, 1953, with the entertainers playing and singing in a small room, separated by a glass window from a live audience of around 30 locals. Holley and Neal, as was expected, performed country and western songs, including hits by Hank Williams, Marty Robbins, and Ernest Tubb, interspersed with gospel tunes, which appealed to their white, conservative listeners. Sometimes, Buddy and Jack invited another local youth, Don Guess, to play bass or steel guitar with them. On occasion, Buddy and Jack would discretely slip a rhythm and blues tune into their show.

Neal, who by now, had a six-day-per-week, full-time job as an electrical contractor, eventually decided that he would rather spend Sunday afternoons with his girlfriend. In 1954, Buddy recruited his old friend and former bandmate, Bob Montgomery, to replace Jack. Before he married his girlfriend and moved to Ruidoso, New Mexico, Neal would make occasional guest appearances on the *Sunday Dance Party*. The renamed *Buddy and Bob Show* opened with Buddy's self-composed instrumental tune, entitled the *Holley Hop*.

Buddy enjoyed hanging around the radio station, and often sat beside the DJs while they were on the air, educating himself about the control panel, microphones, turntables, and tape recorders. At *KDAV*, Buddy first met a disc jockey and young musician, who would later play a prominent role in Holley's life. Waylon Jennings, a year younger than Buddy, was a native of Littlefield, Texas, 40 miles distant from Lubbock, who had dropped out school at age 11, harboring aspirations of becoming a country and western singer. Before long, Buddy, Waylon, and others were conducting jam sessions in a backroom at the radio station.

Jennings immediately recognized that Buddy was the "highlight of the *Sunday Party*." In time, Waylon sensed that bigger things lay on the horizon for Holley: "He wasn't as impressive as a singer in country music. But man, the minute he hit that rock and roll, he was something else."

Appearing regularly on radio, Buddy and Bob gained greater name recognition. The band was soon invited to perform at parties and other social functions. They also played at grand openings of new businesses, like Henry's Superette (earning $10) and Furr Food Store. Quite often, they performed without pay, forcing both to work as carpenters' helpers for L.O. Holley or tile layers for Larry. As Bob remembered it, the duo needed to make additional money so they could "lay down tunes." An entrepreneurial Hi Pockets Duncan grew concerned that his young protégées were often performing for free.

In 1954, after the band played at a private affair for an affluent Lubbock resident, Duncan approached Buddy: "That old party boy is using you."

"Well, we always get fed," Buddy replied.

"Look, I'm willing to be your manager," Duncan offered.

"Fine. What does that mean?" Buddy asked.

"You need to beef up the act. Get someone on bass—maybe Larry Welborn. We'll organize a trio—Buddy, Bob, and Larry," Duncan proposed.

"Where are we going to get a bass fiddle?" Buddy inquired.

"I'll have to buy you a bull fiddle to get you started," Duncan replied.

"I'm going to draw up a contract on you where anybody that uses you, will have to come through me. That will save you from doing any more free parties," Duncan continued.

An additional written contract was executed, specifying that if the group's success spread outside the immediate area of Lubbock, Duncan would relinquish his managerial role. Buddy also self-promoted the band, sending a two-page, hand-printed letter to area high schools. Buddy proposed splitting gate receipts evenly with the schools for their own use, "and at the same time, raise money for us to pay our way through college."

The 15-year-old, Oklahoma-born, Larry Welborn proved to be a gifted and well-timed addition to the group. Eventually, Buddy's old friend and fellow late-night R & B radio listener, Sonny Curtis, joined the band. Born on May 9, 1937, the 17-year-old Curtis, who hailed from Meadow, located 30 miles southwest of Lubbock, was an aspiring singer and song-writer, who played both the guitar and fiddle.

For a time, after the addition of Welborn and Curtis, the band retained its original name, as evidenced by their printed business cards: *BUDDY AND BOB—WESTERN AND BOP.* The card denoted Hi Pockets Duncan as their manager and listed *KDAV* as the band's business address.

At some point in 1954, Welborn dropped out of the band and was replaced by Buddy's friend, Don Guess, who was a song-writer, bassist and steel guitarist. In September of that same year, the band changed its name to the "Rhythm Playboys."

As promised, Hi Pockets Duncan booked paying gigs for the group, such as high school dances, skating rinks, store openings, and car lot sales. The Rhythm Playboys also performed a show in Brownfield, Texas, where they were handsomely rewarded with one-half of the gate receipts. In addition, Buddy and his bandmates often played at Lubbock's Lindsey Theater—earning $50 for playing a 30-minute set before the previews. Because the band members were all underage, Duncan could not book performances for them at the honkytonk joints, just outside Lubbock.

Duncan generously refused to accept a managerial fee. *KDAV* did, however, conduct live remote broadcasts at the venues where the Rhythm Playboys performed.

While the band was playing primarily country and bluegrass music, Buddy remained infatuated with the R & B sound. He would frequently travel to the black section of Lubbock and listen to musicians play the blues in cafes, front porches, and yards. Buddy often quizzed black musicians about how they played certain chords.

Buddy Holley began his senior year of high school in the fall of 1954. Still somewhat nerdish in appearance, Buddy was nonetheless a high-spirited youth. He and his underage friends would pay older boys to buy them beer or a quart of bootleg whiskey. Buddy also developed a taste for Winston cigarettes or menthol Salem, the latter of which he smoked, when suffering from respiratory infections.

Though still in love with the chaste Echo McGuire, who he hoped to marry one day, Buddy indulged his adolescent libidinal urges. His sexual encounters occurred with less respectable local girls, and it is quite possible that Buddy and his friends may have crossed the Mexican border to visit brothels.

Baptized at age 14, Buddy struggled with the sinful nature of tobacco, alcohol, and premarital sex. "I'm ashamed of a lot of the stuff we do, but it's not going to stop me. I like girls and like to get out and be noticed," he confided to a pal. Buddy also rationalized his sins, telling that same friend: "Yeah, (it) looks like every time you screw up, God is there to put His arms around you and say, 'Let's get going again!'"

His devoutly religious parents naturally opposed smoking and drinking. For a time, Buddy smoked behind their backs, until his mother told him that if he was going to smoke cigarettes, he shouldn't try to hide it. Though he developed a taste for alcohol, Buddy was often forced to limit his consumption because of chronic dyspepsia—perhaps a yet undiagnosed peptic ulcer.

While Buddy sometimes fell victim to temptation, he never abandoned his faith, as evidenced by his underlining New Testament passages from the Book of John. He also kept the lyrics of his favorite hymn, *What a Friend We Have in Jesus*, close at hand. Future bandmate, J.I. Allison, described Buddy's philosophy on Christianity: "Oh yeah, Buddy was very religious, I mean, when we were playing together, he didn't go to church every Sunday or preach to everybody. But, I knew he felt very deeply about his convictions." While retaining his spirituality, Buddy rejected rigid edicts concerning personal behavior and the church's hypocritical support of racial segregation.

Buddy always seemed to be in a hurry. In December of 1954, Holley accumulated so many unpaid speeding tickets that he was summoned to court. When Buddy failed to show up for his designated appearance, an arrest warrant was issued by the City of Lubbock. After paying a $13 fine and enduring a brief suspension of his driver's license, Buddy escaped more severe punishment.

Even though he was reticent by nature, Buddy was angered by imperfections, particularly when it came to music. When the band practiced at the Holley's house, Buddy's mother was troubled by the way her youngest son berated fellow musicians about failing to measure up to *his* standards. "Now Buddy, they're just kids—you can't yell at people like that—you've got to get along with them," Ella warned him.

"Mother, they just don't care. They don't take it seriously enough. But, it's got to be right, and so I have to get after them to play it like it should be played," Buddy protested.

Larry Holley thought Buddy was spoiled, and annoyed by his younger brother's tendency to disrespect L.O. and Ella. Eventually, Larry confronted Buddy: "Now look, they're my parents too, and I'm not going to have you talking to them like that. I want that to stop, right now." Larry remembered that Buddy immediately became more deferential and polite to his mother and father.

When provoked, Buddy's temper fuse was short. While playing a gig in San Angelo, the band was heckled by oil field workers in the audience. By the end of the performance, Holley was enraged. Even though the performers were underage, someone bought them a six-pack or two of beer to quench their thirst during the drive back to Lubbock. After downing a couple of beers, Buddy unsuccessfully challenged his bandmates: "Well, let's go back. I want to whip them son of a bitches that didn't like us." Sonny Curtis remembered that Buddy, after a few drinks, became "loud, a smart Alek, and headstrong."

For reasons that are unclear, Holley once got into a knock-down, drag-out fight with a fellow student in his high school Distributive Education Class. Robert Knight, who taught the class, remembered that "I had to grab them both by the collar," until the teenagers calmed down. "Buddy was cocky, but he had a lot to be cocky about…He was very self-confident and got things done. Students who weren't that self-confident were irritated by him and took the attitude, 'I'll knock your head off.' Buddy was a visionary young man and had difficulty with them," Knight recalled.

At the same time, Knight viewed Buddy as "unusually thoughtful, especially for a teenage kid." When Knight was bed-ridden with the mumps, Buddy and Bob Montgomery came to his house at night and played dominoes with him for two hours, just to provide their teacher with company.

Buddy, like many young people, possessed a false sense of invincibility. On one occasion, when Jack Neal was driving, Buddy thought his friend and one-time bandmate was going too slow. Without warning, Buddy placed his foot on top of Neal's and pushed the gas pedal to the floor. Jack recalled the sudden acceleration "scared me half to death."

While he was far from a juvenile delinquent, Buddy was certainly more interested in music than academics. "To Buddy, school was like a prison," his mother remembered. He did, however, participate in extra-curricular activities including acapella choirs and clubs that studied arts and music.

During Buddy's senior year of high school, he served as vice-president of the Distributive Education Club; a program, which allowed students from poorer families to attend classes in the morning and work in the afternoon. Consequently, Buddy became a part-time employee, first at Glen Decorating, followed by Davidson Printing Works. In 1955, during the second semester of his senior year, Davidson fired Buddy for chronic lateness. After his mother intervened, Buddy was re-hired, thus allowing him to graduate high school on time. Even though he was guilty of tardiness at the work place, Buddy used his musical talents to benefit the Distributive Education program, playing and singing during club functions at other high schools in west Texas.

Buddy's lanky frame was not suited for varsity sports. Instead, he preferred hunting and fishing as recreational activities. The hand-eye coordination that enabled him to master the guitar, also lent itself to other hobbies, like leather crafting. More than once, Holley hand-crafted wallets for family members and friends. Buddy also designed a leather cover for his Gibson acoustic guitar (he had purchased the instrument for $35, in October of 1953), embroidering his name and musical notes on the bottom, front side of the instrument. His other leisure activities included painting and drawing blueprints (for "make believe" houses). Buddy eventually became a talented draftsman, which he considered as a back-up occupation if he failed to make it in the music world.

In the summer, he helped his father with residential construction and worked with his brothers in Larry's tiling business. Buddy's specialty was setting tiles, which was well-suited to his eye for detail. "He could lay tile real well," L.O. Holley recalled.

Larry seconded his father's observations: "When I laid tile, I took a lot of care, but went real slow. Travis went fast, but sometimes used to skimp the work. Buddy could go fast and take care."

Music, however, remained Buddy's abiding interest. In addition to practicing with his bandmates, he would often hone his skills while home alone. When practicing by himself, Buddy would typically play just a portion of a new song, rather than the entire tune. After practicing a few chords, he would announce: "Yep, I can play it."

A restless Buddy found it difficult to accept America's growing infatuation with television. "I'll go into somebody's house and they'll be sitting and watching the TV—they don't look up or anything. And, if they're eating, they practically put the food in their ears. I just can't understand it," he complained to a friend. In later years, the Holley family could only remember one occasion when Buddy focused on the television set—Elvis Presley's first appearance on the *Ed Sullivan Show* (in 1956).

On May 6, 1955, Buddy registered for the draft; coincidently, it was the same day that the United States test exploded a nuclear bomb in the Nevada desert. The Eisenhower Administrations, spanning most of the 1950s, were a time of peace. The lack of wars, coupled with his poor eyesight and gastrointestinal problems, kept Buddy from being called into military service.

Twenty-one days after failing his military induction physical, Buddy became the first member of his immediate family to graduate from high school. He now faced an uncertain future. Holley's long-time love, Echo McGuire, was planning to attend a religious school in Abilene, Texas, 165 miles southeast of Lubbock. Many, including Buddy's brother, Larry, "felt like he might marry her," after the couple graduated from high school. Echo's departure for college, however, was significant step toward ending their adolescent relationship.

Now a high school graduate, Buddy was faced with the prospect of earning a living. Before settling for a job in the family construction/tiling business or pursuing drafting as a vocation, Buddy was serious about making music a career.

At different times, both in 1954 and 1955, after a talent scout for Columbia Records attended one of their performances, Buddy and his bandmates travelled 100 miles to Nesman Studios in Wichita Falls, Texas, and recorded a handful of predominately country and western or bluegrass songs, including, *Soft Place in My Heart, You and I are Through, Door to My Heart, Baby Let's Play House, I Gamble My Heart,* and *Queen of the Ballroom,* as well as a rockabilly tune, *Down the Line,* the latter of which was co-written by Buddy and Bob. Holley and Montgomery paid for the recording session with money earned from their public performances. The recordings were pressed into acetate records, but did not impress Columbia executives enough to offer the band a recording contract.

On February 4, 1955, Buddy and Bob signed a publishing contract with Ridgeway Music and music publisher, O.B. Woodward. They received no advance for recording *I Just Don't Care,* which was apparently never made into a record, and their contract was not renewed.

Buddy's interest in rock and roll and rhythm and blues eventually blended with his country and western roots, creating a hybrid, which would become known as "rockabilly." Elvis Presley, the biggest name to emerge in the burgeoning genres of rockabilly and rock and roll, hailed from Tupelo, Mississippi. Buddy was already an admirer of Presley, who identified himself as the "Hillbilly Cat, King of Western Pop." Holley had listened to Presley on late night radio and was a huge fan of his single, *I Forgot to Remember*. Elvis' leather guitar cover inspired Buddy to design his own. Even before he met Presley face-to-face, Buddy informed Waylon Jennings that Elvis was his favorite singer.

On January 2, 1955, *KDAV's* Hi Pockets Duncan booked Presley to play at the Cotton Club; a 1,400-square-feet Quonset hut-like structure that was the Lubbock-area's largest dance hall. At the time, Presley had only recorded two hit records, *That's All Right Momma* and *Blue Moon of Kentucky*, which limited his performance fee to just $35. Two other promising young performers, Johnny Cash and Carl Perkins, also appeared on the bill with Elvis.

Between shows, Buddy first met Presley, while Elvis was backstage, drinking a Coca-Cola. Already impressed with Presley's star power, Buddy found him equally amiable: "You know, he's a real nice, friendly fellow."

The following day, when Presley performed at the opening of a new car dealership, Buddy's band played as his opening act. From that point forward, Holley's interest in performing bluegrass evaporated, and his country and western roots severely eroded. "The day after Elvis left town, we turned into Elvis clones. And we was (sic) bookin' out as an Elvis band," Sonny Curtis recalled.

Curtis soon abandoned his fiddle for a Martin D-28 acoustic guitar, while Don Guess traded his steel guitar for a slap bass. Buddy, who already knew how to play rock and roll, became more animated on the stage. "Buddy never moved around much until then. In country, you just stood still and did your thing. But, after seeing Elvis, there was no holding him; (as) soon as he picked up a guitar, he was way out front and all over the place," Curtis recalled.

When Elvis returned to Lubbock, on February 13, 1955, Buddy and Bob Montgomery intercepted his tour bus outside the city limits, and showed Presley around town. That night, at the Fair Park Coliseum, Buddy and his band opened for Elvis and Ferlin Husky. In just a few short weeks, Presley's popularity had rapidly increased, such that his performance fee had grown to $75.

During the show, Hi Pockets Duncan hobnobbed with Presley's flamboyant manager, Colonel Tom Parker. Duncan understood that Parker's promotional skills had much to do with Elvis' rapid accession into stardom. Even then, Duncan preferred his own client: "...As far as actual talent goes, I'd put Buddy Holley up against Elvis Presley."

Bob Montgomery, who also met Parker, thought Presley's manager was impressed by Holley, but had adopted a policy of not representing more than one performer at a time. However, Parker did inform Nashville-based talent scout, Eddie Crandall, about Holley. While Crandall was not immediately interested, he eventually would be captivated by Buddy's raw talent.

The night of the Fair Park concert, Hi Pockets Duncan convinced Presley and the other entertainers to perform a second show at the Cotton Club, which was a more raucous, honkytonk atmosphere. Sonny Curtis vividly recalled what happened next: "We opened for Elvis. Bales of cotton were stacked around the stage to protect him from the audience. The most beautiful girls in Lubbock were trying to climb the bales to get at him. That's what impressed us as much as the music. We'd been hillbillies, but after the Cotton Club, we were rockers like Elvis."

After their performance at the Cotton Club, Larry Welborn recalled that Elvis nearly got into a fight: "Somebody was wanting to whip Elvis outside the Cotton Club; Elvis was stealing his girl or something." Presley managed to slip away with the girl, and took Holley along. "Buddy and Elvis got along pretty good," Welborn explained.

After performing on the same bill with Elvis Presley, Buddy and his band began playing more rockabilly songs on their radio program and during stage performances. "Without Elvis, none of us could have made it," Buddy readily acknowledged.

Waylon Jennings was certain that Presley had "changed Buddy." "It was the beginning of kids really starting to think for themselves, figuring things out, realizing things that they would never even have thought of before," Jennings opined.

Sonny Curtis, for one, never forgot the image of the hip-wiggling Presley: "Elvis looked like a motorcycle headlight coming at you—white buck shoes, red pants, and an orange jacket." "Presley just blew Buddy away. None of us had ever seen anything like Elvis; the way he could get the girls jumping up and down, and that definitely impressed Holley. But, it was the music that really turned Buddy around. He loved Presley's rhythm. It wasn't country and it wasn't blues. It was somewhere in middle and it suited (us) just fine. After seeing Elvis, Buddy had only one way to go," Curtis remembered. Before long, Curtis purchased a Les Paul Gold Top solid-body electric guitar—a favorite among rock and rollers.

Bob Montgomery seconded Curtis' assessment: "Buddy had a unique sense of rhythm. He was doing his best to be an Elvis imitator, but it became his own thing."

Elvis' performances in Lubbock affected how other performers structured their bands. D.J. Fontana, who was Presley's drummer, greatly impressed the amateur musicians in the area. Roy Orbison, a future rock and roller, who hailed from Wink, Texas, and was about to form a new band, the Teen Kings, recalled a key change in back-up musicians: "We got a drummer, and I think it's a matter of instruments that defined whether you were playing C & W or rock."

Buddy agreed with Orbison, and already had in mind who he wanted to add as his percussionist—Jerry Ivan Allison. Born in a west Texas farmhouse on August 31, 1939, Allison and his family moved to Lubbock in 1950. Buddy first met Allison at J.T. Hutchinson Junior High School. Shortly after Elvis left town, Buddy visited the 16th and J Club, where J.I. Allison was performing with a C & W group, Cal Wayne and the Riverside Ranch Hands.

After Wayne agreed to let Buddy jam with his band, Holley demonstrated how to play rock and roll music; the other musicians followed his lead while performing *Rock Around the Clock*. The audience was entertained by the up-tempo performance, which featured J.I. and Buddy feeding off each other's energy. Consequently, Allison became a convert to rock and roll and his musical compatibility with Buddy appeared instinctive. Holly biographer, John Gribbins, noted Allison's unique skill set: "J.I. played the drums like a lead instrument."

At his parent's house, J.I.'s bedroom became a regular location for Buddy and his band to practice. Even though he was a newcomer, Allison correctly sensed that neither Bob Montgomery nor Sonny Curtis seemed as enthralled with rock and roll as Buddy.

The remarkable chemistry between Buddy and J.I. improved the more they practiced together. When just the two of them played at a local skating rink, many listeners remembered that they were louder than Buddy's entire band. "We'd both play the same rhythm lick that somehow made our music sound fuller," J.I. later recalled.

After Allison formally joined the band, he discovered that Buddy and his group played almost every available gig. "We'd play at the opening of a pack of cigarettes," J.I. joked.

There were still some disappointments along the way. When Elvis performed in Lubbock for the second time, he had invited Buddy and his band to travel to Shreveport, Louisiana where he would arrange for them to play on the *Louisiana Hayride*, which was broadcast, far and wide, every Saturday night, by radio station *KWKH*. The *Louisiana Hayride* was second only to the *Grand Ole* Opry in prestige, counting not only Elvis, but also the late Hank Williams among its alumni. Between 1954 and 1956, Elvis performed on the show nearly 50 times.

Naively, Buddy and his bandmates made 534-mile drive from Lubbock to Shreveport in Holley's 1955 Oldsmobile, arriving unannounced at the municipal auditorium. The *Louisiana Hayride's* program director, Horace Logan, was unimpressed when the boys from west Texas announced that "Elvis sent for us."

Unfortunately, Presley was on tour and could not vouch for Buddy and his band. "Heck, we couldn't even get in the door," Larry Welborn recalled.

The disappointment in Shreveport proved short-lived. Sid King, leader of the Five Strings, invited Buddy's band to play on the same bill with his bluegrass band at Lubbock's Cotton Club. King was a rocker of sorts, performing a bluegrass version of Carl Perkin's *Blue Suede Shoes* (a song made most famous by Elvis Presley) during his show. King was impressed by Buddy and his bandmates, and promised to get them on the *Big D Jamboree* in Dallas, which was broadcast by radio station *KRLD*, every Saturday night.

One Friday, Buddy and his band drove 323 miles east to Dallas, showing up unannounced at Sid King's residence. King, who had expected forewarning, nonetheless allowed the boys to spend the night at his residence, and managed to book them on the following night's *Big D Jamboree*.

Buddy and his bandmates performed *Down the Line* during the popular show. Even though the gig was unpaid, *KRLD* exposed them to their largest audience ever.

Buddy Holley's long-awaited chance at stardom began on October 14, 1955, when his band appeared on the same show as Bill Haley and the Comets, as well as Jimmie Rodgers Snow (son of the legendary Hank Snow). Eddie Crandall, the Nashville talent scout who had heard about Holley from Colonel Tom Parker, was travelling with Haley and Rodgers when they performed in Lubbock. Crandall was immediately impressed by Holley's ability to play and sing both C & W and rock and roll.

Two weeks later, Buddy's band again performed at the Fair Park Coliseum, as the opening act for a *Grand Ole Opry* Show, featuring Marty Robbins, Porter Wagoner, Slim Whitman, Mitchell Torok, Autry Inman, and Hank Locklin. Crandall, who also managed Robbins, was now convinced that Holley had the potential to become a hit-maker. Marty Robbins added his two-cents worth, advising Crandall that Buddy possessed "what it takes."

After returning home to Nashville, Crandall sent a telegram, dated December 2, 1955, to *KDAV* manager, Pappy Dave Stone: *DAVE, I'M VERY CONFIDENT I CAN DO SOMETHING AS FAR AS GETTING BUDDY HOLLY A RECORDING CONTRACT...*

A day later, Crandall telegrammed again, asking Stone to send him four demo records, "as soon as possible (by) airmail." Crandall included specific instructions about recording Buddy—"don't change his style at all."

On December 7, 1955, Buddy and Bob, along with Don Guess on bass, Sonny Curtis on lead guitar, and J.I. Allison playing the drums, cut four acetate demo records at Nesman Studios in Wichita Falls. The recordings, which included two established songs and a couple of new tunes, included *Love Me, Don't Come Back Knockin'* (co-written by Holley and Lubbock native, Sue Parrish), *I Guess I was Just a Fool*, and *Baby Won't You Come Out Tonight* (Buddy's first known solo composition).

Meanwhile, Crandall approached Elvis' manager, Colonel Tom Parker, about landing a record contract for Holley. Parker, however, was preoccupied with the sale of his star performer's contract from the Memphis-based, Sun Records to RCA Victor.

Crandall then turned to Jim Denny, an agent who booked acts for the *Grand Ole Opry* and owned Cedarwood Publishing Company. After listening to the demo records, Denny believed Holley had potential, and agreed to seek a record contract for him.

At that time, three prominent record companies had C & W divisional offices in Nashville—Columbia, RCA Victor, and Decca. Denny first approached Columbia, whose executives had no interest in rockabilly artists. Since RCA Victor had just signed Elvis Presley, Denny called on Decca's Director of Artists and Repertoire (A & R), Paul Cohen.

Decca was a powerful record label in the mid to late 1950s, whose contracted artists included C & W acts, Red Foley, Kitty Wells, and Ernest Tubb, as well as the only major white rock and roller, Bill Haley. The record company also controlled 40 percent of the jukeboxes across the United States, which significantly influenced when and where records were played.

After listening to the demos, Cohen agreed to offer Buddy Holley a record contract, but excluded his bandmates. In January of 1956, Jim

Denny telephoned Pappy Stone with the good news. In the Decca contract Buddy's last name was written as *Holly* (just as it had been misspelled in Denny's initial telegram).

From that point forward, the world would come to know the young man from Lubbock, Texas as *Buddy Holly*.

CHAPTER 3

The Decca Debacle

BUDDY HOLLY'S CONTRACT WITH DECCA started out on the wrong foot, and never recovered. Even though the record label made it clear that they only wanted Holly, Buddy felt loyalty to his group, particularly his long-time friend, Bob Montgomery. Holly's agent, Jim Denny, behaved as if the other band members did not exist, and was less than sympathetic about Montgomery's exclusion. "Well, you can bring him along if you want, but he can't sing on the records. We want one singer, not two," he matter-of-factly informed Buddy.

When Buddy threatened to back out of the record contract, Montgomery, who realized that this was his friend's shot at stardom, graciously stepped aside. Besides, Bob had never been as enthusiastic about rock and roll or rockabilly as Buddy, preferring to play and sing C & W tunes. Even though their partnership ended, Buddy and Bob remained life-long friends, and Montgomery would enjoy a rewarding career as a singer, song writer, music publisher, and record producer.

As promised, Hi Pockets Duncan voided his managerial contract with Holly. "I wasn't able to travel with him, and I didn't want to hinder his success in anyway," Duncan explained. Unfortunately, Buddy would never again have a manager or promoter who was as loyal and trustworthy as Duncan.

Before his inaugural recording session, Buddy reconstituted his band. Don Guess would play the bass fiddle, which Holly had to rent from Lubbock High School for six-dollars (the prior bass, belonging to Hi Pockets Duncan, was apparently in use elsewhere). Sonny Curtis would play lead guitar, while Buddy sang and played rhythm guitar. When the band rehearsed, Allison played the drums, but since he was a year younger than Buddy and still in high school, J.I. would not be able to join Holly, Guess, and Curtis for the first Decca recording session.

Lubbock disc jockey and song writer, Ben Hall, gave Holly a newly-written song to record in Nashville. *Blue Days, Black Nights* chronicles the plight of an individual down on his luck; though his days are never good, his nights are even gloomier.

Buddy asked his brother, Larry, for a $1,000 loan to purchase equipment and attire for the forthcoming recording session and anticipated touring appearances. "Why don't you just ask for the moon?" a surprised Larry responded. Realizing that his brother was determined to become a star "or bust a gut," Larry agreed to loan him the requested funds.

Buddy had long wanted to replace his Les Paul Gold Top electric guitar, which he had purchased in 1954 at Adair Music Company in Lubbock, with a Fender Stratocaster. Invented by Californian, Les Paul, the Stratocaster was a solid body guitar with a built-in vibrato, capable of generating a louder volume. The Stratocaster, which was the successor of Fender's Broadcaster, was largely considered a country and western instrument, but Holly would pioneer its use in rock and roll. Joe B. Mauldin, who later played bass with Buddy Holly and the Crickets, was mightily impressed with Stratocaster, describing it as the first guitar that he had ever seen with a "gear shift."

At a Lubbock music store, Buddy used $249.50 of his borrowed money to purchase his first Fender Stratocaster. He also bought a Pro Amp amplifier to accompany his new guitar.

Unable to find suitable performing outfits in Lubbock, which catered to the C & W crowd, Holly, Curtis, and Guess drove 357 miles to Oklahoma City to purchase more colorful clothes. "That's how we ended up being 'Buddy Holly and the Two Tones.' We bought white trousers, but one of us got a blue shirt and one got an orange one; hence the Two Tones," Curtis recalled. Larry Holley vividly remembered Buddy's new wardrobe: "He bought green, pink, and red sports jackets and some red shoes and some suede shows."

In late January of 1956, Buddy, Don Guess, Sonny Curtis, and local drummer, Charles Hill, departed Lubbock for the 900-mile, two-day-excursion to Nashville in Buddy's black and white 1955 Oldsmobile (like J.I. Allison, Larry Welborn was still in high school, and could not make the trip). Initially, luck was on Holly's side. After Buddy graduated from high school, his parents had turned over payments for the Oldsmobile to their youngest son, who was already in arrears. The quartet just managed to skip town, before a collection agency arrived to re-possessed the vehicle.

On the way to Nashville, Buddy and his bandmates stopped in Memphis, hoping to see Elvis Presley. When he discovered Elvis was on tour, Buddy left him a gift at the Sun Records studio—a hand-crafted leather wallet.

On January 26, 1956, Buddy arrived at Bradley's Barn for his first recording session. The Decca studio was inside a former military Quonset hut, located on 16th Avenue South—Nashville's famed Music Row.

From the start, Decca's Director of Artists and Repertoire, Paul Cohen, and the session producer, Owen Bradley, were determined to record Buddy Holly as a C & W singer, with perhaps a bit of rockabilly, but certainly not as a rock and roll artist. As amateurs, Sonny Curtis remembered that they were in no position to argue with the producer: "We were just nice boys from Texas and we were trying to put our best manners forward. We were on our toes, and it was, 'Yes sir, Mr. Bradley' and 'Whatever you say, Mr. Bradley!'"

The situation quickly grew contentious, when Bradley told Curtis, Guess, and Hill that they were not up to industry standards, and replaced them with session musicians. Grady Martin, who played rhythm guitar, and Doug Kirkham, the drummer, made it even worse, treating the west Texans with condescension. Bradley also insisted that Buddy stand and sing into the microphone, absent his guitar, something Holly had never done before. When Buddy resisted the changes, Bradley was patient, but

Cohen openly berated Holly: "You don't have the voice to be a singer. You should forget about a musical career."

The tense session, lasting from 7:15 p.m. to 10:15 p.m., yielded four recordings. Without playing his guitar, Buddy sang Ben Hall's *Blue Days, Black Nights, Midnight Shift* (written by Earl Lee and Jimmy Armstrong), and a pair of songs written by Buddy's friend and Lubbock native, Sue Parrish, entitled *Don't Come Back Knockin'* and *Love Me*. The recording session cost $386, which would be later deducted from Holly's royalties. For Sonny Curtis, the only highlight from the first Decca recording session was "hanging out" at country star Marty Robbins' office and travelling to downtown Nashville, where they "chased chicks." During the return trip to Lubbock, the cash-strapped group stopped to eat with Buddy's aunt, who lived in east Texas.

For Buddy, the time between the first Decca recording session in January and the second one in July seemed endless. He eagerly awaited a phone call from Decca or the opportunity to hear one of his records played on a juke box. When he could stand it no longer, Buddy wrote Eddie Crandall for an update. The agent's response was not what Buddy had hoped to hear: "I can't say anything good at the present time. "Don't get discouraged. I know it's tough, but the break will come sometime. You have a fine little group." In March, Buddy's frustration and envy heightened, when Elvis Presley's *Heartbreak Hotel* became the first record in history to hit Number One on all three American charts—Pop, Rhythm and Blues, and Country and Western.

On April 16, 1956, Decca finally released Holly's first record. *Blue Days, Black Nights* appeared on the A side of the disc, while *Love Me* occupied the record's flip side. Decca, however, did little to promote the record, except for sending out pictures of an unsmiling Buddy Holly. The company also failed to designate a specific genre, so the record was released only in C & W markets. Sonny Curtis was particularly skeptical: "...They probably sent 25 (records) to San Francisco and called it a release."

When Holly finally received a royalty statement, he learned the single had sold 10,000 copies—7,500 45-RPM and 2,500 78-RPM records.

By industry standards, the sale of only 10,000 copies was hardly a promising start to a musical career. The song writing royalties, split among the composers, netted each about $225. *Billboard* magazine offered lukewarm enthusiasm for the single: "If the public will take more than one Presley or (Carl) Perkins, as it may well, Holly stands a strong chance."

In May of 1956, Buddy and the Two Tones embarked on Faron Young's *Grand Ole Opry* Tour, which also included Ray Price, Carl Perkins, Tommy Collins, and Red Sovine. As the opening act and background musicians for the established stars, they were excluded from the tour bus, and had to follow along in Buddy's car. Earning $10-per-day, Holly opened two shows each night, performing both songs from his newly-released record.

Hoping to improve his stage appeal and following established tradition, Holly tried to perform without his eyeglasses. Impaired by 20/800 vision, Buddy was unable to see his bandmates, much less the audience. On one occasion, after dropping his pick, he had to crawl on hands and knees to find it.

After the tour, Buddy spent $125 to purchase a pair of contact lenses—a vision-improving advance that was still in its infancy. The contacts were not only hard to insert and remove, but also so uncomfortable that Buddy could only wear them for a few minutes each day. At that point, Holly decided that he would perform wearing his glasses, not yet knowing that they would eventually become his trademark and serve as an inspiration for other near-sighted rock and rollers.

With his second Decca recording session not scheduled until July 22, an impatient Buddy wanted to record demos for a song he had recently composed, *Because I Love You*, as well as *It's Not My Fault*, written by Ben Hall.

Much to the chagrin of his original manager, Hi Pockets Duncan, in February of 1956, Buddy traveled to Clovis, New Mexico, 90 miles northwest of Lubbock, where a man named Norman Petty had constructed a first class recording studio. Holly had earlier heard about Petty from his bandmate, Don Guess.

"Whatever you do, don't go to Clovis. Norman Petty has a bad reputation for taking advantage of kids," Hi Pockets warned Buddy. A headstrong Holly, not yet 19-years-old, disregarded Duncan's advice; a decision he would later regret, many times over.

When Holly told Petty that he wanted to "cut some professional-sounding demos," the Clovis producer told him to form a studio-quality band, practice some songs, and then return for an actual recording session. Petty later recalled his initial encounter with Buddy Holly: "My first impression was of a person ultra-eager to succeed. He had the eagerness of someone who has something on his mind and who wants to do something about it."

Decades later, Norman Eugene Petty remains an enigma. Born in Clovis, in May of 1927, Norman was the son of an Oklahoma oil field worker, who had moved to New Mexico, hoping the higher elevation and dryer air would lessen the severity of his tuberculosis.

Sydney, or Pa Petty, as he was often called, operated a two-story gas station and garage, assisted by his wife, Margaret. Next door, a single-story building housed a general store, managed by Norman's maternal aunt and uncle. Norman had two sisters, Edith and Shirley, and an older brother, Billy, who died of leukemia at age 18—the same illness would claim Norman's life, many years later. After Billy's death, Margaret spoiled her surviving son, who she affectionately addressed as "Normie."

Pa Petty was a mechanical whiz, repairing not only cars, but also appliances, cameras, and radios. This mechanical aptitude was passed along to his youngest son. Before he turned 10, Norman hooked up a microphone to the family radio, such that he could host mock broadcasts over the instrument's speakers.

Both of Norman's sisters were musically inclined; one played a harmonica, and the other a guitar. Norman, however, proved to be a musical prodigy, learning to play the piano by ear as a youngster. Before long, he could play any musical piece, after hearing it just once.

Norman's ears were so sensitive that he later worked part-time as a piano tuner. "He'd walk into a hall or a room before a concert, look around it once, and say, 'An octave up from middle C, about F sharp, there's a dead spot. When they checked it on the piano, he'd always be right. And, if he ever heard a bad note, it almost brought him out in a rash," a friend recalled.

During his teen years, Norman was hired as a disc jockey at Clovis radio station, *KICA*, where he hosted the *Musical Mailbag*, which aired twice-per-day. Petty also organized and recorded his first musical ensemble, the "Torchy Swingers." He eventually saved enough money to purchase a disc-cutter; a first for Clovis. With his new machine, Petty earned money recording political campaign spots that were subsequently broadcast on the radio; he also cut 78-RPM discs, which allowed military personnel and their families to exchange long-distance greetings.

At Clovis High School, Norman first met Violet Ann Brady. Vi, as she was known to her family and friends, was born September 17, 1928. A gifted pianist, whose uncle had been a Professor of Music at the University of Oklahoma, she was classically trained and learned to read music. Vi, who was petite, with reddish-blonde hair, began dating Norman when he was 18 years old, and she was a year younger. After graduating from high school, while Norman served a stint in the military, Vi studied music for two years at the University of Oklahoma. On June 20, 1948, 21-year-old Norman and 20-year-old Vi were married.

Vi, whose mother had been institutionalized for mental illness during her daughter's childhood, was an anxious and uncertain person by nature. Norman exploited her fragility and dependency, to the point of dictating Vi's hairstyles and attire. More importantly, he maintained strict and secretive control over the family's finances. While Vi later played piano on studio recordings, when summoned by her husband, she mostly gardened and tended to nearly a dozen pet cats.

Petty's financial control within the family was never really challenged. In the early years, when his parents still operated their gas station and garage, Norman's mother empowered her son to sign checks drawn on her account at the Clovis National Bank.

Standing five-feet, eleven-inches tall, with brown eyes and a broad smile, Norman readily charmed newcomers. What lay behind the smile puzzled some and angered others.

Norman and Vi eventually teamed with their friend, Jack Vaughn, to form the "Norman Petty Trio." In 1954, with Norman playing the organ, Vi on the piano (while also serving as vocalist), and Jack playing the guitar, the group recorded *Mood Indigo*, (a song composed by Duke Ellington). *Mood Indigo* eventually climbed to Number 14 on the national record chart. Three years later, the trio released a less successful instrumental record, *Almost Paradise*, composed by Norman.

The Norman Petty Trio grew popular enough to perform at various venues, travelling to and from Clovis in a blue transfer-like truck, which contained enough space for their instruments, as well as a dressing room for Vi. Childless, Norman and Vi always brought along their surrogate offspring, a black Chihuahua, named "Speedy."

The trio first recorded under the Columbia record label. Norman, however, was dissatisfied with Columbia's producers, who failed to measure up to his exacting standards. He also disliked the fact that studio sessions were always time-limited, which interfered with his creativity and perfectionism.

Using royalties earned from *Mood Indigo*, Norman built his own recording studio, so that the group would no longer be dependent on other facilities and their producers. The studio was also an ideal spot for Norman, Vi, and Jack to practice between live performances. Having established key contacts with high-ranking officers in the U.S. Air Force, Norman arranged for his group to play concerts at various military bases throughout the country. To augment his income, Petty also worked as a professional photographer at weddings and other area functions.

Realizing that there were no other well-equipped recording studios in the area, Norman soon formed his own publishing company, Nor-Va-Jak Music, deriving its name from the original members of the Norman Petty Trio. Petty eventually utilized his studio facilities and personal expertise to produce records for promising young performers.

At 1313 West 7th Street, the up-and-coming producer developed a compound of sorts, fronted by a sign that read *Norman Petty Studios*. The two-story, flat-roofed building, which still served as his parent's gas station and garage, housed an apartment for Norman and Vi. The loft space of that structure functioned as an echo chamber for the studio next door.

The building that once housed his aunt and uncle's grocery store was transformed into a state of the art recording studio, reportedly costing Petty nearly $100,000. The front door of the one-story structure opened into a reception area with a dime Coca-Cola machine. Norman's pride and joy, his control room, was equipped with two Ampex tape recorders (Petty and famed guitarist, Les Paul, were the first two people in America to own such recorders), filters to improve sound quality, a lathe disc-cutter that converted tapes to demo disc records, glass-cased cabinets containing headphones and connecting wires, Western Union time clocks (a compulsive Petty insisted that all of his clocks be synchronized to the second), a RCA microphone, and an Altec single-channel master control board. While a window looked inside the recording studio, Petty positioned his gray leather chair and control board such that he was not facing the window; the configuration allowed only his ears to be exposed to the music.

The main studio, 10 by 20 feet, contained two Telefunken microphones, a Fender Pro amplifier, a Baldwin grand piano, a Hammond organ, and a celesta. To ensure more fluid acoustics, the walls of the studio were rounded. A separate, smaller studio sat to one side, with windows viewing both the main recording area and control room.

A short hall led from the main studio to a kitchen and a small room with two beds, which could be folded out to create four sleeping places. With these added accommodations, recording artists benefited from a home-like atmosphere, where they could spend the night at the studio.

In the attic echo-chamber next door, studio sound was delivered by a speaker on one end, captured by a microphone on the other end, and then delivered back to the control room. Petty was no doubt innovative, both in creating his own echo chamber, strategic microphone placement, and volume control adjustments. He even installed a small microphone inside stand-up bass guitars, which better captured the throbbing sound quality of the instrument.

A common patio area was located behind Petty's twin buildings. Cookouts were held there, and Norman's loyal bookkeeper, Norma Jean Berry, often served as the chef.

Berry, who had abandoned her career as a local journalist to work for Petty, was totally devoted to her boss. Five-feet, two-inches-tall, the pleasantly plump, bespectacled Berry appeared mannish, especially when dressed in blue jeans and penny loafers. She kept two of Norman's large key rings securely attached to her belt; any financial or business-related secrets Petty may have related to Berry remained confidential.

Norman Petty Studios offered another perk. While most studios charged by the hour, artists who booked sessions with Petty, paid only a flat-rate $75-fee. Norman believed that singers and musicians created superior recordings when they were not rushed. Petty, however, more than recouped lost studio fees by taking his cut from royalties generated by artists' successful records.

While he granted unlimited performance time to recording artists, a frugal Petty expected background musicians and vocalists, who typically lived in the Clovis area, to work for free. John and Bill Pickering, who had been friends with Norman since high school and were part of a vocal trio, the Pics, sang on many Petty-produced recordings. "Norman would be nice as pie. He'd talk to you, encourage you, praise you, and feed you—I mean real good food—steaks and everything. But, he'd never give you a dime," John Pickering recalled.

Soft-spoken and unassuming, with a receding hairline and eyeglasses, Petty was not particularly effeminate; nonetheless some people believed that he was gay or bi-sexual. Others opined that the husky-voiced, masculine appearing Norma Jean Berry was engaged in a lesbian affair with Vi Petty, and possibly including Norman in ménage trois.

Norman was prone to disappear for long-stretches of time between recording sessions. He had clandestine offices located at different places in Clovis, where he maintained separate bank accounts, office stationery, and telephone numbers, all of which was kept secret from Vi.

Jimmy Self, Petty's first outside recording artist, remembered the producer's suspicious behaviors: "When Norman was working with musicians in the studio, he'd be there all the time, taking care of every detail, but in between sessions, he'd disappear completely." "Norman would be in one of these secret offices, doing gosh-only-knows what, for hours on end," Self added. Petty sometimes flew to New York City, the west coast, and Europe, his whereabouts unknown to his wife, conducting unspecified business.

Petty's mysterious actions were heavily clothed in piety. An active member of the Clovis Central Baptist Church, Norman would not allow artists to drink or curse in his studio. He also frowned when singers and musicians lit cigarettes in his presence. Petty kept a Bible handy in the control room, and often asked artists to hold hands and pray after they completed a successful recording.

Friends, acquaintances, and recording artists viewed Norman Petty in different ways. He was no doubt a master technician, who could recognize raw talent and shape performers into stars. Fellow church members saw him as devout and generous. Others, like Hi Pockets Duncan, considered him an opportunist, who took advantage of young recording artists.

Buddy Holly's brother, Larry, who would later have considerable contact with the Clovis record producer, offered a blunt and less than flattering assessment: "During World War II, when I was with the military over on Saipan, I can remember falling asleep, one night, in a foxhole with water up to my chin. Over there, you know, you get snails, measuring about 10-inches to a foot across. When I woke up in the foxhole, there was a giant snail crawling right cross my face...Well, I tell you, I used to get just the same kind of feeling when I was around Norman Petty."

Jimmy Self and the "Sunshine Playboys," a C & W group, were the first outside musical artists to record at Petty's studio. Norman successfully negotiated Self a record contract with RCA Victor. Before long, other aspiring artists flocked to Clovis, hoping to fulfill their dreams of stardom. Norman's sound engineering expertise, the studio's well-stocked refrigerator, and available sleeping quarters made the performers feel right at home.

Any recordings made at Petty's studio and later picked up by one of the many record labels that did business with Norman, came at a high cost to performers. Petty not only shared in the profits from record sales, but also insisted on a portion of the song-writing royalties, even when he had no role in their composition. Nor-Va-Jak also secured publishing rights for any records produced at *Norman Petty Studios.*

Rock and roll, still in its infancy, eventually made its way to *Norman Petty Studios.* Roy Orbison, a bespectacled young performer from Wink, Texas, and his band, the "Teen Kings," recorded several demos in Clovis. Orbison's first hit, albeit a modest one, *Ooby Dooby*, was recorded in Clovis. Dissatisfied with Petty's contractual arrangements, Orbison soon moved to Sun Records in Memphis, where the careers of Elvis Presley, Johnny Cash, Carl Perkins, and others were launched. By the early 1960s, Orbison had achieved stardom, recording such classics as *Only the Lonely, Crying,* and *Oh, Pretty Woman.*

Petty's first genuine hit-maker was Buddy Wayne Knox, a 23-year-old graduate of West Texas State College. Knox explained to Petty that he had written a song, *Party Doll*, and was eager to record it with his band, the "Rhythm Orchids;" Knox was the lead vocalist and rhythm guitarist, backed by Donnie Lanier on lead guitar, Jimmy Bowen on bass, and percussionist, Don Mills.

At Petty's studio, in mid to late-1956, Buddy Knox and the Rhythm Orchids recorded *Party Doll.* Jimmy Bowen also recorded his own single, *I'm Sticking with You.* Petty not only produced both records, but he also secured record deals for the artists. Bowen's *I'm Sticking with You* climbed to the Number 11 spot on *Billboard's* music chart in April of 1957. Of greater note, *Party Doll*, made it all the way to Number One in March of that same year, establishing Norman Petty as a legitimate record producer. Knox, on his first try, had released a best-selling record, well before his more experienced counterparts, Buddy Holly and Roy Orbison.

Meanwhile, an ambitious and impatient Buddy Holly strictly followed the recommendations Norman Petty made during their first meeting. In April of 1956, between his first and second Decca recording sessions, Buddy returned to Clovis. Backed by Sonny Curtis, J.I. Allison, and Don Guess, he recorded six self-composed songs—*Baby, Won't You Come Out Tonight, I Guess I was Just a Fool, Because I Love You, I'm Gonna Set My Foot Down, I'm Changing All Those Changes*, and *Rock-a-Bye Rock*.

Naively, Buddy hoped that Decca would allow him to record in both Clovis and Nashville. In Petty's studio, Holly had far more artistic freedom, in contrast to the tightly-controlled conditions in Nashville. However, he would soon learn that his Decca contract was exclusive.

After Buddy's inaugural recording session in Clovis, Norman Petty took the most interest in Holly's guitarist, Sonny Curtis. Jack Vaughn had recently ended his professional relationship with the Norman Petty Trio, and the group needed a new guitarist, or risked losing their profitable air force base performance contract. Petty covertly telephoned Curtis in Lubbock, asking him to return to Clovis. Curtis vividly remembered the ensuing discussion: "Norman invited me up to that apartment he had above the garage, and gave me cookies and milk. I'm sitting there, eating these macaroons, feeling as comfortable as a hog upstairs. Norman's telling me if I'll be in his trio, he'll buy me my own electric guitar and I'll be headed for the big time, and I'm thinking, 'Hey! Great gig man!' Then, he takes me across to the studio for an audition, and I realize that if I joined up with him, I'd have to spend my life playing slow, old things, like *Honeysuckle Rose*. Buddy begged me not to quit (Holly's group), as well, so I turned it down. And, after that, I don't believe Norman liked me until the day he died."

While waiting for his next Decca recording session, Buddy was forced to earn a living. Hi Pockets Duncan, who had resigned from *KDAV*, was now operating the Clover Club, located in Amarillo, Texas, 123 miles north of Lubbock. Duncan soon booked Buddy and his bandmates for a teenage dance at the Clover Club. Surprisingly, when the band played the up tempo, *Midnight Shift*, not only the youngsters, but also the chaperoning parents hit the dance floor.

Holly and his bandmates played as many gigs as possible, including shows at the lesser known Bamboo Club in Lubbock. They also appeared as the opening act for C & W star, Faron Young, at Bronco Stadium in Odessa, Texas.

Both rock and roll and rockabilly remained twin enemies of many conservative Texans. On June 17, 1956, Lubbock's *Avalanche-Journal* printed the first of a series of articles about the immorality of modern music. The reporter noted that audience members at the Bamboo Club, on a night when Holly played, were dancing the "dirty bop." Ella Holley, in defense of her youngest son, wrote a protest letter to the newspaper, but it was never published.

On Thursday, May 31, 1956, Buddy, Sonny, and J.I. went to the State Theater in Lubbock to see the debut of a John Ford western, *The Searchers*. During the movie, John Wayne, whose character is searching for his niece who has been captured by Indians, repeatedly utters a line of bravado: "That'll be the Day." A few days later, when Buddy and J.I. were practicing in Allison's bedroom (a convenient location, since J.I.'s drum set was already in place), Holly suggested writing a song. J.I., who had never composed a song, replied in John Wayne-style: "That'll be the day."

"Yeah, that sounds like a good one," Buddy replied. Much to J.I.'s surprise, it took Holly "about 30 minutes" to write *That'll Be the Day*. From day one, Buddy was certain that his new song would become a hit.

As the time approached for his second Decca recording session in Nashville, Buddy dealt with the emotional fall-out of Echo McGuire's transfer from Abilene Christian to another church-affiliated college, located in York, Nebraska. The new school was 700 miles distant from

Lubbock, further lessening chances of reconciliation between the high school sweethearts.

Perhaps Buddy should have been concerned about Echo's Christmas gift to him in 1955. *Must the Young Die Too?* was a book written by Fort Worth author, Wyatt Sawyer, and its title would prove prescient about Buddy and Echo's relationship, Holly's record contract in Nashville, and even his own lifespan.

On Sunday, July 22, 1956, Buddy, Sonny, Don, and J.I. (who had since graduated high school), returned to Nashville. Buddy's old friend and former bandmate, Bob Montgomery, tagged along to offer emotional support.

The session stared out badly, when Buddy and his bandmates arrived without a bass fiddle—the previous source for their rented instrument, Lubbock High School, was closed for the summer. Owen Bradley tersely informed them that if they could not find a bass within 20 minutes, he would cancel the entire recording session. The boys hustled to radio station *WSM,* and were lucky enough to borrow a stand-up bass from a session musician.

Buddy's recording session, which began at 10:30 p.m., involved significant changes in the format. J.I. Allison, instead of session musician, Doug Kirkham, played the drums. Sonny Curtis was also allowed to play rhythm guitar. Holly even talked Bradley into letting him play lead guitar while singing.

That'll Be the Day, which Buddy was eager to record, required 19 takes, none of which proved to be satisfactory. In J.I.'s opinion, Decca wanted a country-sounding version of a rockabilly song, and instructed Holly "to sing high, which was out of Buddy's range, at that time." The producer also failed to provide a back-up chorus, which was a key component in the song. Sonny Curtis, who played rhythm guitar, offered his own critique: "We just didn't get the right feel. I don't think that song really needed a rhythm guitar." Owen Bradley added insult to injury, describing *That'll Be the Day* as "the worst song I've ever heard."

Paul Cohen, Director of A & R, expected singers and musicians to follow his advice to the letter, leading to repeated arguments with a headstrong Buddy. Jim Denny had to intervene to stop shouting matches between the two, but not before Cohen characterized Holly as "the biggest no-talent I've ever worked with." As a parting shot, Bradley and Cohen condescendingly advised the expanded band to change their name to "Buddy Holly and the Three Tunes."

Holly did record four other songs that turned out more to his liking. *Rock Around with Ollie Vee*, is a jaunty rock and roll anthem, written by Sonny Curtis, and named after an elderly black woman, who assisted Curtis' mother with housework. It took eight takes before Holly was satisfied with *Rock Around with Ollie Vee*. Buddy and his band also recorded *Girl on My Mind* (written by Don Guess), *I'm Changing All These Changes* (written by Holly), and *Ting-A-Ling* (written by Ahmet Ertegun, who would later become President of Atlantic Records).

After Decca chose not to release *any* of the four recordings, Buddy expected to be dropped from the record label. Then, much to his surprise, Holly was invited for a third recording session in November of 1956.

That summer, while Elvis Presley dominated the radio air waves and juke boxes, Buddy helped his brother, Larry, lay tile and assisted his father with framing houses. With Echo McGuire now in distant Nebraska, Buddy began to date other local girls, but none amounted to serious relationships. Buddy and his bandmates continued to play local gigs, including the Hi-D-Ho drive-in, where they would sometimes perform on the restaurant's roof.

On August 24, 1956, Little Richard performed at Lubbock's Cotton Club, a rare venue where rigid segregation was not enforced. The 24-year-old, Georgia-born rock and roller had scored a handful of hit records, including *Tutti-Frutti, Long Tall Sally*, and *Slippin' and Slidin.'* Black, flamboyant, effeminate, and allegedly homosexual (or possibly bisexual) Little Richard performed songs with "suggestive" lyrics—none of which was welcome in west Texas. Earlier that same month, Little

Richard had been arrested in Amarillo on a trumped-up charge of vagrancy, even though he had $2,700 in his possession.

Buddy and J.I., however, loved his music, and stood on the front row among a mixed-race crowd of 500, who were cheering and dancing. As expected, many locals were offended, and fist fights erupted in the parking lot. Lubbock's *Avalanche-Journal* headlined: *ROCK 'N' ROLL DANCE IS SHUT DOWN AFTER DISTURBANCE*. The newspaper reporter wrote that the manager of the Cotton Club eventually "stopped the blaring beat of the Negro pianist's band."

Even though most west Texans were unwelcoming, Buddy and Little Richard hit it off immediately. The flamboyant performer recalled that Holly invited him to dinner at his parent's house, but L.O. would not permit him to enter the residence because of his race and rumored homosexuality. Little Richard also claimed that Buddy stepped to his defense, informing his parents: "If you don't let Richard in, I'll never come back to this house again." Feeling decidedly unwelcome, the black rock and roller said that he refused to enter the Holley's home. Conflicting memories have emerged about this racially-charged incident. Later in life, Buddy's brother, Larry, was hazy about whether Little Richard visited his parent's house, but if so, it was a "fictitious lie" that he was turned away. "Mother would never not let Little Richard in." Did the black performer eat a meal at the Holley's house? "I'm sure he did, if he came over there," Larry opined.

Buddy and Little Richard not only shared their love of music, but also commiserated about the conflict between rock and roll and their fundamentalist religious upbringings. A Seventh-Day Adventist, Little Richard experienced recurring thoughts like Buddy's: "If you want to live with the Lord, you can't rock 'n' roll it, too. God doesn't like it."

Buddy was in an uncomfortable bind. He had befriended a black and possibly gay musical artist; taboo in the eyes of his fellow Tabernacle Baptist Church members. Throughout the country, many white Americans continued their condemnation of rock and roll as not only Satanic, but also as a facilitator of dreaded "race-mixing." While

Buddy had clearly rejected racial bigotry, he would continue to struggle with the seeming incompatibility of rock and roll and fundamentalist Christianity.

As he faced the prospect of losing both Echo McGuire and his Decca record contract, Buddy grew more rebellious. He not only drank and smoked more, but he also befriended what his brother, Larry, described as a "rough crew." One member of Buddy's circle of new friends and acquaintances was a chain-toting motorcyclist. "Anytime anybody tried to beat up Buddy, he would take his chain and whip them..." Larry recalled.

Buddy's choice of companions was, in part, a matter of self-protection. Many Lubbock-area musicians and singers, who were less-skilled than Buddy, resented Holly's Decca record contract. "Buddy liked everybody, but everybody didn't like Buddy," Larry explained.

Larry, however, was not a total apologist for his baby brother, believing that Buddy was acting "snobbish," staying out all night without concern for his mother's worries, and treating his parents with disrespect. As he had done earlier in Buddy's life, Larry confronted him: "I want you to start treating Mother better. She's come to me several times crying and telling me how impudent you talked to her. She's my mother, too, and I love her and I'm just talking to you like a big brother, and I want you to start acting like you're going to have to—you're liable to go someplace in this world and you're going to change your ways."

Buddy, who greatly respected his older brother, and most often heeded his advice, simply responded: "Thank you." A few days after this confrontation, Ella approached Larry: "I don't know what you said to Buddy, but he's a different person since then."

On Sunday, September 9, 1956, a rarity occurred for Buddy—he watched television. That night, Elvis Presley appeared for the first time on the *Ed Sullivan Show*. The stodgy and snobbish Sullivan, who did not care for rock and roll, gave Presley a less than a welcoming introduction, informing *CBS* viewers to "judge for yourself." Nonetheless, Elvis' popularity was so great, that Sullivan granted him the rare opportunity to perform four songs in a single show, *Don't Be Cruel*, *Love Me Tender*, *Hound Dog*, and *Rip It Up* (first popularized by Little Richard). While Sullivan may have been unimpressed, young Americans were mesmerized. Buddy was one of 54,000,000 people who watched the show—a viewership that would not be surpassed until the Beatles performed on the *Ed Sullivan Show* in February of 1964.

On October 23rd of that year, Buddy received a modicum of publicity from the local press. Holly's picture appeared in the pages of the *Avalanche-Journal*, after his band performed at the Cotton Club. In the accompanying article, the reporter described Buddy's "fancy sports coat," and noted that he "was singing rock and roll exclusively." Recognition of any sort from Lubbock residents, however, would remain a rarity for Holly.

Prior to what would be his last recording session with Decca, Holly's old friend and former bandmate, Jack Neal, met with Buddy and Don Guess, asking for their help completing a song. Tongue-in-cheek, Neal informed them that *Modern Don Juan* was inspired by Buddy's sexual exploits.

On November 15, 1956, Buddy returned to Bradley's Barn in Nashville. On this occasion, he was accompanied by Don Guess, only; for reasons that are not entirely clear, Sonny Curtis and J.I. Allison did not make the trip. On their way to Nashville, the pair took a detour, so Buddy could visit with Echo McGuire at her college in Nebraska.

Session players, Floyd Cramer, who played the piano, and E.R. "Dutch" McMillan, a saxophonist, as well as Harold Bradley, Grady Martin, and Farris Coursey (playing other instruments), joined Buddy and Don in the studio.

During the recording session, which started at 9:30 p.m. and cost $485, Buddy performed *Modern Don Juan*, even though he had not yet secured permission from Jack Neal. Though miffed, Neal later signed a release, to keep Buddy from breaching his contract with Decca. *You Are My One Desire*, written by Guess, was another by-product of that session.

Holly also re-recorded Sonny Curtis' *Rocking Around with Ollie Vee*; this time, famed saxophonist, Boots Randolph, played in the background.

By all appearances, the relationship between Buddy Holly and Decca was nearing its end. In later years, Owen Bradley viewed the debacle as a joint failure: "He (Holly) needed somebody else to produce him, not us. He wanted to make things not as country, as we were instructed to do, but he didn't fight it that strong." "We had been very successful with a country format. We were all into country, and it's hard to change patterns. Buddy couldn't fit into our formula any more than we could fit his. He was unique, and he wasn't in a pattern. We didn't understand; he didn't know how to tell us," Bradley added. Studio musician, Harold Bradley, offered a similar assessment: "We thought we could make him rich and famous; he's a hillbilly and we know what to play. We didn't realize that he was trying to create a new sound…"

Nonetheless, on December 24, 1956, Decca released *Modern Don Juan*, with *You Are My One Desire* on the record's flip side. The holiday season was hardly the most fitting time of the year to promote a record, and sales were disappointing.

On January 9, 1957, Buddy, along with Don Guess, Sonny Curtis, and J.I. Allison, toured for 15 days with Hank Thompson and the Brazo Valley Boys. Other tour members included George Jones, Justin Tubb, Cowboy Copas, Wanda Jackson, Hank Locklin, and Mitchell Torok.

Holly now considered himself a rock and roller, seemingly unconcerned that most country stars detested that musical genre. Some C&W performers would later adopt a middle ground, rockabilly, but many remained true to their roots. From the start, Buddy and his bandmates were fish out of water. "We were just Elvis clones. We sounded just like Elvis," Sonny Curtis recalled.

The mercurial and hard-drinking George Jones, who was on his way to becoming a country music legend, ridiculed Buddy for his up-tempo guitar playing and bright stage clothes. As a new-comer among established professionals, Buddy initially held his tongue. Eventually, he could take no more, and Holly informed Jones that the country crooner could never appreciate rock and roll, because he couldn't sing it. Buddy extracted further revenge when Jones was singing his Top 10 hit, *Why Baby Why*; Holly played his guitar at such a fast pace that Jones was forced to perform the number in rockabilly style.

Irrespective of disagreements over style and substance with Jones and other performers, Buddy remained in good spirits during the tour. At restaurants, he would fill water glasses to different depths and then play tunes with his eating utensils. Sonny Curtis remembered going to the movies to see *Wuthering Heights*, starring Laurence Olivier and Merle Oberon. "There's a line in it, 'If you come over to my house, I'll let you hold my hand beneath my fan.' Buddy leans back in his seat, throws out his arms, and says, 'Have mercy!' Well the whole place just broke up," Curtis recalled.

With a sense of foreboding, Buddy and his bandmates continued to play Lubbock-area gigs. As Buddy expected, in January of 1957, Decca formally notified him that the record label was not renewing his option.

At this point, Buddy and the Three Tones fell apart. Don Guess was the first to leave the band. Money was tight, and Guess could not purchase his own bass fiddle; the one previously rented from Lubbock High School was now battered from travelling many miles strapped on top of Buddy's car. "Well, I'm not cut out be a bass player," Guess informed Buddy, when he departed.

Sonny Curtis, who had never been as enthralled with rock and roll as Buddy, was the next to leave. "I wasn't getting along with Holly that well; we sort of had a conflict in personality. But, the main reason I quit was because we weren't making any money." By now, Curtis, whose family was poor, had graduated high school and he needed a steady income, which could not be generated from playing sporadic gigs with Holly. "Buddy had great faith in the future, but I honestly felt we weren't really going anywhere," Sonny recalled.

J.I. Allison, who stuck with Buddy, offered his own take on Curtis' departure: "The reason that we changed people was usual personal things—like Sonny didn't particularly like to play rhythm guitar; he liked to play lead guitar. So, when Buddy got wanting to play lead, Sonny said, 'Well, shoot, I don't want to play rhythm, so I just won't play gigs.'"

Sonny soon joined Slim Whitman's band as a guitarist. Curtis later enjoyed a productive career as a singer, musician, and song-writer.

With the rejection from Decca and his band decimated, Buddy seriously questioned if he was going to be successful as a musical entertainer. Ella Holley remembered that her youngest son "came darn near quitting for a time or two."

Broke and down on his luck, Buddy nonetheless believed *That'll Be the Day*, which had flopped in Nashville, remained his ticket to stardom. From that point forward, he was determined to focus on rock and roll, and create his *own* sound.

The most likely path to success led Buddy back to *Norman Petty Studios*.

CHAPTER 4

Clovis, Petty, and the Crickets

HI POCKETS DUNCAN, WHO WOULD always hold Buddy Holly's best interests at heart, was unhappy when he heard that his former client planned to cut more records at *Norman Petty Studios*. "I'm advising you again not to go to Clovis," Duncan warned Buddy.

Duncan's concerns were not unwarranted; he already knew, in part, how the Clovis producer operated. Petty would no doubt help Buddy, but in exchange, would demand partial song-writing credits for any recordings made in his studio, thus sharing in the royalties for compositions he had no role in creating.

Holly, at age 19, was simply too impatient and immature to think about money or seriously question Petty's shady reputation. At this point in his life, Buddy was focused on three things—he wanted complete creative control in the recording studio, he was certain *That'll Be the Day* was destined to become a hit, and he knew that Norman Petty had transformed Buddy Knox and *Party Doll* into overnight sensations.

"If you can get a hit for that Buddy (Knox) you can get a hit for this Buddy," Holly assured Petty.

"It's the talent, not the studio," Petty replied, refusing to take responsibility if Holly bombed.

Buddy wasted no time, recruiting Larry Welborn, at least on a temporary basis, to replace Don Guess as his bass player. In late January of 1957, Buddy, J.I., and Larry drove to Clovis and recorded two songs, *Brown-Eyed Handsome Man* (a Chuck Berry original) and *Bo Diddley* (written by Bo Diddley; the only artist known to have named a song after himself).

Norman Petty was impressed by Buddy's "intensity, honesty, and sincerity." "He wasn't the world's most handsome guy, he didn't have the world's most beautiful voice, but he was himself." Vi Petty thought the trio from Lubbock look "real gangly" in their blue jeans and tee shirts, but was charmed by their politeness and professionalism. At the end of the recording session, Norman instructed Buddy to write two new songs and return in late February, at which time they would cut an actual record.

While J.I. Allison was fully on board, Larry Welborn was already playing in another band, and Buddy needed to find a full-time bass player and rhythm guitarist. To replace Sonny Curtis on rhythm guitar, Holly recruited 19-year-old Niki Sullivan.

Born on June 23, 1937, in South Gate, California, Sullivan and his family moved to Lubbock when he was two-years-old. In 1954, Niki, already a talented singer and guitarist, returned to California, where he appeared on the *Rocket to Stardom* television program, performing *Baby Let's Play House.* After moving back to Lubbock, Sullivan and fellow musician, Bobby Peeples, recorded a less than successful record, *Piddle-De-Pat.*

Nikki's mother and Ella Holly were close friends, which facilitated the introduction between their sons. Lanky and bespectacled, Sullivan was similar in appearance to Buddy, and was flattered to join Holly's band, without first having to audition. As far as Niki was concerned, Holly was "the nearest thing to Elvis Presley" in Lubbock.

A year younger than Buddy, Sullivan was energetic and eager to prove his worth during the lengthy rehearsals leading up to Holly's first full-fledged recording session in Clovis. "We worked on *That'll Be the Day* several times, just for me to learn the parts and everything, because I had never heard it played publicly. Everything we played was in the key of A. Buddy decided on the vocals and the arrangements; he was in total charge of everything. Whatever changes were made from how it sounded in Nashville, Buddy did it." Sullivan was further impressed by

Buddy's confidence and grace under fire; Holly waited until the night before they travelled to Clovis to start composing *I'm Looking for Someone to Love* (the flip side to *That'll Be the Day*).

On a sub-freezing Sunday night, February 24, 1957, Buddy, J.I., Larry, and Niki headed for Clovis in two cars. Their caravan included three other Lubbock natives, June Clark, Garry Tollet, and Tollet's wife, Ramona—all of whom would serve as back-up singers in the recording studio (Niki Sullivan would also sing background vocals). While the 100-mile, two-lane blacktop appeared flat to the naked eye, it gradually ascended to an elevation of 4,300 feet, by the time the group reached Clovis, located just 10 miles west of the Texas and New Mexico border. At the state line, clocks changed from Central to Mountain Time. The gain of one hour, coupled with lax enforcement of speed limit laws, enabled lead-footed drivers to brag that they reached Clovis before departing Lubbock. The journey might have been fast, but the scenery was monotonous—cotton fields and pasture land, occasionally interrupted by isolated farm houses.

On that frigid February night, Larry Holley was driving a used, red 1955 Cadillac that he helped finance for his youngest brother. Larry would make the trip from Lubbock to Clovis more than once, functioning not only as his brother's chauffeur, but also as a peacemaker and body guard: "Buddy and Jerry (J.I.), together, were quite a handful. They'd holler or make signs at guys in other cars; the other guys would chase us, waiting to fight. I'd have to get out and calm things down. One or two times, I'd end up having a fight, myself."

While Larry drove, Buddy sat in the back seat, completing the lyrics to *I'm Looking for Someone to Love*. As they crossed over a set of train tracks at the state line, Buddy confessed that he was struggling to compose the first verse of the last stanza. "The bump-bump of our tires over the railroad tracks gave me an idea," Larry later recalled. He suggested that his brother adopt the adage that one of their uncles frequently used to foreshadow danger. Buddy managed to incorporate the incongruent phrases in the first four verses of the final stanza (listen for yourself).

"Yeah, that might do pretty good," Buddy replied, completing the song with the out of place, but prophetic verses.

After Buddy and his entourage arrived at *Norman Petty Studios*, they spent the first few hours practicing. Actual recording sessions could not be conducted until late at night, after noisy trucks and freight trains were no longer passing nearby, and the town's electric amperage was at its maximum.

Unlike the take-charge producer at Buddy's Decca recording sessions in Nashville, Petty merely positioned the microphones and ran the control board, allowing Buddy to arrange the music—the total artistic control Holly had long-craved. "When we started, Buddy had the whole arrangement worked out. All Norman did was set up the microphones," back-up singer, Gary Tollet recalled.

That'll Be the Day, the record's A side, was completed in only two takes, and would eventually become Buddy Holly and the soon-to-be-christened Crickets' best-selling single. "We were cutting *That'll Be the Day* just as a demo to send to New York, to see if they liked the sound of the group—not for a master record. So, we just went in and set up and sort of shucked through it. I think we cut it two times…And, we didn't get it perfect, because we never suspected that the (demo) record would ever come out," J.I. Allison remembered.

That'll Be the Day is a classic example of early rock and roll; a style some refer to as the "Texas Shuffle." The Clovis recording is far more energetic and lower-pitched than the country-style version previously recorded in Nashville. *That'll Be the Day* asserts the bravado of John Wayne's classic line in *The Searchers*, through the voice of a lover, who is supremely confident that he will decide how and when the couple's relationship comes to an end.

The bulk of the recording session, which lasted until 3:00 a.m., was devoted to Buddy's newly-completed B-side to the record, *I'm Looking for Someone to Love.* Holly's trademark vocal hiccups are prominent in this tune, which, in many ways, reflected his own personal life. Now that Buddy's relationship with Echo McGuire was seemingly on the ropes, he was once again on the prowl.

Buddy had not intended for Norman Petty to negotiate a record deal for *That'll Be the Day*, and hoped to follow the same path as background singer, Gary Tollet. It just so happened that Gary and his wife were repaying Buddy and J.I. for performing as background musicians during Tollet's own recording session, three days earlier, in the studio at Lubbock radio station *KDAV*. Tollet ultimately secured his own record contract with Roulette, a company where his cousin was employed.

At the end of Buddy's recording session in Clovis, a savvy Norman Petty provided Holly with two alternatives: "I'll give you the acetate, and you peddle it, and that will be $500, or I'll go get you on a record label, and for that, I want the publishing rights." Even though he was an independent producer, Petty was well known to major record companies in New York City, more so than many of his peers. The Norman Petty Trio was under contract to Columbia Records, and he had an established relationship with the label's A & R director, Mitch Miller. Petty was also well-acquainted with Murray Deutch, an executive at Peer Southern Publishing; at that time, Peer Southern served as Nor-Va-Jack's selling agent.

As Hi Pockets Duncan had predicted, Petty's offer to sell Holly's record came at a steep price—both *That'll Be the Day* and *I'm Looking for Someone to Love* would be published by Nor-Va-Jak, insuring that Petty received his share of the royalties. Petty also insisted that his name be added to the song-writing credits, explaining that disc jockeys who recognized an established performer's name on the record would be more apt to give it playing time. Such a move guaranteed that Petty would receive an equal share of the song-writing royalties, which an eager and naïve Buddy did not yet fully appreciate.

Even though he was a year younger than Holly, J.I. Allison recognized the addition of Petty's name to the song-writing credits as outright deception. Buddy and J.I. composed *That'll Be the Day* months earlier, while Holly completed *I'm Looking for Someone to Love*, just minutes before arriving in Clovis. Petty had not contributed lyrics to either song.

Niki Sullivan clearly recalled Petty's sales pitch, delivered in the wee hours of that Monday morning: "He said that people in the music industry knew him because of his trio, so record companies and disc jockeys and people would be more likely to take an interest if they saw the name 'Norman Petty' instead of just some unknown kid from west Texas. And, anyway, he claimed he helped to write the songs in a way, by getting them to sound right in the studio and making suggestions, all along the line. Buddy didn't care; he was just delighted to think that the songs were going to be published, and someone like Norman believed in him and was going to push him in New York. And, Norman told us that was the way it always happened. We had no choice but to take him at his word..."

Holly, who was the band's leader, agreed to Petty's proposal. Little did he know just how much this hasty decision would come back to haunt him.

After granting Norman Petty publishing rights and partial song-writing credits for his first Clovis-recorded record, Holly was eager to assemble a committed band, both for studio recording sessions and for stage performances. J.I. and Niki were fully committed to the band, even though they were already at odds with each other. Sullivan believed that Allison, who was determined to remain Buddy's best friend, deliberately kept him from developing a closer relationship with Holly.

After Larry Welborn returned to his existing band, Buddy quickly searched for a permanent bass player. On March 1, 1957, Buddy and J.I. attended a dance where a local band, the Four Teens, was performing. Allison was already familiar with the band's diminutive bass player, Joe Benson Mauldin, Jr., who was commonly addressed as Joe B. Born in Lubbock, on July 8, 1940, Mauldin and his family moved to Dallas when he was very young. After his parents divorced, four-year-old Joe B. returned to Lubbock with his mother. At age 13, he suffered a serious head injury, when a car struck the motor scooter he was riding. After being hospitalized, Joe B. recovered, but family and friends henceforth adopted the role of his protector.

As a young adolescent, Joe B. learned to play the piano, trumpet, and steel guitar. His mother, who recognized her son's potential, hoped Joe B. would eventually pursue a career in classical music.

Impressed by his energetic and enthusiastic bass thumping, Buddy and J.I. stopped by Joe B's house the day after first seeing him perform, and asked if he would play with them during a gig in Carlsbad, New Mexico. That very night, the foursome, Buddy, J.I., Nikki, and Joe B., who would eventually become known as the Crickets, played together for the first time at an Elks Club dance. It took only one performance for Buddy to realize that Joe B. was the perfect complement to round out his quartet.

After equally splitting their $65 performance fee, the group drove back to Lubbock, during which time Buddy and J.I. lobbied Joe B. to join their band. Mauldin was impressed by Buddy's sales pitch: "We've cut a record called *That'll Be the Day*, and it's going to be a stone hit. And, we're going to get rich." "Big things are going to happen," Buddy further promised.

Joe B. was naturally skeptical: "Man, what makes you think that? It's not even out yet. How do know it's going to sell?"

"Oh, that's all right. It'll be a hit. And, we're going to get rich," Buddy reiterated.

"Well, how long do you think that's going to take?" Joe B. asked.

"How long did it take Elvis?" Buddy responded.

Joe B. was hooked by Buddy's enthusiasm, even though he had not participated in the recording of *That'll Be the Day* or *I'm Looking for Someone to Love*. Everyone seemed to be happy, except for Joe B.'s mother, who advised her son that he would regret his decision to join the other rock and rollers. With the addition of Joe B., Buddy had unknowingly established the base line-up employed by rock and roll bands for years to come—lead guitarist, rhythm guitarist, bass player, and drummer.

Before *That'll Be the Day* could be released by a record label other than Decca, certain legal issues had to be resolved. Even though Decca had not renewed his option, Holly's original contract prohibited him from re-recording songs that had originally been cut in their studio, until five years had elapsed. When Buddy telephoned Paul Cohen in Nashville, on February 28, 1957, asking for permission to release *That'll Be the Day* under a different label, Decca's Director of A & R declined his request. Norman Petty taped the phone call, which preserved Cohen's response: "We got money tied up in this thing, and they may go ahead and release them. I don't know what they're liable to do. They'll play them over and may salvage them. You can't record them for another company. You can record anything else you want to—any other new songs." Buddy remained calm throughout the phone conversation, other than to complain that this a "heck of a way to treat a guy."

Even though Buddy and J.I. had composed *That'll Be the Day*, and Holly had been the lead vocalist, if his name appeared on the record, he faced legal reprisal from Decca. Furthermore, the song had been written while Buddy was also under contract to Cedarwood Publishing, who had first claim to any royalties the record generated. Norman Petty would later convince Cedarwood's President, Jim Denny, to trade 50 percent of the royalties from *That'll Be the Day* for the full rights to a future Holly song, *Think It Over*—ultimately a huge loss for Cedarwood. In addition, the Petty-negotiated settlement specified that in the unlikely event that Decca's Nashville affiliate ever decided to release the original, countrified version of *That'll Be the Day*, Holly would not be entitled to any royalties.

Since this agreement had not yet been negotiated, *That'll Be the Day* would have to be released under a group name, without Buddy's name appearing on the song-writing credits. Gathering at Allison's house, Buddy, J.I., Niki, and Joe B. consulted an encyclopedia and perused the names of insects, like spiders, grasshoppers, beetles, and crickets. The insect theme may have come from Buddy, who was a fan of the R&B group named the Spiders. After J.I. referred to a grasshopper as "a little black bug you step on," the quartet agreed to use the name the "Crickets;" Allison described crickets as insects that "make a happy sound by rubbing their legs together."

Before Norman Petty took their demo record to New York, the Crickets recorded two new songs, *Maybe Baby* (written by Buddy, and later re-recorded as an improved version) and *Last Night* (written by Joe B.). Patience was never Holly's long suit, so he had the new songs, along with *That'll Be the Day* and *I'm Looking for Someone to Love*, pressed into 78-RPM acetates and sent to Roulette, in hopes the Crickets might be as fortunate as Gary Tollet, who had secured his own record contract.

After Roulette rejected the group's efforts to promote themselves, Buddy, more than ever, was convinced that Norman Petty was the man who could secure a recording contract for the Crickets. It appears unlikely that Petty was aware of the Crickets' unsuccessful attempt to broker their own record deal with Roulette. Even though Petty demanded publishing rights and a share of the song writing royalties, Buddy informed his bandmates that Norman was their best shot at stardom. "We were about as far down as you get already," Buddy later told disc jockey, Freeman Hoover.

More than ever, Buddy believed *That'll Be the Day* would become a hit. Niki Sullivan remembered that Holly was the only Cricket who was supremely confident the song would be a future best-seller.

Norman Petty eventually flew to New York City, where he maintained an office and an apartment, hoping to find a record company that was interested in *That'll Be the Day*. His first stop was Columbia Records, the label that had issued the Norman Petty Trio's *Mood Indigo*. Columbia's Director of A & R, Mitch Miller, however, had no interest in the Crickets' record. "Rock and roll is just a passing fad; I give it six months," Miller predicted.

Petty then called on Peer Southern, the publishers of the Norman Petty Trio's *Almost Paradise*. Murray Deutch, a Peer Southern executive, was known to have a good eye for talent, and had scored record deals for the Platters, among others. Deutch, who had received "some good songs" from Petty in the past, never established a kinship with the New Mexico record producer: "Warmth wasn't something you got with Norman Petty. He was the kind of guy who'd give you ice in the wintertime."

Deutch, however, was greatly impressed with *That'll Be the Day*, believing "that it had something special." "I just flipped for it," Deutch recalled, and he readily agreed to shop for a record label. Like most music industry executives, Deutch was savvy. If he secured a record contract for the Crickets, Deutch informed Petty that Peer Southern wanted 50 percent of the publishing rights. With little room for negotiation, Petty agreed to those terms.

Deutch took the record to Larry Newton, the A & R Director for ABC Records, and Jerry Wexler, who held the same position at Atlantic, but neither of the labels were interested. Undeterred, Deutch called Bob Thiele, Coral Records' A & R Director.

Born in Brooklyn, on July 27, 1922, Thiele had played clarinet in a jazz band as a teenager. Inspired by music, Thiele created a successful mail order company, Signature Records, before he went to work for Coral Records in 1952.

Ironically, Coral was a subsidiary of Decca, who earlier in the year, had failed to renew Buddy Holly's Nashville recording contract. Decca had widely established spin-off labels, like Coral, to compete with independent record companies. Deutch informed Thiele that both ABC and Atlantic had rejected a potential hit record. After he listened to the demo, Thiele recalled that a distressed Norman Petty telephoned him: "Please, I don't want any money for it. Just get this record released!"

Thiele, who was initially unaware of Holly's past contract with Decca, was favorably impressed with *That'll Be the Day*. Much to Petty's surprise, Thiele thought the demo was good enough and he did not need to listen to a master recording.

When Thiele played *That'll Be the Day* for Decca's President, Milton Rachmil, and Vice-President, Leonard Schneider, both were decidedly unimpressed with the record, ridiculing it as "junk" and a "joke." Since Coral typically released adult-oriented records, like those by the Lawrence Welk Orchestra, Rachmil and Schneider were concerned *That'll Be the Day* would offend both the label's established performers and its record buyers. Decca producer, Dick Jacobs, informed Thiele that he was taking a big chance on an artist who had already been dumped from the record company's C & W division in Nashville.

After Thiele literally threatened to quit his job if *That'll Be the Day* was not given a shot, Decca's executives allowed him to release the record on Brunswick, the company's least prestigious subsidiary label. Anticipating sluggish sales, Brunswick agreed to press only 1,000 copies of *That'll Be the Day*.

On March 18, 1957, Decca assigned master numbers to *That'll Be the Day* and *I'm Looking for Someone to Love*. A day later, just three weeks after the demo was recorded in Clovis, Brunswick payed Petty $100 for two master copies. While the advance money was small, the negotiated royalty rate, between two and three-cents-per-record-sold, was a bit higher than most new artists received at the time; the royalty concession was likely based on Brunswick's belief that the record would never be a top-seller.

Still uncertain about the legal ramifications of releasing *That'll Be the Day* on Brunswick, even though it was a subsidiary of Decca, Buddy Holly did not sign the record contract. Instead, J.I., Niki, and Joe B. inked the agreement on behalf of the Crickets. Buddy couldn't help but be amused that Brunswick was a Decca affiliate, describing the deal as "kind of going out the front door and coming in the back."

Hi Pockets Duncan was distressed to learn that Holly and his fellow Crickets had allowed Norman Petty to claim song-writing credits on their first two recordings. From that point forward, Petty's name would appear as a song-writer on most of the records released under the name Buddy Holly or the Crickets, absent any proof that he helped compose the lyrics for those songs. Among the most egregious examples of Petty's claiming partial song-writing credits included *That'll Be the Day* (written by Holly and Allison), *I'm Look for Someone to Love* (written by Holly), *Down the Line* (written by Holly and Bob Montgomery), *Peggy Sue* (written by Holly), and *Oh Boy* (written by Bill Tilghman and Sonny West).

Petty claimed that Murray Deutch endorsed his decision to take partial song-writing credit on *That'll Be the Day*, as a protective measure against Cedarwood Publishing Company's original copyright. In later years, Deutch vehemently denied Petty's assertion: "Never, in 30 years in the business, did I ever suggest anything like that to anybody." Another time, Petty declared that Buddy wrote the music, but he wrote the lyrics to *That'll Be the Day*; a blatant lie.

Niki Sullivan was fully aware of Petty's song-writing deceptions. "I really don't mean to put Norman down, but I honestly do not remember Norman making any serious changes that even stick out in my mind. I cannot remember any songs that Norman had a hand in..." Sullivan summarized the song-writing process: "Buddy was the major contributor, or the originator on the idea of the song. We (the Crickets) would all contribute, but it was Buddy who was the basic creator..."

Eager to release a hit record, Buddy rationalized that the band had to make certain concessions to achieve their goal. Joe B. Mauldin attributed their lack of foresight to youth and innocence: "Norman says, 'We'll spread it around, and that way everybody will get a little publicity.' And, we were all just having such a good time and never paid attention. We'd say, 'Let's put so-and-so's name on that one.' And, I don't think Buddy cared that he might be giving away money. I don't think money was that big (of) an interest to him. If it had been, things wouldn't have gotten as screwed up as they did. We didn't have a lawyer—we just did everything on trust in each other."

Petty further deceived his young recording artists. He falsely led the Crickets to believe that they would be offered shares in Nor-Va-Jak Publishing, once the band generated a hit record.

Until Petty reached an understanding with Cedarwood Publishing about song writing royalties on *That'll Be the Day*, Buddy Holly's name could not appear on the record. Consequently, on May 16, 1957, Bob Thiele, who realized that Holly could be successful, with or without the Crickets, signed Buddy to a separate record contract with Coral Records. From that point forward, Brunswick would release records recorded by the Crickets, while Coral would issue recordings by Buddy Holly. The separate labels were legally cosmetic; it was acknowledged by all parties that Buddy was the leader of the band; even J.I.'s drum set was imprinted with the logo: *BUDDY HOLLY AND THE CRICKETS.*

While Petty made more than one self-serving decision that negatively affected Buddy Holly and Crickets, he continued to present himself as a devout, church-going Christian. Norman secured a pledge from the Crickets that they would tithe a portion (traditionally 10 percent) of any future earnings to their respective churches. To seal the bond, Petty had the group place their hands atop the Bible he kept in his control room, and together, they offered a prayer of thanksgiving.

While waiting for *That'll Be the Day* to be released by Brunswick, the financially-strapped Crickets took whatever jobs were available—Niki Sullivan drove a flower delivery truck, Joe B. shined shoes, J.I. was employed at a grocery store, and Buddy laid tile and worked construction. Continuous manual labor convinced Buddy that he needed to add some muscle to his lean frame, and he began lifting weights; one of many self-improvements that he would initiate in the months to follow.

The Crickets continued to play at every available venue. Several of those performances were on the state fair circuit. Ever in a rush, Buddy was pulled over for speeding by a law enforcement officer in route to a Texas fair ground. J.I. remembered Holly was indignant, and informed the officer that he was hurrying to perform a public service for the county's economic benefit: "And, you're going to stop me?"

On one occasion, Holly managed to combine both work and music. Along with his brother, Larry, Buddy drove an 18-wheeler to San Angelo, Texas to pick up a load of tiles. During their trip, the pair stopped to eat at a café in the predominately black section of a small town. After gobbling down a hamburger, Buddy discussed music with the black combo entertaining the diners. Consequently, one of the band members asked Buddy if he wanted to join them during their next number, *Sexy Ways*.

"I don't mind if I do," Buddy replied.

"It was rocking before we left," Larry remembered, as other patrons began packing the restaurant.

Buddy's guitar performance that day was an epiphany for both brothers. Larry had always known that "he (Buddy) was good, but not that good." After they were back on the road, Buddy told his brother he was now certain that his life's calling was to entertain people.

Norman Petty eventually allowed the Crickets to practice and record in his studio without paying a fee. Petty's actions were not entirely benevolent; in a rare moment of self-disclosure, Norman informed another of his artists, Jimmy Self, that he could "almost smell the dollar bills here."

Holly and Petty were both night owls, which fit perfectly with the need to record during the late-night and early-morning hours in Clovis. When other artists booked the studio, Buddy readily volunteered to play the guitar and sing background vocals. Holly's voice and guitar playing can be heard on albums Petty produced for Tex-Mex artists, including Jack Crawford and Ray Ruff.

About a month after recording *That'll Be the Day* and *I'm Looking for Someone to Love*, Buddy and the Crickets cut two more singles, *Maybe Baby* and *Last Night*. Buddy's mother had written the first part of the lyrics for *Maybe Baby*, "just to prove I can write a song, too." Insisting that her contribution had been small and unbecoming of a Christian lady, Ella Holley asked not to be recognized as a composer on the record.

Maybe Baby, smooth and fluid, is more pop than classic rock and roll, revealing the hopes of someone who is smitten with a yet unattainable love interest. If the singer can be patient, just maybe, his dreams will come true.

Buddy was clearly on a song-writing roll. In a six-month period during 1957, he composed *Words of Love, Everyday, Listen to Me, Tell Me How,* and *Peggy Sue*.

While awaiting the release of *That'll Be the Day*, Buddy and the Crickets recorded more than a dozen songs at *Norman Petty Studios*. Between June

29th and July 1st, Holly recorded four songs that ultimately charted in *Billboard's* Top 100—*Peggy Sue,* Oh Boy, *Listen to Me,* and *I'm Gonna Love You Too.* "Buddy just loved to record," Petty marveled.

The Crickets made use of the kitchen and sleeping facilities at the studio, often crashing there for a few days, rather than making the 200-mile round-trip from Lubbock to Clovis. Buddy's parents were naturally curious about where their youngest son was spending so much of his time. When L.O. and Ella finally drove to Clovis, they were impressed by Norman Petty's professionalism and repeated references to his religious faith.

It didn't take long for Petty to recruit members of the Holley family to perform tasks on his behalf. L.O., Travis, Larry, and Buddy brought over a truck load of tiles, left-overs from previous jobs, and laid them on the floor of the attic echo chamber next door, helping soundproof the space. "We figured it was the least we could do, because of all that Norman seemed to be doing for Buddy," Larry recalled.

Early on, there was a genuine and mutual respect between Petty and the Crickets. Norman utilized his innate microphone-placement skills during recording sessions. The microphone Petty positioned between the strings and body of Joe B.'s stand-up base captured more of the instrument's natural percussion. Using the equipment at hand, he maximized the Crickets' innate talents. "Many people give me credit for creating Buddy Holly. I didn't. I exaggerated or captured various peculiar and natural things he did," Petty truthfully admitted.

It was a comfortable situation for the young musical artists and their producer. "The one thing Norman did for us was just to let us ramble. If there was an idea there, and we had it worked out in song form, then we could go into the studio and work on it until we got it the way it sounded good to everybody. Norman just kept us going; however long it took; it didn't make any difference. There was never any pressure at Petty's studio, and Buddy felt relaxed. Buddy was able to sing natural—the songs just came natural—ideas came natural. And, Norman never stood in the way. He might offer a suggestion here or there, or want us to add this or take that away, but he never pressured Buddy to hurry up, or to change what Buddy was trying to present," J.I. remembered.

Buddy's skills as a composer continuously improved. No longer having to compete against Bob Montgomery, Sonny Curtis, and Don Guess, who were also skilled song-writers, Holly capitalized on the opportunity to hone his craft.

When Buddy wrote songs at his parent's house in Lubbock, his mother remembered that he would suddenly leave, during or just after their evening meal. After Buddy drove around for an hour or so, Ella described what happened next: "Then he'd come back, go straight to his room, pick up his guitar and start to sing it—something he had been thinking about, while he was out in the car by himself."

When the boys stayed over in Clovis, an opportunistic Norman made sure they stayed busy between recording sessions. Buddy and the other Crickets were not only expected to keep the premises neat and clean, but also weed the rose garden and mow the lawn.

Money never strayed far from Petty's mind, and he mistakenly assumed Holly felt the same way. Norman reminded Buddy that he was the star of the show, and by all rights, should keep the group's royalties, while placing J.I., Niki, and Joe B. on straight salaries. Buddy immediately nixed this proposal, believing each band member deserved an equal share.

"Buddy was the most giving person to the people around him that I've ever known. Other stars kept their musicians on salary, but Buddy said, 'No, man—share and share alike. You're as much a part of this group as I am. If it wasn't for you guys, I couldn't perform what I put on.' When we started out, it was Buddy, Jerry, Niki Sullivan and me. Buddy wanted to split everything four ways flat—25 percent for everybody. And, Norman said, 'Hey, wait a minute. You're the star, they're the sidemen. Put them on salary.' And, Buddy said, 'No, I wouldn't do that to a dog…'" Joe B. graciously recalled.

"We divided everything into equal shares, 25 percent apiece, the records and the touring. Buddy did insist on that. I can remember

Norman saying, 'Buddy is the singer, the leader, and he's entitled to a larger share.' And, Buddy, at that point, said, 'No I want it equal. I'd rather have it that way,'" Niki added.

Petty was not impressed by Buddy's generosity. He considered a four-way split on live performance fees marginally acceptable, but believed that Holly was neglecting his own self-interest, when he insisted on equal distribution of money generated from record royalties.

Petty recognized that Buddy was not only the most talented member of the group, but also performed a disproportionate amount of work, releasing his own songs under Coral Records and performing as the star on the Crickets' Brunswick Records. Only a handful of his later Coral solo records contained vocals other than Buddy's. In contrast, *all* the Crickets' Brunswick records required background studio vocalists. Apart from Niki Sullivan's vocals on *That'll Be the Day* and *Not Fade Away*, none of the Crickets ever sang during studio recordings.

When the Crickets later released their first Brunswick LP, entitled *The Chirping Crickets*, the Picks (brothers John and Bill Pickering, along with their friend, Bob Latham) performed as background vocalists. On later Brunswick recordings, the Picks were replaced by the Roses—Bob Linville, Ray Rush, and David Bigham.

"When we started to record sometimes, we didn't know if it was going to be a Crickets' record or a Buddy Holly record," J.I. Allison explained. Norman Petty concurred: "Every time that we would record, there would be some songs that were conducive to just being a solo, and some that needed backing." Bob Thiele, who landed the Brunswick and Coral Record contracts, confirmed that neither the Crickets' records nor Buddy Holly's solo releases were targeted to appeal to a specific listening audience. Niki Sullivan, however, noted one constant: "Buddy was always the leader in our group. Buddy had something in mind, frankly, I don't think all of us quite understand. Buddy was looking for a sound to record."

Whether it was a Brunswick or Coral Record, Buddy Holly was the lead vocalist, most often the lead guitarist, and quite often the song-writer. Hence, his willingness to split the royalties four ways was truly charitable.

While Buddy Holly was kind and generous, he was by no means a saint, and found it difficult to suppress his active libido. During one of her husband's late night excursions, perhaps a rumored liaison with a male lover, Vi Petty allegedly invited Buddy to the couple's next door apartment. When an astonished Buddy returned to the studio, he told Niki Sullivan: "I can't believe it. I made love to Vi." Others, like Sonny Curtis, considered the story "ludicrous." "Guys tell each other things like that, I would have known about it," Curtis explained.

Norman's friend, Dr. Jerry Fisher, also doubted that a dependent Vi was capable of infidelity: "For the episodic schizophrenic Vi was, it would have been impossible for her ever even to contemplate having sex with anyone but Norman." Niki, who was actually present at the studio complex when the alleged sexual liaison occurred, refuted the doubters: "Buddy was never a braggart about that kind of thing. If Buddy said it happened, it happened."

Beginning in 1957, there is considerable evidence that Buddy did become romantically involved with a married woman. The relationship began when the Crickets started rehearsing at the Lubbock home of their friends, James "Nig" Clark and his wife, June.

In their late 20s, the Clarks were rock and roll fans, and from the very beginning, ardent supporters of the Crickets. The couple, who had married when June was only 16, had an 11-year-old son, but their relationship was less than harmonious. Some of their friends believed that Nig and June remained married, solely for the benefit of their child.

Buddy, whose relationship with Echo McGuire was nearing its end, was smitten with the slim, attractive, and vivacious June. Holly's attraction to June, however, appeared to be driven by more than just youthful lust. "I knew he liked me, because he was a normal young guy. But the thing he always wanted to do most when we were together was just talk to me," June remembered.

Buddy's infatuation was such that he would linger for hours at Hull's Drug Store, where June worked behind the cosmetics counter. June grew concerned that Buddy's conspicuous behavior would alert Nig to their clandestine affair. Buddy, who seemed to care little about what others thought, told June that he would give up music, if she would leave her husband and run away with him. Whether that promise was made during the height of passion or represented genuine devotion, it was truly a profound statement; Buddy would be abandoning his long-standing dream of becoming a professional entertainer, just as he was on the cusp of achieving stardom.

Larry Holley, hoping to avert scandal and rectify an impulsive, career-ending mistake by his younger brother, eventually intervened. He took Buddy on a fishing trip to Colorado, hoping to separate the couple long enough for Buddy to reassess his priorities. Larry's timely intervention may have saved Buddy's career.

"One day, in this little Colorado town, we passed a record store and there was (Paul) Anka's picture in the window, and a caption saying how *Diana* was shooting up the Top 10. After that, Buddy couldn't keep his mind on fishing, at all. 'I know I can beat this Paul Anka kid.' He kept saying, 'I know I can beat him!'" Larry recalled. While his affair with June continued for several more months, Buddy never again talked about giving up his musical career for her.

Beginning on a Tuesday night, April 8, 1957, Buddy and the Crickets recorded a new song composed by Buddy. *Words of Love* reveals the private exchanges of a couple very much in love. The melodic, opening acoustic guitar chords set the stage for a song that has captivated many listeners over the years, including rock and roll legend, Paul McCartney.

The simple, yet complex tune, required six hours to complete—by far, the Crickets longest single recording session. The echoing quality of Buddy's voice sounds distinctly different from any of his previous recordings; the result of overdubbing, which allowed Holly to harmonize with himself.

Lacking multi-tracking technology, *Words of Love* was Buddy's first experience with overdubbing. The original song tape was replayed at the same time as additional vocal and instrumental sounds were added to it. Afterwards, the combination was recorded on a second tape machine. In the master recording, it appears that Buddy's vocals, the rhythm guitar, drums, and bass were recorded first. Next, Buddy overdubbed with his lead guitar and repeated the lyrics. At this point in music history, the technique was innovative. Holly biographer, John Goldrosen, wrote that "Holly was probably the first rock 'n' roll artist to use vocal and instrumental overdubbing..."

J.I. Allison credited Holly with the idea of overdubbing *Words of Love*: "Buddy had two guitar parts worked out, that he wanted to play, before we even started to record that. I don't know just how he got the idea, but he planned to do it that way. It wasn't like he came over to the studio and somebody said, 'Hey, why don't you do this?' Because, he figured it out before."

The B side *to Words of Love*, which took only one take and about 10 minutes to record, was *Mailman, Bring Me No Blues*. Norman roused Vi Petty from bed to play piano on the recording; Vi's annoyance at being awakened appears to have been loudly taken out on the ivories. The song was composed by Decca's Bob Thiele (under the pseudonym, Stanley Clayton), along with composers, Ruth Roberts and Bill Katz. Thiele informed Buddy that *Mailman, Bring Me No Blues* had been written especially for him.

For whatever reason, Norman Petty sent the record directly to Peer Southern, rather than Coral. Within their rights as music publishers, Peer Southern then gave *Words of Love* to a Canadian group, the Diamonds, who had recently recorded a million-selling single, *Little Darling* (which climbed to Number Two on the charts).

The Diamonds immediately recorded *Words of Love*, which was released on May 20th. Buddy's rendition of *Words of Love* was not issued by Coral until a month later—by then, the Diamonds version of the song had amassed an insurmountable lead in record sales. Consequently,

Buddy's first success and significant royalty payments came from his role as a song-writer, rather than a recording artist. Interestingly, on the Diamond's single, the composer's name appears spelled as Buddy *Holley*.

The weeks and months passed slowly after the release of *That'll Be the Day*. The record label was responsible for much of the delay. Decca, still not sold on rock and roll, did very little to promote Holly's dream song.

Even though he was frustrated and impatient, Buddy worked even harder. He was determined the Crickets were not going to be entirely a studio band, and wanted them to sound just as good during stage performances. The band practiced religiously at J.I.'s and Larry Holley's house, Nig and June Clark's residence, and at a rented space in south Lubbock. Their efforts proved worthwhile; in the future, the Crickets would not always have to lip sync during television performances. The only difference between the band's live performances and studio recordings was the absence of background vocals, except for a few occasions when Niki Sullivan sang harmony on stage.

Absent a hit record, the Crickets had little money in their pockets. Only three months after his brother, Larry, had made the down payment, Buddy realized he could not keep up the installments on his used Cadillac, and secretly returned it to the car lot. The following day, the owner of the dealership appeared at Larry Holley's house, demanding full payment, after discovering that Buddy had naively abandoned the Cadillac. Ever the dutiful older brother, Larry assumed payments, enabling Buddy to keep his automobile.

Eager for recognition, on May 11, 1957, the Crickets auditioned for the *Arthur Godfrey Talent Scouts*, a nationally broadcast show, which featured promising new performers. The closest regional location for the audition was at the *KFDA* television studio in Amarillo, Texas, a three-hour drive from Lubbock. At 3:45 p.m. the Crickets opened their audition with a Little Richard song, followed by some of their own numbers. Godfrey's scouts, who were unimpressed with rock and roll music, did not offer the Crickets a spot on the show, just as they had done when Elvis Presley auditioned in 1955. "When we finished, the guy that was in charge of the audition said, 'Oh my gosh, what is music going to?'" Joe B. laughingly recalled.

That same month, likely when both groups were playing at the same concert venue, the Crickets made friends with Phil and Don Everly. The Everly Brothers' *Bye Bye Love*, release by Cadence Records, had recently exploded onto the charts. The Crickets' kinship with the Kentucky-born siblings would last for a lifetime.

Buddy, who was impressed by the rhythmic harmony of Phil and Don, offered to let them record his newly-written song, *Not Fade Away*. The duo had no choice but to turn him down, because their manager, Wesley Rose, insisted that his rising stars record only songs by a select writing team. Before long, the Everly Brothers scored yet another hit, *All I Have to do is Dream*. Nonetheless, Don was appreciative of Holly's offer: "It was nice for Buddy to do that for us."

Ever observant, Buddy believed the Everly Brothers' success bode well for the Crickets. Their styles were so similar that Holly believed his solo voice sounded like Phil, but when overdubbed, he mimicked the brothers' harmony.

During the summer of 1957, Buddy and one of the other Crickets, either J.I. or Joe B., entered a *Battle of the Bands* contest in Lubbock; the winner to be determined by the performers who received the loudest applause from the audience, When Buddy first appeared on stage, an envious member of another group shouted: "There comes old turkey neck!" Larry Holley, who was in attendance, experienced conflicting emotions: "I didn't think he was going to win after hearing all them (sic) other guys. They was (sic) booing and hollering and carrying on, but Buddy didn't let it bother him at all. Of course, I was there and it made me mad, but Buddy got up there just as professional-like, and started playing, and it wasn't any comparison to them other guys. He started shuffling across the floor, not like Chuck Berry, where he gets down low and squats, but just shuffling along like he was playing for the King of England, and could care less what they thought. He was going to do the best he could, and the crowd went wild, and he won. That's when I knew that Buddy had the quality that it would take to overcome the heckling…"

On May 16, 1957, not yet aware of *That'll Be the Day's* fate, Buddy was informed that *Words of Love* and *Mailman, Bring Me No Blues* would be released as a 45-RPM record in 11 days. Decca executives were impressed by the quality of Holly's voice on *Words of Love*, and released it on the more prestigious Coral label. The song, which had already been a hit for the Diamonds, failed to crack *Billboard's* Top 100. The record's B side, *Mailman, Bring Me No Blues*, also failed to chart.

Thirteen days later, during a return visit to Clovis, Buddy recorded his self-composed *Everyday*. During a break, Buddy experimented with the studio's celesta (an instrument akin to a harpsicord), before announcing: "You know, that's what this song needs."

After Vi Petty wrote out the score, the celesta, played by Norman, became the lead instrument in *Everyday*. Only one other early rock and roll-era song, *It's Too Late*, performed by Chuck Wills and released in 1956, is known to have used a celesta as part of its instrumentation.

While Buddy was practicing *Everyday*, J.I. kept time by tapping his hands on his knees. "Hey, that sounds good," Buddy remarked. Consequently, the master recording features J.I. slapping his blue jeans as the song's sole percussion. "On *Everyday*, I patted my knees. Buddy was playing guitar and I was keeping rhythm; so, we recorded it like that. (I) never set a finger on the drums on that record; being lazy, I guess," J.I. recalled.

The gentle, but upbeat tune, describes an unconsummated love affair. With patience, the day will finally come.

Even though Buddy did not have a songwriting contract with Cedarwood, Norman Petty had not yet reached a final settlement with Decca's Nashville division. As a precaution, Holly used a pseudonym, Charles Hardin (his first and middle name) on *Everyday's* song-writing credits.

Everyday might have become a bigger seller, had it not later been released as the B-side to the mega-hit, *Peggy Sue*. While it failed to chart in the U.S., *Everyday* later climb to Number 16 on the *New Musical Express*—a compilation of the 30 best-selling singles in Great Britain. Even though *Everyday* was never a contemporary chart favorite in America, rock and roll music critic, Jonathan Gott, later described it as one of "Holly's deepest, wisest, and seemingly least complicated songs," which "expresses the unadorned confrontation of beauty and love with time." *Everyday* not only became one of the most popular cover songs for future artists, but it also was one of Buddy's personal favorites.

The same day that *Everyday* was recorded, Buddy and the Crickets recorded *Not Fade Away*—the song he had first offered to the Everly Brothers. The hard-driving, classic rock and roll score features a Bo Diddley-like beat, charged by Buddy's uninhibited guitar strokes and his wide vocal range. The overdubbed vocals of both Holly and Nikki Sullivan add texture to the background. *Not Fade Away* featured another unconventional source of percussion; just as he had done in Holly's cover of Elvis Presley's *Baby I Don't Care*, J.I. pounded out the rhythm on an empty cardboard box, rather than his drum set.

Not Fade Away is a bold anthem. Rather than singing about hopeful anticipation, it is a boastful declaration, foreshadowing a night of unbridled passion.

Even though Buddy wrote *Not Fade Away* (with some help from J.I.), it would not appear as such on the record. Norman Petty listed himself as the co-composer, completely omitting J.I.'s name from the song-writing credits. "Buddy and I wrote *Not Fade Away*, and again, my name isn't on it. The verse about *my love* being *bigger than a Cadillac* is mine..." J.I. recalled.

In the early summer of 1957, Buddy and the Crickets recorded two more songs in Clovis, neither or which proved to be best sellers. *Ready Teddy*, written by Robert Blackwell and John Maralsco, had initially been released by Little Richard in 1956, but the cover version by Elvis proved to be more popular, and many listeners came to associate the song with Presley. Buddy's version, no less raucous, features lively vocals and a driving instrumental beat.

The second recording of the night, *Valley of Tears*, was more in tune with a C & W ballad—another indication of Holly's versatility. Though Buddy was never enamored with the organ, Norman insisted on playing it in the background. *Valley of Tears* never charted in the U.S., but in 1961, two years after Holly's death, it was released as the B side to *Everyday*, which climbed to Number 12 on the chart in the U.K.

By now, it was clear *That'll Be the Day* (with *I'm Looking for Someone to Love* on the B-side), which had been released by Brunswick on May 27, 1957, was not going to be an overnight hit. On June 10th, *Billboard* magazine, in its "reviews of new pop records," assigned both songs a mediocre 72 (out of 100) rating. The *Billboard* reviewer described the Crickets first record as a "medium beat rockabilly," whose "performance is better than the material."

The course followed by *That'll Be the Day* was quite unusual; most new records either moved up the charts quickly or failed to sell. In the latter case, disc jockeys deemed the single a flop, and gave it little or no play time. *That'll Be the Day*, however, started out slowly on the national level, before regional market sales eventually drove it to the top.

The unconventional route followed by *That'll Be the Day* can largely be credited to the actions of two American disc jockeys. George Woods, who spun records at Philadelphia's *WDAS*, which catered to a predominately black listening audience, played the Crickets' record so often that it became a hit in the surrounding area. In Buffalo, Tom Clay, whose *WWOL* DJ name was Guy King, was so enamored with *That'll Be the Day*, he played the single several times per day, including a continuous 20-minute stretch.

Both Murray Deutch and Bob Thiele gave most of the credit for the record's latent success to George Woods. "For weeks and weeks nothing happened—there were no orders. And, then I got a call from Norman

Weinstroer, the sales manager for Brunswick. He said, 'Georgie Woods wants to play the record.' And, it busted wide open. Woods was the one who broke the record," Deutch recalled. Deutch was delighted, but amazed: "All of a sudden, the record started to sell; the sales department called, and they had one order from Philly, alone, for 20,000 copies!"

The rising popularity of *That'll Be the Day* was not yet known to Buddy and the Crickets, who continued to record songs at a manic pace. On a blistering hot day, June 30, 1957, the band returned to Clovis and recorded what would turn out to be a monster hit. *Peggy Sue*, written by Buddy, was originally entitled *Cindy Lou*, in honor of Holly's niece, Cindy, and his sister's middle name, Lou. Just three weeks earlier, Patricia Lou Weir had given birth to a daughter named Cindy. The original score featured a slower-tempo, Latin beat, until J.I. intervened.

Allison pleaded with Buddy to change the name of the song to *Peggy Sue*, in honor of his former girlfriend. Peggy Sue Gerron had broken-up with J.I. in the summer of 1956. Afterwards, Peggy Sue moved to Sacramento, California and lived with her older sister and brother-in-law. After arriving in California, she attended her senior year of high school at an all-girl's Catholic school. "Jerry wanted to do something to get me back," Peggy Sue later recalled.

Buddy tentatively agreed to J.I.'s proposal, but only if the percussionist could maintain a driving drum beat throughout the song, such that it could be recorded in only one take. Instead of the previously envisioned Latin tempo, Buddy wanted Allison to play paradiddles—a practice drum roll that percussionists often employ while warming-up, using only the snare drums, absent the cymbals. To keep the percussion from overwhelming the guitar and vocals, J.I.'s drum set was moved into the reception area. The repetitive, driving drum rolls were also filtered through the echo chamber next door.

Peggy Sue featured Buddy playing both rhythm and lead guitar. While singing, he played rhythm, but changed to treble lead at the first instrumental break. Because he was unable to play and change the switch on his Fender Stratocaster at the same time, Niki Sullivan knelt at his side in the studio. "Buddy couldn't switch from playing rhythm on the chorus to playing lead on the bridge; he couldn't get his hand to the switch fast enough, without breaking rhythm and having it show up on tape," Sullivan recalled. Holly eventually learned to maneuver the switch on his own, as evidenced during stage and television performances.

J.I. was highly impressed with Buddy's skill as a guitarist: "I've never seen anyone, since, who plays it that way. Every other guitar player strums it back and forth with his pick—down-up-down-up, like that. But, Holly did it with just down strokes—down-down-down-down-down-down." Buddy's vocals also feature his trademark hiccups and stutters; at one point, he manages to stretch the name Sue into six syllables.

While J.I. was playing paradiddles, Norman Petty constantly adjusted the volume control, generating a throbbing quality. While it required two takes for Allison to perfect his role as a percussionist, it still only took 20 minutes to record *Peggy Sue*, and Buddy was more that satisfied with the song's name change. When the record was eventually released, its unique sound captivated listeners. Author, Paul Williams, offered a memorable tribute in the book, *In Rock 'n' Roll: The 100 Best Singles*: "There is something perfect about the sound of *Peggy Sue*. It gets into the blood. Buddy Holly could have been a country singer, or pop crooner, could have and probably would have fitted his talent to whatever music was happening in the world when he came along. It happened to be rock 'n' roll. But, it only fully became rock 'n' roll the day Buddy Holly started singing it."

"Buddy Holly would change the mood of the song with the chords. He was one of the first to match lyrics to music…" musician, Gary Murphy, proclaimed. Singer, song-writer, and playwright, Andy Wilkinson, summed up the up the unique qualities of the song: "*Peggy Sue* works so well exactly because it doesn't tell us a thing about her; it shows us, instead. So, instead of being preached to, when the song's over, we feel about *Peggy Sue* the same way that the singer does. That's the best kind of writing."

While Buddy (with some assistance from J.I.) composed *Peggy Sue*, Norman Petty immediately recognized the song's hit potential. Predictably, he placed his own name on the song-writing credits. By the time the record was released, it listed only Petty and Allison as the composers, completely excluding Holly. *Peggy Sue* would eventually climb to Number Three on *Billboard's* pop chart and Number Two on the R&B charts, selling more than 1,000,000 records.

Throughout the summer of 1957, Buddy and the Crickets continued to churn out recordings in the Clovis studio. *Listen to Me*, written by Buddy, features double-tracking, echoing both Holly's voice and guitar. The song effectively validates the profound nature of true love. The almost eerie quality of the recording mimics the chords on Mickey and Sylvia's Number One hit, *Love is Strange*, which was one of Buddy's favorites. The influence of *Listen to Me* can be heard in 1960s' records by the Beatles, the Byrds, and the Mamas and Papas.

As had been the case with *Everyday*, Holly used the song-writing pseudonym of Charles Hardin on *Listen to Me*. Yet again, Norman Petty added his name as co-composer, even though Buddy had written the entire song before it was recorded.

During the recording of another song, *I'm Gonna Love You Too*, a cricket somehow made its way into the echo chamber and eluded capture. On the LP, *Buddy Holly*, and the cassette tape, *Oh Boy*, the insect is audible, not to mention in rhythm, near the end of the song. *I'm Gonna Love You Too* is a bold declaration of sorts—a former lover will eventually return to the fold.

Oh Boy, written by Sonny West and Bill Tilghman, was yet another single recorded by the Crickets in the prolific summer of 1957. One of the best known of Buddy Holly's recordings, the opening lines promise a would-be lover a night (or perhaps even longer) of unforgettable passion.

Buddy continued to appear remarkably unconcerned about song-writing credits. Not yet aware that he had a hit record in the making, Holly either ignored or did not yet appreciate the significance of future royalty payments. He apparently believed what Norman had told him earlier—the presence of Petty's name would increase a record's playtime. Larry Holley offered a simpler explanation: "It wasn't just to Norman. Buddy would give a song away to anyone, because he knew he could write a new song every night."

The song-writing credits on the Crickets' and Buddy Holly's records are difficult to decipher, except for the fact that Norman Petty's name appears on most of them. *Peggy Sue*, written by Buddy, except for one bridge contributed to J.I., originally credited Petty and Allison as the co-composers. On *Maybe Baby*, both Nikki and Joe B. contributed to its composition, but Petty and Holly were listed as the song writers. *Not Fade Away*, written by Buddy and J.I., was released under the names Charles Hardin and Norman Petty. *I'm Gonna Love You Too* and *Well All Right* (yet to be recorded, and written solely by Buddy), listed the names of Holly, Mauldin, Allison, and Petty as joint composers.

Even though he had recorded a treasure trove of songs during the summer of 1957, Buddy Holly had little to show for his efforts. Six long weeks had passed since *That'll Be the Day* had been released by Brunswick, and Buddy was anxious and uncertain about the song's fate. While laying tile with his brother, Buddy openly shared his frustration.

"Why don't you call the guy in New York, direct, and just ask him?" Larry suggested. After the pair headed to their parent's house and Buddy telephoned the record company, Larry described the ensuing events: "And the guy there says, 'Hey, baby! They're playing your record on the streets of New York City!' So, Buddy says, 'Well can you send me five-hundred dollars? 'Cause I'm broke!'"

A few days later, while the Crickets were sleeping late after another all-night recording session in Clovis, Norman Petty awakened them to read a telegram from Murray Deutch—*That'll Be the Day* had already sold 50,000 records, and the Crickets should be prepared to come to New York City. Nikki Sullivan recalled that the news was slow to sink in; only Buddy was interested in reading the telegram, while "the rest of us just went back to sleep."

On July 29, 1957, *Billboard* magazine named *That'll Be the Day* as a "best buy record." By September 23rd, the song had rapidly ascended to the Number One ranking on *Billboard's* pop chart, and to Number Two on the rhythm and blues chart. A week later, the Crickets' first record became a million-seller. For three consecutive months, *That'll Be the Day* remained in *Billboard's* Top 30.

Bob Thiele soon offered a $600 advance for the master recordings of *Peggy Sue* and *Everyday*. The Crickets were suddenly in demand for stage performances, radio and television interviews, and record store promotional appearances.

Norman Petty informed the band that they were now in need of a manager. An enthusiastic Buddy quickly replied: "We've got a manager."

"Oh? Who is it?" Petty replied.

"You are," Buddy answered.

Petty later downplayed his spontaneous appointment as the Crickets' manager: "I did not force myself on them. I didn't say, 'Hey, I'm going to be your manager.' They asked me; and, in fact, I tried to convince them I really wasn't a manager."

"I don't remember if we asked him, or if he just sort of became our manager..." J.I. Allison recalled. Excited, youthful, and inexperienced, Niki Sullivan recalled that "the four of us literally pushed ourselves on Norman—we insisted that he do it."

Petty's management fee was set at 10 percent of Buddy Holly's and the Crickets' total earnings. He also promised to tithe 10 percent of each band members' performance and royalty fees to their respective churches. In retrospect, it appears unlikely that Petty made any direct payments to their churches; in that case, he pocketed far more than his

10 percent managerial fee, not to mention his unmerited share of the song-writing royalties.

Petty soon opened an account "for the band" at Clovis National Bank. It was, however, an account that only *he* could access.

Even though Petty later described his managerial role as a "glorified babysitting job," he immediately exercised rigid control over his charges, while reaping generous monetary benefits.

CHAPTER 5

The Big Time

AS THEY PREPARED FOR THEIR national debut, the Crickets were hardly models of sartorial splendor. In the studio, they wore blue jeans and tee shirts, or if the weather was oppressively hot, Bermuda shorts. During stage performances, Buddy adopted the flashy, Elvis look. "The first time I saw Buddy on stage, I was quite shocked. I saw him sporting a bright red jacket, bright shoes, and white trousers. And, after I saw that, I decided that it would have to go, because he was playing for adult audiences, too," Norman Petty concluded.

At a men's clothing store in Lubbock, Petty updated the Crickets wardrobe. When they departed for New York, Buddy, J.I., Niki, and Joe B. were outfitted with conservative slacks, sports coats, and suits.

Even before the Crickets boarded a commercial flight from Amarillo to the Big Apple, Petty had begun exerting rigid managerial control over their lives. Each of the four was given a detailed letter with 19 specific instructions, some of which were mundane, while others had far-reaching implications. Included in Petty's specific directives were: 1. What time to be at the airport for departure; 2. Instructions to take along $30 to $40 in cash, but otherwise use traveler's checks; 3. A warning to carry proper identification; 4. Instructions to "sign only engagement contracts and nothing more;" 5. What type of clothes to pack; 6. A reminder to take extra guitar strings and drum sticks; 7. Instructions to take a cab upon arrival in New York City and go "directly" to the Edison Hotel; 8. Advice to purchase "at least two dozen Dramamine and take at least one before your departure;" 9. A reminder to take a small Bible and "read it;" 10. "Be sure to send money back to Clovis for bank account."

The young and naïve Crickets had no idea just how much Petty's final instruction would ultimately impact their lives. For now, the boys from west Texas seemed far more comfortable with an experienced hand guiding their every move.

When the Crickets landed in New York City, they were no doubt excited, but also intimidated. Following Petty's instructions to the letter, the wide-eyed rock and rollers took a taxi to the Edison Hotel, located between 46th and 47th Streets, near Times Square. The Edison's rooms, priced at $27.70-per-night, were comfortable, but far from luxurious; a subtle reminder that Buddy and the Crickets were not yet established stars.

A telegram from Petty awaited the Crickets at their hotel, offering congratulations and reminding them that he would soon visit in person. The cable was signed "Papa Norman"—an innocent, but eventually dreaded moniker.

Coral Records' Director of Artists and Repertoire, Bob Thiele, who had dealt with Petty in the past, sensed there would be future problems in the relationship between the band and its manager. Thiele considered Buddy Holly to be a "nice guy," but likened Petty to a "cop," who always maintained strict control.

The Crickets were in awe of the sights and sounds of Manhattan. At Jack Dempsey's famed restaurant, they ordered bourbon and Coke cocktails, much to the amusement of the waiter and bartender, who treated them like country bumpkins.

After their first promotional appearance at a Manhattan record store where *That'll Be the Day's* sales had been brisk, Buddy and his bandmates hobnobbed with a prestigious group. "We were introduced to the head of Coral Records, Bob Thiele, and he invited us to his home in upstate New York—a beautiful place with two-inch carpeting. There were about six to ten people at the party including Steve Lawrence (the popular television comic, who was accompanied by his well-known wife and singer, Eydie Gorme), but mostly Coral-Brunswick executives…We were asked to perform and did a four-piece vocal of an old song. Norman Petty had given us this barbershop quartet song, something like *'O Baby Mine,* just to prove that we were a group and could sing. We did it without any instruments. (The) whole bunch was (sic) nice people, so comfortable and pleasant, but New Yorkish, elite enough to be upstate for relaxation," Niki Sullivan remembered.

In early August of 1957, after traveling from New York City to Philadelphia for another autograph-signing session at a record store, the Crickets began their first tour. Much has been said and written about this initial tour, some of which is apocryphal. For unknown reasons, perhaps his inexperience as a manager, Norman Petty had booked the Crickets for a series of performances in three cities, where they would be the only white performers on the bill.

It is questionable as to whether the tour promotor realized that Buddy Holly and the Crickets were white. Adding to the confusion, an all-black group from the Bronx, who had recently disbanded, Dean Barlow and the Crickets, were well-known for their hit record, *Fine Wine*. One of the former black Crickets, Early "Speedy" Carroll, had since joined the Cadillacs, who were part of Holly's first tour, and recently scored a hit record, *Speedo*. Buddy felt it necessary to apologize to the other tour acts about his lack of awareness that there had been another band named the Crickets. Adding to the confusion, an all-black group, the Ravens, had earlier recorded a song, entitled *That'll Be the Day*.

Others believe that fellow performers and audiences were fully aware that Buddy Holly and the Crickets were an all-white ensemble, even prior to the start of the concert series. In the beginning, a few black performers had their doubts about the west Texans, believing *That'll Be the Day* was a fluke, and the white Crickets were simply one-hit wonders. For the most part, the black artists were welcoming and friendly. As J.I. remembered it, the other entertainers were "always real nice to us." Joe B. was particularly grateful to the star of the show, Clyde McPhatter, who treated them warmly. Mauldin sensed that most of the other acts were aware of the Cricket's discomfort and "tried to help us."

Nonetheless, audiences in the *Around the World* tour, which featured stops in Baltimore, Washington D.C., and New York City, were expecting to be entertained by rhythm and blues' performers. During those three weeks, the Crickets would play in front of almost exclusively black audiences.

On August 2, 1957, Norman Petty was present for opening night at the Royal Theater in Baltimore. On the third day of the tour, Buddy developed laryngitis, forcing Niki Sullivan to fill in as lead singer until Holly regained his voice. A snide Petty was less than supportive of Buddy's misfortune, while also dismissing his importance: "*Anyone* can sing *those* songs."

After over overcoming confusion about the Crickets' racial make-up and the band's own anxiety, the shows in Baltimore and Washington D.C.'s Howard Theater went well. "It was really great—they were great audiences. There wasn't any tension, at all," J.I. remembered. Niki concurred: "Everybody made us feel right at home." The only real mishap involved someone stealing Niki's Gibson electric guitar, forcing him to hurriedly purchase a replacement instrument.

The final and most imposing stop on the *Around the World* tour was Harlem's Apollo Theater. The 1,600-seat venue was housed within a three-story building, with 15-feet-high, flashing purple lights, spelling out *APOLLO*. For over two decades, the biggest names in black entertainment had performed in the theater, including Billie Holiday, Ray Charles, Lena Horne, and Sammy Davis, Jr. The maxim of the day was: "If you can work the Apollo, you can work anywhere."

During their week-long engagement at the Apollo, the performers were scheduled to play four-shows-per-day; 12:30 p.m., 3:30 p.m., 6:30 p.m. and 9:30 p.m. On Wednesday, Saturday, and Sunday, a fifth show was added at midnight.

At a total cost of $76.65, Buddy, J.I., Nikki, and Joe B. were booked in the Theresa Hotel for a week. During their stay at the hotel, located on the corner of Harlem's 7th Avenue and 125th Street, the Crickets were likely unaware that they were the only Caucasians for miles around.

The hotel, however, was a convenient distance from the Apollo Theater, which was located at 253 West 125th Street.

While still feeling somewhat out of place, the Crickets had gained self-confidence from their solid performances in Baltimore and D.C. Contrary to popular lore, the Crickets were not the first white act to play at the Apollo, and black listeners had bought enough copies of *That'll Be the Day*, to make the song a hit on the rhythm and blues chart. J.I., however, was under the impression that the Apollo audience expected the Crickets to be an all-black band. Judging by the crowd's initial response, Allison may have been correct.

Before their opening show on August 16th, the Crickets received a telegram from Murray Deutch: "Congratulations and welcome back. I know you will knock them dead." Before a predominately black audience, excluding a few white booking agents and talent scouts, the Crickets were the second act during the matinee show.

After the emcee announced, "It's show time at the Apollo," Buddy and the Crickets had the misfortune of following Clyde McPhatter, whose hits included *Have Mercy Baby* and *Without Love*. When curtains opened, the Crickets encountered complete silence. Niki Sullivan vividly recalled what happened next: "There was this big lady, about 400 pounds, sitting right in front. Before we hit a note, she hollered out, 'You better sound as good as the record!'" After the Crickets performed *That'll Be the Day*, the audience offered mild applause, but was mostly unresponsive when the band performed their follow-up songs. Describing their early performances as "flops," Niki was alarmed: "I don't think five people clapped."

After two days of underwhelming performances at the Apollo, the Crickets were demoted to the show's final act. Adding insult to injury, the band was assigned to a malodorous, roach-infested dressing room.

On August 19th, four days before their final performance at the Apollo, Buddy tried a different approach to connect with the lackluster audience. Instead of opening with *That'll Be the Day*, Holly turned to his bandmates: "Ah, hell with it, let's given them *Bo Diddley*." Buddy's well-timed, extemporaneous decision proved that he was developing a sense of what listeners wanted to hear.

"…And, we went into *Bo Diddley*, cutting up and working our buns off. I was dancing around in a big circle, going through a bunch of gyrations, and Buddy was all over the stage, and Joe B. was bouncing that bass back and forth and laying it down, and I've never seen Jerry work harder on those damn drums. And, when we finished that song, the people just went bananas. From then on, we were accepted at the Apollo…" Niki vividly recalled. Sullivan was not bragging; black singing star and actress, Leslie Uggams, who was among the audience members that day, recalled that Buddy Holly was "terrific," "sexy," and "wonderful."

During their first professional tour, the Crickets had experienced a myriad of conflicting emotions—anxiety, disappointment, and adulation. As new-comers, they were also poorly compensated for their efforts. Booked at a rate of $1,000-per-week, after the union took its cut, promoter Irving Feld was paid, and Norman Petty shaved off his commission in advance, the performers were left with around $200 each.

The Crickets' next concert performances occurred during Alan Freed's *Grand Labor Day Rock 'n' Roll Show*, held at the 4,400-seat Paramount Theater, located at the corner of Brooklyn's Flatbush and DeKalb Avenues. Beginning in 1955, Freed, the widely popular disc jockey at New York City's radio station *WINS*, had promoted and hosted holiday rock and roll shows coinciding with Easter, Labor Day, and Christmas. The 35-year-old Freed, whose nickname was "Moondog," was perhaps the most influential promoter of his day, and boasted that *he* was the one who had invented the name rock and roll.

In late August, prior to the Labor Day shows, the Crickets appeared on television for the first time, performing on *Alan Freed's Rock 'n' Roll Show*, aired by the *ABC* network. On Monday, August 16th, Buddy and his bandmates appeared on another *ABC* show, *American Bandstand*, which was still in its infancy. Hosted by 27-year-old Dick Clark, who would eventually become a legend in the entertainment world, the program was telecast at 2:30 p.m. each day. Inside *American Bandstand's* studio in Philadelphia, around 200 teenagers sat on bleachers, primed to hit the cramped dance floor, when the guest artists began playing. The Crickets played *That'll Be the Day* in front of 20,000,000 television viewers—their first nationwide performance and largest audience, by far. The same day the band debuted on *American Bandstand*, That'll *Be the Day* passed the 500,000-mark in record sales.

Joining the Crickets on the *Great Labor Day Rock 'n' Roll Show* were several popular and more-established artists, including Little Richard, Buddy Knox, Eddie Cochran, Chuck Berry, the Del Vikings, Mickey and Sylvia, and the Diamonds (who had scored a hit with Holly's composition, *Words of Love*).

The Labor Day performances, seven-days in duration, were marathon sessions, lasting from 11:00 a.m. to 2:00 a.m., during which time the rock and rollers were required to play five to seven sets per day. After paying a one-dollar admission fee, audience members were entertained by up to 20 different artists per show. Between sets, while the crowds shuffled in and out, western movies were projected onto a big screen. Performers used the house microphones and lights, and unless they were a self-contained group, like the Crickets, were backed by the Alan Freed Orchestra.

The Crickets contract specified that they were to play "a minimum of 29 shows in any one week." Each act was allowed only a few minutes of stage time, long enough to play the A and B sides of their current hit record, and if lucky, a soon-to-be-released single.

The Crickets were well received during the Labor Day shows. In addition to wider recognition, their compensation improved five-fold from their first engagement, with each band member netting $1,000.

During the Crickets one-week appearance at the Brooklyn Paramount, June Clark, responding to repeated calls from Buddy, travelled to New York City with her son, under the guise of visiting her sister. Convinced that J.I. was also infatuated with June, Buddy kept her visit secret from Allison, even though Nikki and Joe B. were aware of the forthcoming liaison. Buddy and June had several trysts, either at her sister's apartment or a hotel. June recalled Buddy informing her that he wanted more than just an affair—a permanent relationship, but not at the expense of abandoning his musical career. Admitting that she "seriously thought about it," June was unwilling to risk the prospect of losing her son as the result of divorce and a potentially-nasty child custody proceedings. After June departed New York City, Buddy and his married lover never spoke again.

After performing on the Freed Labor Day shows, the Crickets settled into the Edison Hotel, preparing to join a rock and roll road show, arranged by promoter, Irving Feld. During the forthcoming tour, the Crickets would be joined by other rockers, including Paul Anka, Chuck Berry, Fats Domino, the Everly Brothers, and Frankie Lyman.

When Norman Petty visited their New York City hotel room, he was alarmed to see Buddy and J.I. leafing through a stack of cash, representing performance fees they had not forwarded to Clovis, as previously instructed. Petty reminded the Crickets that he was responsible for depositing their earnings in the bank. Joe B., ordinarily the most amenable of the Crickets, briefly challenged Petty, wanting to know if individual band members could withdraw funds from the bank account. Norman indicated that only he would have access to account, but the Crickets could submit their bills to him for payment. From that point forward, Petty instructed the Crickets to keep only $1000-per-week from their performance fees, and promptly send the balance to Clovis.

Their youthfulness and naiveté—Joe B. and J.I. were teenagers, while both Buddy and Niki were only 20—made them more susceptible to Petty's manipulations. It was a decision they would rue; the Crickets would never know how much of their earnings Petty kept on deposit.

Petty justified his actions based on the boys' immaturity, and their actions, in part, reinforced his supposition. During a water squirting contest, the underlying tension between Nikki and Jerry exploded into verbal warfare. The angry shouting match eventually degenerated into a fist fight. A few days later, when the band posed for the cover photo on their first long-play album, *The Chirping Crickets*; J.I. had a visible cut on his left cheek from the altercation with Niki.

Even though they played pranks on one another and had their share of disagreements, the Crickets nonetheless developed a compassionate kinship. On August 31, 1957, J.I.'s 18th birthday, his bandmates threw him a surprise party, including a cake that spelled out his middle name, Ivan, with candy decorations.

In New York City, the Crickets renewed their friendship with the Everly Brothers. Don, the older of the two brothers, remembered the Crickets were "nice guys" and "like brothers." Phil described the bond that the Everly's developed with Buddy and his bandmates: "We were all from the South; we'd all started out in country music. It was like belonging to a fraternity." Don never forgot Buddy's earlier offer to let them record *Not Fade Away*: "He was the most generous person with his music I've ever met in this business."

Further along in their careers, Phil and Don Everly were more sophisticated in the ways of the world, and quickly determined that the Texans needed a wardrobe update. Don took the Crickets to Phil's Men Shop, located on Manhattan's 3rd Avenue, and had them outfitted in single-breasted suits—the so called "Ivy League" look, replacing the more conservative attire purchased by Norman Petty in Lubbock. Phil and Don also talked Buddy into replacing his half-rim silver eyeglasses with a black horn-rimmed pair, which would eventually become his trademark. Now that he had the means to afford new clothes, Holly, who had always been a fastidious dresser, would maintain an even more stylish appearance.

Buddy also became a regular patron of Manny's Music Store in Manhattan, establishing a close relationship with sales clerk, Henry Goldried. Between 1957 and 1958, Holly purchased two Stratocasters, a Guild F-50 Navarre acoustic guitar, a Gibson J-200 acoustic guitar, a Magnatone Custom 280 amplifier, and a Gibson Stereo GA amplifier.

Irving Feld's *Biggest Show of Stars for 1957* tour, sponsored by General Artists Corporation (GAC), left New York on September 6, 1957, for an 80-day, cross-country swing, covering 10,000 miles, while visiting 24 states and five Canadian provinces. Because of the Freed Labor Day concert, the Crickets missed the first two stops, Pittsburgh and Norfolk, before joining the tour buses, which crisscrossed the United States and Canada. From September 9th through November 24th, the Crickets would perform 67 out of 77 days on the road, usually two-shows-per-day. Most of the performances were one-night stands, which included stops in places like Akron, Cincinnati, Columbus, and Hershey. "It was a bus loaded with everybody in the Top 10," Phil Everly recalled.

During the two-hour shows, there were so many performers that each act was limited to a 10-minute set, and the Crickets only had time to play three songs—*That'll Be the Day*, and two of the following, *Ready Teddy*, *Peggy Sue*, or *Oh Boy*. Many of the concerts were held in smaller auditoriums, where audience members paid three to four dollars to gain admission. The enthusiasm of the small-to-medium-sized audiences was infectious, and on one occasion, when the crowd cheered for an encore, Buddy turned to his bandmates: "Wasn't that fun?"

Even though the Crickets had very few days off and the most they earned for any given show was $1,000, Buddy was thrilled with the opportunity to perform. "I think the real Buddy Holly was there, behind the mike. Away from the mike, he was quiet, reserved, business-like, shy, introverted, if you will. Behind the microphone, he was just like a bolt of lightning. He had to be happy while he was doing it; that's what he always wanted to do. It was one-hundred percent, the real Buddy Holly, the minute he walked on the stage," Niki recalled.

Performing seemed to fulfill most of Holly's needs while on the road. Niki never saw Buddy with a girl during this tour. Joe B., who agreed that Buddy "was never hustling girls," remembered Holly's behavior between shows: "Every once in a while, he'd have some beer, or go get a couple of drinks, but even that was sparingly..." On the lengthy bus trips, Buddy often relaxed by shooting dice. After two and one-half months on the road, Holly was regarded as one of the rock and rollers' best crapshooters.

The entertainers, irrespective of background, race, and gender, got along well within the tight confines of the buses. Famed rhythm and blues singer, LaVern Baker, became the group's official mother, patching tears and sewing buttons on stage uniforms.

Sometimes, the performers were lucky enough to steal a few hours of sleep in a hotel, but the hectic pace often necessitated all-night bus rides. Phil Everly, who was only 18-years-old, enjoyed the adventure of the tour experience, including sleeping in luggage racks and making up silly songs with his fellow entertainers. Along the way, the entertainers had fun with pillow fights and good-natured pranks, like de-pantsing someone.

"I don't recall much drinking. We didn't have time—usually we were too tired. As for dope—zero on dope. I didn't even know what marijuana was, until years later. There were girls around, but you know, at any time we had to jump on a bus after a show and travel three to five-hundred miles, that was out…" Niki recalled, "We didn't need booze or drugs. We were all on a natural high…"

J.I., however, found the tour experience to be less than glamorous: "It really was a draggy tour. I think we missed about five states (*a bit of an exaggeration*). We'd get on a bus and ride and get off and pick, then get back on and ride."

During the era of Jim Crow, the rock and rollers discovered their shared musical bond transcended racism. "My whole life of education seemed to occur right there on that 80-day tour. The most outstanding thing to me was the camaraderie—everybody living and working together. Color just didn't come up. The Drifters treated me as kind of a white sheep of the family. If I had a trouble, or worry, or loneliness, they would always sit down and talk to me. After we got back to New York, we had our farewell party, and when they all went out and got on the bus to leave, I cried," Niki recalled.

Joe B. established a particularly close relationship with Chuck Berry. During the tour, after receiving a royalty check, Berry purchased a Cadillac. From that point forward, he would occasionally ask Joe B. to ride along with him in his new car. Joe B. not only enjoyed a temporary reprieve from the cramped buses, but also found the 31-year-old Berry to be a mentor and a friendly source of advice. Even though Berry was nearing the height of his fame, Joe B. found him to be "a super guy" and "would talk to me about anything."

There were a few mishaps during the lengthy tour. Fourteen-year-old Frankie Lyman, who had parted with his group, the Teenagers, after scoring a major hit, *Why Do Fools Fall in Love,* was on the fast track to delinquency, abusing drugs and sleeping with prostitutes. In Canada, Lyman was confronted by the police with heroin in his hotel room. His celebrity profile likely kept him from being arrested. The singer's manager wasn't so lucky; he was arrested by Canadian law enforcement officials for possession of drugs. Even though he was still a young teenager, Frankie Lyman's career was on a downward spiral, and he would die of a heroin overdose at the age of 25.

Canadian star, Paul Anka, who was only 16-years-old, but had already charted a Number One song, *Diana,* got off on the wrong foot with Buddy Holly. Hyperactive by nature, Anka accidently knocked a plug from an electrical outlet on November 6th, while the Crickets were performing at the Kiel Opera House in St. Louis, killing the stage microphones. An enraged Buddy cursed as he exited the stage. Holly soon forgave Anka, who was a gifted song-writer, and the two eventually worked out an agreement to compose tunes for one another.

The month of September proved to be highly successful for Buddy Holly. Coral Records released his first solo record, *Peggy Sue,* accompanied by *Everyday* on the flip side. *Cash Box* magazine hailed Holly as "a newcomer who's broken into the star category."

On September 23rd, *That'll Be the Day* reached Number One on *Billboard's* pop music chart, replacing Jimmie Rodgers' *Honeycomb. That'll*

Be the Day remained on top for one week, before it was displaced by the Everly Brothers, *Wake Up Little Suzie*.

In the U.K., *That'll Be the Day* succeeded Paul Anka's *Diana*, and remained Number One for three consecutive weeks. The success of the Crickets first single in the U.K. was quite remarkable. Vogue Coral Q did not release the single until September 10th, and it only took *That'll Be the Day* seven weeks to climb to Number One. The Brits ultimately purchased 431,000 copies; population adjusted, this would have been equivalent to 1,700,000 sales in the U.S.

The jubilant Crickets crammed inside a phone booth on September 23rd, and called Norman Petty in Clovis, to confirm the news about *That'll Be the Day*. On a separate line, Petty telephoned Decca executives in New York City and Los Angeles, who verified the song was a chart-topper. That same night, Buddy announced to the audience that the Crickets had the Number One record in the land. The crowd appeared equally thrilled; the Crickets played four encores, more than anyone else on the tour.

Three days earlier, when Coral released *Peggy Sue/Everyday*, *Cash Box* magazine lauded the new single as a "hot two-sider that could establish Buddy Holly as a name to be reckoned with." Meanwhile, on *Billboard's* Rhythm and Blues chart, *That'll Be the Day* eventually climbed to the Number Two spot. *Peggy Sue* and *Oh Boy*, would later climb into R&B's Top 10.

The Crickets' excitement was soon tempered by ugly reality. When the tour reached the Deep South, the entertainers' travel and performing arrangements were disrupted. Between Atlanta and New Orleans, law enforcement officers stopped the two tour buses and unceremoniously segregated them by race. In Georgia and Louisiana, state laws prohibited blacks and whites from travelling in the same vehicle or lodging in the same hotels.

In Columbus, Georgia, Birmingham, Alabama, and New Orleans, Louisiana, racially integrated acts could not even perform on the same stages. From September 23rd through September 27th, the white rock and rollers, including the Crickets, the Everly Brothers, and Paul Anka, were forced to withdraw from the tour, until the entertainers exited the Deep South. By now, the black entertainers were their friends and confidants, which angered and frustrated the Crickets.

As the exhausting tour progressed, seeds of discord were being sown. Niki Sullivan's initial enthusiasm for rock and roll stardom had rapidly waned. He found the touring "life-style", including cramped buses and no ready access to laundry facilities, both tiring and unregimented.

Raised as an only child, Niki never felt comfortable with the prank-pulling and carousing of his bandmates. He felt that J.I., Buddy, and Joe B., too often made fun of him. Niki, who loved to eat waffles at any meal of the day, took offense when his bandmates castigated him for not ordering a steak.

Sullivan also began to question his value to the group. Nikki was technically the rhythm guitarist, but after Buddy mastered both rhythm and lead roles, Sullivan's guitar often wasn't picked up by the microphones. When Niki made subtle hints about leaving the group, his fellow Crickets made no special effort to talk him out of it.

After *That'll Be the Day* reached Number One, Brunswick Records was pushing for an album by the Crickets. To complete an LP, the band needed to record additional songs, but were distant from the studio in Clovis.

On September 28th, the Feld tour reached Tulsa, Oklahoma. The Norman Petty Trio happened to be playing at Tinker Air Force Base, just outside Oklahoma City, and only a hundred miles or so west of Tulsa.

Petty, who had brought along his recording equipment in the same truck that the Norman Petty Trio used to transport their instruments, negotiated access to the Officer's Club after the facility closed for the night. Surprisingly, the acoustics in one corner of the club were near studio perfect.

To complete their album, entitled *The Chirping Crickets*, the band recorded a handful of songs, including *An Empty Cup* and *A Broken Date*, both of which had been written by Roy Orbison. Buddy also recorded a solo single, *You've Got Love*, written by Orbison and fellow Teen King band member, Little Johnny Wilson. While *You've Got Love* was never a success for Buddy, it later emerged as a rockabilly hit for Wilson.

The Crickets also re-recorded *Maybe Baby*, as neither Holly nor Petty were pleased with the quality of the Clovis original. Joe B. later claimed that he had played some role in writing the lyrics for *Maybe Baby*, but if so, he was pushed aside by the Crickets' manager—the only song-writing credits were attributed to Petty and Holly.

Before the air force base session was completed, the Crickets' completed another recording. *Rock Me My Baby* is an up-tempo combination of lines from two classic nursery rhymes—*Hickory Dickory Dock* and *Rock-a-Bye Baby*.

While touring in Oklahoma, Buddy ran into Carl Perkins, who had written and first recorded the widely-popular *Blue Suede Shoes* at Sun Studios in Memphis (the song eventually became a much bigger hit for Elvis Presley). Like others, Perkins recognized the dichotomy between Holly's modest and unassuming private personality and his on-stage persona. When Buddy performed in front of an audience, Perkins noted that "he was on fire."

Holly entertained a special audience in Oklahoma City. On September 29th, L.O., Ella, and Larry Holley drove to the Sooner State to see Buddy perform.

The tour eventually made its way to Texas, stopping in Dallas, Fort Worth, San Antonio, Houston, Corpus Christi, Austin, El Paso, and Waco. Conservative Lubbock made no effort to book the rock and roll show, even though the Crickets were a featured act. The closest Buddy, J.I., Nikki, and Joe B. made it to home was Waco, 209 miles southeast from Lubbock (adding insult to injury, Waco was only half the size of Lubbock). During a matinee performance in Waco, Buddy and Niki first learned that they were third cousins. "There were about 35 people in the audience for the afternoon show and they were all related to Buddy and me," Niki amusingly recalled.

While performing in Corpus Christi in early October, Buddy and his bandmates discovered that their hotel room was infested with live crickets. J.I. insisted that it would be bad luck to kill the insects; instead, the Crickets used brooms to sweep the crickets out of the room.

While the Crickets were still in Texas, *Peggy Sue* was rapidly ascending the *Billboard* chart, which placed Buddy in an enviable position—he was the only tour performer to have simultaneous hit records. *Peggy Sue* eventually climbed all the way to Number Three, and became a million-plus seller.

After receiving their $1,000-per-week performance fees, the Crickets deducted expenses and faithfully sent the remainder of the money to Clovis, as instructed by Norman Petty. Larry Holly bitterly recalled how cash-poor Buddy and Crickets were: "Norman Petty was actually taking their money. Buddy told me, 'I can't even tithe, because I don't have any money for the church!' Norman told Buddy, 'Well, I'm tithing with ya'll's money here at our church and it goes to the same place,' which it didn't. Norman kept them broke all the time, having to ask for money. He got all the money in, and did what he wanted to with it. He built that big pipe organ in that church up there (Petty's regular place of worship in Clovis), with some of the money."

From Texas, the Feld tour headed to California, where line-up changes were made. The Bobettes, the Spaniels, and Johnnie and Joe exited; their replacements included Eddie Cochran, Buddy Knox, and Jimmy Bowen and the Rhythm Orchids. Buddy and Eddie Cochran immediately developed a close relationship, and often occupied adjacent hotel rooms, when the performers were fortunate enough to avoid all-night bus trips.

While the tour moved through California, Norman Petty was busy in his Clovis studio. Employing the Picks as background vocalists, Petty mixed his rising stars' first long-play album, *The Chirping Crickets*.

By the time the performers reached Sacramento on October 18th, J.I. Allison's mother had obtained permission from Peggy Sue Gerron's parents for her to attend the rock and roll show. Gerron, who was a senior in high school, was still living with her sister and brother-in-law in California's capitol city.

J.I. greeted Peggy Sue at the backstage door of the Sacramento Memorial Coliseum and escorted her to a seat near the front of the stage. Peggy Sue had not heard any of the Crickets songs, either on a record or the radio, and she never considered the possibility that one of them had been named in her honor.

The Cricket's opened with *That'll Be the Day*, followed by *Oh Boy*. "Buddy never stood still. He would swing up to the microphone, lean in to sing, then rock back on his foot, and spin around to play his guitar to the band, before pivoting back to sing to the audience again…" Peggy Sue vividly recalled.

Before the Crickets performed their third number, Buddy offered an introduction: "This is a special show tonight, and we're playing this song for a special person." J.I.'s invited guest, surrounded by fellow audience members, was caught totally unaware. "My heart pounded, and my cheeks were on fire. With all the people around me bouncing, swaying, and singing my name over and over, I sank down in my seat, and covered my face with my hands, and cried out to myself, what have ya'll done to me?" an astounded Peggy Sue remembered.

"Aren't you glad your mother named you after my song?" Buddy teased Peggy Sue after the show. Years later, Gerron's embarrassment had abated, and she freely admitted that she was "thrilled to have been a part of it."

In late October of 1957, Brunswick released another Crickets single, *Oh Boy*, with *Not Fade Away* on the record's flip side. Sales in the U.S. did not match those for *That'll Be the Day* or *Peggy Sue*, but *Oh Boy* still climbed to Number 10 on *Billboard's* Top 100. While *Not Fade Away* failed to chart in 1957, to date, it and *Peggy Sue* have been covered by more artists that any of Buddy Holly's songs.

On October 23rd, during a tour stop in Vancouver, British Columbia, Buddy was interviewed backstage by disc jockey, Red Robinson. Holly told Robinson that he was ready to return to Lubbock, where the temperature wasn't as "cool," and the weather was "drier." While he had been energized by the Crickets' records sales and the crowd's applause,

Buddy confessed to Robinson that he wasn't certain if rock and roll music was here to stay.

Nine days later, while sitting in Eddie Cochran's room at the Albany Hotel in Denver, Buddy was again interviewed by a local disc jockey, who asked him if a movie was in his future. Buddy smiled at Cochran, who had previously appeared in the low-budget film, *Go, Johnny, Go!* The movie had also featured appearances by Chuck Berry, Jackie Wilson, and Ritchie Valens, along with disc jockeys Alan Freed and Jimmy Clanton. In jest, Holly said he would try and sweet talk Cochran into landing him a movie contract.

Cochran had, in fact, tried to get the Crickets a cameo role in *Go, Johnny, Go!* While the movie was being shot, Cochran spoke with Alan Freed, whose manager, Jack Hook, telephoned Norman Petty. While the Crickets would not have been compensated for appearing in the movie, the promotional value and excitement factor were priceless. Petty, however, declined—no money, no Crickets.

"We never did any rock and roll movies, because Norman Petty was waiting for big parts. We wanted to do *Go Johnny, Go!* But, Norman said, 'No, no, we will wait for a legit movie.' I don't think he liked rock and roll movies; sometimes, I didn't think he liked rock and roll," J.I. quipped.

On November 4th, the tour played at the Civic Auditorium Music Hall in Omaha. Perhaps hoping their romantic flame was not completely extinguished, Buddy tried to telephone Echo McGuire, who was attending college in York, Nebraska. Echo, however, was in class, and could not directly speak with Buddy. "He was hoping I could come over to Omaha; it was like a two-hour drive. By the time they got hold of me, it was already too late to go over," Echo remembered. A rendezvous between the high school sweethearts would likely have been inconsequential; Echo was already dating a classmate that she would soon marry.

The *Biggest Show of Stars from 1957* concluded on November 24, 1957, after 80 consecutive days on the road. That same day, *Cash Box* magazine named the Crickets as the "Most Promising Vocal Group of 1957."

On November 27th, Brunswick released the band's first LP, *The Chirping Crickets*, which included *That'll Be the Day, Oh Boy, Not Fade Away, Maybe Baby, You've Got Love, It's Too Late, Tell Me How, I'm Looking for Someone to Love, An Empty Cup, Send Me Some Lovin', Rock Me My Baby*, and *Last Night*. Even though they were now nationally known, the Crickets were nonetheless exhausted by the physical and mental toll of stardom.

What did the future hold for Buddy Holly? While three of his or the Crickets' songs had already cracked the Top 10 in the United States, record sales were even brisker in the United Kingdom and Australia. In early November of 1957, Buddy simultaneously had three records in England's Top 10. *That'll Be the Day* was Number One, Oh *Boy* had climbed to Number Three, and *Peggy Sue* held the Number Six spot. In Australia, all three records had also made the Top 10, each peaking at Number Two.

More television time and a tour abroad awaited the boys from Lubbock.

CHAPTER 6

The Price of Fame

ON DECEMBER 1, 1957, BUDDY Holly and the Crickets appeared on America's most watched television entertainment program, the *Ed Sullivan Show*. Entertainers relished the opportunity to appear on the show, which *CBS* broadcasted from New York City to a live, nationwide audience at 8:00 p.m. EST, every Sunday night. An appearance on the *Ed Sullivan Show* was proof positive the Crickets were indeed stars.

Appearing on the variety show was not without its problematic aspects. The 55-year-old Sullivan, a former sportswriter and gossip columnist, was gruff in demeanor, stiff in appearance, and expressionless in countenance; the latter of which earned him a less than flattering nickname, "The Great Stone Face."

Sullivan was rigid and uncompromising about his one-hour television show, which featured all forms of entertainment, including singers, stand-up comics, jugglers, magicians, and animal acts. He insisted that no performer's act exceed the length of a single commercial break.

Niki Sullivan, still a Cricket, but just barely, was decidedly unimpressed. The studio, later renamed the *Ed Sullivan Theater* (where David Letterman, would later host his late-night talk show program), appeared enormous to television viewers. The theater, however, only seated 300 to 400 people, and the performers' dressing rooms were cramped. Niki recalled that the Crickets were paid $1,600, but had to pay $1,800 in union fees—a net loss of $200. "We were all let down. We expected so many thousands of people in the audience, because that's how it looked when we'd seen it on TV. But, when we walked out there, we just couldn't believe it—it was a very small theater, with a couple of hundred people."

During the Crickets' practice session, J.I.'s drum set had been placed on a 10-feet-tall platform. At that elevation, Allison couldn't hear the other instruments: "If you can't hear, you can't play together." After rehearsal, Buddy ordered a change: "I can't hear the drums good; just take that thing down."

Golden-voiced Sam Cooke, whose *Send Me* was the Number One record in the United States, and *Collier's* All-American college football team were among the guests booked on the show with the Crickets.

During their first, nationally-televised live television appearance during prime time, the Crickets were nattily attired in dark tuxedos and matching bow ties. Holly, the only one who sang, wore a microphone looped around his neck. Niki's guitar was not even plugged in, but it did not keep him from shuffling his feet in time with the music and mouthing inaudible background vocals. Buddy sang *That'll Be the Day* during the band's first set, followed by *Peggy Sue* on the second go-around.

After the Crickets completed *Peggy Sue*, while the stage crew was clearing J.I.'s drum set and the band members were exiting the stage, Ed Sullivan beckoned Holly. "Buddy Holly, Buddy, Buddy, Buddy, come back here," Sullivan monotonously ordered.

When Sullivan asked the ages of the Crickets, Buddy informed him that two were 18, one was 20, and he was 21. Sullivan, who was no fan of rock and roll music, was nonetheless impressed by Holly's polite manners and sincerity. He inquired about Lubbock and asked if all the band members had graduated from high school. Sullivan also wanted to know if the Crickets had become instantly famous. Holly admitted to some "rough times," but indicated the group had been "real lucky." Sullivan ended the interview by calling Buddy "Tex," and when Holly offered his hand, like a true Texas gentleman, the surprised host stiffly shook it.

After the *Ed Sullivan Show*, the Crickets flew from New York City to Lubbock for a three-day break; their first visit home, since August of that year. Anticipating formal recognition of some sort, Buddy rented a limousine to take him from the airport to his parent's house. Much to his disappointment, Holly discovered there was no welcoming party at airport, no fans lining the streets, and his parents weren't even at home. Buddy later complained about wasting his money on a limo.

The conservative citizens of Lubbock seemed unimpressed that the Crickets had toured a sizeable portion of the country (and parts of Canada) and appeared on television three times. The local newspaper had recognized them only once since they left town—a tiny group picture, after the band appeared on the *Ed Sullivan Show.*

Rather than quiz her son about the places he'd been or the things he'd seen and done, Ella Holley was more interested in knowing about what it was like to tour with "Negros." Buddy quickly informed her that there were no issues, and astonished Ella by telling her that he felt like he was black. Buddy was further disappointed, when he discovered his parents had forgotten to watch him on the *Ed Sullivan Show.*

One of the Crickets, however, managed to win over his harshest critic. After telling him earlier in the year that he would regret joining a rock and roll band, Joe B's mother was now his biggest fan. "She kept a scrapbook at home, with just about every piece of publicity that was ever put out on us in the United States, like in *Billboard* and *Cashbox*, and with all the publicity photos that we had. And if we played in Oklahoma City or somewhere in New Mexico or Texas, she and Dad would drive hundreds of miles to wherever we were, just to see us perform," Joe B. recalled.

Larry Holley kidded Buddy that he sounded like a New Yorker, and warned him not to lose his Texas accent. Buddy laughed, promising his brother that he would not become a Yankee. The Holley family was proud, but did not yet fully appreciate how rapidly Buddy's star had ascended.

Coral/Brunswick had recently sent Norman Petty a check for $192,000, representing record sales from *That'll Be the Day* and *Peggy Sue.* When Buddy inquired about the $50,000 in song writing royalties and remuneration from Broadcast Music Incorporation (the company that processed payments each time an artist's song was played on radio or television), Petty told him that the Crickets had already spent that amount, but offered no itemized paperwork to substantiate his claim. Consequently, the money trouble between Buddy Holly and Norman Petty officially took root.

Now that he finally had some cash in his pocket, Buddy repaid the $1,000 loan to his brother, Larry. He also reimbursed various people in Lubbock who had loaned him money, accompanied by a gracious thank you: "I appreciate your carrying me." Buddy was generous with his money, not only buying his parents a brand new, red and white Chevrolet Impala, but also purchasing new pews for the Tabernacle Baptist Church.

As a bonus, Buddy took Larry and his father on a fishing trip to Ballinger, located in central Texas. During the drive to Ballinger, an exhausted Buddy was asleep in the car, when Larry and L.O. stopped for a cup of coffee at a restaurant. When the jukebox started playing *That'll Be the Day*, L.O. informed the waitress that the singer and composer of that song was sleeping in their car. To prove that he wasn't lying, Buddy's father went outside, awakened his youngest son, and brought him inside to meet the astonished waitress.

The Crickets were busy during their brief return to Lubbock. Even though they were beginning to question Norman Petty's handling of their money, the band returned to Clovis on December 17th. While at the studio, Buddy recorded a remake of Elvis Presley's *You're So Square—Baby I Don't Care*. As he had done in *Not Fade Away*, J.I. pounded an empty cardboard box rather than his drums. While never a hit for Buddy, Waylon Jennings liked Holly's version of Elvis' song the best, believing it most clearly epitomized the unique sound of first generation rock and roll.

The Crickets also recorded *Look at Me*, featuring Vi Petty on the piano. While never a best-seller, *Look at Me* reminds a former lover that her spurned paramour still cares deeply for her. The lively medley was composed by Buddy and J.I. Not surprisingly, the final song-writing credits included Norman Petty's name.

The brief return home also marked the end of Niki Sullivan's tenure as a Cricket. Niki simply could not envision a life filled with repeated tours: "When we got back home to Texas, and I got some good food, I said there ain't no way I'm going to live like this."

From the beginning, Niki had always felt somewhat like a misfit, and never acclimated to his bandmates' teasing and horseplay. "Remember, I was an only child, until I was 17; an only child who used to play golf by himself just to entertain himself; do a lot of things by myself; I was a loner," Sullivan explained.

"We got back, and I was very tired. We all were. We were over at Clovis, and I just said, 'Buddy, I want to quit. I'm just not happy.' Buddy didn't understand why, but he didn't pursue it. He just said, 'Well, Niki, if that's what you want to do.' So, we had a meeting of everyone in Norman's office, and I said, 'Fellas, I enjoyed it and everything, but that's it,' and I walked out and went home," Niki remembered.

Sullivan did not hold ill-feelings toward his former bandmates, but regretted that "Norman did not make any effort to take something that was broken and try and piece it back together." Petty, however, had a different take on Nikki's departure: "The biggest rub was between Jerry and Niki, and Buddy went along with Jerry." "What was there to patch up? I knew Jerry and Joe B. and Buddy wanted him to leave, and on the other hand that Niki wanted to leave," Petty stated, even though none of the other Crickets ever indicated that they wanted to push Sullivan out of the band.

J.I.'s recollections clearly did not jibe with Petty's: "We never did really have a fight with Niki or say that we wanted him out of the group. Oh, he and I had a good fight one time, when we were playing the Brooklyn Paramount. We got to squirting water at each other, something like that, and we had a fist fight. In fact, my eye was swollen up on *The Chirping Crickets* album cover photo, because he got me good around the eye.

But, that had nothing to do with him leaving, that was just silly kid stuff. None of us were uptight when he split. He wanted out; it was a mutual thing."

Joe B. agreed that Niki left of his own volition: "After about three months on the road, Niki, on a few occasions, mentioned to me that this kind of life was not for him, and that he was going to try and get out and make a record deal on his own. And, my response was, 'Hey man, do whatever you need to do.' When Buddy and Jerry and I would discuss it, they'd say, 'If he wants out, all he has to do is walk.' Buddy and Jerry never forced or pushed him out."

If anyone other than Niki wanted to shrink the band, it was likely Norman Petty, motivated by financial self-interest. Sullivan claimed that Petty offered him 10 percent of all money (record sales and royalties) generated by *That'll Be the Day*, if Niki agreed not to make claims on any other Crickets' recordings. When Petty later reneged on this deal, Nikki took his father to Clovis and asked to audit the Crickets' financial records. Petty put them off twice, indicating on one occasion that the records were in the possession of his accountant. "As I always say, Jesse James wasn't killed in the 1880s. He was still alive Clovis, New Mexico until the 1980s," Niki bitterly recalled. Out of their own pockets, the Crickets gave Sullivan $1,000 in severance pay.

Niki remained bitter about Petty's financial exploitation, and his failure to make the previously-agreed-upon tithe to Sullivan's church. "My Dad was right in what he said the first time he ever met Norman. 'Son, never trust a businessman who keeps a Bible on his desk.'" Niki recalled.

After Niki left the group, Petty managed to convince Buddy, who was undoubtedly the star of the show, to alter the Crickets' original financial agreement. From that point forward, Holly would receive 50 percent of record sales and live performance fees, while J.I. and Joe B. would split the remaining half equally.

Exactly how the new financial arrangements impacted the Crickets have since remain clouded in mystery. Petty continued to bank the band's earnings in a single account; one that only he could access.

Buddy, J.I., and Joe B. all had checking accounts at Lubbock banks, but their registers revealed little activity. If any one of the Crickets made a major purchase, he sent the invoice to Petty for payment. On December 20th, when Buddy purchased his parents a new Impala coupe from Stewart-Meadors automobile dealership in Clovis, Petty not only made the $500 down payment, but also paid off the $3,648.55 balance before the end of the month.

For a time, the Crickets were seemingly content to buy whatever they wanted, and simply forward the bills to Petty. "It was a change from not having enough money to buy gas for a car to being able to buy a new car with cash," J.I. marveled.

Buddy's newfound stardom was offset by a heart-breaking visit from Echo McGuire, who had returned to Lubbock for the holiday break. If Holly believed there was still a flicker in their adolescent romance, it was immediately extinguished.

During a face-to-face meeting, she informed Holly of her plans to marry fellow classmate, Ron Griffith, the following spring. "I told (Buddy) what I had decided. From that point on, I put him aside," Echo recalled. The wedding came sooner than forecasted; Echo and Ron were married on Valentine's Day, 1958.

The Crickets briefly contemplated asking Buddy's former bandmate, Sonny Curtis, to replace the departed Nikki Sullivan. Curtis, however, was on the verge of landing his own record contract and likely would not have been interested in the Crickets' proposal. Consequently, Nikki's spot in the band remained open.

Buddy Holly had previously established the standard four-man line-up, which served as the model for future rock and roll bands. After Niki Sullivan departed, the Crickets were down to a guitarist, a bass player, and a drummer, representing yet another innovation. The transition from a quartet to a trio appeared seamless. Buddy had always been the lead vocalist and could play all guitar parts, while J.I.'s spirited percussion and Joe B.'s relentless thumping of the bass fiddle masked the absence of a regular rhythm guitarist. During subsequent stage performances, audiences detected no difference in the sound quality of the music performed by the three-man band.

At year's end, the Crickets were back in New York City. On December 28th, the band appeared on the *Arthur Murray Dance Party*. The televised program, hosted by the famed grand ballroom dancer and his wife, Kathryn, usually featured big band music. Consequently, Kathryn Murray carefully introduced the Crickets as "rock and roll specialists." "Now, whatever you may thing of rock and roll, I think you have to keep a nice open mind about what the young people go for—otherwise, the young ones will think you don't understand them," Murray instructed the primetime television audience.

Standing in front of a row of young women clad in ballroom gowns, the tuxedo-clad Crickets performed *Peggy Sue*. While it was a most unusual venue, Buddy and his bandmates earned $2,000 for their performance.

A day earlier, Buddy had received good news; *Peggy Sue* had reached Number Three on the *Billboard* chart and surpassed the 1,000,000-mark in sales. At the same time, *Oh Boy* was steadily climbing the charts.

From late December through early January, the Crickets performed on Alan Freed's *Holiday of Stars Twelve Days of Christmas Show* held at Brooklyn's Paramount Theater. Screaming teenagers stood in line for several blocks, braving sub-freezing temperatures, to see many of rock and roll's hottest artists, including Fats Domino, Paul Anka, Jerry Lee Lewis, Danny and the Juniors, and the Everly Brothers. Like other Freed holiday shows, the entertainers played short sets, six to seven times per day. With Brunswick and Coral having both released records that charted in the Top 10, for the first time, Buddy Holly and the Crickets were billed as separate acts.

"That was the high point for me—the New York Paramount Show. There were all kinds of people on the show, like maybe 20 acts, and we did better than anyone else, as far as encores and all that—like nobody else would get an encore, and maybe we'd get two or three, sometimes…" J.I. Allison recalled. The *Holiday of Stars* show grossed $300,000; from those net receipts, the Crickets were paid $4,200.

At Christmas, Buddy rewarded himself by purchasing a long-coveted F-50 Navarre acoustic guitar from Manny's Music Shop—the instrument would be featured in the yet-to-be-recorded *Well All Right*. Months later, Buddy was approached by a young amateur musician, who raved about the guitar. Typical of Holly's innate generosity, he handed the instrument over: "Here, man, you keep it." Joe B. recalled there were many other times when Buddy behaved in a like manner; he simply like spreading happiness and good fortune, to the point of spontaneously giving away his expensive and prized possessions.

As 1957 neared its end, J.I. and Joe B. sensed a change in Buddy's personality, perhaps a direct result of the Crickets' stardom. Holly grew moodier and much less interested in being a prankster. J.I. was surprised when Buddy berated him for knocking off Holly's glasses during horseplay.

J.I. believed that Buddy "didn't want to fool around anymore—it was like he was there to work." Murray Deutch and Bob Thiele thought Holly had developed a measure of sophistication and was, more than ever, dedicated to improving his music. "Buddy was a very quiet kid, who said little until he got to know you. He kept things inside. He never talked too much, but he was a very bright guy—I mean business-wise, about the music business. But, he stayed the same person," Deutch later reflected.

Holly made serious efforts to upgrade his personal appearance. During the Crickets' Christmas holiday visit to Lubbock, he paid a dentist $600 to have his stained and crooked front teeth capped. He also experimented with different hairstyles, including a short-lived permanent. After returning to New York, Buddy consulted a dermatologist, who removed acne scars from his face, either by dermabrasion (a scraping process) or a chemical treatment involving phenol—both procedures were quite painful.

Buddy also visited a Manhattan optometrist to have the frames of his horn-rimmed eyeglasses squared, making them appear more prominent. J.I. took partial credit for this change: "I said to him, 'If you're going to wear glasses, then really make it obvious you're wearing glasses...'"

Dick James, Holly's future producer at Coral Records, who described Buddy as a "marvelous person" and a "sweet classic soul," noted his progressive sophistication. "I first met him when he was appearing in Brooklyn. He had silver-rimmed glasses, gold-rimmed teeth, and looked like a hick from Texas. The next time I saw him, he wore a three-piece suit, horned-rim glasses, had had his teeth recapped, and looked like a gentleman," James recalled.

Even with his self-improvements, Buddy never became a teen idol, the likes of Elvis Presley or Frankie Avalon. Holly's subtle charm and sincerity tended to attract members of the opposite sex more so than his looks. After his death, Buddy's mother remembered getting more condolence letters from men than women; a tribute to Holly's music, rather than his appearance.

On December 31, 1957, Buddy, J.I., and Joe B. stood atop the Paramount Theater and watched the ball drop in Times Square, signaling the beginning of a new year. In less than 12 months, the Crickets had emerged from obscurity to become the central characters in a real-life, rags-to-riches story.

At the beginning of 1958, Buddy Holly was Decca's top recording artist; quite the turn-around from a record label that had previously rejected him. On January 6th, Holly recorded two new songs, *You are My One Desire* and *Love Me*. Though neither single charted in *Billboard's* Top 100, both received positive reviews. *Cash Box* magazine described *You are My One Desire* as "an emotional love story with great feeling," and *Love Me* as a "swinging rock-a-billy jumper."

On January 8th, the Crickets began GAC's *America's Teenage Performing Stars* tour, promoted by Irving Feld. Seventeen days in duration, the tour also featured the Everly Brothers, Danny and the Juniors, Paul Anka, and Jimmie Rodgers. Now considered legitimate stars, the Crickets commanded $1,200-per-*show* (as compared to $1,000-per-*week*, during the 1957 Feld-promoted tour). The $53,000 the Crickets earned seemed like a whole lot more; with Niki Sullivan's departure, after Norman's 10 percent fee off the top, the money was split only three ways. The Crickets also received "100 Percent Billing," which meant their names appeared in the largest font on all tour advertisements.

During two plus weeks on the road, Buddy, whose relationship with Echo McGuire had ended, found himself the target of female groupies. His charm allured women, and he was overwhelmed by more seductresses than he could possibly handle. Phil Everly benefitted from the surplus of women: "Buddy Holly put me to bed with a girl. And, he laughed."

Storm clouds, however, were brewing on the horizon. Ardent segregationists still regarded rock and roll as "Jungle Music," and conservative Christians continued to condemn it as the "Devil's Music." During the Feld tour, even more enemies emerged. At a concert in Hazelton, Pennsylvania, a young woman removed her blouse and bra, and then asked both Everly Brothers to sign her naked breasts. Eager reporters immediately circulated the sensational story. Consequently, many radio stations banned rock and roll music from their airways; some even destroyed their entire stock of rock and roll records.

A newspaper photograph of Buddy Holly, the Everly Brothers, and the Shephard Sisters (three attractive blondes, who had recorded a hit record, *Alone*), featured the caption: "The only way you can tell the difference between rock 'n' roll girls is the boys have longer hair." The *New York Times* quoted a local psychiatrist, who characterized rock and roll as "cannibalistic and tribalistic." The *New York Daily News* described the music as a "barrage of primitive, jungle-beat rhythms." A racist in Alabama declared that rock and roll was the "means by which the white man and his children can be driven to a level with the Niggers." Some journalists went so far as to predict that rock and roll would precipitate a national teenage crime wave.

Ignoring public outcry, Decca could not do enough for its rising star. Bob Thiele, head of A & R, who had been responsible for both the Crickets' and Buddy's recording contracts, was planning to release a solo LP entitled, *Buddy Holly*. Accordingly, Thiele wanted Buddy to record *Rave On*, a single composed by Sonny West and Bill Tilghman (co-writers of *Oh Boy*), at Bell Sound Studios, located on Manhattan's West 54th Street. When Norman Petty got wind of this proposal, he immediately vetoed it.

Buddy was angered by Norman's refusal, and for the first time, thought about firing Petty. Larry Holley remembered Buddy's ire: "He called me from New York and asked if he should do this or that. He wanted me to be his manager. He offered me a tremendous sum of money just to go with him everywhere and keep him out of trouble, sort of like a bodyguard, but I couldn't leave. I was running the (tile setting) business." Buddy also telephoned Hi Pockets Duncan, who more than once, had tried to warn him about Norman Petty's shady reputation. Duncan remembered Buddy was "steaming mad."

In his first bold act of defiance against Petty, Buddy stopped sending money from tour performances to Clovis. He also bucked Norman by opting to record *Rave On* at Bell Sound Studios. The only concession Holly made was allowing Petty to participate as a studio musician during the recording.

After reading the lyrics, Buddy was eager to record *Rave On*. Co-writer, Sonny West, had previously released his version of the song on Atlantic Records, but it failed to generate sales. West described the subsequent route followed by *Rave On*: "We sent it to Norman, as usual. And, as usual, when it came out in published form, it had his name added to it. Norman's original plan was for a group called the Big Beats from Dallas to record it. But, Buddy said, 'No way. I've got to have this song.'"

Bob Thiele remembered the events surrounding their recording session: "Buddy had been saying how much he'd like the two of us to work together. I booked him a session at Bell Sound Studios, and got Milton de Lugg, the orchestra leader, in as a producer, with extra session men... We had a vocal group, the Jivetones, in on it, too. Petty, I know, got really uptight, thinking I was moving in on his boy. To be diplomatic, we had to let him be there as backup pianist. All the time, I could feel the vibrations of jealousy."

The first two hours of the session, beginning at 8:00 p.m., on Saturday, January 25, 1958, involved recording vocal tracks by the Jivetones. From 10:00 p.m. to 2:00 a.m., Buddy recorded *Rave On*, followed by another new song, *That's My Desire*.

Rave On was Buddy's first up-tempo song where he did not play the guitar. Instead, Norman Petty's jazz-style piano playing, for which he was unceremoniously paid $44 (the normal union fee), the lead and rhythm guitars of session musicians, Al Cailo and Donald Artone, Joe B.'s driving bass, and J.I.'s enthusiastic percussion perfectly complemented both Holly's lead and the Jivetones' background vocals. *Rave On* is a spirited anthem about the power of love, beginning with Buddy's six-syllable stuttering of the word "well" in the opening stanza.

"*Rave On* was a great record, full of power and very exciting and I am not surprised it still appeals to people today. His records sound as fresh and exciting as when he made them. There's such a strong personality in his voice and even though it's good paunchy rock music, there's a plaintive melancholy quality that I like," song-writer, Geoff Goddard, later opined.

The second recording of the night *That's My Desire*, was a ballad Frankie Laine had transformed into a million-seller in 1947. With the Jivetones singing back-up, Buddy recorded the song in two takes, but was so dissatisfied with the outcome, that he asked Decca not to release it. J.I. concurred with Buddy about *That's My Desire*: "We weren't happy with that song. I mean, we didn't consider it a record. We sort of said, 'Okay, we'll try that later.'"

The flip-side to *Rave On*, *Take Your Time*, was recorded later in the year in Clovis. When Coral released the single on April 20, 1958, *Rave On* was the first Buddy Holly featuring background vocalist. The single made it to Number 37 on the *Billboard* chart, and climbed all the way to Number Five in the United Kingdom; since 1958, it has been a popular cover song for numerous artists.

For Norman Petty, the recording of *Rave On* was bittersweet. As usual, he managed to finagle both publishing and song-writing credits, entitling him to a share of those royalties. At the same, he realized that Buddy Holly no longer needed him or his studio in Clovis to produce records.

The night after the Bell Sound Studios recording session, the Crickets made their second appearance on the *Ed Sullivan Show*. Buddy asked that the Picks, who sang background on *Oh Boy*, be flown to New York, so the live performance would sound just like the studio recording. The Picks, however, did not belong to the Musician's Union. "Norman Petty never paid us a cent for doing that session. And, we never got any credit on the record label. But, Buddy liked what we'd done so much that he sent us money to fly up to New York for the Sullivan show. Then, at the last minute, we were told the Musician's Union wouldn't let us go on," Bill Pickering recalled.

From there, the situation deteriorated further. During dress rehearsal, J.I. and Joe B. missed their cues when Buddy went on stage. When an impatient Sullivan asked where the rest of Crickets were, Holly merely shrugged his shoulders.

An angry Sullivan retaliated by cutting the Crickets' scheduled play time from two songs to one, and instructed them not to perform *Oh Boy*, because the lyrics were too vulgar. When Buddy, J.I., and Joe B. returned to the studio for their live television appearance, Sullivan demanded to know what song Buddy had substituted for *Oh Boy*. A defiant Holly informed the humorless host that his fans wanted to hear *Oh Boy*, and if he couldn't perform that song, he would not go on stage. Unaccustomed to having his orders disobeyed, Sullivan passive-aggressively set in motion a plan to disrupt the Crickets' performance.

When he appeared on the *Ed Sullivan Show* for the second time, Holly's appearance was strikingly different. Instead of a tuxedo, he wore an Ivy League suit and sported a brighter smile, along with black, square-framed, horn-rimmed glasses.

When the Crickets opened their act, Sullivan extracted his revenge. He instructed engineers to turn down the studio sound and dim the overhead lights. When Holly figured out what Sullivan was up to, he was determined not be hoodwinked by the angry host. To compensate for the loss of volume, Buddy simply played faster, added an unplanned chorus, spun his entire body around at the guitar break, and unleashed a wolfish howl. After the Crickets finished *Oh Boy*, the audience applauded loudly, but when the camera shifted back to Sullivan, he masked his rage behind a stiff smile. Despite their contentious engagement, the Crickets were paid $2,000 for their performance.

Even though Sullivan was enraged by Buddy Holly's defiance, the Crickets popularity was at an all-time high. Sullivan soon swallowed his pride and invited the group back for a third appearance.

Unwilling to Sullivan's devious acts of sabotage, Holly now possessed enough self-confidence to turn down an offer to appear in front of 50,000,000 television viewers.

CHAPTER 7

The American Invasion

ROCK AND ROLL FANS OUTSIDE the United States were clamoring for additional hit records, and even more eager to eyeball American performers. Buddy Holly and the Crickets were particularly grateful to fans in Australia and the United Kingdom, where their records consistently charted higher than in the United States. By early 1958, the timing was perfect for the Crickets to tour abroad.

On January 27th, one day after their second performance on the *Ed Sullivan Show*, Buddy, J.I., and Joe B. boarded a propeller-driven, Pan-Am Constellation airliner in New York City (commercial jet-powered flights out of the United States would not begin until later that year). Joining them was Norman Petty, ostensibly functioning as their manager, but behaving more like a tourist. For Petty, it was essentially a free vacation, funded by the band's earnings. A color, home movie, presumably shot by Petty, recorded the Crickets smiling and waving as they boarded the aircraft.

The first stop was in Los Angeles, where Jerry Lee Lewis and Paul Anka joined the tour. It was a tumultuous time for Lewis, who was aptly nicknamed "The Killer." Critics of rock and roll music had widely condemned Lewis' marriage to his 13-year-old cousin. The unpredictable entertainer was in a foul mood, making it known that he could earn more money playing concerts in the U.S., rather than travelling abroad. Never amused by Jerry Lee's antics, on or off the stage, Buddy Holly tried to keep his distance from Lewis.

An adolescent Anka, whose self-composed *Diana* had been a monster hit in 1957, was considered the star of the tour. The fact that Anka was billed as the lead performer did not faze Holly. "Buddy was always one for saying, 'The hell with billing, man, I want the money,'" Joe B. recalled.

Hawaii, which would become America's 50th state on August 21, 1959, was the next stop. After landing in Oahu, the performers checked into a hotel on Waikiki Beach. The first show, held at Honolulu's Civic Auditorium, drew nearly 10,000 fans. While Paul Anka received the only glowing review in the *Honolulu Star-Bulletin*, Buddy was satisfied with the Crickets performance, writing his sister and brother-in-law in Lubbock, and informing them that Hawaiians were true rock and roll fans. The Crickets also performed a concert at the Schofield Barracks, near Pearl Harbor.

In Hawaii, Ritchie Valens joined the tour. Only 16-years-old, Valens was the first Chicano rock and roll star. Holly's and Valens' paths would intersect the following year; this time, with a tragic outcome.

From Hawaii, the performers flew overnight, some 6,000 miles, to Australia. As the Constellation approached the small island of Canton to refuel, the aircraft developed engine problems; in retrospect, an eerie foreboding for both Buddy Holly and Ritchie Valens. Once on the ground, it took several hours to make the needed repairs.

During the long flight to Australia, a new rift emerged between the Crickets and Norman Petty. J.I. informed Petty that he had proposed to Peggy Sue Gerron (the sweethearts had reunited after *Peggy Sue* became a hit). Petty, who believed marriage would be detrimental to the star power of rock and rollers, unsuccessfully tried to resolve the issue by driving a wedge between Buddy and his drummer. "Norman came over and sat down by Buddy and me. He looked at Buddy and said, 'Well, who are we going to get to play drums after Jerry gets married?' And, Buddy looked at me and said, 'Well, who are we going to get to manage us, since Norman's already married?' We both started to laugh. Norman didn't think it was funny," J.I. recalled.

On January 30th, the Constellation landed in Sydney, where the Americans were joined by Johnny O'Keefe, Australia's leading rock and roll entertainer. The seven-day tour of the continent, billed as *The Big Show*, included paid stops in Sydney, Melbourne, Brisbane, and Newcastle, as well as a charity performance at the Nurses Memorial Center (in Melbourne); the latter was sponsored by the Colgate/Palmolive Company and recorded for later broadcast on the radio.

The Australian tour director, Lee Gordon, was a pioneer in promoting rock and roll shows. A year earlier, Gordon had arranged a similar tour for Bill Haley and the Comets, Little Richard, Eddie Cochran, the Platters, and Gene Vincent.

Buddy Holly and the Crickets were the hottest artists at that time—*That'll Be the Day*, *Peggy Sue*, and *Oh Boy* had all peaked at Number Two on the Australian hit list. Even though Jerry Lee Lewis had demanded lead status on the promotional posters, largely based upon his recent hit single, *Great Balls of Fire*, Paul Anka's name was the one printed in the biggest and boldest letters. Holly cared little about the font size on the posters; he was already aware the Crickets were being paid more than any of the other acts on the tour.

Trouble seemed to follow Jerry Lee Lewis wherever he went. Before one performance, Holly reluctantly drug Lewis from an Australian bar and forced him into a hotel shower, until he was sober enough to appear on stage.

The Crickets first appearance was in an 11,000-seat arena in Sydney. Having never played in front of such a large audience, Buddy confessed to feeling "overwhelmed," and J.I. admitted that the band's performance was not up to their usual standards. A reviewer for the *Brisbane Courier-Mail* concurred, describing Holly as "ill-at-ease" and "inexperienced." The Crickets, however, gradually acclimated to both the venue and crowd size. "The first few shows went badly for us," J.I. wrote in a letter to home, "but the last three days, we have been stealing the show, as Norm would say."

From Sydney, the tour group traveled by bus, 105 miles northeast, to Newcastle. On January 31st, the performers played two shows in an open stadium. Unlike a year earlier when American rockers toured the city, there were no riots during or after the concerts. Instead, the *Newcastle Morning Herald* reported that the audience "rocked in the aisles and stomped their feet" to the music.

After the shows in Newcastle, a local disc jockey, Pat Barton, interviewed Holly, who was polite and direct in his responses. When asked how long he had been playing rock and roll, Buddy explained that he and J.I. were long-time friends, who had played together for five years, while Joe B. had joined the band within the past year. Holly clarified that it was the same band performing songs recorded on both the Brunswick and Coral Labels, and that every member of the Crickets was a song-writer. Asked if Elvis Presley was his favorite singer, Buddy replied: "I guess he's one of them." Lastly, Barton wanted to know if there was a conflict in the band. Holly carefully responded that Niki Sullivan had "stayed behind," as opposed to having left the band.

Throughout the Australian tour, Norman Petty continued to oversee the Crickets' lives, as if they were small children. On one occasion, when Buddy was eating spaghetti, Norman tucked a napkin under Holly's chin, so he wouldn't stain his clothes.

On February 1st, when the tour returned to Sydney, the Crickets had become accustomed to larger crowds, and performed much better. Two days later, the group played in Brisbane, located some 200 miles north of Sydney. The combined attendance at two shows at the Cloudlana Ballroom was 8,000.

While Jerry Lee Lewis was uncouth (his antics included urinating into a beer bottle at a bar) and insulting to his guests, Australian record executive, Ken Taylor, was impressed by the politeness of the Crickets. In his book, *Rock Generation,* Taylor wrote about Holly: "To meet him, Buddy was the perfect representation of a somber American person—ascetic, serious, (and) dignified, behind the horn-rimmed glasses he perpetually wore. His personality, innate decency, and talent added up to an American legend."

After Brisbane, the tour group took to the air again, flying just over 1,200 miles to Melbourne, for a February 4th concert at the Stadium (later renamed Festival Hall). The Crickets were in particularly fine form that evening, and the entertainment reviewer for the *Melbourne Herald* wrote that Holly "shook the stadium" when performing *Oh Boy* and *Rip It Up*. The article described Holly as the "undoubted star of the show with his clever display of guitar techniques." The reviewer's observations were prescient; Australians would remain Holly fans for many years to come.

Meanwhile, in the United States, Coral had released a new Buddy Holly single, *I'm Gonna Love You Too*, with *Listen to Me* on the B side of the record. Coral's timing was poor; Buddy and the Crickets still had active hits on the chart, and disc jockeys were reluctant to play multiple records by the same artist. Neither *I'm Gonna Love You Too* nor *Listen to Me* made it into *Billboard's* Top 100. In England, however, *Listen to Me* climbed to Number 16, while *I'm Gonna Love You Too* cracked Australia's Top 40.

The performers departed Australia on February 6th. During a lay-over in Honolulu, Buddy met with local disc jockeys, helping promote the Crickets' records. The tour group also played one show at the Kaiser Hotel, before returning to the mainland.

The Crickets arrived in Lubbock on February 10, 1958, encountering wintertime weather, much different than Australia's summer season and Hawaii's tropical climate. Once again, there was no welcome wagon to greet the local rock and roll stars.

Two days later, *Maybe Baby* (re-recorded at Tinker Air Force Base) and *Tell Me How* were released by Brunswick Records. While *Tell Me How* failed to chart, *Maybe Baby* climbed to Number 17 on the *Billboard* chart. In the U.K, *Maybe Baby* made it all the way to Number Four.

On February 12th, the Crickets returned to Clovis for a week-long recording session. A Holly solo, *Take Your Time*, was slated to be the B side of *Rave On* (previously recorded in New York City). Written by Holly, *Take Your Time* incorporated a single line written by Norman Petty. This simple addition allowed Petty to claim 50 percent of the song-writing royalties. The added line, however, proved difficult for an exhausted Holly to articulate. "I just can't get it Norm," Buddy is heard saying on the tape, complaining that the "page just blurs." He goes on to complain that he "can't even see the words," even though he is "looking right at them." A feminine voice soon emerges on the tape, either Vi Petty or J.I. (mimicking a woman): "Take your time." Buddy reacts with laughter and vows to "beat the crap out" out of the tongue twisting lyric.

With Petty playing his Hammond organ in the background, the song counsels patience when dealing with affairs of the heart. While Norman was proud of his contributions to the song, *Take Your Time* failed to chart.

Think it Over, written by Buddy and J.I., but with Petty's name added to the song-writing credits, was recorded by the Crickets, and featured a new background vocal group, the Roses, who had previously sung on recordings by the Norman Petty Trio. Unlike their predecessors, the Picks, the Roses were paid $65 by Petty to participate in the session. Robert Linville, a member of the Roses, captured one of the clearest visual images of Buddy Holly at work in the studio; "a skinny guy with a pack of cigarettes rolled up in his tee shirt sleeve."

Think it Over cautions a lover to reconsider a hasty decision to end their relationship. The Crickets also recorded another Holly composition, *Tell Me How*, where the singer simply asks a lover what he needs to do to retain her affection.

The final song from that session, *Fool's Paradise*, was another Holly composition. It questions the thoughts and feelings of a lover, who is seemingly far away.

While the Crickets' recording session failed to generate a Top 10 hit like *That'll Be the Day*, *Peggy Sue*, or *Oh Boy*, it was not a total loss. *Tell Me How* failed to chart, but *Think It Over* climbed to Number 27 on *Billboard's* chart and reached Number 11 in the United Kingdom. *Fool's Paradise* topped at Number 58 on *Billboard*'s Top 100.

The Clovis recording sessions in February of 1958 also featured another single composed by Holly, entitled *Well, All Right*. The song's title originated from a phrase Little Richard often shouted after performing a hit: "Well, All Right!" The instrumentation, simple in structure, involves Buddy's Guild F-50 Navarre acoustic guitar (inside of which Norman Petty had installed a microphone to more intimately capture the instrument's sound), Joe B.'s bass, and J.I. playing a lone cymbal; the lyrics describe the reactions of lovers to their parents' accusations of rashness and immaturity. Much to Buddy's disappointment, *Well, All Right* failed to chart in *Billboard's* Top 100.

Before the week in Clovis concluded, J.I. Allison recorded his only solo record. The A side featured *Real Wild Child*, written and originally recorded by Australian rock and roller, Johnny O'Keefe. J.I, was backed by Bo Clarke on drums and Joe B. on bass, while Buddy played guitar and joined the Roses on background vocals. Norman Petty also contributed to the record, playing a series of wine glasses filled with water.

On the flip side, Allison sang a rock and roll version of the classic tune, *Oh You Beautiful Doll*. Norman Petty explained the basis for J.I.'s solo recordings: "At the time, the Crickets were so hot that Coral was ready to release anything we gave them."

J.I. thought both recordings were "atrocious," and insisted upon using only his middle name, Ivan, as the performing artist. *Real Wild Child* was more humorous than classically artistic, but in October of that year, the song climbed as high as Number 68 on *Billboard's* Hot 100 and Number 10 on regional charts. J.I., however, would never be pleased with his version of the song: "It started out at the bottom of the charts and worked its way across."

Nonetheless, Norman Petty booked Allison a solo concert appearance in Charleston, West Virginia. A quarter of a century later, recording artist, Iggy Popp, scored a hit with *Real Wild Child*.

Between the Australian tour and the forthcoming one in the states, Buddy found himself, once again, struggling to reconcile his conservative Christian upbringing with rock and roll music. Turning to his dutiful brother, Larry, Buddy asked how he could be a rock and roll star and still serve God.

Larry, who always supported his younger brother's musical ambitions, was equally unwavering in his Christian faith. He explained to Buddy that *no one* could put *anything* before God—either themselves or their careers. While Buddy would never completely walk the straight and narrow, he continued to contribute money to Tabernacle Baptist Church; while the church condemned Buddy's music, the pastor never failed to accept Holly's generous financial offerings. Buddy informed Larry that he eventually planned to record a gospel album; a means of proving that a rock and roll singer could also be a Christian.

From February 20th through the 25th, the Crickets joined the Everly Brothers, Bill Haley and the Comets, the Royal Teens, and Jerry Lee Lewis on the *Big Gold Record Stars* tour of Florida. Phil and Don received top billing, which meant they would close each show. When the performers arrived at their first stop, the Everly brothers, who did not have a traveling back-up band, discovered that local teen-aged musicians had been recruited to play with them. Phil was panicked at the prospect of following the raucous Jerry Lee Lewis' stage performance, while the Everly Brothers were "backed by three high school kids, who could hardly play a note." Buddy ultimately saved the day, announcing that the Crickets would back the Everly's. Phil later recalled that he and Don were saved "only by the grace of God and Buddy Holly."

During the last week of February, Coral released the LP, *Buddy Holly*. The album selections included *Peggy Sue, Everyday, Listen To Me, I'm Gonna Love You Too, Words of Love, Rave On, Look At Me, Valley of Tears, Ready Teddy, Mailman Bring Me No Blues, You're So Square*, and *Little Baby*.

Immediately after the Florida tour, the Crickets boarded an airliner in Miami, for an overnight flight to England. Norman Petty, accompanied by his wife and ubiquitous movie camera, joined the travel party. Joe B., quiet, but observant, couldn't help but wonder if the Crickets were directly paying for Norman and Vi's vacation to the United Kingdom.

When the group landed at Heathrow Airport on March 1, 1958, they were greeted by young fans hungry for rock and roll music. In the late 1950s, teenagers and young adults in the United Kingdom, unless they came from wealth, had limited and staid entertainment venues; even the British pubs closed at 8:00 p.m.

The *BBC*, which controlled the content of almost all television and radio programs, had banned rock and rock roll music, forcing young Brits to listen to records or tune into broadcasts (after 8:00 p.m.), originating from Radio Luxembourg's powerful signal. A year earlier, Bill Haley and the Comets, had the first American rock and rollers to visit the United Kingdom.

Future British rocker, Jerry Wayne, was among those eager to see the American performers: "I was knocked out when I saw the cover of *The Chirping Crickets* LP with those Fenders on the front. We'd never seen those in this country, and you couldn't even buy them in shops. You saw them and knew you wanted one!"

The Crickets tour of the U.K. was arranged by the Grade Organization and emceed by singer and comedian, Des O'Connor. Billed as a variety show, the tour included jugglers, Ronnie Keene's big band orchestra, the Tanner Sisters (easy-listening singers, akin to America's Andrews Sisters), and balladeer, Gary Miller. The Crickets were the sole rock and roll performers.

The programs sold at each venue were hardly elaborate, depicting a cartoon drawing of a cricket, which served as an inexpensive way of promoting the American rockers. Buddy and his bandmates were expected to play for 25 minutes at each stop, choosing from 10 songs they had selected in advance.

After interviewing Buddy, a U.K. reporter, described him as "very cautious." Holly explained that he was grateful that the British audiences and record buyers "seem to like us." He also predicted that the Crickets would remain viable if they did not "make any mistakes."

British comedian, Mark Kelly, later admitted that he had preconceived and unrealistic mental images of the American rock and rollers:

"Buddy Holly didn't look cool and didn't dress cool. He wasn't like Elvis or Eddie Cochrane. He looked like a nervous office clerk, fronting a band who only booked weddings…" Outward appearances aside, it was an ideal time for the Crickets to be visiting the United Kingdom. Their recent 45-RPM record, featuring *Maybe Baby/Tell Me How*, was zooming up the British charts and would eventually crest at Number Four. *Listen to Me/I'm Gonna Love You Too* was rated Number 16. Adding icing to the cake, *That'll Be the Day*, *Peggy Sue*, and *Oh Boy* were still in the U.K.'s Top 10.

The Crickets, along with Norman and Vi Petty, settled into London's Cumberland Hotel, where rooms rented for a bit over three-pounds-per-night (five dollars). Buddy, who wanted a radio in his room, paid an additional nine-pence-per-day (15 cents).

Since the Brits had never eyeballed the Crickets, and the band's pre-publicity had been minimal, Buddy, J.I., and Joe B. roamed the streets of London without being recognized. One of their few promotional appearances was hosted by the Whiskey-a-Go-Go, a club in Soho, where Buddy was photographed holding a wicket and standing alongside English National cricket players, Dennis Compton and Godfrey Evans.

The 25-day tour of the U.K. was a hectic one, allowing for no days off. On Saturday, March 1st, the Crickets played their first two shows at London's Trocadero Cinema in the Elephant and Castle neighborhood, located near the Thames River. Orchestra leader, Ronnie Keene, remembered opening night, where 1,500 people attended the first show, followed by 3,000 at the second performance: "The place was packed to the rafters. It was obvious that no one had come to see us, or any of the other British acts. We were just cannon fodder. Still, we weren't booed; they listened to us and clapped politely. But, when Buddy and the Crickets were announced, the whole place erupted. At that moment, I realized it was all over for musicians like me. This was the future."

The Crickets' volume was limited by the range of the house microphones and the amplifier they brought on stage. By today's standards, the band's 50-watt Fender Bassman amp, with four 10-inch speakers, seems primitive, but could still generate an ear-piercing volume. Comedian, Des O'Connor, attested to the American rockers ability to raise the roof: "We were touring with the Ronnie Keene Orchestra, which had 28 musicians, with a front line of 16 brass (players), then out come the Crickets, just three of them, and I couldn't make out how they were making 10 times as much noise. It was so exciting and vibrant, and I knew that something exciting was happening."

The audience was amazed that the Crickets' stage performances (absent the background vocalists on some recordings) sounded just like their records. Buddy's animated gyrations on the stage made the concerts even more entertaining. After the opening two shows in London, nearly 300 teenagers waited outside the back stage exit to greet the Crickets and ask for their autographs.

English music critics offered mixed, but largely positive reviews. The complaints included high ticket prices and the band's short performances (only 20 to 25 minutes long). One reviewer was scornful, writing that Buddy Holly was "obviously out of his depth," and that his stage movements drew "scornful laughs" from the audience; an observation unsubstantiated by the crowds' boisterous reactions.

Most of the reviews were laudatory. Keith Goodwin, critic for the *New Musical Express* wrote: "If enthusiasm, drive, and down-to-earth abandon are the ingredients necessary for success in the rock 'n' roll field, then Buddy Holly and the Crickets are all set for a long and eventful run of popularity! They rocked their way through a tremendous, belting, 25-minute act without letting up for one moment…Take my word for it, this is rock 'n' roll like we've never heard it before in Britain!" Another reviewer declared that the Crickets' stage performance of *Peggy Sue* was "every bit as good as on the disc."

J.I. was certain the normally-stoic British were roused by the Crickets on-stage antics. While Joe B. laid on his back playing the bass fiddle, Buddy, who had been jumping around, leaned down and sang into Mauldin's microphone. While the audiences were "marveling," J.I. was of the proud opinion: "Aren't we the ones!"

The following day, Sunday, March 2nd, was a notable and busy one for the Crickets. During the daylight hours, they played two shows at the Gaumont State Cinema, located in northern London. During one of their performances, an excited audience member recalled that Holly "literally exploded onto the stage."

That night, the Crickets joined comedian, Bob Hope, famed ballerina, Alicia Markova, and actor, Robert Morley, to celebrate the 100th telecast of *Val Parnell's Sunday Night at the London Palladium*. Televised by the *Associated Television Corporation (ATV)*, an independent network, the variety show drew England's largest weekly viewership.

Buddy, J.I., and Joe B., already nervous about performing on live television in a different country, were somewhat disappointed in their performance. The technicians failed to adjust the microphone volume and balance correctly, which added to the Crickets self-critique; from that point forward, Norman Petty took control of the sound board at each concert venue.

Even though the Crickets were less than satisfied with their performance, many television watchers, some of whom would be household names within a decade, were mesmerized. John Lennon, a 17-year-old student at the Liverpool School of Arts, who had already formed his own band, the Quarrymen, was a huge Buddy Holly fan. Lennon carefully studied the television screen in his parent's house; Buddy's Fender Stratocaster was the first one he had ever seen. He also watched closely while J.I. played paradiddles during *Peggy Sue*. Like Holly, Lennon was terribly near-sighted, but resisted wearing eyeglasses on stage. After watching Buddy at the Palladium, Lennon concluded that it was acceptable for rock and rollers to perform in glasses.

"Until Buddy came along, any fellow with glasses took them off to play," Paul McCartney remembered. After Holly played the Palladium, Lennon began wearing his eyeglasses on stage, and according to McCartney, could "see the world for once."

The 15-year-old McCartney, also a native of Liverpool, was a budding guitarist, songwriter, and a member of John Lennon's Quarrymen.

He pressed his face close to the television, watching Holly maneuver his fingers on the guitar strings. McCartney was particularly interested to know if Holly used a capo while playing *Peggy Sue*; Buddy; Holly sometimes, but not always, employed a capo (a tool, which is laid down on an entire fret, allowing a guitarist, who only knows certain chord shapes, to play in different keys; using a capo, guitarists without classical training or expert knowledge of the instrument can play different keys and create different voicings). From that night forward, McCartney "always loved Buddy's music."

Fifteen-year-old Keith Richards, who lived in Dartford, located 16 miles southeast of London, also watched the Crickets on television. Richards and his childhood neighbor, Mick Jagger, would later form their own band—the Rolling Stones. Richards was impressed that Holly was "self-contained, wrote his own songs, had a great band, and didn't need anyone else." Richards later surmised that Buddy wrote "working music," which could both be recorded in the studio and performed on stage. "Buddy got us to writing songs," Richards recalled, highlighting one of Holly's most enduring influences on budding British rock and rollers.

In Ripley, located in the Village in Surrey, 13-year-old Eric Clapton admired "the style, the look, (and the) individuality of Buddy Holly." After watching the Crickets perform on television, Clapton asked for a guitar on his next birthday. While practicing in the stairwell of his parent's house, Clapton discovered that he could create an echo-effect akin to Holly's.

Like John Lennon, eleven-year-old Reginald Kenneth Dwight (later known to the world as Elton John), focused on Holly's eyeglasses. He soon began wearing glasses, not out of necessity, "but in homage to Buddy Holly."

Denny Laine, who was 12-years-old in 1958 and would later become a guitarist in Paul McCartney's post-Beatles band, Wings, credited Holly as "my first real inspiration." "In fact, the guitar lick on *That'll Be the Day* made me want to learn to play," Laine remembered.

Another Cricket caught the eye of future rock and roll drummer, Bob Henrit. "Jerry Allison was a schooled drummer and we weren't. Every drummer played *Peggy Sue* hand to hand, but he played a paradiddle. We didn't even know what a paradiddle was! And, the way he played *Oh Boy* was subtle. He was putting something into rock we weren't seeing. We were emulating him without realizing what he was doing," Henrit recalled.

At the Palladium, Holly became a fan, himself, and was thrilled to meet the legendary Bob Hope. He wrote about hobnobbing with the comic and actor in a letter to his parents.

Unfortunately for music historians and rock and roll aficionados, *Sunday Night at the Palladium* was not videotaped. Consequently, the history-making concert can only be actively relieved through the eyes and ears of surviving audience members and television viewers. However, a series of black and white photographs were taken of Holly while he was performing during the concert; one of those pictures would be used three decades later, as a promotional poster for the musical, *Buddy*.

On March 3rd, the Crickets, accompanied by Norman and Vi Petty, departed London via bus. For the next three weeks, they played a series of one-night stands. The group's designated road manager, Wally Stewart, was largely a yeoman, mostly confining his duties to driving the bus and unloading luggage. The concert venues included Stockton on Tees, Southampton, Sheffield, Newcastle on Tyne, Wolverhampton, Nottingham, Bradford, Birmingham, Worcester, Croydon, East Ham, Woolwich, Ipswich, Leicester, Doncaster, Wigan, Hull, Liverpool, Walthamstow, Salisbury, and Cardiff (located in Wales). At one point, when travelling by train, the Crickets were surprised by a hand-held banner along the rail bed: *BUDDY HOLLY IS GREAT.*

At Stockton on Tees, the band's second road tour stop, the audiences were far less boisterous, and the Crickets wondered if something was lacking in their performance. It was simply an aberration—the teenagers and young adults in attendance were more subdued than the crowds in London. After the concert, hundreds of fans stood in line to obtain the autographs of Buddy, J.I., and Joe B. "Buddy Holly and the Crickets were absolutely marvelous, because they were the loudest we ever heard," Brian Poole, a future U.K. rock and roller, proclaimed.

The U.K.'s entertainment critics continued to occasionally share their disdain for rock and roll in written reviews. Peter Holdsworth, a reporter for the newspaper in Bradford, referred to Buddy Holly as "a screeching guitar player," with lyrics that were often "indecipherable." Holdsworth found the Crickets' "fantastic reception" distasteful, and could not understand why the British did not prefer to hear an "articulate vocalist." "Where on the earth is show business heading?" Holdsworth questioned, a view shared by many conservative Americans.

Another reviewer, however, wrote a more descriptive and far less critical account, following the concert in Birmingham: "Buddy Holly, leader of the group, is a studious-looking young man who totes his electric guitar like a sawn-off shotgun and carries a giant-sized amplifier, which even makes the Town Hall organ pipes flinch. Mr. Holly is 70 percent of the act. He plays and sings with brash exuberance, and a few Presley-like wiggles, which had the teenage audience squealing with delight. The rest of the group consists of a bass player, whose ability was lost in the noise, and a drummer who plays with sledge hammer precision."

During the daytime hours, the Crickets mostly slept on the bus, while Norman Petty compulsively filmed the passing scenery. Buddy, J.I., and Joe B. did not sleep all the time, as Petty's color home movies can attest: 1. The Crickets standing on a bridge over the Cam River at Cambridge; 2. Buddy writing a letter to his parents at the Old George Hotel in Salisbury, while the rest of the group drank hot chocolate by the fireplace; 3. A stop in Birmingham, where Buddy insisted on visiting the Morris and Austin automobile production facility; 4. A tour of the British Motor Corporation factory and showroom.

While in England, Norman Petty purchased an Austin Healey coupe and had it shipped back to Clovis, paying $2,303.94. Throughout the U.K. tour, Petty was a compulsive shopper—in addition to an automobile, he bought fine china and swaths of worsted wool (large enough to be tailored into suits). Based on his history of financial machinations, were these purchases funded, at least in part, by money due Buddy and the Crickets?

While the Crickets were enjoying themselves, they were homesick and disliked the cold and rain. On March 10th, in Birmingham, and the following day, in Gaumont, Worcester, Buddy played both concerts despite a head cold and fever. In Gaumont, fans broke into Holly's dressing room window to gain access to the star. A British girl was so infatuated that she later sent handwritten letters to Lubbock implying that there was an unsubstantiated romantic connection between the two; Holly never answered the missives.

Overnight stops along the way were decidedly un-American—small beds, coin-activated heaters, and no restaurant service after 9:00 p.m. Joe B. remembered that some of the rooms were unheated and the only warmth in many hotel lobbies was generated by coal fires.

With Norman Petty along for the ride, alcohol was not permitted as a lubricant to combat homesickness and the chilly dampness. Near the end of the second week of the tour, Buddy sent his sister, Pat, a postcard: "We're getting a bit tired of England. It's awfully cold over here. (It) seems like it could never get summer here…Well, so long for now. Love, Buddy."

Irrespective of the weather, the Crickets' spirits were buoyed by the responses of their audiences along the way. The enthusiasm of concert attendees clearly overshadowed negative reviews from stodgy critics. "We had a really good time here. It was cold and the beer was warm, which was the wrong way for us. The British audiences were more reserved during the songs, but they really grooved afterwards," J.I. explained.

The west Texans also bonded with their English touring partners. Ronnie Keene was impressed by Holly's friendliness and down-to-earth nature: "I used to sit next to him on the bus. He was a lovely lad—lovely. There were no big star affectations about him, at all. He used to talk to the boys in my band, just as if he was one of them."

The tour returned to London on March 12th and played four shows at two different venues. While there, Buddy took the opportunity to visit Saville Row and update his increasingly-fashionable wardrobe. After departing London, yet again, the Crickets played tour stops in Ipswich, Leicester, Doncaster, Wigan, and Hull.

On March 20th, they played Philharmonic Hall in Liverpool. The seaport city of 500,000, home to John Lennon and Paul McCartney, was a hotbed of youthful enthusiasm for rock and roll. McCartney and Lennon were unable to attend the Crickets' concert in Liverpool; it is quite possible that the Quarrymen had previously booked a gig that same night. The crowds in Liverpool were raucous by British standards, and the Crickets fed off the excitement; during the second show, J.I. threw his drumsticks into the crowd, while Buddy played the guitar above his head and duck-walked across the stage.

A few years later, when Lennon and McCartney, joined by George Harrison and Ringo Starr, formed the Beatles and transformed the world of music, Liverpool would become known as the "birthplace of British rock." After Buddy Holly's visit to the United Kingdom, Lennon and McCartney grew more ambitious and rebellious, skipping school to play their guitars and write songs. While playing, singing, and composing at McCartney's house, Paul remembered the pair were endeavoring "to figure out how Buddy did it."

"The attraction wasn't hard to fathom. Buddy Holly had everything they'd wanted, everything they'd been struggling to create musically: melodic songs; a crisp, clean sound; impeccable rhythm; unforgettable riffs, and monster appeal..." Beatle's biographer, Bob Spitz, wrote. "More germane to their discovery of Buddy Holly was that he wrote his own songs," Spitz added.

In November of 1959, the Quarrymen entered a *Star Search* competition at the Manchester Hippodrome. Performing under a different stage name, Johnny and the Moondogs, Lennon and McCartney chose to cover Holly's *Think It Over*.

Lennon wrote J.I. Allison's mother in Lubbock, inquiring about the origin of the name the Crickets. Adopting the same insect theme, Lennon decided to rename his band the "Beatles;" to more accurately describe their sound, Lennon replaced the second "e" with an "a."

On March 21st, the Crickets were back in London and played two shows at Walthamstow's Granada Theater. The next three days were occupied by one-night stands at the Garmount Theater in Salisbury, Colston Hall in Bristol, and Capitol Cinema in Cardiff.

On March 25th, the entertainers returned to London. During the day, fulfilling the stipulations of their tour contract, the Crickets appeared on television again. Buddy lip-synched *Maybe Baby* on *Off the Record*, televised by *BBC* and hosted by former big band leader, Jack Payne. Even though he was exhausted, Holly played with great enthusiasm. Holly's taped performance aired on television three days after the Crickets had departed the United Kingdom.

That same night, the Crickets played two shows at the Hammersmith Gaumont Theater. After the first performance, while Buddy and J.I. lounged in their dressing room, Joe B. entered the room with an unlit cigar in his mouth. When Mauldin announced that he was going to enjoy a smoke to commemorate the conclusion of the group's British tour, both J.I. and Buddy objected. Holly was particularly opposed, fearing the smoke would irritate his vocal chords. Ignoring his bandmates' protests, Joe B. lit the cigar, precipitating what Buddy later described as a "friendly scuffle." During the resulting physical altercation, Joe B. accidently struck Holly in the mouth with his forehead, knocking the caps off two of Buddy's top front teeth. The impact was so forceful that Joe B. retained a permanent scar on his forehead.

Joe B. remembered what started out as horseplay resulted in a "traumatic incident." Buddy immediately wanted to cancel the final show, as he did not want to perform snaggle-toothed. Norman Petty, however, was unwilling to risk the loss of any revenue, and convinced Holly to cover the gap with chewing gum. "I don't know how he sang with a wad of chewing gum up over his lips, but he did it, and we completed the show," Joe B. recalled.

Afterwards, Petty tactlessly chided the Crickets for having delivered their "worst" performance, ever. By now, Buddy held little regard for Norman's criticism or praise; a harbinger of the break-up that would occur within the year.

On March 25, 1958, when the Crickets departed London for the United States, they left behind immediate and lasting impacts. Their record sales soared in the United Kingdom (for an entire week, during their 25-day tour, *Peggy Sue, Oh Boy, Maybe Baby,* and *Listen to Me* simultaneously charted in the U.K.'s Top 30). In addition, guitar sales sky-rocketed while the Crickets were in the U.K. Of even greater importance, young British performers, more than ever, were inspired to follow the lead of Buddy Holly.

It is fair to say that Buddy Holly's *American Invasion* of 1958 was clearly a catalyst for the much-acclaimed British Invasion of the early 1960s.

CHAPTER 8

Buddy and J.I. Say I Do

AFTER TOURING THE UNITED KINGDOM, Norman and Vi Petty returned to Clovis, but the Crickets only had two days of rest, before joining Alan Freed's 44-day *Big Beat Show*. Other artists on the tour included Chuck Berry, Jerry Lee Lewis, Larry Williams, Frankie Lyman, the Chantels, the Diamonds, Screamin' Jay Hawkins, Danny and the Juniors, and the Alan Freed Band. Their stardom now clearly established, the Crickets were now being paid $5,000-per-week.

Beginning with an appearance in Brooklyn's Paramount Theater, the tour group performed on 68 separate occasions. In larger cities, the entertainers played two or three shows in a single day.

In the era of package shows, the individual or group designated as the closing act was a matter of pride. Unlike many other performers, Buddy Holly was seemingly disinterested in the Crickets' position in the line-up. On this tour, the battle of closers came down to Chuck Berry and Jerry Lee Lewis. Much to the Killer's displeasure, Alan Freed picked Berry to conclude each show, as he was the senior-ranking rock and roller.

Lewis extracted revenge in an outrageous manner during the opening show at the Paramount Theater. After concluding his penultimate act, the Killer poured gasoline from a Coca-Cola bottle on his piano, before setting it on fire. More than one listener clearly recalled Lewis greeting Berry as he exited the stage: "Follow that Nigger!"

After several shows at the Paramount, the tour moved to Loew's Paradise in Brooklyn on March 31st, followed by the New York Coliseum in Manhattan, two days later. The *Big Beat Show* then visited 19 states, as well as a few cities in eastern Canada.

Despite the hectic schedule, the pace was less tiring than previous tours, because the entertainers often flew. Their aircraft, however, were less than luxurious—World War II-era propeller-driven DC-3 airliners that shook fiercely when encountering turbulence. While many of the passengers were terrified and airsick by the rough rides, Buddy Holly seemed unfazed, shooting craps with Danny Rupp, the lead singer of Danny and the Juniors. The same day the group landed in Cincinnati, Ohio, a helicopter crashed outside the city, killing its pilot; a harsh reminder of the dangers associated with air travel.

Rupp, whose group would score the biggest hit of 1958, *At the Hop*, enjoyed Holly's company. He described Buddy as an "all around great guy," whose talent was "way before his time," and the forerunner of "what the Beatles came out with." On a secondary level, Rupp admired Holly's skill at shooting craps, where Buddy sometimes won up to $3,000-per-game.

The first 10 days of the tour went well, before the group encountered a series of problems. While the entertainers were eating at a restaurant in St. Louis, their bus was broken into, and Buddy's Fender Stratocaster and part of J.I.'s drum set were stolen. For a brief period, Buddy was forced to use a borrowed guitar. After placing an emergency phone call to Manny's Music Store in New York City, Holly ordered an identical Stratocaster, which was shipped to him, just prior to the Crickets' performance in Waterloo, Iowa.

Complicating matters, three separate rock and roll shows were traveling the country simultaneously. As a result, ticket sales declined, so much so, that one of the other tours, the *Rhythm and Blues Cavalcade of 1958*, was forced to shut down early (on April 27th).

On April 22nd, when the Freed show played in Waterloo, Iowa, Jerry Lee Lewis disappointed fans by failing to show up for his performance. That same night, the lead singer of Dicky Doo and the Don'ts got into a fight with an audience member, precipitating a melee.

When the tour reached its final week, scheduled to begin in Boston, all hell broke loose. Two years earlier, Freed's rock and roll show was marred by altercations between raucous teenagers and the Boston police. Freed carelessly inflamed an already tense situation by characterizing the lawmen as a "bunch of red-necked old men." When the Freed tour returned to Boston in 1957, fights broke out in the city's subways, leading city officials to ban further rock and roll shows.

Reluctantly, Boston Mayor, John B. Hynes, lifted the ban just before the *Big Beat* show debuted on May 3, 1958. Two shows were scheduled for opening day, and much to Hynes' chagrin, his leniency led to repeated chaos.

The arena, located in a high-crime area of the city, was perfectly situated for disaster. Nearly 60 percent of the audience in the 7,200-seat arena were white; many were racists, who jeered and heckled the black entertainers. The situation reached the point of no return, when a young white girl leapt on stage and grabbed the crotch of a black performer. After the crowd grew louder and more menacing, the police refused to lower the theater lights for subsequent performances. Alan Freed stepped to the microphone and tried to restore order, but his announcement did nothing to promote reconciliation: "I guess the police don't want you kids to have a good time." Afterwards, a policeman angrily informed the promoter: "We don't like your kind of music here."

When Chuck Berry opened his act, white crowd members began throwing objects at him, including chairs from the balcony. A frightened Berry was forced to seek protection behind his drummer.

At this point, policemen and security officials forced the crowd into the streets, where fights broke out among the expelled audience members and law enforcement officers. Before order could be restored, several people were injured by beatings and stabbings, accompanied by looting, arson, and vandalism. After police paddy wagons were dispatched, numerous rioters were arrested. A writer for *Variety* magazine chronicled the chaos: "Fifteen persons, including six women, were stabbed, slugged, beaten, or robbed by berserk gangs of teenage boys and girls following the jam session."

Freed and the performers were forced to seek refuge in the Hotel Statler, before flying out of town, bound for Montreal. An angry Mayor Hynes immediately issued another decree: "If the kids of Boston are hungry for this music, they'll starve for it, until they learn how to behave like citizens, instead of hooligans. Boston will have no more rock and roll."

Freed was subsequently indicted by a Suffolk County grand jury for trying to overthrow the government, based on the state of Massachusetts' statute prohibiting anarchy. Even though the charges against Freed were eventually dropped, the district attorney, Garrett H. Byrne, publicly railed against "rock and roll paganism." State Senator, William D. Fleming, introduced legislation banning the playing of rock and roll music in all government buildings.

Following the riot in Boston, the remaining concerts in the United States (New Haven Connecticut, Newark, New Jersey, and Troy, New York) were cancelled. Alan Freed was the ultimate scapegoat. The promoter Newark, who had already sold out the scheduled May 10th performance, went berserk; he stormed into the *WINS* radio studio, while Freed was on the air, and threatened the disc jockey with a handgun. Fearing a backlash of negative publicity, *WINS* fired Freed, irrevocably damaging his career as a disc jockey and promoter. From that point forward, there would not only be fewer rock and roll tours, but also a smaller roster of entertainers.

The chaos in Boston served as a springboard for wider criticism of modern music. The city's Archdiocese issued a statement condemning rock and roll. FBI Director, J. Edgar Hoover, declared that rock and roll was a "corrupting influence on America's youth," while the *New York Herald* likened it to the plague.

After the remainder of the Freed Tour was canceled, Buddy and the Crickets returned to Texas for much-needed rest; their first real break in 10 months.

As an act of defiance against Norman Petty, Holly had not sent the Crickets' recent performance fees back to Clovis. Consequently, on May 28, 1958, when the trio landed at Dallas' Love Field, Buddy had a pocketful of cash.

Eager to enjoy themselves, Buddy, J.I., and Joe B. immediately headed to the Harley Davidson motorcycle dealership in Dallas. Even though Buddy had $5,000 to spend, the sales representative was condescending to the blue-jean clad Crickets. When Buddy ask about the cost of one model, the snotty salesmen not only told him that he couldn't afford a Harley motorcycle, but also refused to answer any further questions.

Insulted, the Crickets took a taxi to Ray Miller's Triumph Motorcycle Sales, where the owner recognized Buddy, J.I., and Joe B. A gracious Miller told them that they could test drive any of the motorcycles in his showroom. Consequently, Joe B. selected a Triumph Thunderbird, while J.I. chose a Trophy model. Buddy opted for an Ariel Cyclone. The Crickets also outfitted themselves with denim jackets and leather motorcycle caps, emblazoned with the silver-winged Triumph emblem—by the time they left the motorcycle dealership, Buddy had spent just over $3,000.

"We had always dreamed of having motorcycles. In fact, Buddy had had a Triumph before, because we went and saw *The Wild Ones* with Marlon Brando, and no time after that, Buddy somehow had a motorcycle. Anyway, Buddy was carrying all kinds of cash from the tour we had been on..." J.I. explained. Allison giddily recalled their impulsive purchases: "It sure was fun."

While the Crickets were motorcycling 323 miles to Lubbock, thunderstorms and tornadoes were menacing west Texas. "None of us had ever ridden bikes that powerful before. And, on the journey, it came on to rain real hard. We got soaked through, and had to stop and buy ourselves more new sets of Levi's," Joe B. remembered.

After returning to Lubbock, the Crickets tooled about town on their new toys. J.I.'s brother, James, took home movies of the boys and their motorcycles in the Allison's front yard. In one sequence, J.I. can be seen chasing Buddy (wearing dark glasses and his leather motorcycle cap) with a pocketknife, playfully re-enacting a fight scene from the movie, *Rebel Without a Cause.*

On May 28, 1958, Buddy was served with another selective service draft notice, and ordered to undergo a physical fitness examination. The physicians classified Holly as 4F, and excused him from military service because of a "stomach ulcer" and uncorrected 20/800 vision.

In what turned out to be the last summer of his life, Buddy relished the opportunity to relax. He took time to visit with old friends, including his former bandmate, Bob Montgomery, who was still playing country and western gigs in the Lubbock area.

At long last, Holly's family seemed to appreciate just how far their sibling and son had come in such a short time. After explaining how audiences in England had received him "with open arms," Larry recognized that his younger brother was a "star." "I don't think we realized it before that," Larry recalled.

Buddy was nonetheless disappointed that most of Lubbock's residents seemed indifferent about his success. There were no welcome home celebrations for the Crickets; unlike Jerry Lee Lewis' hometown, Ferriday, Louisiana, where the rock and roller was presented a key to the city.

That summer, the Crickets' newly released single, *Think it Over,* climbed to Number 27 on *Billboard's* chart, and the record's flip side, *Fool's Paradise,* charted at Number 58. As might have been expected, the record sold better in England, reaching the Number 11 spot.

On May 25, 1958, Buddy and the Crickets returned to Clovis to record a handful of new songs. *It's So Easy* was written by Holly, but as usual, Norman Petty added his name to the composers' credits. Once again, Buddy relinquished the lead guitar, inviting 26-year-old Tommy Allsup to assume that role. Born in Oklahoma, on November 24, 1931, Thomas Douglas Allsup was the 12th of 13 children. As a young adult, he played lead guitar for a western swing band headed by Johnnie Lee Wills, brother of Bob Wills, whose band, the Texas Playboys, were legends in the Southwest.

For the first time since Nikki Sullivan's departure, the Crickets played together as a quartet. In addition to singing lead vocals, Buddy strummed an acoustic guitar. Ever the innovator, Buddy had seamlessly changed the instrument line-up while recording *It's So Easy*.

"Buddy was a star and he knew it, and he didn't mind anybody else sharing the stardom with him. He loved the way Tommy played; he thought he was a fantastic guitar player. Tommy knew a lot about music, too. And, he was a very likeable, enjoyable person. It was just one of those things, where you meet somebody and you really hit it off—it seemed like we all hit it off good with Tommy," Joe B. remembered.

When the group recorded *It's So Easy*, the Roses provided background vocals. The jaunty tune is self-explanatory—it requires little effort for some people, as Buddy Holly would soon prove, to fall in love.

The flip side to *It's So Easy*, *Lonesome Tears*, also featuring Tommy Allsup on lead guitar, was a disappointment, so much so, that Norman Petty uncharacteristically refused to add himself as a co-writer with Holly. Much to Buddy's disappointment, when Brunswick released *It's So Easy*, the record failed to chart in *Billboard's* Top 100.

The following day, Buddy recorded a solo single, *Heartbeat* (written by his former bandmate, Bob Montgomery), which would be paired with the forthcoming Coral release of *Well All Right*. Even though Bob Montgomery, was the sole composer of *Heartbeat*, Norman Petty once again added his name to the song-writing credits. Joe B. was not available that day, so George Atwood played bass, accompanied by J.I. on drums and Tommy Allsup on lead guitar. The song, a favorite among Holly fans over the years, describes the visceral reaction to a lover's kiss.

Heartbeat crested at Number 82 in *Billboard's* Top 100. Yet again, another Holly song was better received in the United Kingdom, with *Heartbeat* climbing as high as Number 30.

By now, the Crickets could afford an apartment in Clovis, such that they did not have to make daily commutes from Lubbock or crash at Petty's studio. In addition to recording his own songs, Buddy graciously volunteered to play as a session guitarist for several recording artists, including Fred Crawford, Jack Huddle, Jim Robinson, and the Norman Petty Trio.

On June 6th, Buddy lent a hand to Carolyn Hester, a singer he met in New York City, who had recently landed a record contract with Coral. Hester, whose style could best be described as folk, was backed by Holly on guitar and George Atwood on bass during her recording session at *Norman Petty Studios*. Hester sang *Take Your Time* (written by Holly) and *A Little While Ago* (self-composed), as well as two holiday songs—*Christmas in Killarney* and *Hurry, Santa, Hurry*. By this stage in his career, Buddy was interested not only in performing, but also in promoting the careers of up-and-coming artists.

While taking a vacation from touring, Buddy remained active, both writing and recording new songs. Holly and Bob Montgomery co-wrote *Love's Made a Fool of You* and *Wishing*. Buddy believed both songs were ideally suited for the Everly Brothers, but Phil and Don were still legally bound by their manager, Wesley Rose, to only record songs written by the husband and wife team, Boudleaux and Felice Bryant, thus preventing them from accepting yet another generous Holly offering. Consequently, Buddy recorded both songs in Clovis.

Love's Made a Fool of You and *Wishing* feature Buddy's vocals and acoustic guitar, backed by Tommy Allsup on lead guitar, Bo Clarke on drums, and George Atwood on bass. Atwood, a decade older than his counterparts, was an experienced musician, having played with several jazz ensembles, including the Gene Krupa Band. Neither J.I. or Joe B. played on these recordings. The vocals were subsequently double-tracked, mimicking the Everly Brothers' melodic harmony.

In the final version of *Wishing*, which would be among Buddy's favorite recordings, Allsup's guitar sounded much like a fiddle—a reflection of his country and western roots. The song expresses heartfelt longing for the affections of an unattainable love.

Love's Made a Fool of You is remarkable for its Latin rhythm, enhanced by Allsup's lead guitar and Buddy's spirited vocals. It warns the listener about the joys and pitfalls associated with matters of the heart.

By the middle of 1958, Norman Petty realized that he was losing control of his most important star. No longer willing to subsist on a salary doled out by the Crickets' manager, Buddy had already begun pocketing all earnings from their tour performances, rather than forwarding the money to Clovis. At the same time, Buddy, J.I., and Joe B. were not yet confident enough to completely sever ties with Petty, or prepared to confront Norman about his management of their song-writing and record sales' royalties. J.I. explained their dilemma in simple terms: "We were just kids."

Buddy continued to share his good fortune with family, friends, and even strangers. During a fishing and hiking expedition to Brazos Box Canyon in New Mexico, accompanied by his brother, Larry, Larry's friend, Bill Edwards, his father, and his cousin, Sam, Buddy purchased new fishing gear for the entire group. On another occasion, while Buddy was getting his boots shined in Lubbock, the black attendant told Holly how much he liked his wristwatch. Buddy spontaneously gave the shoe shine man his watch, concluding that anyone who admired the timepiece more than he did, should have it.

By June of 1958, Buddy realized the survival of his solo and the Crickets' group careers hinged on having the right kind of manager—one who was willing to be an active promoter and explore new musical genres. His concerns were not without foundation; neither Holly nor the Crickets had cracked America's Top 10 since *Oh Boy* was released in November of 1957.

The Chirping Crickets, Brunswick's first long play album was a success, climbing to Number Five in American sales. *Buddy Holly*, released by Coral as Buddy's first solo LP, however, failed to chart in the United States (even though it climbed to Number Eight in the U.K.). Buddy was unhappy with the sloppy promotion of both albums; the design of Buddy's solo LP confused buyers, picturing the singer without his trademark glasses. Adding to Holly's concerns, the liner notes for both *The Chirping Crickets* and *Buddy Holly* mistakenly listed the performers' hometown as *Bullock*, Texas. Buddy concluded that a proactive manager, intent upon promoting his biggest stars, would never have permitted those mistakes to occur.

While there was no doubt rock and roll was booming in the United Kingdom, particularly after the Crickets' tour, Buddy wanted to recapture the magic in America. Consequently, Holly was open to exploring new musical avenues, which might appeal to a wider range of listeners.

In June of 1958, Decca offered Buddy a second opportunity to record in Coral's New York studio. Fearful that his star was drifting away from him, Norman Petty insisted upon accompanying Holly to the recording session in the Big Apple.

Dick Jacobs, who had succeeded Bob Thiele as Coral/Brunswick's Director of A & R, recommended that Buddy record a song written by Bobby Darrin—*Early in the Morning*. The song, featuring both gospel and rhythm and blues, was characterized as "rock and soul." As a bonus, Jacobs agreed to produce the record himself.

On June 19, 1958, Buddy recorded *Early in the Morning* at Coral's studio in Manhattan's Pythian Temple, located on West 50th Street. A small auditorium and recording studio were located inside the large building, which was owned by the Masons' Knights of Pythian. In place of the Crickets, Buddy's background performers included a black gospel chorus, The Helen Way Singers, saxophonist, Sam "The Man" Taylor, drummer, Panama Francis, two guitarists, and a pianist. The flip side of the record included another Bobby Darrin composition, *Now We're One*.

Bypassing the usual waiting period, Jacobs pressed the record and released it immediately. *Now We're One* failed to chart, but *Early in the Morning* reached Number 31 on *Billboard's* Top 100, Number 17 in the U.K., and Number 22 in Australia. Of perhaps greater importance, Buddy had proven that he was capable of further expanding his musical repertoire. "He really thought that it was an excellent record. He liked having the black chorus singing on it. When I heard the record, I thought at the time, 'This is the best record, so far.' My feelings weren't hurt by not playing on it; after all, I wasn't even in New York when he cut it," J.I. Allison recalled.

The Pythian Temple recording session reinforced Buddy's ties to New York City. Even though Norman Petty had witnessed the making of a record outside of his control, he was unwilling to voluntarily cede his role as the producer and manager of Buddy Holly and the Crickets.

In 1958, a monumental event occurred in Buddy Holley's life—he fell in love. While in New York City, in 1958 (the exact month is in question), the Crickets would drop in on their Peer Southern Music Publishing benefactor, Murry Deutch. The details and chronology of Holley's courtship with his future wife, Maria Elena Santiago, vary according to the source.

Maria Elena, a lively attractive, petite, and opinionated receptionist at Peer Southern, remembers that she first met Buddy, when he, J.I., and Joe B. visited Deutch on that early summer day. At age 25, Maria Elena was four years older than Buddy; the age difference, however, was trumped by mutual attraction.

Maria Elena, who was born in Puerto Rico in January of 1933, lost her mother when she was only eight years old. After his second wife passed away, Maria Elena's father, who was a detective with the San Juan Police Department, decided that his daughter was entitled to the best possible education, and would benefit from a female mentor. Consequently, he sent Maria Elena to live with her unmarried maternal aunt, Provi Garcia, who lived in New York City.

Rare for a Hispanic woman in the 1950s, Garcia held an influential position at Peer Southern Publishing, heading the company's Latin American Music Division. Maria Elena settled into her Aunt Provi's apartment, located on 10th Street in Greenwich Village, and completed school in New York City. After graduating from high school, she worked for a time at St. Vincent's Hospital as a translator for Spanish-speaking patients. Maria Elena also served as her aunt's assistant, packing luggage, purchasing clothes, and serving as a hostess during the cocktail parties Provi held at her apartment for Peer-Southern song-writers.

While Provi often traveled with her job and left her niece alone, she was nonetheless very strict, often chaperoning Maria Elena during social outings. Even though she grew to be quite sophisticated in the ways of the world, Maria Elena was remarkably innocent in affairs of the heart, and later admitted that she did not kiss a man until she was 25-years-old. In the early summer of 1958, Maria Elena was working as a receptionist at Peer Southern, her desk stationed just outside Murray Deutch's office.

Maria Elena, who is the primary source concerning her whirlwind romance with Holly, vividly recalled the very first time she supposedly met Buddy: "He came in with the other two Crickets, Jerry and Joe B. He introduced himself and said he was going to see Murray Deutch—he had an appointment. I said, 'All right.' I called in and Murray said for him to wait a few minutes; he had another client in there. In the meantime, while Buddy was waiting, he started a conversation, just to get my attention, I guess. That was when he asked me to go out to dinner with him."

When Buddy asked her out on a date, he meant that very night, which was not surprising, given his impulsive nature. A high-spirited Maria Elena was surprised by Buddy's bold invitation, but equally attracted by his charm and direct manner; as Holly biographer, Ellis Amburn, wrote, "women were often quick to sense that a veritable 'Superman' lurked beneath his 'Clark Kentish' exterior."

After the Crickets met with Deutch, Buddy once again approached Maria Elena, and asked what time she would be free for lunch. She indicated that it was a couple of hours until her lunch break, but explained that Peer-Southern employees were not allowed to date the record label's clients.

Buddy ignored her warning: "Okay, we'll be waiting for you."

Maria Elena thought he was joking, unaware that Buddy had secretly recruited the assistance of others. When the lunch hour arrived, Jo Harper, who handled Nor-Va-Jak contracts for Peer Southern, asked Maria Elena where she planned to eat. Having planned to dine at a downstairs' restaurant in the building, Maria Elena changed her mind after Harper intervened: "No, come out with me. Let's go over to Howard Johnson's."

"Why there?" Maria Elena asked.

"I've got to bring some papers over to Norman Petty, and he's waiting for me there," Harper replied.

When the pair arrived at Howard Johnson's, Norman Petty and the Crickets were already waiting, seated at the same table; Marina Elena soon learned that Buddy had orchestrated their lunch rendezvous. "There were two empty seats, and the Crickets were arguing about where I was going to sit. I wound up next to Buddy, on his right. The others were fooling around, playing footsie and grabbing for my hands, while Norman was looking under the table, trying to figure out what was going on. Finally, Buddy grabbed my hand and said, 'Okay, you guys, you cut it out, because I've got her now...'" Maria Elena clearly remembered.

"You see this girl? I'm going to marry her. I'm going to get her to agree in the next two days, before we leave New York," Buddy announced to his dining companions.

Maria Elena was surprised, but not offended: "I liked him right away. As quiet and shy as he appeared to be, when he made up his mind, that was it."

Once again, Maria Elena explained to Buddy that her Aunt would never permit her to date clients: "She doesn't want me to go out with musicians. She feels that they are not 'all there;' that they're mostly crazy people."

Maria Elena, however, was eager to accept Buddy's dinner invitation. At the same time, she was afraid to directly seek her aunt's permission, and asked Jo Harper to call Provi and vouch for Holly. Later in the afternoon, Murray Deutch also phoned Provi: "Buddy is a very nice boy, and it will be okay for you to let Maria Elena go out with him." Neither Harper nor Deutch succeeded with their appeals. "That didn't sit very well with my aunt," Maria Elena recalled

Finally, Maria Elena worked up the courage to telephone her aunt. "Buddy's very nice. I like him," she pleaded.

"You know, I really don't believe you should get involved. I don't think you will be very safe with those people," Provi replied.

Maria Elena was persistent, and finally obtained Provi's approval. "There's just one condition. I want you to come home early, at least by twelve, not later than that," her aunt insisted.

Maria Elena was both elated and anxious: "Earlier in the afternoon, Buddy had phoned me and said that if I could go out, to meet him at his hotel at 6:30 p.m." When she finally secured her aunt's permission, it was already 5:30 p.m. Maria Elena hurried to a nearby clothing store and purchased a new outfit, showered at the office, donned her new clothes, and rushed to Holly's hotel, arriving just as his limo was pulling away. Fortunately, Buddy caught sight of her, and instructed the driver to stop.

At P.J. Clarke's, a popular pub on Manhattan's 3rd Avenue, Buddy and Maria Elena had their first official date, which was quite proper; he ordered a Coca-Cola and she had a glass of water. Over dinner, the couple developed an immediate rapport, sharing not only their past successes and frustrations, but also their future ambitions.

Buddy found Maria Elena to be unlike any other woman he had met—attractive, intelligent, articulate, sophisticated, and a good listener. Likewise, Maria Elena felt an immediate connection, as if she had known Buddy "for years already." She was particularly impressed by his maturity: "A young man of 21 going on 50."

During dinner, Buddy suddenly got up from the table: "Excuse me a minute, Maria Elena. I'll be right back." He then stepped outside the pub and purchased a red rose from a street vendor.

When he returned to the table, Buddy handed his date the rose: "This is for you, and would you marry me?"

Astonished, Maria Elena thought he was joking: "Oh, sure! When do want me, now or later?"

"I'm serious about this," Buddy replied.

"Well, I guess you are," she said, searching for an appropriate response, "I'll tell you what you need to do. Tomorrow morning, you come over to my aunt's apartment, and you tell her that you want to marry me."

After the couple parted company for the evening, Maria Elena was not yet convinced that Buddy was serious: "I was still taking it as a joke. I thought, this guy is not going to come." But, he did.

At 9:00 the following morning, Holly arrived at the multi-story building, located on the corner of 5th Avenue and 10th Street, and asked the doorman to ring Provi Garcia's apartment. After being escorted upstairs, Buddy learned that Maria Elena's aunt was still asleep.

Once Provi awakened, Buddy came straight to the point: "We want to get married."

Like her niece, Provi was stunned. "Well, don't you think you should wait a little longer and make sure that this is what you want?" she advised.

"No, no, no. I don't have time for courting. I know I want to marry Maria Elena. I know she wants to marry me," Buddy asserted.

Surprisingly, Provi was easily swayed by Holly's conviction and sincerity: "Well, if that's what you people want, I couldn't say no, because no matter what I say, it would be worse if I say no and you just go right ahead and do it." Maria Elena, who had already made up her mind to accept Buddy's proposal, was delighted by Provi's approval.

Provi, who was about to embark on a business trip, offered Maria Elena her credit card to purchase a wedding dress and other accessories: "Go out and get whatever you need." Buddy cavalierly objected, promising to pay for whatever items his fiancé might need.

While the couple's romance was no doubt whirlwind, was it as sudden and dramatic as later recounted by Maria Elena? In an early 1959 interview with *Sixteen* magazine, Maria Elena indicated that she had first met Buddy Holly in *January* of 1958, some five months before their supposed first date, when he proposed to her.

Sonny Curtis informed the author he was in New York City in *March* of 1958, recording at Dot Record studios and inking a song-writing contract with Peer Southern Music Publishing. During that same visit, Curtis remembered that Buddy asked him to escort Maria Elena to the Crickets' performance at the Brooklyn Paramount.

Depending on the source, Buddy and Maria Elena met as early as *January* (and apparently no later than *June*) of 1958. Irrespective of the exact month of their first introduction, the couple's courtship was speedy courtship, and they married in August of that same year.

Anticipating family resistance to his engagement, Buddy talked to his brother, Larry, before breaking the news to his parents. In conservative Texas, interracial marriages were still considered taboo, and it was unusual, if not sinful, for an older woman to marry a younger man. Larry took his brother's surprising news in stride: "He was looking to get married, anyway, anyhow. Jerry was about to do it, and Buddy didn't want to be left behind. And, I know he'd been real heartsick since it ended with Echo…" In the months to come, Larry's assertion that Buddy's sudden interest in marriage was a means of competing with J.I. was not without merit.

Even though Larry supported Buddy, Ella Holley was reflexively opposed to the marriage. When Buddy's parents later traveled to New York to meet Maria Elena, Ella was polite and friendly, but no less approving, finding it difficult to overcome the issues of race and her future daughter-in-law's Catholicism. L.O., however, was charmed by Maria Elena and immediately started treating her like a daughter. "Buddy's father and I hit it off, boom, right from the beginning. He was a very sweet, easy-going kind of man. His mother was different; she was the one who directed traffic in that family. But, they both made me feel welcome right away. They said Buddy had found a gorgeous girl. They thought I was a little doll with my clothes, my accent. They made me feel like something breakable."

The Crickets were fully supportive of Buddy's decision to get married. J.I. understood the contentious religious issue; Peggy Sue Gerron was also Catholic. As best friends, Buddy and J.I. planned to schedule a double wedding. An easy-going Joe B. voiced no opposition: "I was pretty surprised by the suddenness of it, but if it was going to make Buddy happy, I was for it 100 percent."

Nonetheless, the engagement remained low key, so much so, that many of Holly's fans did not know he was married until after his death. The lovebirds set a wedding date for later in the summer, after the Crickets completed their upcoming tour.

As had been the case with J.I.'s engagement, Norman Petty was totally opposed to Buddy getting married. He warned Holly that a married rock and roll star would lose many of his female fans. Petty, however, was more likely concerned that Maria Elena and her Aunt Provi, who worked in the music publishing and record industry, would eventually discover how he had financially leveraged Buddy.

"Norman never liked me from the beginning. He saw danger in me. He knew the problems I was going to cause him. He knew I was going to take over. In his mind, Buddy was his and nobody else's," Maria Elena candidly recalled.

From the very beginning of their relationship, Buddy confided to Maria Elena about his growing dissatisfaction with Petty: "I'm not happy with Norman, because Norman does not want to spend money on publicity. He never wants to put money out to promote us." Marina Elena understood Buddy's discontent: "Norman didn't want to spend a red cent, because he didn't want the money out of his hands. I don't care what anybody says, you need to be promoted. I don't care how good, how wonderful you are, you need the exposure. And, sincerely, the man never did that. Buddy was not happy with it. Everybody else was always out there, and Buddy always had to struggle to make sure that the people knew about him…"

Petty, in fact, had done little to increase the Crickets' public exposure. The only promotional pictures of the group were black and white shots taken by Petty's loyal bookkeeper, Norma Jean Berry. Unlike the managers of contemporary rock and roll stars, Petty was reluctant to invest the time and money to make the Crickets' name more recognizable. Buddy, J.I., and Joe B. had been sorely disappointed when Petty refused to allow them to appear alongside other rock and rollers in the movie, *Go, Johnny, Go!* "Buddy had always trusted Norman and believed in his judgment. But, when he got to New York and started talking to people there, he realized how backward Norman was," Maria Elena added.

Buddy was equally frustrated by Petty's exclusive control of the Crickets' money. While he faithfully paid their bills, Petty never revealed how much money was deposited in the Crickets' bank account, which he, alone, managed. Petty would only tell Buddy, J.I., and Joe B. that the sum was *less* than they thought.

By mid-1958, approximately 2,000,000 Coral and Brunswick-released singles had been sold in the United States. With their two percent contracted royalty rate, that amount, alone, equaled $20,000 (equivalent to $167,000, in the year 2016). In addition, Petty had collected money for the band's records sales in the U.K. and Australia, song-writing royalties, and fees from the Broadcast Music International (BMI) for songs played on radio or television. Still, Petty was the only one who knew how much money was deposited on behalf of the Crickets.

Petty's control over the Crickets' funds was such that Buddy was forced to send him a bill for Maria Elena's engagement ring. Holly grew angry when Petty insisted that he purchase a one karate diamond, rather than the larger stone he had selected for his fiancé.

While Maria Elena believed that Petty's lack of promotion of *Heartbeat* and *It's So Easy* had prevented them from becoming hits, she was not the sole force behind Holly's later decision to fire Norman Petty. She recalled that Buddy "wanted to break with Norman, even before he met me," which can be substantiated by Holly's earlier statements. At the same time, she possessed considerable insight into the record business and understood how disingenuous it was for Petty to "put his name on every song that Buddy wrote," especially the chart-topping *That'll Be the Day.*

Petty, however, was certain that Maria Elena was exerting undue influence over Buddy and distancing him from his Clovis roots. In time,

Petty believed she would push Buddy to abandon J.I. and Joe B, opting for a solo career.

Maria Elena later claimed Petty told Buddy that she was a "cheap girl," who "picked up" numerous singers. This scurrilous rumor had supposedly been passed along to Petty by an executive at Peer Southern.

Up until the day of Buddy's wedding, Petty tried to talk him out of marriage. "Norman knew that once I got involved, I would be finding out things that he didn't want me to find or Buddy to find, and that once I was in the picture, things would turn around," Maria Elena opined.

The seeds of discontent between Holly and Petty had been sown well before Buddy met Maria Elena. The couple's engagement, no doubt, drove the two men even further apart.

By the end of June, Buddy and the Crickets were feeling cash poor. Consequently, they agreed to join the *Summer Dance Party*. The 11-day tour was set to begin on July 4th, in Angola, Indiana, followed by stops in Iowa, Illinois, Michigan, Minnesota, and Wisconsin.

The *Summer Dance Party* was a much different format than previous tours; the Crickets were the only well-known artists on the bill. Tommy Allsup and his four-man Western Swing Band accompanied them as their opening act. At each stop, local bands would complete the concert line-up. For the first time, Joe B. played a Fender Stratocaster Precision Model, electric bass, rather than his usual stand-up fiddle (Buddy, however, insisted that Joe B. continue to play the stand-up bass in the studio, so as not to disrupt sound consistency). Instead of buses, the caravan travelled in two vehicles—Buddy's light blue Lincoln and a yellow Desoto station wagon Holly had recently purchased, the latter of which towed a U-Haul trailer containing both bands' equipment. On occasion, Tommy rode along with the Crickets in Buddy's Lincoln.

This tour was slower-paced, allowing the Crickets to relax between shows. In Waterloo, Iowa, they had enough free time to rent a boat, such that Buddy and Joe B. could water ski on the Cedar River.

In the past, the Crickets had been paid by the tour organizers. During the *Summer Dance Party*, Buddy was responsible for collecting their performance fees at each stop. J.I. recalled that a few promoters deliberately tried to short-change them: "I remember when somebody tried to duck us, Holly would jump right up and say, 'Here's the contract and this is what you owe us. You pay or else.'"

By this point in his career, Buddy realized that his music spoke for itself. In Waterloo, Iowa, photographer, Dick Cole, asked him to remove his eyeglasses. Holly refused: "I'm not trying to be a glamour boy. I'm trying to be a musician."

Until the very end of his life, the state of Iowa seemed cursed for Holly. In Waterloo, when the Crickets playfully attempted to walk across logs floating in the Cedar River, they were unceremoniously dumped into the water. On July 13th, in North Woods, while Buddy was swimming across a lake, he grew fatigued and nearly drowned. After he struggled to reach the opposite shore, a shivering Holly had to be covered with blankets, drink several cups of coffee, and take a long, hot shower to elevate his body temperature.

Even though he nearly drowned and suffered hypothermia, Buddy managed to play two shows that night at the Crystal Rock, located in nearby Rhinelander. During the intermission, overcome with fatigue, Holly took a nap in the back seat of his Lincoln.

When it was time for the second show to begin, Buddy roused himself from the car, splashed cold water on his face, and slowly made his way onto the stage. A teenage boy in the audience immediately shouted: "Hey, Buddy! I'll buy you a beer if you can play *Rave On*." The challenge seemed to energize Holly, who opened with *Rave On* and then rocked through the remainder of the set.

After the show, Buddy walked across the street to a bar and encountered the audience member who had goaded him: "I'm here to collect my beer." "Buddy made my friend buy him that beer," the teenager's acquaintance recalled.

The tour members encountered further obstacles as the *Summer Dance Party* progressed. Buddy had so popularized Fender guitars that the company gave him a pair of newly-manufactured Stratocasters and two amplifiers prior to the start of the tour; Holly gave one of the new guitars to Tommy Allsup. At some point, their instrument trailer was burglarized, and one of the Stratocasters was stolen. From that point forward, Buddy and Tommy were forced to pass the same guitar back and forth, between sets.

Buddy continued to openly challenge Norman Petty, refusing to send the Crickets' performance fees to Clovis. Instead, he kept the money in the glove compartment of his Lincoln and dispensed it to different band members. Holly proved to be an effective road manager, strictly documenting cash payments, gasoline consumption, and other travel-related expenses.

Since he was required to carry so much cash in his car, Buddy had previously purchased a .22 caliber revolver for protection. On at least one occasion, Joe B. remembered that the weapon came in handy. "Right after we'd gotten paid one night, there was a problem in the parking lot. Some headlights came up behind us, real close, and wouldn't let us back out of our place. Buddy reached into the glove box, buzzed down the Lincoln's rear window, turned around, and pointed his gun through it. Those headlights just disappeared!"

After the Crickets returned to Lubbock from the *Summer Dance Party* tour, J.I. was eager to hit the road again, uncertain how much longer the rock and roll gravy train would continue running. When Buddy turned down an immediate tour offer, J.I. was disconcerted. Buddy explained that he wanted to enjoy life a bit, and told J.I. that if he wanted a Cadillac, he (Buddy) would buy it for him. Perplexed by Buddy's reluctance to pursue the Crickets' traditional work ethic, J.I. probed further.

"What if you were killed tomorrow and never took the opportunity to appreciate what you've earned?" Buddy responded.

"You're right," Allison agreed; at that time, neither of them realized the prescience of Buddy's reasoning.

While Holly was technically on vacation, he was rarely idle. Buddy and Joe B. purchased a boat and water ski equipment, which they used on Buffalo Springs Lake, located 11 miles east of Lubbock. While J.I. and Joe B. were in the boat, Buddy tried to jump over the Lubbock Ski Club's ramp. His daredevil trick ended in a crash landing, and Holly lost both his eyeglasses and wallet (one can only ask why he was carrying his wallet while water skiing). Some years after Buddy's death, Ella Holley was surprised when her son's glasses and wallet were recovered while the lake was being dredged; the waterlogged billfold still contained Buddy's cash and driver's license.

Holly also filled his hours with weight lifting and karate, attempting to strengthen his skinny frame. Larry Holley described it best—Buddy enjoyed relaxing with "a lot of fire."

Even though Buddy and J.I. had planned a double wedding, Allison and Peggy Sue Gerron decided to jump the gun. On July 21, 1958, the couple obtained a marriage license at the country courthouse in Lubbock, and a day later, eloped. After driving 320 miles to Honey Grove, located near the Oklahoma border, they were married the following evening by J.I.'s uncle, who was a Methodist minister. The elopement had been J.I.'s idea; he convinced his fiancé that it was the best way to escape family conflicts over whether the couple should have a Catholic or Baptist wedding.

Absent a wedding cake or reception, the newlyweds drove to Dallas for a brief honeymoon, where a sheepish J.I. telephoned Buddy with news of their elopement. Peggy Sue managed to smooth the waters, promising that she and J.I. would postpone their official honeymoon until after Buddy and Maria Elena were married.

"Buddy asked me where I wanted to go. I said, 'Somewhere warm, with white sand. How about Acapulco?' He laughed and said, 'I'll take care of it.'" As promised, Buddy arranged all the details relating to their joint honeymoon.

As Buddy neared his marriage date, Ella Holley continued to raise objections to the interracial union. A frustrated Buddy finally informed his mother, like it or not, that he was marrying Maria Elena in August.

Norman relentlessly opposed the joint marriages of Buddy and J.I. In addition to tarnishing their images as single rock and rollers, Petty insisted that they were too young and immature to get married.

Even though the couple resented his intrusion into their private lives, J.I. and Peggy Sue later concluded that Norman was correct about their immaturity. "There is a warm side to Jerry. Our relationship was extremely stormy; and, it was from the very beginning. There's nothing wrong with the fact that we can all make a decision that is not especially good for us," Peggy Sue admitted, years after she and J.I. divorced.

Maria Elena arrived in Lubbock in early August of 1958. By this time, the entire Holley family, including a heretofore reluctant Ella, had accepted the inevitability of the forthcoming marriage. L.O. and Ella informed their future daughter-in-law that she was free to address them as "Dad" and "Mother."

Religion quickly became a non-issue. Even though she had been raised as a Roman Catholic, Maria Elena did not insist on a priest performing the wedding service or demand that any future children be raised as Catholics. The Holley's own pastor, Reverend Ben D. Johnson, put aside the Baptist's traditional anti-Catholic bias, and agreed to conduct the service. Johnson's decision was perhaps made easier, given the amount of money Buddy had donated to the Tabernacle Baptist Church

In the days leading up to the wedding, Buddy and Maria Elena chastely slept in separate bedrooms at the Holley's house. L.O. was convinced that his youngest son had displayed newfound maturity by choosing an assertive wife. Maria Elena believed Ella had finally come to accept her, and noted that both parents provided her with the "same warmth and affection" they lavished on Buddy.

Peggy Sue Gerron Allison, however, was uncomfortable around Maria Elena, who she claims basically ignored her. The relationship between Buddy and J.I.'s spouses would always remain tense. Peggy Sue remembered that it was not until the eve of the wedding before Maria Elena first spoke to her, asking the newlywed to serve as her matron of honor.

On August 15th, a blistering hot day, when the temperature in Lubbock reached 97 degrees, Buddy and Maria Elena were married at the Holley's house. Buddy's family (his parents, brothers, sister, brother-in-law, cousins, nieces, and nephews), J.I., Peggy Sue, and Joe B. crowded inside L.O. and Ella's living room to witness the ceremony.

It was the simplest of weddings for an accomplished musical star. As expected, J.I. served as Buddy's best man. There were few frills—a single floral arrangement, punch bowl, and a wedding cake.

Maria Elena wore a plain white dress and veil, while Buddy dressed in a dark suit, pinned with a boutonniere. Having lost his regular eyeglasses during the recent water skiing mishap, Buddy was forced to wear his prescription sunglasses. After the coupled exchanged vows, J.I. played Buddy's newly-released record, *Now We're One*, on the turntable. From the limited funds in his personal checking account, bearing the name Charles Holley, Buddy paid Reverend Johnson $100 for conducting the service.

The four newlyweds immediately departed for their joint honeymoon. After driving to El Paso in the Crickets' touring station wagon, they spent the night in a hotel, before flying to Acapulco the following morning. The newlyweds stayed at least one night at the Las Brisas Hotel, before relocating to the El Cano, which was less luxurious, but offered a waterfront view. After discovering a lagoon appropriate for waterskiing, Buddy rented a boat. J.I. and Maria Elena, who were not particularly good swimmers, stayed in the boat, while Buddy skied and an adventurous Peggy Sue attempted to learn.

Unanticipated tensions emerged during the honeymoon. Even before departing for Mexico, J.I. and Peggy Sue were encountering difficulties adjusting to married life. Peggy Sue intuitively sensed that Buddy didn't appear "real happy," believing he and Maria Elena were struggling with their age and cultural differences. Peggy Sue cited one such incident: "He (Buddy) and Jerry and I were in the hotel restaurant one evening, waiting for Maria Elena to come down and join us for dinner. Time passed, she still didn't show, and Buddy got more and more agitated. Eventually, he went off to the house phone to call her up in their room. After a while, he came back and said, 'She's not coming down for dinner, after all. She's going to have it up in the room.' He looked tense and stressed the way I'd never seen him before."

Maria Elena, who was seven years older than Peggy Sue, had little in common with J.I.'s new wife, and continued to make little effort toward establishing a friendship. "She was sophisticated, worked in New York, and wore fashionable clothes. I'd only just hung up my can-can petticoats," Peggy Sue explained.

On the return trip to Texas, the newlyweds stopped in Mexico City. In a photograph taken while all four were dining together, both Buddy and Peggy Sue's smiles appear noticeably forced.

When Buddy and Maria Elena returned to Lubbock, they stayed at L.O. and Ella's house, mainly out of financial necessity. The couple was financially strapped, and both Buddy and his new bride were convinced that Norman Petty was deliberately holding onto his record royalties; perhaps as a means of punishing Holly for getting married. "Norman said, 'No, I have to get together with the accountant.' After we got married, Norman was furious,'" Maria Elena recalled, after she and Buddy drove to Clovis to personally speak with Petty.

Norman Petty remembered the situation much differently, claiming that he received $28,838 in publishing royalties from Peer-Southern in early August of 1958. On August 11th, he recalled paying Buddy ($3,887.93), J.I. ($1,453.82), and Joe B. ($4,877.48). If Petty's financial records can be trusted (a big if), it appears Holly netted less than $4,000 in August of 1958, hardly enough to sustain his wants, needs, and obligations in the coming months.

Maria Elena's memories ran contrary to Petty's: "My aunt was the one supporting us when we got married." "Buddy did not have a red cent to his name. Norman controlled all the monies..." Maria Elena contended.

In the five or so months he had to live, Buddy consistently maintained that Norman was spitefully withholding his rightful share of royalty monies.

CHAPTER 9

A New Direction

THE REMAINING MONTHS OF 1958 were filled with anxiety and uncertainty for Buddy Holly. He was not alone; many other pioneers of rock and roll music were also distracted or had fallen into disfavor with the public. Elvis Presley had been drafted into the Army and was stationed in Germany. The flamboyant Little Richard abruptly turned his back on rock and roll, and was studying to become a Seventh-Day Adventist minister at Oakwood College, in Huntsville, Alabama. Jerry Lee Lewis continued to feel the sting of public scorn after entering a scandalous marriage with his 13-year-old, second cousin. Chuck Berry would soon be in trouble for violating the Mann Act—transporting a woman across state lines for an immoral purpose. His first conviction, in 1959, would be overturned, because the judge made racist remarks. In 1961, after his arrest, trial, and conviction for once again violating the Mann Act, Berry was fined $10,000 and served two years (of a three-year sentence) at the federal penitentiary in Springfield, Missouri.

Buddy was not only dealing with financial pressures, but also fretted about his recent failures to chart a Top 10 record in the U.S., which he blamed, in part, on a manager lacking promotional skills. Holly envisioned a future as a performer, producer, and record publisher, but those dreams could not be fully realized until he was paid the money owed to him by Norman Petty.

Buddy began drafting plans for his own recording studio and publishing company. He had already purchased land near Lubbock, in an area known as Bobalet Heights. One wing of the proposed structure would house the studio and record production center, while the other would serve as a new house for his parents. Plans for the 4,300-square-feet complex included a carport, terraces, walkways, gardens, ponds, and a swimming pool.

Buddy planned to create his own record label and publishing company, Taupe, the color of his Cadillac, but later changed the name to Prism. Holly along with his friend, song-writer, and record producer, Ray Rush, invested $3,500 to become co-partners in the record company. Buddy would serve as President, while Rush would function as Director of Promotions. Having not yet severed ties with Norman Petty, Buddy planned for the Clovis producer to oversee record sales, and surprisingly (if not astonishingly) serve as the company's Treasurer. Early on, Petty agreed to sell Buddy some recording equipment. Any possibility of a joint venture between Holly and Petty, however, would come to an abrupt halt before the end of the year.

Buddy believed there was an abundance of musical talent in west Texas. Accordingly, he planned to produce records for local artists in his Lubbock studio, such that they would not have to travel far from home.

In the early weeks after he was married, Buddy spent considerable time at radio station *KLLL* (or *KL Double L*, as it was often called). Purchased by brothers Sky and Slim Corbin, on May 1, 1958, *KLLL*, which featured a "Hillbilly Top 40" format, was housed atop the 20-story Great Plains Life Building—the tallest structure between Fort Worth and California.

Hi Pockets Duncan, Buddy's one-time manager, had been hired to work as a disc jockey for *KLLL*. The station's most popular DJ, however, was young Waylon Jennings, who was lured away from rival station, *KVOW*. At a salary of $75-per-week, Jennings hosted two shows per day, while still dreaming about a future as a country and western artist. Jennings, who had known Holly before he became a star, viewed Buddy as a hero, and welcomed his visits to *KLLL*.

Avoiding Clovis and further conflict with Norman Petty, Buddy chose *KLLL* as his new hang-out. Arriving at the radio station with his guitar, Buddy would compose songs and occasionally cut demos, using the station's recording equipment. On occasion, Buddy, Waylon, Sky, and Slim would gather in a back room at the radio station and jam for most of the night.

When Jennings recorded radio commercials, Buddy would often sing in the background. Holly also recorded advertisement jingles for *KL Double L*, to the tune of his popular hits, like *Everyday*.

Hi Pockets Duncan, sensing that Waylon Jennings had a realistic chance of becoming a successful musical artist, recruited Buddy to serve as his mentor. Holly, who was appreciative of Duncan's role in shaping his own career and respected his ability to judge talent, readily agreed to help. In fact, when Buddy first introduced Maria Elena to Hi Pockets, he informed her: "Let me put it this way. If it wasn't for him, I wouldn't have you."

Duncan remembered that "Buddy liked Waylon," and immediately went to work improving his image. Holly took Jennings to a Lubbock clothing store, and utilizing his limited funds, updated Waylon's wardrobe. He also introduced Jennings to his personal barber, who gave the disc jockey a more stylish haircut.

Buddy told Peggy Sue Allison about his forthcoming venture: "Norman's going to help me produce a record for Waylon; my debut as a producer. I'm so excited by it! Waylon has lots of talent. He just doesn't know it yet."

Before producing a record for Jennings, Buddy had previously offered to play background guitar for another aspiring singer, Jerry Engler. Engler's recording session in Clovis began on the night of September 6, 1958 and did not conclude until after midnight; by then, it was Buddy's 22nd and last birthday. As a birthday present to himself, Buddy traded his light blue Lincoln for a brand new, taupe-colored Cadillac (Larry Holley teasingly told his brother that the Caddy was pink). "Buddy always said he'd have himself a Cadillac by the time he was 21. So, he did," Bob Montgomery recalled.

On September 10th, Buddy and Waylon drove to Clovis, at which time both cut records. The visit marked the end of an era; it would be the *last time* Holly recorded at *Norman Petty Studios*. Buddy sang *Reminiscing*, written by fellow Texan and tenor saxophonist, King Curtis (whose real name was Curtis Ousley). Curtis' saxophone had been featured on the Coasters 1957 hit, *Yakety-Yak*, which made it to Number One on the *Billboard* chart. Prior to the Clovis recording session, Buddy telephoned Curtis, who he had met during an Alan Freed concert tour, and asked him to play on *Reminiscing*.

"That'll be $500 and plane fare," replied Curtis, who was living in New York City.

"Ain't that a little high?" Buddy asked, aware that his cash reserve was low.

"You're making yours all the time and I gotta make mine. You send the money up to New York," Curtis insisted.

"No, if I was to send $500, and the plane crashed, I'd lose my money and sax player," Buddy proposed.

"Mr. Holly, just send the money and don't talk like that," Curtis replied.

After Holly agreed to Curtis' terms, he picked up the saxophonist at the airport in Amarillo and drove him to Clovis. Determined to add just the right sound to his new recording, Buddy ultimately paid Curtis $600 to play as a session musician on *Reminiscing*. Detailing the woes of a jilted lover, Buddy's characteristic hiccups and Curtis' bawdy saxophone express a sense of longing without being maudlin.

Waylon Jennings, nervously awaiting his opportunity to record, was carefully watching and listening to Holly, while "just marveling a whole lot." Neither *Reminiscing* nor the record's flip side, *Come Back Baby*, were released until after Buddy's death. The record failed to the chart in the United States, but climbed to Number 17 in the U.K.

Buddy intended for Waylon to record *Jolie Blon*, a Cajun song written by Harry Choate in the mid-1940s. In its original form, with French lyrics, the song tells of a beautiful woman, Jolie Blonde (French for "pretty blonde"), who breaks her lover's heart by running off with another man.

Buddy not only produced Waylon's first record, but also played rhythm guitar. The other background artists included King Curtis, two of Norman Petty's house musicians, and the Roses (as vocalists). Even though he was "scared," Jennings found his first recording session to be "a lot of fun." He was impressed with Buddy as a producer, remembering that it "seemed like he was trying tell me everything he could in a short period of time." Jennings noted that Holly appeared "happy all the time," and full of "a lot of energy."

The lyrics to *Jolie Blon* challenged Waylon, who struggled with the Cajun dialect, even though he and Buddy had listened to Choate's record repeatedly, memorizing the words and vocal inflections. Jennings freely admitted that his cover of *Jolie Blon* was less than refined: "I wasn't near ready to start recording then." Waylon also recorded *When Sin Stops*, a country song composed by two local song-writers, which appeared on the record's flip side.

The combination of difficult to understand lyrics, a rhythm and blues saxophonist, and a rockabilly beat was not a winning formula for a hit record. Even though Buddy secured Jennings a record deal with Brunswick, *Jolie Blon* sold poorly. "A lot of people who heard the results got a lot of laughs out of it," Waylon good-naturedly recalled.

Even though Waylon would not achieve stardom until years later, he never forgot the advice Buddy gave him: 1. A performer should never "compromise about his music;" 2. "Do what you feel;" 3. "Leave while you're ahead"—if an artist retires when he is most popular, he won't repeat the same music and diminish his legacy.

On September 12, 1958, Buddy and Maria Elena drove to California, both as a vacation and an opportunity to self-promote *It's So Easy*. While on the west coast, Holly dropped by Ray Charles' house, only to discover that the highly successful, blind singer and musician was on tour. Buddy left behind his telephone number, but apparently never received a return call from Charles.

Norman Petty, sensing that his days with Holly were numbered, began quietly undermining Buddy. He told J.I. and Joe B. that Maria Elena was forcing Buddy to move to New York City. If the Crickets followed him, Norman warned them that they would be financially exploited by New York record executives; Petty's condemnation of New Yorkers was laughable, and nothing less than the pot calling the kettle black.

Maria Elena remembered that when she travelled to Clovis with Buddy, Petty essentially ignored her, much the same way he treated his own wife: "Norman paid no attention to her (Vi). She had no say-so. She was not asked anything; she was just told. The poor woman was just kind of existing in that weird atmosphere."

Maria Elena bristled when Vi and Norma Jean Berry made fun of her accent. Vi explained that they were laughing only because her accent was "cute." "At least I can speak your language. You can't speak mine," Maria Elena retorted.

Maria Elena believed the mannish-looking Norma Jean had sexual designs on her, and kept her distance. During a portion of the late-night recording session, Maria Elena chose to sleep in Buddy's Cadillac, rather than the studio's bedroom.

Petty was proud of the recently purchased *Nor-Va-Jak* lettering on the outside wall of the next-door gas station/apartment. Maria Elena was not impressed; compared to New York recording facilities, she described Petty's studio, a bit too harshly, as "old," "dilapidated," and "horrible."

On September 23, 1958, the Crickets traveled to New York City to appear on Alan Freed's television program, where Buddy lip synched his soon-to-be-released singles *Heartbeat* and *Well All Right*. Afterwards, Holly and Freed chatted for a bit, including an eerily foreboding conversation about the rickety DC-3 airplanes they had flown during the summer tour. Buddy specifically recalled the day when the helicopter pilot was killed in a crash near Cincinnati. Freed concluded the interview: "Buddy, we've had a lot of fun together, and I hope we're going to have a lot of fun together in the future…"

While in New York, Buddy and Phil Everly co-produced two songs for a young Italian-American singer, Lou Giordano. On September 30,

1958, at Beltone Studios, Giordano recorded *Stay Close to Me* (written by Holly) and *Don't Cha Know* (composed by Everly). Buddy and Phil played guitar and sang background vocals (along with Joey Villa) on both recordings. Holly planned for Giordano and Waylon Jennings to become Prism Records first two recording artists. Even though Buddy helped Giordano obtain a contract with Brunswick Records in November of 1958, his single, released the following January, failed to chart. *Cash Box* magazine rated each song as a B plus, and Giordano would never become a huge star.

Even though Buddy was not eager to hit the road again, he needed the money. Consequently, the Crickets joined another GAC tour—*The Biggest Show of Stars 1958, Fall Edition*. Among the entertainers who accompanied them on the 16-day concert series, which began on October 3rd, were Dion and the Belmonts, Clyde McPhatter, Frankie Avalon, Paul Anka, the Everly Brothers, Jerry Lee Lewis, Jimmy Clanton, the Coasters, Little Anthony and the Imperials, Frankie Lyman, Connie Francis, and Bobby Darin. The group travelled across the northeastern United States and into Canada. Performing a total of 14 shows, the Crickets earned $10,000.

The fall tour featured a new face in the Crickets' line-up. Tommy Allsup was added as lead guitarist, expanding the band to a quartet. The Roses also traveled with the Crickets, performing as background vocalists. Even though Peggy Sue Allison did not accompany her husband on the tour, Maria Elena traveled with Buddy.

The presence of Maria Elena disrupted the Crickets' long-standing interpersonal relationships. While Buddy and Maria Elena drove in his Cadillac, J.I., Joe B., Tommy, and the Roses followed in the Desoto station wagon towing their equipment trailer. For the first time, the band was literally and figuratively separated. "On that tour, we weren't as close as we had been before. Of course, now, I can understand why; Buddy was a married man and had his wife with him, and he had to devote more time to her than he did to Jerry and I (sic). But, at the same, I felt like Buddy didn't want to be part of the group anymore. He wanted to be a big shot star, himself. And, I was jealous of Maria Elena, because it seemed that she was taking Buddy away from Jerry and I (sic). Buddy had been like a brother for so long, and suddenly Buddy was no longer a brother," Joe B. recalled.

Maria Elena found life on the road to be distasteful: "There were no roadies to do the work in those days. We had to carry all the luggage ourselves, set up, and dismantle equipment…" In addition to enduring the "terrible" food, Maria Elena hand-washed the band members' "shirts" and "underwear."

Maria Elena's natural assertiveness ultimately proved useful. She was emphatic that the Crickets be paid in full at each venue. Maria Elena also advised Buddy and the other artists to collect their money before performing, or risk being stiffed. She knew that her husband was carrying a pistol in the "scotch bag" where they kept the money, which gave her added confidence when a promoter tried to short change them. "I didn't fool around. I said, 'Okay, pay me now!'" Maria Elena remembered.

J.I. and Joe B., unhappy about spending time with Buddy only while the group performed, began drinking heavily, sometimes in the morning hours. J.I. recalled a later confrontation with Buddy: "We really didn't see each other that much, except at the shows. And, Buddy got kind of put out with us. Things got sort of tense, because we were really shucking it. Sometimes, we'd get drunk in the morning and stay drunk all day. And, Buddy wasn't out-and-out opposed to drinking, but he didn't like us to do it all the time, and the way we were doing it. Anyway, after the tour was over, he talked to Joe B. and me, and said, 'Okay, you guys, I can't take all this. If we're going to do this thing, let's do it right. We're getting older, and we've got to take this more seriously. You guys drink too much; it's obnoxious, and I hate it. If you want to stay with me, great, but you've got to be more interested in what you're doing.' So, we finally said, 'Yeah, okay, we understand; we'll tighten up a little bit.'"

Because Maria Elena did not have a driver's license, an exhausted Buddy had to drive from one tour stop to the next. In the middle part of October, after playing a show in Upstate New York, the Crickets were running late for their next performance in Scranton, Pennsylvania. After Buddy was pulled over while cruising at 95-miles-per-hour, the policeman asked him if he knew how fast he was driving. Holly's smart-aleck retort resulted in his being hauled into the police station, leaving Maria Elena behind in the Cadillac. At police headquarters, where the lighting was better, the cop realized that his prisoner was Buddy Holly. After asking for Buddy's autograph, the officer released him. The group managed to make it to Scranton, just in time for their next performance.

On another occasion, a sleep-deprived Buddy asked Maria Elena, who had "never driven a car before in my life," to take the wheel. Buddy told her that driving "was real easy" and to let truck drivers, who honked their horns, "pass you." Before he fell sound asleep, Buddy instructed Maria Elena to wake him up when they reached a certain turn on the road map. "I found out very quickly that when you have to do something, you do it," she recalled.

When the *Biggest Show of Stars* tour ended in October of 1958, Buddy informed J.I. and Joe B. that he planned to fire Norman Petty. He also wanted his fellow Crickets to move to New York City with him, so the entire band could be closer to their record company, music publisher, and booking agents. Buddy explained that it was imperative for them to hire a manger who would actively promote their careers. "Buddy was unhappy that Norman didn't believe in music magazines or that sort of thing," J.I. recalled.

Even though J.I. and Joe B. were not eager to leave Lubbock, Buddy believed they were on board with his decision. J.I. tentatively agreed, especially after Holly promised him a share in his new record company. A decision was made, or so Buddy thought, to fire Petty when the group returned to Lubbock.

J.I., Peggy Sue, and Joe B. went so far as to search for housing. "We looked at apartments, big enough to accommodate Jerry, myself, and Joe B., because he (Joe B.) didn't want to live alone in New York City," Peggy Sue remembered.

Maria Elena was very concerned about the future of her husband's career. Peggy Sue remembered Maria Elena confronting her after the *Biggest Show of Stars* tour: "Well Peggy Sue, you need to know that Jerry is not paying attention to business! Now, I think he is a really good drummer, but he is just not being a professional. He is making Buddy look bad and the Crickets." "I don't think you understand how this can affect your life, you know…If Jerry Allison thinks he can't be replaced, he should think twice. You need to get hold of him right now—it is unprofessional to get on stage drunk…You know, Buddy isn't going to let him ruin his career. There are a million drummers out there who need a job!" Maria Elena continued. After listening to Maria Elena's admonitions, Peggy Sue held little hope that she could control her independent-minded husband's behaviors.

On October 21, 1958, Buddy recorded four new songs at the Pythian Temple in New York City. Even though he had previously resisted using an orchestra as background musicians (something Norman Petty had proposed), fearing that violins and other symphony-style instrumentation would transform him from a rock and roller into a "pop" singer, Buddy was now confident and bold enough to explore new musical avenues.

Coral Records' Dick Jacobs agreed to produce and arrange the aptly-named "string session." The background musicians included members of the New York Philharmonic and *NBC's* studio symphony orchestras. While the Crickets were not playing on the recordings, they were present at the studio, along with Maria Elena, Peggy Sue, Jo Harper (Murray Deutch's secretary at Peer-Southern), Paul Anka, and Norman and Vi Petty.

At 5:00 p.m., Buddy bustled into the studio, three hours before the session was scheduled to begin. He startled Dick Jacobs by announcing that Paul Anka had just completed a "fantastic" song for him, entitled *It Doesn't Matter Anymore*, and he intended to record it that very night. When Jacobs protested that there wasn't enough time to incorporate another song in the line-up, Buddy insisted: "We gotta do it."

The producer soon relented, even though Buddy did not have a lead sheet. Jacob's copyist was immediately summoned, and wrote the lead sheets as Buddy sang the song, accompanied by his guitar. Jacobs remembered writing the "pizzicato arrangement for the strings;" a technique first used by Tchaikovsky.

The musical arrangement for *It Doesn't Matter Anymore* was completed by the time the orchestra members arrived—eight violinists, two violists, a harpist, a guitarist, a pianist, a drummer, and a saxophonist. Peggy Sue remembered the violinists were "real snobbish," and made it known they had little regard for rock and roll artists. If Buddy was aware of their condescending attitude, Peggy Sue sensed that he "didn't let anybody shake him up." Jacobs concurred; while the orchestra practiced the arrangement, Buddy remained "untemperamental" and "relaxed."

The session recordings were live cuts, with no overdubbing. While Peggy Sue remembered that Buddy was positioned in an isolation booth with a window overlooking the auditorium, Dick Jacobs insisted that Holly stood on the stage, directly in front of the orchestra.

Buddy's melodic voice and trademark hiccups blended perfectly with the classical instrumentation on *It Doesn't Matter Anymore*. The lively tune details the woeful sentiments of a jilted lover. "I'd never heard Buddy sound so good. It was like a mass of energy had engulfed me and I could feel the music all the way down to my toes," Peggy Sue recalled.

After the last note was sung and played, both Buddy and the orchestra members were smiling—they had recorded a hit in just one take. "We came out with a really fine record," Dick Jacobs remembered. *It Doesn't Matter Anymore* would reach Number 13 on the *Billboard* chart and make it all the way to Number One in the U.K., but unfortunately, not until after Buddy's death.

It only took three and one-half hours to record the remaining three songs. *Raining in My Heart* (written by Boudleaux and Felice Bryant), the B side to *It Doesn't Matter Anymore*, was released in January of 1959, and peaked at Number 88 on the *Billboard* chart (after Buddy's death).

True Love Ways, written by Holly, is believed to have been a self-composed love song for Maria Elena. "He (Buddy) wrote *True Love Ways* when we got married. He told me that he had a song started for me. He said it was going to be our song. It's a very difficult song to sing, as it goes up and down," Maria Elena remembered.

Buddy's mother was impressed by her youngest son's ability to sing not only rock and roll, but also romantic tunes, and *True Love Ways* became Ella Holley's favorite song. Released in May of 1960, over a year after Holly's death, *True Love Ways* failed to chart in the U.S., but climbed to Number 25 in the U.K.

Years later, *True Love Ways* remains a fan favorite. "…If you listen to *True Love Ways* on a CD, it's as though you are in the studio; it's wonderful. Buddy Holly recorded so few songs during his short career, and I've never heard one that I didn't like. He sang from the heart and he had a wonderful voice, very stylized. He also was a great song-writer and he spoke to the youth of the world at that time," rock and roll star, Bobby Vee, later recalled.

The string session concluded with *Moondreams*, composed by Norman Petty. While Petty freely added his name as a composer on other song-writers' records, he did not extend that courtesy to Buddy Holly. *Moondreams* was not released until after Holly's death, and failed to chart.

Holly's recordings with the symphony orchestra were indeed innovative. Of equal importance, the string session marked the *last time* Buddy ever recorded in a studio.

Holly was pleased with all four recordings, but still questioned whether rock and roll was ready for violins. In the opinion of Dick Jacobs, the string session proved that Holly could record anywhere with any producer. Peggy Sue Allison remembered that J.I. was less than impressed by Buddy's latest recordings, on which neither he nor Joe B. played. A bored J.I. insisted that he and Peggy Sue leave half-way through the recording session.

"This is Norman's string session that he just couldn't live without! He's always trying to change Buddy and make him a popular star!" J.I.

complained to his wife, overlooking the fact that Petty, who had previously suggested Holly might want to record with an orchestra, had nothing to do with the actual production.

Holly's enthusiasm for trying new things gained momentum; he told Dick Jacobs that he wanted to make a record with the legendary Ray Charles, as well as record a big band-type song, accompanied by brass musicians. Coral Records', Bob Thiele, was so enthusiastic about the latter proposal that he offered to produce the record in New York City. When Norman Petty objected, Buddy simply ignored him.

By now, Petty knew that Holly was most likely heading in a new direction. Consequently, when he flew back to New Mexico, the Clovis producer set into motion a plan to separate J.I. and Joe B. from Buddy.

At the same time, Buddy was taking steps to protect his own interests, writing BMI and asking that the song-writing credits for *Peggy Sue* be changed from Petty and Allison to Holly. Preparing to change managers, Buddy asked Decca to provide him with copies of all contracts that he was party to.

Shortly after the string session, Buddy and the Crickets performed *It's So Easy* on The *Dick Clark Saturday Night Beechnut Show*, which was telecast from Manhattan's Little Theater, located in Times Square. On October 28th, the Crickets appeared on Clark's *American Bandstand*, and once again played *It's So Easy* in front of 8,000,000 television viewers. Before introducing the band, Clark asked Buddy how many songs he had composed. Holly casually replied, "15, 20 songs." When Clark announced that it was time to perform, Buddy calmly replied: "Okey dokey." After performing *It's So Easy* with the Crickets, Buddy sang *Heartbeat* as a solo.

Clark interviewed J.I. during the show, and asked if the Crickets were returning to Lubbock. Allison replied that they were "eager" to get home, "just as soon as we can fly out of New York." Unbeknownst to Buddy, J.I., and Joe B., it was the *final time* all three of them would perform together.

Before the Crickets returned to Texas, Buddy, yet again, reminded his bandmates that he was moving to New York City: "I hope you guys will come along." Concerned that Holly was being "headstrong," and still uncertain about relocating from Lubbock, Joe B. was already reconsidering his commitment. J.I., however, reassured Buddy that he was ready to make the move.

"Buddy said, 'I'm going to move to New York, and I'm going to go out from Norman. There's a lot of stuff I want to do.' We agreed that we'd all move to New York and start our own publishing company, and we had it all worked out. We even called Norman and told him that we were hanging it up and moving to New York," J.I. recalled. Allison likely confused the sequence of events, as it appears that Petty was not informed of his dismissal until the Crickets returned to Texas.

J.I. and Joe B. flew to Texas, while Buddy and Maria Elena elected to make the three-day drive to Lubbock in his Cadillac. After Buddy arrived home, the agreed-upon plan was for the Crickets, in unison, to drive to Clovis and fire Petty.

Buddy believed the decision to leave Petty was timely and justified, even though the Clovis producer had long been his mentor. There was no doubt Norman had done much to kick start Buddy's and the Crickets' careers—free studio time, negotiation of their initial record contracts, and allowing Holly to exert artistic control in the studio, the latter of which enabled Buddy to develop the skills necessary to become a promising producer.

Petty's generosity, however, had come at a steep price. The Crickets granted him exclusive power of attorney to negotiate their contracts and manage their money. All income generated from record sales, record play time, publishing, and song-writing royalties had been paid directly to Petty, who banked the money in an account (or perhaps accounts), which only he could access. He had claimed song-writing credits on most of their records; entitling him to a share of the royalties. From the start, Petty had exercised rigid control, insisting that all performance fees, except for a small weekly salary, be forwarded to Clovis; a rule that Buddy eventually disregarded. Even after the Crickets stopped sending Petty monies earned on tour, they were still forced to send receipts for major purchases to Clovis.

J.I. likened it to a parent-child relationship: "When we needed some tires, we had to go to Norman for the money. And, he'd say, 'Okay, you can get a good deal on the thin white sidewalls at Ward's.' And, we'd say, 'We don't want Ward's tires, we want Sears tires, or Firestone, or whatever.' And, he'd say, 'Nope, you don't want to waste your money like that.' He was trying to do the right thing for us. But, it just seemed like he had too much control."

Petty not only had unchecked control over the Crickets' finances, but he also attempted to direct their personal lives. Both Buddy and J.I. continued to resent Norman's unsuccessful attempts to keep them from getting married.

The Crickets were fully aware that they had empowered Petty—a by-product of youthfulness, inexperience, and naiveté. "Norman kept telling us, 'This is our company; we're all in it together, and we're going to all share from it.' Of course, none of us ever saw a nickel of the publishing money. But, I saw this beautiful studio and all those nice offices he had, and I was thinking, 'Wow, I own a piece of this. I've got it made.' And, I think that's one thing that led us into letting him sign for equal shares on our songs," J.I. explained.

Buddy may have been the only member of the Crickets who saw Norman Petty as a stepping stone in their careers. Nearing the end of 1958, Holly had learned how to collect and distribute tour fees, function as a road manager, produce records, and manage the band's financial affairs, all without Petty's guidance.

By pre-arrangement, after returning to Lubbock, J.I. and Joe B. were supposed to start packing their belongings for the move to New York City and wait for Buddy's arrival. Allison and Mauldin, however, drove to Clovis before Buddy made it back home. When they asked for their rightful shares of money held in deposit, Petty refused to release any funds, until his role as the Crickets' manager was clarified.

When J.I. and Joe B. verified that Petty was going to be fired and the band members were moving to New York City, Norman skillfully went to work breaking up the Crickets. Petty told J.I. and Joe B. that they didn't need Buddy—if the pair stayed with him, he would not only continue to produce their records, but also step up promotional activities on their behalf. Joe B. eventually came to understand that Petty had a broader agenda; he was determined to extract personal and financial revenge on Buddy Holly.

Petty's false promises, threats, and manipulations convinced J.I. and Joe B., who were already ambivalent about leaving Lubbock, to stay put. "We went over to Clovis, and Norman talked us out of splitting; that's what happened. He said, 'You know, you guys better hang down here. When you get to New York, you're going to see, you'll be cheated out of everything;' all that kind of stuff. So, we said, 'Okay,'" J.I. recalled.

Joe B. explained Petty's counterproposal in greater detail: "The feelings that I had on the tour could have been one of the reasons that Norman influenced me as much as he did when we got back to Clovis. But, it's not Maria that broke the group up; I felt like Petty's the one who broke the group up. Norman said, 'Look, let's stay down here, where we have control of everything.' And, he built us up, saying, 'You guys are the Crickets, you will be the Crickets, and you'll keep the Crickets name. And, we'll get another lead singer and a guitar player—so forth and so on. He told us that the Crickets were the ones that had all the hits—Buddy Holly had only *Peggy Sue*, and he couldn't make a living on the name Buddy Holly. So, if we stayed down in Clovis with Norman, we could keep the name of the Crickets, and Norman had 'all his (Buddy's) money in the bank, and we'll starve him to death.'"

It had been relatively easy for Petty to change J.I and Joe B.'s minds, as both were uneasy about "not fitting in," if they moved to New York City. J.I. summarized the situation in simple terms: "Norman Petty talked us out of it." Joe B. was more diplomatic; the Crickets weren't exactly "breaking up," but "just quit playing together."

Unlike Norman Petty, J.I. never blamed Buddy for their break-up: "I am sure in my mind that Buddy wasn't fed up with us. He was fed up with Norman Petty…"

Buddy and Maria Elena arrived in Lubbock on November 2nd. When Buddy called J.I.'s house and discovered his bandmates had already gone to Clovis, he could not understand why they had not waited for him. As Larry Holley remembered it: "Buddy just got livid mad."

In short order, Buddy and Maria Elena drove to Clovis to confront Norman Petty. Maria Elena remembered that Petty attempted to control the situation: "Norman tried to get me to go and talk to Vi, so he could meet with Buddy one-on-one." Buddy objected, indicating that whatever Norman needed to say could be spoken in front of Maria Elena. Buddy informed Petty that he was firing him, in front of Maria Elena, Vi, and Norman Jean Berry.

Petty, who knew he was going to be fired, had already made up his mind to withhold royalty monies due Buddy. "We went to Clovis one day to get our money. Norman definitely said, 'No, I'm not ready. I've got to get the facts and account to the other two boys. I cannot let you have money,'" Maria Elena bitterly remembered.

Petty's recollection of the confrontation was different, and he painted Maria Elena in a negative light; she was the one who said Buddy "could do better" and Norman was "not fit" to manage the Crickets. Petty recalled asking what he had done to justify being fired, and was told by Buddy and Maria Elena that it was more a matter of what he *had not* done for Holly and the Crickets—namely promotion.

After verifying that his decision was final, Buddy demanded all money due to the Crickets, which would be divided equally. At that point, Petty dropped his bombshell—J.I. and Joe B. were staying with him. Buddy was stunned, and in the words of Maria Elena, instantly felt "betrayed."

Maria Elena appealed on behalf of her shell-shocked husband: "I said, 'Well, Norman, you need to let him have at least part of his money. We need to live on something.' He said, 'No, he cannot have his money. You have to wait until I get all the accounting done.'"

Maria Elena recalled that Petty's tone grew instantly stone cold: "Well, to be honest with you, I don't have to pay you anything, until I'm ready." Holly's emotions rapidly transformed from shock to anger:

"Buddy said, 'Well, you know, give me my money, or you're going to be in some kind of a problem.'"

"Oh, I'll tell you what. I'd rather see you dead, first, before I give you any money now," Maria Elena remembered Petty saying. Sensing that her husband was about to punch Norman, she quickly intervened: "Let's go. Let's get a lawyer when we get back (to New York City)."

Later that same day, Buddy spoke with J.I. and tried to convince his best friend to reconsider his decision to remain with Norman Petty. Allison informed Holly that he really wanted to stay in Texas, where he had more freedom, including the opportunity to ride his motorcycle.

J.I. recalled that Holly was disappointed but rational: "We sat in the car and went through it all. And, Buddy was agreeable to the whole thing. He said, 'I wish you guys would go with me. You're going to be sorry you didn't. But, I can understand, if you don't want to, you don't want to.' We weren't uptight or anything like that. And, he said, 'Okay, you guys can have the name of the Crickets, and I'll just work as Buddy Holly.'" Despite Buddy's apparent generosity, ownership of the Crickets' name would soon become a major bone of contention.

Maria Elena recalled that her husband was far more distraught than J.I. realized: "Buddy got real hurt when they did this. He cried, thinking that the boys had betrayed him, staying with Norman." Buddy was inconsolable for a time: "I thought I had treated them fair. I don't know why they should have done that to me."

Buddy was so upset that he told both Marina Elena and his parents that he might abandon his musical career. "Listen, Buddy, they were the ones that left you, and you have a lot of talent of your own and you'll do well," Maria Elena reassured him.

A few days later, Buddy ran into J.I. at a café in Lubbock. Buddy asked, yet again, if his two former bandmates were certain about their decision. J.I. indicated yes, at least for now.

"The person I really worry about in all this is Joe B.," Buddy continued; both he and J.I. had long been protective of their bass player.

"Don't worry, I'll take care of Joe B.," J.I. asserted.

As he adjusted to the sudden and disappointing dissolution of his band, Buddy was developing a new interest—aviation. Larry Holley was already a pilot, and his youngest brother hoped to follow suit. Buddy dreamed of purchasing his own plane and flying to concert venues.

He never shared this plan with Maria Elena, who was deathly afraid of small aircraft. A family friend had once flown her from San Juan to St. Thomas in a private plane; sometime later, that same plane, following the identical route, crashed, killing the pilot and his passengers, some of whom were Maria Elena's friends.

On November 5, 1958, Buddy took a 30-minute flying lesson at Champs Aviation, located at the Lubbock Municipal Airport. For nine-dollars, the instructor allowed Holly to pilot the propeller-driven Cessna. Larry, who accompanied his brother during the flight, remembered that the instructor stalled the engine and allowed the aircraft to free fall for several frightening seconds. Afterwards, Buddy informed his brother: "Man, that stall seemed to last for 30 minutes!" When Maria Elena later learned that Buddy had taken a flight lesson "behind my back," she was appalled.

Years after his brother's death, Larry Holley was rummaging through drawers in his house, where he discovered a dusty flight log book bearing Buddy's signatures. The log revealed that Buddy had taken at least three flying lessons, in August, September, and November of 1958. During those practice flights, he flew with an instructor from Champs Aviation aboard a Cessna 172 (tail number N855568).

With little or no money, Buddy and Maria Elena decided to return to New York City. By now, Maria Elena believed the entire Holley family had come to love and respect her, regardless of race or religious upbringing. She specifically recalled L.O. telling her: "You're the best thing that ever happened to Buddy. You've cut his umbilical cords. When he was younger, he was tied to his mother. Then, he was tied to Norman Petty. But, now, he's come into his own—he's finally a man."

Buddy and Maria Elena were uncomfortable with Lubbock's undeniable prejudice against people of color, as well as interracial marriages.

Holly, however, was not cutting ties with his hometown; he still planned to construct his recording studio in Lubbock, and some people, including Peggy Sue Gerron Allison, believed that Buddy planned to eventually move back to Texas. Before departing Lubbock, perhaps as a token of gratitude for first introducing him to stringed instruments, Buddy gave his brother, Travis, his Guild F-50 Navarre acoustic guitar.

During their drive to New York City, the couple stopped in Wichita Falls Texas, where Buddy's old friend, Snuff Garrett, was a disc jockey at *KSYD*. Garrett, who was in the middle of a marathon broadcast, invited Buddy to join him in the studio. While Maria Elena slept in the Cadillac, the two men chatted while records were being played, and Holly told Garrett that he wanted him, as well as Waylon Jennings, to move to New York City and work for his new record label. On the air, Garrett let Buddy announce a station break, proclaiming that *KSYD* was "the station that other stations listen to."

After returning to New York City, Buddy and his wife were heavily reliant upon loans from Maria Elena's Aunt Provi. Buddy promised Provi he would repay her, as he had done in the past, when others loaned him money. Having to rely on his mother-in-law for financial support, however, was embarrassing and humiliating for Holly.

Heartbeat, released on November 11, 1958, made it only as far as Number 82 on *Billboard's* Top 100—a major disappointment for Buddy. On the bright side, the record climbed to Number 30 in the United Kingdom. The disc's flip side, *Well All Right*, failed to chart in the both the U.S. and U.K., though it reached Number 24 in Australia (ironically, members of the *Buddy Holly Memorial Society*, who were polled in 1977 and 1978, ranked *Well All Right* as their fourth most popular song).

Buddy and Maria Elena settled into a fourth-floor, one-bedroom apartment, at the corner of 9th Street and 5th Avenue, in Greenwich Village. The apartment complex, located in the same neighborhood as Provi's apartment, was the site where Mark Twain's house once stood. A bank occupied the ground floor of the building, while apartments filled the upper stories.

In December of 1958 and January of 1959, Buddy explored the Bohemian culture of Greenwich Village. Between December 3rd and December 17th, he also recorded six self-composed songs, using an Ampex tape machine in the couple's apartment (it was the same reel-to-reel machine that Norman Petty had brought to Oklahoma, when Buddy and the Crickets recorded in the officer's club at the air force base). The purity of Buddy's voice and acoustic guitar are remarkable in each of those recordings.

What To Do details the heartache and uncertainty associated with ending a relationship. *That's What They Say* expresses hope that true love is on the horizon. Another of the aptly-named "apartment tapes," *That Makes It Tough*, details the lingering, unforgettable images of a lost lover.

Yet another apartment recording demonstrates the wide range of Buddy's voice. *Crying, Waiting, Hoping* expresses wishful longing for a reunion with a lost lover. *Learning the Game* is a reminder that wisdom that comes from experience, and seemingly perfect relationships can fail the test of time

Peggy Sue Got Married was composed at the suggestion of Buddy's father, based on the phenomenal success of *Peggy Sue*. Peggy Sue's rumored betrothal is first revealed in this tune, with perhaps a tone of regret in the singer's voice.

On December 11th, Buddy wrote his parents, mentioning he had been writing some "fairly good songs." "The best one is a 'top secret' one titled *Peggy Sue Got Married*. Please don't mention it to anyone. I want it to be a complete surprise," Buddy penned.

Since Decca had not yet approached him about another recording session, Buddy's so-called apartment tapes proved that his financial woes did not impair his creativity. "Those apartment tapes are really wonderful songs; they were going to be on his next album," Maria Elena remembered. None of those songs were released to the public until after Buddy's death.

Buddy looked to a brighter future, and continued designing blue prints for his studio in Lubbock, adding a record store, which would be managed by his father. He also set up the legal framework for his record label and publishing company. Even though the recording studio would be in Texas, Maria Elena believed the couple would make New York City their permanent home.

Without Aunt Provi's generosity, Buddy and Maria Elena would not have been able to afford their $900-per-month apartment rent. The apartment, though small, suited Buddy just fine, and he used his skills as a draftsmen and carpenter to construct kitchen cabinets and a bar that opened onto the terrace.

Both Buddy and Maria Elena enjoyed taking long walks, exploring the nooks and crannies of Greenwich Village. "Buddy and I were like night owls. We couldn't sleep. Both of us were hyper. We just felt like walking. We kept on the move. We went to coffee houses and listened to poetry readings. He loved poetry readings and the folk singers in Greenwich Village…" Maria Elena remembered.

Buddy's taste in music had always been eclectic, and he grew more intrigued by jazz and folk music. Maria Elena noted that exposure to previously unexplored genres triggered creativity: "Buddy was always open to new ideas. He looked into every type of music…He'd always listen to suggestions, and be willing to try something out and see if he could do it—see if it sounded good."

Unable to reach a settlement with Norman Petty, Buddy sought legal counsel. Provi set up a consultation with lawyers representing Peer-Southern Publishing, but since the parent company's royalty payments were in question, conflicts of interest prevented them from representing Holly.

Don and Phil Everly, who were involved in a legal dispute with their manager, Wesley Rose, recommended Buddy consult their personal attorney, Harold Ornstein. Ornstein had a solid track record of representing musicians, including not only the Everly Brothers, but also Pat Boone, Benny Goodman, and Ray Charles.

On November 24, 1958, Ornstein wrote Norman Petty a letter enumerating several points: 1. Buddy Holly had retained him as legal counsel;

2. Holly wished to cancel Petty's power of attorney; 3. A request for "all copyright registrations, certificates, publication agreements, mechanical licenses, and agreements between Mr. Holly and any co-author of any song;" 4. A statement of "any monies" which had been collected "on behalf of Mr. Holly;" 5. A check for the "full balance of any monies due to him."

Four days later, Petty answered Ornstein's letter: 1. He had no written contracts between himself and Buddy Holly or the Crickets—only verbal ones (which was most likely true); 2. There were existing performance contracts that Petty had never seen (most likely untrue); 3. Buddy Holly had been paid fairly, to date (highly questionable); 4. All checks received for Buddy Holly and the Crickets had been placed in an "agency account" (true): 5. Holly would be paid once a full audit had been completed (yet to be seen).

Buddy was appalled to learn that the "agency account" was the *Norman Petty Agency, Incorporated*, which he knew only Petty could access. Trying to maintain a sliver of optimism, Holly still hoped to be paid his share of royalty money before Christmas.

Despite the financial uncertainty, Holly was certain his career could be re-charged. He was equally determined to have robust promotional services in the future. Consequently, Buddy posed for famed photographer, Bruno. The portfolio contained stylish photographs of Holly with new, thicker-framed, square-shaped glasses, and at least one picture of him without his spectacles.

Since they could not afford a secretary, Buddy and Maria Elena kept up with Holly's fan mail. Buddy personally answered each letter and assured his fans that he hoped to reunite with the Crickets. The couple also set in motion plans to establish Buddy Holly fan clubs throughout the country.

Lacking a manager, Buddy offered the position to Peer-Southern's Murray Deutch, who he trusted implicitly. Deutch refused, diplomatically informing Buddy: "I couldn't think of a better way to spoil our good relationship. I don't want to be your mother, your father, your banker, your Rabbi…"

In addition to resurrecting his musical career, Buddy told Maria Elena that he wanted to become an actor: "I want to be like Anthony Perkins, because I'm kind of tall and lanky, like him. I want to do a movie; not only act in it—I want to write the score of the movie." Maria Elena suggested that before Buddy pursued a movie roll, he should enroll in Lee Strasberg's private method acting school, whose alumni included Marlon Brando and Marilyn Monroe.

Buddy was flush with ideas about how he could expand his musical genre. "I want to learn classical guitar and do some kind of classical score for the Spanish guitar," he informed his wife. Buddy immersed himself in Maria Elena's collection of flamenco records. "He started listening to them and said, 'Oh, I could do that, easy.' He started playing his guitar, and soon he picked it up. He was into perfection and said, 'Who do I call?'" she recalled. After Maria Elena introduced him to a teacher in their neighborhood, Buddy started taking flamenco lessons.

When Buddy informed Maria Elena that he wanted to learn Spanish, she tutored him by singing Latin-American songs. Interestingly, one of those tunes was entitled *Maria Elena*, written by Lorenzo Barcelata in 1953—a tribute to the Mexican President's wife.

Buddy revived talk about performing a duet with Ray Charles. He also wanted to produce a gospel album. "I love Mahalia Jackson," he enthusiastically reminded Maria Elena.

Maria Elena was not without her own suggestions; she wanted her husband to learn to dance. At first, Buddy balked, then agreed to enroll at a dance studio in the future.

"Buddy was a 22-year-old, going on 50. He was very relaxed and easy going, but he had this drive, and his mind was so sharp. It was going all the time," Maria Elena recalled. Don Everly seconded her observation, describing Holly as "a thinking man."

Maria Elena was fascinated by her husband's active mind and dreams for the future: "All the ideas that Buddy had at that time! He wanted to open studios in different areas, like London."

Buddy looked forward to becoming a full-fledged record producer, targeting young artists. "Buddy didn't have in mind just writing songs that fit his own style, and then finding someone else to record them. Instead, he wanted to try writing songs meant deliberately for somebody else in particular, and meant to suit that singer's style and potential audience," Maria Elena explained.

In his Lubbock studio, Holly planned to employ a house band, not only for young artists, but also to serve as back-up on his personal recordings. Tommy Allsup was among those who admired Holly's innovation: "He wanted to try out fiddles, steel guitars, and all that, on his own releases." "You have to keep coming up with something new; something they haven't heard before," Buddy informed his old bandmate, Larry Welborn.

In dire need of income, Buddy explored commercial endorsements. The Guild Guitar Company agreed to design a "Buddy Holly" electric guitar, and pay him a percentage of the instruments' sales.

Writing, editing, and recording the apartment tapes kept Holly busy. When not composing in his own apartment, Buddy would go to Provi's residence, where he could use her piano. Holly employed both the piano and guitar, writing the lyrics and music at the same time, with remarkable efficiency. His revisions, however, were more labor intensive—he wanted every song to sound just right. Just as he had done when taking solo drives in Lubbock, Buddy would leave his apartment for lengthy walks, before returning and immediately composing or revising songs. "...He really cared about the way the songs sounded and the words he chose. He'd keep asking, 'Do you think this sounds good? It doesn't sound like I want it to.' Or, 'That's not what I want to say; it isn't what I had in mind...'" Maria Elena remembered.

Even though he remained active and largely maintained a positive outlook, Buddy was likely internalizing stress related to his lagging career and dismal financial situation. In January of 1959, Maria Elena convinced him to drink "a couple of glasses of champagne" to celebrate her

26th birthday. He soon became violently sick, likely a direct result of the alcohol aggravating his existing ulcers. From that point forward, Maria Elena promised to never again tempt her husband with alcohol.

When Buddy approached Irving Feld, complaining that Norman Petty controlled his money and would not relinquish it, the promoter proposed a partial solution: "Why don't we put on a tour for you? You can make some money and save some money."

In September of 1958, Feld's GAC and GAC-Super Productions began organizing tours that mainly featured up-and-coming stars. Each performance was emceed by a local radio disc jockey, and admission rates were inexpensive (around one-dollar), the latter of which lured teenage rock and roll fans. In addition, audience members, who retained their ticket stubs, were eligible to receive discounts from music stores that helped promote the concerts.

GAC was planning a bus tour of the Midwest from late January through mid-February of 1959—the *Winter Dance Party*. While Buddy was less than excited about traversing the interior of the country in the dead of winter, he desperately needed the money. In addition, Maria Elena was pregnant, which meant he would soon have another mouth to feed.

Maria Elena was opposed to the *Winter Dance Party* from the start, describing it as a tour "for beginners," and "not the right thing" for Buddy. Holly reminded her that necessity trumped preference: "I'm not going to continue to ask your aunt to lend us money. It's time to go to work, no matter what it is." Consequently, arrangements for the tour were finalized on December 14, 1958.

Later that month, when his good friend, Eddie Cochran, was playing at the Paramount Theater, Buddy visited with him at the Park-Sheraton Hotel. The Everly Brothers and Lou Giordano (whose first record Buddy had co-produced with Phil Everly) were also present. During the get together, Buddy complained about Norman Petty holding his money, as well as the disappointing record sales for *It's So Easy* and *Heartbeat*.

"He wasn't suicidal about it. I guess you could say his pride was a little hurt, but he was determined to get back up there again. That's why I was surprised when he told me he was going out on the road again. The last I heard, he'd decided to stay in New York and work on his records, until one of them went Top Ten," Phil recalled.

Buddy asked Eddie Cochran to join him on the *Winter Dance Party*. Cochran tentatively agreed, but later withdrew, after receiving an offer to appear on the *Ed Sullivan Show* in early February of 1959. Holly understood Cochran's change of plans—the *Ed Sullivan Show* was a far bigger showcase for his friend.

When Buddy and Maria Elena returned to Lubbock, just prior to Christmas, it would be the *last time* he would see his parents, siblings, and most his lifelong friends. Holly looked forward to spending time with friends and family, and he also needed to recruit a band to accompany him on the *Winter Dance Party*.

In a conversation with his brother, Larry, Buddy shared his frustration about having to tour again: "It's sure getting to be a grind. I'm getting tired of having to run constantly and be in the limelight. I can't lead my life like I want to. I'm getting fed up with it. I'm not fed up with music in general—I like producing and writing songs. But, as far as touring and being in front of the public eye constantly, that really gets to be a drag." He also showed Larry the 24-day *Winter Dance Party* itinerary, which necessitated his performing almost every day, punctuated by lengthy bus rides. "Look at this! It's pathetic, the way they're pushing me; every night in a different town," Buddy grumbled.

Maria Elena remembered that Buddy unsuccessfully tried to telephone J.I. and Joe B. to see if they wanted to reunite, if only briefly, and accompany him on the *Winter Dance Party*. Buddy's former bandmates had relocated to Clovis, where J.I. and Peggy Sue had rented an apartment in mid-November (Joe B. was also living with them). At the time, J.I. was primarily playing as a session musician at *Norman Petty Studios*.

Petty wasted no time reconstituting the Crickets. Earl Sinks, who had previously performed as an opening act for the Crickets, was recruited to replace Buddy as lead vocalist, while Sonny Curtis joined the band as lead guitarist. The newly-formed Crickets had recorded two songs on November 21st, *Love's Made a Fool of You* and *Someone, Someone*; the latter of which was written by Vi Petty, who also played piano on the recording, with the Roses performing background vocals.

Neither of those songs ever charted. The second-generation Crickets were becoming increasingly disgruntled; Petty had yet to book them any stage performances and failed to initiate the promised promotional services.

GAC gave Buddy a $2,500 cash advance before the start of the *Winter Dance Party*, a portion of which he used to buy his family Christmas gifts. Larry Holley later recalled the 1958 holiday season was a particularly joyous one for Buddy's family.

Even though he was unhappy about the forthcoming tour, angered by Norman Petty's refusal to relinquish his royalties, and hurt by J.I.'s and Joe B.'s betrayal, Holly maintained a smiling face. "When Buddy came home at Christmas, it seemed like it was one of the happiest times in his life. He was free, and he had it pretty well made; he could do just about what he wanted to do," L.O. recalled, apparently unable to sense his youngest son's underlying turmoil.

Buddy lavished his family with Christmas presents. "I think he blew just about all the money he had on coming here to impress us," Larry recalled. A silent home movie, shot inside the Holley's house, preserved images of Buddy's final Christmas Day.

On December 27th, while visiting the *KLLL* studio, Buddy remarked that it was not very difficult to write a song. An unbelieving staff member quickly bet Holly that he couldn't write a song in 30 minutes. Buddy accepted the challenge and composed *You're the One* in just 15 minutes. While Buddy played his guitar and sang the newly-written song, Waylon Jennings and Slim Corbin clapped their hands to keep time. When the record was pressed, the song-writing credits read Holly-Jennings-Corbin. *You're the One*, released as the B side to *Love is Strange* in 1969, made it to Number 105 on the *Billboard* chart.

On December 28th, an unseasonably warm day in Lubbock, with the temperature climbing into the lower 60s, Buddy treated his father, both of his brothers, and a cousin to a fishing trip. Beforehand, he took the group to a sporting goods store and paid for any fishing gear they needed. "We had some good times. It just didn't last long enough," Larry sadly reflected.

During his Christmas vacation, Buddy met his old friend and fellow musician, George Atwood, for a cup of coffee at Walgreen's drug store. Atwood remembered Holly discussing his proposed studio in Lubbock: "He was going to have his own pressing plant there. He was going to have his own trucks deliver the stuff. He was going to do it from square one."

Buddy also shared a meal with his first singing partner, Jack Neal, at the Nite Owl restaurant. Holly informed Neal that he had already purchased the land for his Lubbock studio complex, which L.O. was going to construct. Holly explained that he eventually hoped to expand his operations to other cities in the U.S. and abroad. Neal was among the local performers Buddy wanted to produce at his Lubbock studio. "Jack, there's a real mess of talent here in west Texas, if only they could get a start. I want to do something to help them along. Maybe I can make you a star, too!" Buddy declared.

While in Lubbock, Buddy performed during a live *KLLL* remote broadcast at the grand opening of a new fruit and vegetable store. Afterwards, Buddy asked KLLL's co-manager, Slim Corbin, to set up a homecoming concert for him, the following summer.

Even though he was angry and frustrated with Norman Petty, Holly refused to outwardly disparage his former manager. "Buddy never really told us why he had broken with Norman. Once, when he was home and some of his friends were over, somebody started to make some remark about Norman, and Buddy cut it right off, 'I don't want anyone bad-mouthing Norman. I don't want to hear anything about it,'" Ella Holley recalled.

Buddy made a trip to Clovis to meet with Bob Montgomery, who was working as a sound engineer at *Norman Petty Studios*. Buddy hoped to recruit his old friend to work for Prism, serving as the director of the New York City publishing division. Holly and Petty had a brief encounter in Clovis, but no harsh words were exchanged. Still angry and hurt, Buddy apparently made no further efforts to contact either J.I. or Joe B.

Buddy eventually assembled a band to join him on the *Winter Dance Party*. During one of his frequent visits to *KLLL*, Holly offered his friend, disc jockey, and aspiring country and western artist, Waylon Jennings, the opportunity to play bass during the upcoming tour. Waylon, who had never played a bass guitar, was somewhat intimidated. Buddy assured Jennings that he would teach him how to play the instrument after he arrived in New York City, just before the tour commenced.

Jennings was eager to play with Holly, but his pregnant wife was opposed to a road tour. When station manager, Sky Corbin, granted Waylon a leave of absence, Jennings agreed to join the band, even though his wife was "awful disgusted."

Buddy drove to Odessa and visited with Tommy Allsup, who was playing at the Saddle Club with country piano star, Moon Mullican. After listening to Buddy's proposal, Allsup agreed to join Holly's band during the *Winter Dance Party*.

In Clovis, Buddy saw Carl "Goose" Bunch playing drums for a local band, the Poor Boys. Born in Big Springs, Texas on November 24, 1939, the 19-year-old Bunch was a gifted percussionist. Holly asked Allsup, who was well-acquainted with Bunch, to recruit the drummer to join their touring band.

Having assembled his band, Buddy instructed Jennings, Allsup, and Bunch to fly to New York in mid-January, so the quartet could practice for a week, before embarking on the *Winter Dance Party*. Holly decided to call his new band the Crickets—a legal maneuver, staking his claim to the band's original name, in the event he was forced to sue Norman Petty for his share of outstanding royalty monies.

On December 31, 1958, Buddy and Maria Elena flew back to New York City. Buddy would never again see Lubbock or his immediate family.

At some point in January of 1959, Buddy recorded additional songs, which were captured on his Ampex tape machine—the 1905 classic, *Wait 'Til the Sun Shines Nellie*, Little Richard's *Slippin' and Slidin'*, *Dearest* (self-composed), Mickey and Sylvia's *Love is Strange*, *Smokey Joe's Café* (written by the prolific composing team, Jerome Leiber and Mike Stoller), *Leave My Woman Alone* (a Ray Charles' instrumental), and *Buddy's Guitar* (another instrumental). *Buddy's Guitar* may well have been the *last* composition of Holly's young life.

On January 5th, Coral released *It Doesn't Matter Anymore*, with *Raining in My Heart* on the flip side of the record. *Cash Box* magazine was enthusiastic about the single: "Buddy Holly has a pair of winners back to back that could join hands to give him his biggest money-maker since *Peggy Sue*." Holly could only hope the *Cash Box* reviewer was prescient.

Meanwhile, Holly wrote Norman Petty about the status of his royalty money. In the missive, he maintained a polite tone, closing with: "Thanking you in advance, Buddy Holly."

On January 20, 1959, Waylon Jennings, Tommy Allsup, and Carl Bunch landed at New York City's Idlewild Airport. Allsup and Bunch checked in the Edison Hotel, while Jennings bunked on the couch in the Holly's small apartment.

It was Waylon's first trip to the Big Apple: "Talk about culture shock. We went down the very next day after we got there, and Buddy bought suits, blazers, ascots…We were hot!" After purchasing Waylon an electric bass, Buddy informed him: "You've got two weeks to learn this." With the assistance of Tommy Allsup and two long play albums, *The Chirping Crickets* and *Buddy Holly*, Waylon familiarized himself with the bass guitar. "I very quickly memorized everything Buddy did. I didn't learn to play the bass; I memorized the notes," Jennings explained.

In a music hall Buddy had rented for a week, he practiced with his newly-formed band. The musicians worked diligently to sound like their predecessors. "It was hard work for me. I was a perfectionist and I wanted to get it perfect and I couldn't. I was scared that I wouldn't be able to please Buddy," percussionist, Carl Bunch, recalled. When not practicing, Bunch repeatedly listened to Buddy's and the Crickets' records.

The rehearsals proved highly productive. "When we left New York City, you could listen to us and we sounded like J.I., Joe B., and Niki Sullivan. We were good," Bunch proudly concluded.

Waylon enjoyed the private time he spent with Buddy and Maria Elena. He and Buddy held frequent jam sessions in the Holly's apartment, playing a variety of songs. Jennings was particularly gratified when Holly allowed him to play his Stratocaster.

One night during Waylon's stay, Maria Elena announced that she was going to cook rice, red beans, and broiled steaks. Buddy was surprised; his wife was not domestic, and the couple usually went out to eat. Waylon nearly spit out his first mouthful of the badly burnt beans, until Buddy kicked him under the table.

"Aren't they good! You did a good job," Buddy exclaimed.

Waylon simply got up from the table: "Well, I'm full."

"Buddy didn't want to hurt my feelings. He knew I was trying. I just didn't know how to cook. He wouldn't hurt my feelings for anything," Maria Elena recalled. Waylon, whose own marriage was troubled, believed his host couple had established a tight bond: "Maria Elena was a sweet girl, and you could see that Buddy was very much in love with her."

Like her husband, Maria Elena appreciated Jennings' talent as a singer and a musician. "Waylons, you could be a pop singer. Every time I listen to you sing, it gives me goose bumples," she announced, amusing Buddy with her mispronunciation of Jennings first name, and substituting *bumples* for pimples.

Before departing New York City to begin the *Winter Dance Party*, Buddy informed Waylon that he was going to produce the buddying artist's next record, which Holly was convinced would establish Jennings as a rising star. Holly planned to hire a studio band, including steel guitar and fiddle players, to augment Waylon's distinctive country and western sound.

"Buddy was the first guy who had confidence in me. Hell, I had as much star quality as an old shoe. But, he really liked me and believed in me. He said, 'There's no doubt you're going to be a star. I know. The way you sing, there's no limit. You can sing pop, you can sing rock, and you can sing country,'" Waylon remembered. Buddy urged his protégé to be flexible: "You don't ever have to be restricted as a country artist, because you can cut rock records, if you ever want to."

Buddy, however, could not open his proposed studio in Lubbock, until he received the money Norman Petty owed him, which Holly estimated to be as much as $50,000 to $80,000. Consequently, in mid-January, Holly sent Petty a registered letter, asking for his share of the royalties. When Petty once again refused to release the money, Buddy was enraged: "I'm going to Clovis and break everything in sight, including Norman's neck."

On January 9th, Petty, ever-protective of his own financial interests, wrote Isabelle Marks, a Coral Records executive: "Buddy Holly is no longer a Cricket, as of the first of the year." Petty indicated that "all new recordings by the Crickets will feature the new lead voice (18-year-old Earl Sinks)," and "Buddy will be heard only on his Coral recordings."

The unfortunate legal wrangling would continue until well after Buddy's death. By now, Holly's original attorney, Harold Ornstein, had delegated much of Buddy's representation to his colleague, George Schiffer. On January 12th, Schiffer wrote Petty, requesting, yet again, an accounting of how much money was owed to his client, and inquiring as to when Norman would be in New York City, so the two of them could have a face-to-face meeting.

That same day, Schiffer learned about Petty's earlier letter to Isabelle Marks. Buddy's lawyer promptly dispatched a terse telegram to Clovis: STRONGLY OBJECT TO YOUR LETTER OF JANUARY 9 TO CORAL RECORDS. BUDDY HOLLY HAS FULL RIGHT TO USE THE NAME "THE CRICKETS" AND WILL CONTINUE TO USE THAT NAME. STRONGLY OBJECT TO MISLEADING USE OF THE NAME IN CONJUNCTION WITH SINGER OTHER THAN HIMSELF. LETTER

FOLLOWS. PLEASE BE ADVISED THAT IN VIEW OF THE FACT THAT YOU NO LONGER REPRESENT MR. HOLLY YOUR ATTEMPT TO GIVE INSTRUCTIONS TO CORAL RECORDS REGARDING HIS FUTURE RECORDING IS UNWARRANTED AND UNAUTHORIZED.

A day later, Isabelle Marks wrote Petty: "Our contract covering the performance of the Crickets is with Buddy Holly, Jerry Allison, and Joe Mauldin. We must insist that the performances by the Crickets be with the individuals who are parties of the contract and we cannot accept any substitutions."

On January 14th, after receiving Schiffer's telegram, Petty sent a return letter that bordered on the absurd: "It would seem obvious that Buddy Holly was never actually a member of 'The Crickets.' All personal appearances, all recordings, and any other artistic presentations by Buddy Holly with 'The Crickets' were usually billed and shown to be two separate entities; that is 'Buddy Holly' and 'The Crickets.' We feel constrained to advise, therefore, in behalf of 'The Crickets,' who now consist of Joe Mauldin, Jerry Allison, and a new member, that Mr. Holly is definitely not at liberty to use the name 'The Crickets' in any artistic presentation without their expressed written consent."

Petty was splitting legal hairs. There were never two bands—it was either Buddy Holly and the Crickets or Buddy Holly backed by the Crickets (even though the Crickets did not perform on all of Holly's singles, such as the string session recordings). The decision to release records under the separate Brunswick and Coral labels was made at a time when Buddy's contractual obligation to Decca's Nashville division had yet to be resolved.

Schiffer's return letter to Petty declared that Buddy "has as much right, and probably more, to the use of the name 'The Crickets,' and had "no intention of surrendering his rights." Schiffer correctly pointed out that the Crickets' "name and reputation were built primarily on Buddy Holly."

In a separate letter addressed to Petty, dated January 16th, Schiffer returned to the issue of royalty payments. He demanded "immediate payment of all sums presently held by you, which belong to Mr. Holly, together with a full accounting and copies of all contracts between Mr. Holly and the other members of The Crickets, between Mr. Holly and you, and between Mr. Holly and Nor-Va-Jak."

Three days later, Schiffer wrote the Clovis National Bank informing officials that Norman Petty was no longer Buddy Holly's power of attorney and was not authorized to withdraw or deposit funds designated as belonging to Holly. On January 19th, the bank responded by letter, stating that Buddy Holly had no account at their institution, and the "money deposited here is under the heading of the *Norman Petty Agency* and we cannot honor any signature other than Mr. Petty's." The bank verified what had been long-suspected; Petty had exclusive control over Buddy Holly's and the Crickets' funds. On January 20th, Schiffer wrote Petty another letter emphasizing that Holly had equal claim to the name "The Crickets." The attorney also warned the Clovis producer that the issues concerning ownership of the band's name and Petty's failure to pay Holly could result in Schiffer filing a law suit on behalf of his client.

After all the letters, telegrams, and legal posturing, nothing had been resolved concerning Buddy's royalty money by the time he was scheduled to leave for the *Winter Dance Party* tour. Thus, while Buddy was on the road, Maria Elena would remain financially dependent on her Aunt Provi. "Buddy was very concerned with the fact that my aunt was supporting us. We were married, and he felt terrible about it," Maria Elena remembered.

Between travel expenses, Christmas gifts, outfitting his new band, and setting up a payroll for Waylon, Tommy, and Carl, Buddy had exhausted the advance money paid to him by GAC. Absent Provi's generous loans, Buddy and Maria Elena were essentially penniless.

Despite his dire financial straits, Buddy's spirit remained unbroken. In late January, just before the *Winter Dance Party* tour commenced, Holly had lunch with Dick Jacobs, who had been promoted to Director of Artists and Repertoire at Coral Records. During their final meeting,

Holly gave Jacobs the apartment tape demos, which he planned to use in future recording sessions.

On January 22nd, Buddy recorded a promotional commercial to be played on radio stations in the cities and towns where the upcoming tour would be visiting: "Hi, this is Buddy Holly. The Crickets and I are really happy to be coming your way on the *Winter Dance Party*. We certainly hope to see all our old friends and to be making some new ones, too. Also, I hope you like my latest Coral release, *Heartbeat*. See you soon."

Even though he did not want to tour the frozen Midwest, Holly needed the money and could not idly wait for Petty to release his royalty payments. Phil Everly clearly remembered the last time he saw Buddy; both were at their lawyer's office. Everly was convinced that if Holly "had the money, he wouldn't have gone out (on the *Winter Dance Party*)." Waylon Jennings was also aware of Holly's unfortunate bind: "I know Buddy wouldn't have taken that tour if Norman Petty hadn't tied up his money..."

Maria Elena, who was experiencing severe morning sickness in the early stages of her pregnancy, was in no condition to accompany Buddy on a lengthy, frigid, and sleep-deprived bus tour. As the time for her husband to leave approached, Maria Elena had a change of heart. After experiencing a premonition that Buddy would somehow end up flying on a small plane, Maria Elena was certain her physical presence would keep him from boarding anything but a commercial airliner. Buddy, however, vetoed her plan to travel with him: "No. This is just a very short tour, and you're not feeling well."

The night before Buddy left New York City, Maria Elena dreamed that a huge fireball sped in her direction, narrowly missed her, crashed into the ground, and left behind a crater. Buddy also had a frightening dream—he and Maria Elena were passengers in a small plane piloted by his brother, Larry. When Larry told Buddy to discard his wife, Buddy defiantly refused: "Anywhere I go, Maria comes with me." Taking matters into his own hands, Larry landed atop a skyscraper and forced

Maria Elena to exit the aircraft. Before he awakened, Buddy remembered crying out: "Don't worry. I'll come back and get you." When the couple shared their separate, but mutually disconcerting dreams, it represented an eerie sense of déjà vu.

In distant Clovis, New Mexico, Peggy Sue Allison was trying to interpret her own frightening dreams about Buddy. Three times, between September and December of 1958, she had disturbingly prescient nightmares of a white plane, with a brown stripe and V-tail, crashing into snowy farmland. In her dreams, Peggy Sue could see Buddy in the front seat of the aircraft, with two unidentifiable people occupying the rear seats.

Drummer, Carl Bunch, who had overheard Buddy and Maria Elena discussing their respective dreams, interpreted the conversation as foreshadowing. "Buddy had a premonition about his death," Bunch later opined, without elaborating.

The morning of Buddy's departure, January 22, 1959, Marina Elena was nearly hysterical. "I kept saying to him, 'I don't want you to go, I don't want you to go...'" she recalled.

When he left the couple's apartment building for the final time, Buddy kissed Maria Elena: "I want you to take care of yourself and my baby."

CHAPTER 10

A Deadly Winter

ON JANUARY 22, 1959, BUDDY, Waylon, Tommy, and Carl boarded a train in New York City, bound for Chicago. Even though Buddy was less than thrilled about participating in the *Winter Dance Party*, he maintained a positive attitude. At Grand Central Station, Holly and Jennings had their picture taken in a photo booth; Waylon was wearing sunglasses, as both smiled and smoked cigarettes. Buddy had tried to curtail his smoking after he was married, but recent stresses had made it difficult for him to completely stop. When nicotine cravings arose, Buddy would laughingly inquire: "Waylum, you gotta a Salem?"

The entire tour group, which included Buddy Holly and the newly-formed Crickets, Ritchie Valens, J.P. "the Big Bopper" Richardson, Dion and the Belmonts, and Frankie Sardo gathered at a hotel in Chicago. Sam Geller, who Irving Feld had hired to serve as tour's traveling manager, was there to greet them. The *Winter Dance Party* was scheduled to begin the next day, January 23rd, and conclude on February 15th.

Unlike past tours, Holly would receive a salary, as well as a share of the tour's profits. Buddy's salary, approximately $3,000 to $ 3,500-per-week (out which he paid wages to Waylon, Tommy, and Carl), was the highest among the performers. Dion and the Belmonts were paid $1,000 to $1,200-per week, while Valens and the Big Bopper earned $700 to $800-per-week.

At age 22, Buddy was six years younger that the oldest tour member, the Big Bopper, but he was the most established star, and emerged as the tour's unquestioned leader. After a brief rehearsal, Holly informed the other performers that his band (Jennings, Allsup, and Bunch) would serve as the background musicians for each act. *Winter Dance Party* promotional posters also gave Buddy Holly and the new Crickets top billing.

Among his fellow entertainers, Buddy was most concerned about 17-year-old Ritchie Valens, hoping that he would not have to babysit the adolescent. Holly had met Valens during the Australian rock and roll tour in early 1958, but did not know him very well. Born in California, Richard Valenzuela, who was of mixed Mexican and Indian ancestry, was rock and roll's first Chicano star. His manager, Bob Keene, aware of mid-20th century racial prejudices, ultimately changed Valenzuela's stage name to the less ethic-sounding Ritchie Valens. Valens was clearly a rising star, and some fans had christened him as the "New Elvis."

Valens' first single *Come On, Let's Go*, had been a modest hit, but both sides of his second single, *Donna* and *La Bamba*, exploded onto the charts in December of 1958. Raised in a housing project by his single-parent mother, Valens was thrilled when he earned enough money from his record sales to purchase her a new house. Valens' rise to stardom had been so rapid that the *Winter Dance Party* was one of his first major domestic tours.

Buddy need not have worried about Valens; they bonded from the very start. Shy and reserved when not performing, Valens personality was much like Buddy's, and he had long-admired Holly. "Ritchie Valens and I really hit it off well," Buddy soon informed Maria Elena over the telephone.

Buddy recognized Valens' undeniable talent, considering him an ideal artist for his future record label. "Buddy was talking to Ritchie. Ritchie asked Buddy if he would record and produce him. He had a few ideas to do some of the Spanish songs," Maria Elena remembered.

Waylon Jennings formed a close relationship with another of the tour's featured acts—the Big Bopper; even though he was better known by that stage name, Jiles Perry Richardson was often called "Jape" by his friends. The son of a Texas oil field worker, the crew-cut Richardson was a chunky five-feet, 10-inches-tall, and weighed 200-plus-pounds. Like Buddy Holly, Richardson was married, and his wife Adrianne, nicknamed "Teetsie," was six-month's pregnant with the couple's second child.

Richardson earned his performing name while working as a disc jockey at radio station *KTRM* in Beaumont, Texas: "Bee-bop's big, and I'm so big, so why don't I become the Big Bopper?" In May of 1957, the Big Bopper hosted a "Disc-a-Thon," where he stayed on the air for *six* consecutive days. During that time, he played 1,821 records, lost 35 pounds, and earned $746.50 in overtime pay. During the *Winter Dance Party*, he proudly wore a wristwatch with an engraved back: *KTRM CHAMPION DISC-A-THON, 122 HOURS, 8 MINUTES, J.P. RICHARDSON, 5-4-57.*

The Big Bopper added "singer" to his disc jockey resume when he began writing and recording gimmicky records. In August of 1958, Mercury-Sun Records released his first single, *Purple People Eater Meets the Witchdoctor*. While this song was not particularly successful, the record's B side, *Chantilly Lace*, climbed all the way to Number Six on *Billboard's* Top 100.

Colorful by nature, the Big Bopper often donned a Stetson and an ankle-length, leopard skin jacket that he named "Melvin." He sometimes enthusiastically greeted others with a classic line from *Chantilly Lace*: "Hello Baby!"

While his follow-up single, *Big Bopper's Wedding*, failed to chart, Richardson was a gifted song-writer and had an excellent ear for music. By touring on the *Winter Dance Party*, the Big Bopper would earn additional income and hoped to increase his name recognition. He envisioned a future as a successful song-writer and a radio station owner.

Led by Dion DiMucci, a native of the Bronx, Dion and the Belmonts (Carlo Mastrangelo, Freddy Milano, and Angelo D'Aleo) had scored several hits, including *I Wonder Why* and *A Teenager in Love*. The handsome quartet were a huge attraction to teenage girls, or as Waylon Jennings described in his distinctive, blunt manner: "A doo-wop group made good."

Even though he was Texas boy, Buddy developed a bond with the streetwise DiMucci, who had a history of alcohol, marijuana, and heroin abuse. Having battled his personal demons, Dion considered Holly a role model: "...I admired how together he was."

The fifth act on the tour, New York-born Frankie Sardo was of Italian descent. A Korean War veteran, Sardo had yet to score a successful hit, but his sex appeal attracted female fans. ABC/Paramount had just released his new single *Fake Out/Class Room*, and hoped the *Winter Dance Party* would promote record sales and jump-start Sardo's heretofore lackluster career.

"He was the worst singer you've ever heard in your life," Waylon bluntly opined. At same time, Jennings appreciated Sardo's sense of humor and was respectful of the Italian singer's rumored Mafia connections.

On January 23, 1959, the tour group left Chicago, and for the next 10 days, haphazardly zig-zagged across the frozen Midwest, during the region's worst winter in 30 years. The tour's route defied any geometric configuration, and the performers often backtracked over the same icy roads. Some of the night-after-night performance venues were 400 to 500 miles apart. Worse yet, there were no interstates, but mostly two-lane roads, many of them winding through sparsely-inhabited areas.

Travelling in what Dion DiMucci accurately described as "a converted school bus," the entertainers headed for the Million Dollar Ballroom in Milwaukee, Wisconsin. "It snowed on us from the time we left Chicago. I don't know why we got such lousy buses—such lousy, old buses," Tommy Allsup recalled.

Cold, bitter cold, was the operative word. Waylon Jennings described how he dealt with the frigid temperatures: "What you do is you hold your breath from the time you left the bus until you get in the dressing room door."

The answer to the bus dilemma was simple, but unsatisfactory. Bob Ehlert, who worked out of GAC's office in Chicago, had leased the unreliable buses from the lowest bidder; they were nothing more than old school buses, lacking bunk beds or toilets (except for buckets). Over the course of a week and a half, the entertainers had to change buses at least six or seven times, due to mechanical problems. Even before the entertainers reached their first destination, tour manager, Sam Geller, who traveled with the performers, was appalled: "The bus was third class. We had ample room, individual seats and all that, but I had never made a tour in the wintertime..."

Traveling north to Milwaukee in the snow and driving winds, the entertainers discovered the vehicle's heating system was inadequate, and they could soon see steam rising from their breath. Holly's drummer, Carl Bunch felt his feet progressively growing numb; an early indication of frostbite. "It was so cold on the bus that'd we'd have to wear all our clothes—coats and everything. My feet were constantly freezing," Waylon Jennings recalled.

Throughout the *Winter Dance Party*, the rock and rollers rarely had any break between performing and traveling to the next gig, absent opportunities to perform the most basic of necessities, like laundering their stage performance outfits. "We tried to hang our wrinkled suits in the aisle (of the bus), and after a while, it got kind of ripe in there. We smelled like goats," Jennings remembered.

When the group arrived in Milwaukee, they discovered a long line of teenagers outside the Million Dollar Ballroom, braving minus-25-degree temperatures. In Milwaukee, and other stops along the way, the performance venues were often ill-suited for professional entertainers. The lighting in the auditoriums was sometimes poor, and if the building did not have a public-address system, the musicians had to use their own portable amplifiers.

The group's inaugural show established the order of performers. Frankie Sardo opened and played for approximately 15 minutes, followed by the Big Bopper and Dion and the Belmonts. Ritchie Valens came on stage next, before Buddy Holly closed the show. Between sets, the entertainers signed autographs and posed for photographs with audience members.

The crowd in Milwaukee embraced Buddy and his newly-formed band. Waylon, Tommy, and Carl were dressed in gray pants, black jackets, and silver ascots; their second stage outfit consisted of brown pants and jackets, accompanied by gold ascots.

Buddy opened the set alone, and for the duration of the tour, began with Billy Grammar's Top 10 hit, *Gotta Travel On*, before he was joined by Waylon, Tommy, and Carl. From that point forward, he sang a mix of his own hits, as well as other rock and roll classics, like *Be-Bop-Lu* and *Whole Lotta Shakin'*. There was no set order following *Gotta Travel On*, and Holly often played crowd requests or songs he sensed the audience wanted to hear. Buddy later added a few country and western and blue grass songs from his pre-Cricket days, like *Salty Dog Blues*. At each tour stop, Holly gave out 10 free copies of *It Doesn't Matter Anymore*.

Opening night was a learning experience for the new Crickets. At first, Waylon had difficulty keeping pace with Buddy and Tommy's skilled guitar playing. On four occasions, Buddy tried to verbally communicate with Waylon, who could not hear him. Holly finally moved closer and shouted into Jennings' ear: "Turn that Goddamn bass down!" Waylon recalled that the most amusing part of the show was Carl Bunch trying to keep his eyeglasses from sliding down his face, while simultaneously playing the paradiddles accompanying *Peggy Sue*.

Just before his initial performance, Buddy telephoned Maria Elena: "I'm going on stage now. I'm leaving the hook off. I want you to hear something." "He sang *True Love Ways*, which was our song. It became a ritual. He called me every night from wherever he was," she later recalled.

After spending the night in a Milwaukee hotel, a rare luxury during the tour, the *Winter Dance Party* headed south, to Kenosha, Wisconsin. The inside of the bus remained alarmingly cold, and the signs and symptoms of frostbite were clearly afflicting Carl Bunch's feet, even though he was wearing several pairs of socks.

Buddy and Dion sat close together, sharing body heat. Along the way, the pair picked their guitars and sang. When Dion serenaded the group with Hank Williams' classic, *Hey, Good Looking*, in his Bronx accent, Buddy and the other Texans burst into laughter.

When they could briefly endure the bitter cold, some of the entertainers played poker or shot craps. Even though he was only two years older than Carl Bunch, Buddy was protective of his drummer, and warned him not to gamble: "I'm not paying you enough."

On the night of January 24th, the group played at the Eagles Ballroom in Kenosha. It was after midnight when the entertainers left Kenosha, bound for Mankato, Minnesota, 350 miles to the northwest. Back stage at Mankato's Kato Ballroom, while talking to his wife on the telephone, Buddy told her that he was excited by the prospect of producing Ritchie Valens' future records. At one point, Holly put Valens on the line, allowing the young rocker to personally introduce himself to Maria Elena.

"You could tell that Buddy missed Maria Elena. After the show, Waylon, the Bopper, and me would usually go for a beer, but Buddy didn't come. He didn't drink at all on that tour," Tommy Allsup remembered.

The tour members madly rushed to their next stop, Eau Claire Wisconsin, and because of distance and time constraints, had to eat their meals from snack machines at gas stations along the way. During another cold and dreary bus ride, Ritchie Valens circulated a tape recorder, asking each performer to say hello to his mother.

It was minus-25-degrees on the night of January 26th, when the entertainers played at Fournier's Dance Hall in Eau Claire. The audience members, who were seated in chairs and wooden bleachers, were undeterred by the winter chill and enthusiastically welcomed the *Winter Dance Party* performers. After the show, Buddy, Ritchie, and the Big Bopper ate a late dinner at Sammy's Pizza.

In Eau Claire, Carl Bunch inadvertently left his gray and black stage outfit in the dressing room, which meant that he, Waylon, and Tommy would be forced to wear a single set of performing clothes for the remainder of the tour. Bunch, who was afraid to admit that he had lost his outfit, approached Buddy: "Oh, God! I don't know what happened. Somebody must have gotten on the bus and stolen them." A disbelieving

Holly was less than amused: "I wouldn't dig that hole any deeper, son. You're going to have to crawl out of it."

From Eau Claire, the tour bus headed 250 miles to Montevideo, Minnesota. At the Fiesta Ballroom, a frustrated Buddy telephoned Maria Elena, complaining about the poorly organized tour, as well as the "dirty and cold" buses. Buddy also informed her: "If you get a call from Jerry and Joe B., tell them I'll be back in two weeks, and I want to talk to them, alone." Marina Elena believed that her husband wanted to resume touring with the original Crickets, while employing session musicians in the studio. She also remembered that J.I. called her to obtain the *Winter Dance Party* travel itinerary, so he could telephone Buddy. "Buddy still hoped to patch things up with the Crickets. He tried to call them once, in fact, from New York (before the tour started), but they weren't home; they were in Clovis. He felt that if he could just talk to them, they could get back together..." Maria Elena recalled.

Not everyone agreed with Maria Elena's prediction of a potential Crickets' reunion. "I think it was another fictitious thing," Larry Holley opined. Norman Petty, of course, refuted any notion of reconciliation: "They (J.I. and Joe B.) were going to stay with me, and I was going to produce them as the Crickets."

As frustrated as he was about the tour conditions, Buddy did not allow it to negatively impact his performances. At the Fiesta Ballroom, Scott Harding, a teenage resident of Montevideo, along with two other members of their newly-formed garage band, were excited to see the professional rock and rollers in action. Harding and his bandmates soon began performing Holly's *Peggy Sue* and Valens' *Donna*, when they performed at high school proms and other venues.

21-year-old Bob Bunn, a guitar player in another local band, stood at the foot of the stage and admired Holly's skill with his Fender Stratocaster: "Everybody just stood and watched him. He played pretty much one song after another. He didn't talk too much; he just said, 'Thank you!'"

Later that night, when Buddy ran into Bob Bunn at a local café, he asked: "Does it always get this cold in Minnesota?"

Listen to Me

"No, it gets a lot colder," Bunn chuckled.

On January 27th, the same day Buddy was in Montevideo, his attorney, George Schiffer, spoke with Norman Petty by telephone. Unbeknownst to Schiffer, Petty tape-recorded the call, which Norma Jean Berry later typed into a transcript. When Schiffer asked Petty if he planned to travel to New York City in the foreseeable future, the Clovis producer answered in the negative, but invited the lawyer to come to New Mexico, if he desired a face-to-face meeting.

For the first time, Petty talked about numbers with Schiffer, indicating that Buddy Holly had a balance of *$35,296* due to him. At the same time, Petty maligned Buddy's character, describing him as child-like, with "a tendency to want to make contracts and get out of them." He further alleged that Holly held back performance fees, gambled some of the money away, and did not produce receipts for tax purposes. Petty also complained that Buddy had not paid him $2,000 for the Ampex tape recorder he purchased in the fall of 1958. "Technically, Buddy has stolen equipment, as far as my insurance company is concerned, if we wanted to get nasty," Petty tersely informed Schiffer.

Petty also told the attorney that he had instructed record magazines, like *Billboard*, not to recognize the band currently travelling with Holly as the Crickets, until all legal matters were resolved. Schiffer held his own, reminding Petty that he had not yet received a full list of songs composed by Holly and published by Nor-Va-Jak. After Petty indicated that he would send all the contracts to Schiffer, he asked the attorney not to freeze royalty payments from Coral and Brunswick records; not surprisingly, Schiffer refused.

The next night's tour stop was at the Prom Ballroom in St. Paul, Minnesota. There, Ritchie Valens purchase a copy of the latest issue of *Variety* magazine, and was delighted to learn that *Donna* was Number Four on the hit list and *La Bamba* had climbed to Number 17.

In St. Paul, Bob Diehl, a disc jockey at *WDGY's* 50,000-watt rock and roll radio station, emceed the show. Much to the delight of Diehl and the local promotor, the paid attendance at the Prom Ballroom, nearly 2,000, was one of the *Winter Dance Party's* largest audiences.

Diehl, who had briefly met Holly during Alan Freed's *Big Beat* tour in 1958, ate lunch with Buddy. "He remembered everything. That impressed me," Diehl recalled. Back stage, Diehl watched Buddy pat Ritchie Valens on the back, encouraging him to relax before his performance. Diehl described Holly as "this tall, slender fellow," who assumed a take-charge role. "He'd make sure that the lighting was right, that the band instruments were right, and that all the speakers were working. He was a very, very, thorough fellow," the disc jockey added.

The *Winter Dance Party* next headed south to Davenport, Iowa, as temperatures plunged; the result of a Canadian cold front dipping into the Midwest. On the poorly-heated bus, the performers put on extra layers of clothes, while some drank straight out of whiskey bottles.

In Davenport, located on the banks of the Mississippi River, the group played two shows at the Capitol Theater—7:00 p.m. and 9:00 p.m. *KSTT* disc jockey, Mark Stevens, emceed both performances. Stevens was busy setting up equipment to audiotape the shows, when the performers arrived. Stevens described Ritchie Valens' appearance as haggard, as if he were coming down with the flu.

That night, the rock and rollers relished the opportunity to grab a few hours of sleep at a local hotel. During their brief respite from the bus, Buddy visited Waylon in his hotel room, informing him that he planned to reunite with J.I. and Joe B., and tour England. Buddy told Waylon that he wanted him to accompany the Crickets to the U.K., and perform as their opening act. Holly also cautioned Jennings to keep quiet about their chat, as he did not plan to include Tommy Allsup as a tour member.

Even though the roads were covered with ice, resulting in multiple automobile accidents, and flights were cancelled at the nearby regional airport, the *Winter Dance Party* headed to Fort Dodge, Iowa in the early morning hours of January 30th. The next leg of the tour involved traversing nearly 200 miles of sparsely-populated woodlands, farms, and small towns. Inside the perpetually cold bus, the frostbite damage to Carl Bunch's feet was rapidly progressing.

During the bus ride, Waylon and the Big Bopper huddled together, sipping vodka, and composing *Move Over Blues*, a song written specifically for country and western star, George Jones (as proof of his skill as a composer, two songs written by the Big Bopper, *White Lightening*, recorded by Jones, and Johnny Preston's *Running Bear*, would reach Number One on the C & W charts before the end of 1959). Because of the hazardous conditions of the roads, Waylon and the Big Bopper had ample time to write song lyrics; the bus driver could not safely exceed 25-miles-per-hour.

Thirty miles west of Davenport, with the temperature in the teens, the heaters on the bus completely stopped working. After the bus stopped at Gaul Motor Company in the small town of Tipton, population 2,100, a mechanic discovered that all nine heaters on the vehicle were frozen solid. While waiting several hours for the heaters to defrost, several of the entertainers explored the town. Buddy, however, remained in the showroom of the Ford dealership. At one point, he jokingly informed those within earshot: "I'm a reindeer salesman."

By now, Carl Bunch was concerned that his frostbitten feet would develop gangrene, which might require life-saving amputation. Bunch, who was a fundamentalist Christian, had convinced himself that Satan was coming "to kill, to steal, and destroy" the members of the *Winter Dance Party*.

Because of the unexpected delay in Tipton, the bus was late arriving in Fort Dodge. "We were worried," Dick Derring, the assistant manager of Laramar Ballroom, remembered. Bob Geer, the teenage son of the ballroom's owner, was appalled by the *Winter Dance Party's* primitive travel arrangements: "They had a bus that smelled bad. I'm sure it was no fun travelling on it." *KWMT* disc jockey, Bill McCollough, who emceed the Fort Dodge show, was also on hand when the entertainers arrived: "It was an old ratty-looking bus. It was pretty tacky."

Braving frigid temperatures and four inches of new snowfall, nearly 1,000 people jammed into the Laramar Ballroom. Eddie Simpson, who was a freshman at Callendar High school, watched the show from the balcony. "…I remember when they announced Buddy Holly, he stepped out on the stage. He had been standing in the backdrop, and everybody went nuts when he started singing."

After the show, Bill McCullough had the opportunity to chat with Holly: "He was complaining about the bus—how it was drafty and everything, and he was going to catch his death cold, he thought."

"Well, why don't you let me fly you," McCullough off-handedly remarked.

"That's a really great idea," Holly immediately replied.

"I can't really," the disc jockey was forced to admit; he was still taking flying lessons and had not yet undertaken a solo flight.

"Could you call somebody and get us a plane?" Buddy asked.

"Yeah, I can do that," McCullough replied, hoping to save face.

The disc jockey telephoned his flight instructor, who was unwilling to fly 360 miles to Duluth under the cover of darkness. The ballroom owner, Larry Geer, who had piloted small airplanes for 22 years, informed Holly that it was too risky to fly at night in the frigid and uncertain weather conditions.

Carl Bunch, who overheard the conversation, knew Holly was serious: "Buddy was flying crazy. Buddy believed you could land a small airplane on a housetop, if you had to. He had been bugging us for days." Tommy Allsup concurred with Bunch's assessment: "We'd talked about it several times. Buddy liked to fly. He thought there was no way a small plane would crash. He was used to flying out there in west Texas, where you could land in a field." The only consolation for Holly was the opportunity to spend the night in a warm hotel bed, before boarding the cold and rank-smelling bus the following day.

The morning of January 31st, the entertainers headed north to Duluth, Minnesota, 350 miles distant from Fort Dodge. Just as the group was reaching Duluth, their bus broke down. The trip had taken most of the day, and the entertainers arrived just in time to take the briefest of naps at a hotel, before the 8:00 p.m. show.

In Duluth, Buddy telephoned his good friend and fellow rock and roller, Eddie Cochran. Holly was depressed; a month after its release, *It*

Doesn't Matter Anymore had not cracked *Billboard's* Top 100. Concerned about Buddy's despondency, Cochran reassured him: "You're the best there is. You'll be back up there again soon."

Buddy was not the only one who was unhappy. A warm-blooded Californian, Ritchie Valens was sick and tired of riding in cold buses. "Tell everybody I'm flying," Valens complained to a local newspaper reporter. When he telephoned his manager, Bob Keene, who lived in Santa Monica, California, Valens complained: "It's 35-degrees-below-zero back here and I'm freezing."

Keene told his star to "finish that evening and then come home, if things were that bad." As the youngest member of the ensemble, and determined to prove his mettle, Valens quickly changed the subject. "No. I just wanted to tell you. Tonight, I got two curtain calls! How about that!" he exclaimed.

Nearly 2,000 people braved the sub-freezing temperature and paid two-dollars-each to attend the concert at the National Guard Armory. That night, Buddy debuted new performing attire—a different colored ascot and a yellow, leather jacket, trimmed with a fur collar. Waylon, Tommy, and Carl, however, were forced to wear the same wrinkled, dirty, and malodorous stage outfits.

Bobby Zimmerman, a teenager from Hibbing, Minnesota, located 50 miles north of Duluth, was among the audience members. In later years, Zimmerman would become known to the world as Bob Dylan. "I saw Buddy in Duluth at the armory. Buddy was incredible," the legendary folk singer and song-writer later remembered.

The following day included two scheduled performances—a matinee in Appleton and an evening show at the Riverside Ballroom in Green Bay (both in Wisconsin). To accommodate such a tight schedule required yet another all-night bus trip.

About 130 miles south of Appleton, the bus abruptly died; a piston had gone completely through the engine block. It was 1:30 a.m., and the tour group found themselves stranded in a remote area of Wisconsin, known as North Woods. "The bus finally broke down, out there in the middle of the wilderness," Carl Bunch clearly recalled.

Outside, the temperature was minus-40-degrees. With no help in sight, some of the entertainers burned newspapers in the aisle, vainly hoping to generate a measure of warmth. "It was cold—really cold," Tommy Allsup remembered. Periodically, a small group would exit the bus, brave the bitter wind, stand in the middle of Highway 51, and hope to flag down a passing motorist; not the likeliest of possibilities during a frigid night in the middle of nowhere. When a southbound vehicle eventually approached, the tour members vainly waved their arms at the passing tractor-trailer truck.

Inside the bus, Carl Bunch was at the height of his misery. Even though he was wearing six pairs of socks, Bunch's feet were frozen solid, and he could barely walk.

After another two hours, a convoy of vehicles, organized by the County Sheriff's Office in Hurley, located 15 miles to the south, suddenly appeared. Even though the semi failed to stop, the driver had notified law enforcement officials about the stalled bus. Just before the break of day, on February 1st, the entertainers were dropped off at the Club Carnival Café in Hurley. Their black driver, who could not enter the segregated restaurant, was forced to eat his breakfast at an Iron County Garage, where the bus had been towed.

At this point, Carl Bunch had to be transported to Grandview Hospital, seven miles east of Hurley. Over the next several days, physicians painstakingly treated his severely frostbitten feet, such that Bunch escaped the horror of amputation.

After the bus became inoperable, the matinee performance at the Cinderella Ballroom in Appleton was cancelled, but GAC still expected the entertainers to perform the evening show in Green Bay. At 11:30 a.m. the *Winter Dance Party* entertainers boarded either a Greyhound bus or a Chicago Northwestern train, both of which were bound for Green Bay. When they finally arrived at their hotel, late on Sunday afternoon, Ritchie Valens was overjoyed by the simplest of pleasures—a winter coat his mother had mailed from California.

That night, teenagers stood in line for three blocks to gain admission to the Riverside Ballroom, which featured a large dance floor. With

Carl Bunch confined to a hospital bed, Ritchie Valens stepped in to play drums while Dion and the Belmonts performed. The Belmonts' Carlo Mastrangelo served as percussionist for the remaining acts. Two teen-age girls, positioned near the front of the stage, nearly fainted when Dion and Buddy reached out to hold their hands while performing. "We were in love with those guys," Sharon Larscheid explained.

Holly was impressed that the audience knew the lyrics to all his songs and joyously sang along with him. After the conclusion of the show, the last known picture of Buddy, while not performing on stage, was taken by a local photographer. Holly was seated on a small staircase, perhaps stage side, dressed in his yellow jacket with the fur collar. His chin resting on his left hand, and perhaps unaware that he was being photographed, Buddy appeared contemplative.

On February 2nd, the members of the *Winter Dance Party* were scheduled to have their first vacation day. The planned respite, however, was pre-empted. Carroll Anderson, the 39-year-old manager of the Surf Ballroom in Clear Lake, Iowa, located some 400 miles southwest of Green Bay, contacted GAC and arranged for an impromptu tour stop. For a fee of $25, local disc jockey, Bob Hale, had agreed to serve as the emcee. Anderson, who paid $850 for the performers to come to Clear Lake, was convinced that the presence of Buddy Holly would shatter the Surf Ballroom's attendance record.

The Surf was then part of a chain of ballrooms; the Clear Lake venue was built in 1933, by skating rink magnate, Carl Fox. The original Surf ballroom was located on the lakefront, with a deck over the water and a rooftop garden. After being heavily damaged by fire in April of 1947, the structure was relocated across the street from the original building. The newly-constructed Surf Ballroom was designed to be fire-resistant, with exterior brick walls bound to tile, as well as brick and cypress wood interiors. Carroll Anderson, who hosted the *Winter Dance Party* concert, had assumed management of the Surf in 1950.

Buddy Holly was none too happy that his much-needed day off had been cancelled. As Carroll Anderson later recalled, Holly felt "just like a high-class bum being kicked around on the road." In Green Bay, Buddy's mood further soured after he received a telegram from Norman Petty, warning Holly and his current bandmates to "stop using the name the Crickets, because the Crickets are Jerry and Joe B." That same day, Petty had released his most recent audit, indicating that the Crickets were only due *$5,000*; far less than the *$50,000 to $80,000* Holly had anticipated, and *much less* than the figure Petty shared with George Schiffer during their January 27th phone call. Tommy Allsup remembered that Buddy was infuriated with Petty's inconsistent and nefarious bookkeeping: "When this tour is over, I'm going back to Clovis and I'm going to kick Norman Petty's ass. I'm going to get my money out of that studio, one way or the other."

To make it to Clear Lake in time, the performers had to leave immediately after the Green Bay show. There was no time to take a shower, much less launder their soiled stage outfits. In Hurley, a replacement engine had been installed in the same bus, which was driven to Green Bay, just in time to transport the entertainers to Clear Lake.

During the drive to Clear Lake, the supposedly-repaired bus developed heater problems, forcing the group to stop at a service station in Praire du Chien. While the heater was being repaired, the Big Bopper purchased an insulated sleeping bag and a bottle of whiskey.

At another stop along the way, Buddy called his attorney in New York City, to discuss the ongoing dispute with Norman Petty. "He came back on the bus and was mad. I mean he was bad mad; the maddest I ever saw him," Waylon recalled.

Buddy also phoned Maria Elena and shared his displeasure. When she suggested he come home, Buddy refused: "Maria, you know me. I have to finish." "We need the money," he reminded her.

With yet another bus malfunction, the entertainers were forced to cancel a scheduled 4:30 p.m. appearance at a record store in neighboring Mason City. It was 6:00 p.m. before the group reached Clear Lake—named for the 3,600-acre lake located just south of the Surf Ballroom. Even though it was bitterly cold, teenagers, some of whom were accompanied by their parents, were already standing in line for first show, scheduled at 8:00 p.m.

By now, Holly was determined that he was going charter a plane to Fargo, North Dakota, which was the closest airport to their next tour stop, in Moorhead, Minnesota. Buddy told Tommy that he would carry the entire group's dirty clothes aboard the plane and have them laundered or dry-cleaned before the next concert, including the Big Bopper's leopard skin coat and Valens' black jeans performing outfit. "We only carried three shirts and we'd had no laundry for a couple of weeks, and the shirts could have stood up on their own," Allsup noted.

Waylon understood Holly's mounting frustrations: "Buddy was exhausted, and we didn't have a clean shirt among us." "That was the only time I saw Buddy that he was adamant. Nobody was going to talk him into getting back on that bus—nobody," Frankie Sardo recalled.

In the lobby of the Surf Ballroom, Buddy telephoned Maria Elena and informed her that he was travelling ahead of the other tour members, but mindful of her fear of small airplanes, did not clarify his mode of transportation. She wanted to know why her husband was assuming so much responsibility. "There's nobody else to do it," Buddy answered.

In addition to getting the band members' uniforms cleaned, Holly also looked forward to sleeping in a hotel room and having extra time to set up for the next night's show. Once the plane landed in Fargo, North Dakota, it was only a 10-minute drive across the Red River to Moorhead.

Having made up his mind to fly to the next tour stop, Buddy approached the ballroom manager, Carroll Anderson: "How far is the airport from here?"

"It's only one and a half miles," Anderson replied.

After Holly asked the manager to arrange a charter flight to Fargo, Anderson first tried to telephone Jerry Dwyer, who owned a flying service at the nearby Mason City Municipal Airport. After learning that Dwyer was at a Chamber of Commerce meeting, Anderson called Roger Peterson, who was a charter pilot for Dwyer's Flying Service. Even though he had been working all day, Peterson had the next day off, and agreed to pilot the passengers to Fargo.

The flight departure was scheduled for 12:30 a.m., after the conclusion of the second show at the Surf Ballroom. The plane could accommodate up to three passengers, and the total cost of the three-and-one-half-hour flight was $108.

Peterson was tired; by departure time, he would have been working for 17 straight hours and was concerned about making the seven-hour, round trip flight. He briefly reconsidered his decision, and telephoned another area pilot, Cerro Gordo County Deputy Sheriff, Duane Mayfield. Mayfield was not interested in piloting the rock and rollers: "No thanks, I'm a Lawrence Welk Fan." At this point, Peterson, who was only 21-years-old and excited by the prospect of flying the entertainers, particularly Buddy Holly, concluded that he was alert enough to pilot the aircraft.

In in the interval before take-off, Peterson and his wife of four months, DeAnn, had Charles E. McGlothlen (Dwyer Flying Service's chief mechanic) and his wife, Judye, over to their house for pie and coffee. McGlothlen was concerned about the weather and Peterson's level of fatigue: "We kept asking him if he really thought he ought to take the flight. I told him not to go that night. His wife told him not to go, and Judye told him not to go…"

Peterson would not be deterred, and when Charles and Judye departed the Peterson's house at approximately 10:00 p.m., McGlothlen did not sense that his friend was overly-fatigued. As McGlothlen remembered it, Peterson had been "in a very good mood, all the time."

Back at the Surf Ballroom, teenagers paid $1.25 to attend either of the two shows. Parents, who were admitted for 10 cents, served as chaperones; Anderson wanted to prove that rock and roll was not just for juvenile delinquents. By the end of the night, 1,200 teens and 300 adults had been admitted, generating nearly a $700 profit for Anderson.

Even though it was 18-degrees outside, the Surf Ballroom was decorated like a Florida night club. Palm trees greeted visitors in the lobby and were positioned on either side of the stage. The vaulted ceiling, overlying the 6,300-square-feet maple wood dance floor, was blue, with projected images of drifting clouds. Wooden booths, with green, padded leather upholstery, lined the periphery of the room, to accommodate non-dancers.

Bob Hale, the 25-year-old morning disc jockey at *KRIB* in Mason City, who served as emcee, remembered, years later, how impressed he was by Holly: "From the moment the bus arrived, Buddy took charge. He directed the equipment set-up, discussed the upcoming event, discussed and decided the performance order, and did so while sitting at the piano playing as he spoke. He was only 22-years-old, but possessed the leadership of a modern-day CEO. Buddy was clearly in charge of everything and everyone. It was equally apparent that those he led respected and liked him, while looking to him for direction."

Hale remembered that GAC tour director, Sam Geller, told him that Holly "is going to be the biggest influence in the history of the entertainment industry." Geller pointed out that Holly was not only a performer, song-writer, and producer, but was also essentially running this tour. "Someday soon, he will have his own recording studios, record label, and television show. We'll all be working for him…" Geller opined.

Before the first show, Hale chatted with Buddy and the Big Bopper, sharing a common bond; all three of their wives were pregnant. Holly openly discussed his ongoing dispute with Norman Petty: "I've got to get this stuff straightened out. One problem with being on the road, you don't know what's going on back there."

While obviously stressed, Buddy remained confident. When Carroll Anderson inquired as to what was in store for him, Buddy answered: "Well I'm either going to the top, or else I'm going to fall. But, I think you're going to see me in the big time."

When Hale opened the first show, he was amazed by the size of the audience: "It was the biggest crowd that Carroll Anderson had ever had in the Surf. It was the biggest thing I'd ever seen. We had people that had driven in from St. Paul; others had driven in from Illinois and Minneapolis. The place was filled to rafters."

During both shows, Carlo Mastrangelo played the drums when Buddy was performing; otherwise, Holly served as the replacement percussionist. When Valens took the stage, Hale remembered "the girls went crazy over Ritchie." Buddy's performance, however, "almost blew the roof off." "They didn't want to let him go," Hale recalled.

During the break between the first and second shows, when the stars were signing autographs, Holly received the most requests. Bob Hale was busy throughout the intermission, interviewing the performers for his *KRIB* radio show. When he asked for the identity of "the guy with glasses," playing drums behind Dion and the Belmonts and partially obscured by the symbols, a voice spoke up: "My name is Mr. Holly, Mr. Hale."

Ritchie Valens mentioned Buddy's recent record, *It Doesn't Matter Anymore*, bragging that Holly was the first rock and roller to use violinists. Valens jokingly informed Hale that Buddy should be performing in a cutaway with tails, because he would be conducting a philharmonic orchestra by year's end.

While the performers drank sodas and coffee during the intermission, a newspaperman from the *Clear Lake Mirror Reporter* wrote that the rock and rollers were "full of pep," and "reacting joyously to the big crowd of young people." The same reporter noted that Valens and the Big Bopper "playfully Indian-wrestled between acts." Years later, Bob Hale remembered the *Winter Dance Party* in Clear Lake as "the biggest thrill of my life."

The second show started at 10:30 p.m., and before he took the stage, Buddy asked Carroll Anderson to verify that the charter flight to Fargo was on schedule. After telephoning Dwyer's Flying Service, Anderson informed Holly that the plane would be ready by midnight.

When Buddy Holly stepped on the stage for his second show, he opened with Billy Grammar's hit, *Gonna Travel On*. As the audience shouted for him to play their favorites, Holly kept them dancing and applauding with many of the hits that had made him famous, including, *That'll Be the Day*, *Peggy Sue*, *Oh Boy*, *Rave On*, and *Everyday*.

Among the audience members was young Robert Wobbeking, a native of Dows, Iowa, located south of Clear Lake. At the time, Wobbeking was attending business school in Mason City, and accompanied a friend to the Surf Ballroom. Even though he was more familiar with Elvis Presley than the *Winter Dance Party* entertainers, after the concert, Wobbeking told his companion: "Buddy Holly is my new favorite singer."

Bob Hale remembered that Buddy's final performance was "fantastic," and described the audience as "one big surge" crowding toward the stage. With *Winter Dance Party* stops yet to follow in Moorhead, Sioux City, Clear Rapids, Waterloo, Dubuque, Spring Valley, Chicago, Peoria, Springfield, Louisville, Canton, and Youngstown, no one could have anticipated that this was Buddy Holly's *last* performance.

When Buddy concluded his set with Chuck Berry's *Brown-Eyed Handsome Man*, the other performers joined him on stage. Bob Hale fittingly described it as a "farewell." The crowd shouted for an encore, but Holly informed them that he was in a hurry to catch a plane. While others have claimed that Buddy and the other performers joined together to sing Ritchie Valens' *La Bamba*, Tommy Allsup, who was on stage at the time, agreed with Bob Hale—Buddy's *final* song was *Brown-Eyed Handsome Man*.

When Buddy Holly exited the stage for the last time, it was the unknowing end of an incredible 18-month professional career. In that short time, Buddy had played at approximately 200 different venues, performing publicly 500 or more times.

The original passenger manifest for the charter flight to Fargo included Buddy, along with his bandmates, Waylon Jennings and Tommy Allsup. As the time neared to leave the Surf Ballroom, the Big Bopper approached Waylon, telling him that he was coming down with the flu, and wanted to get to Moorhead in time to see a doctor. "Those bus seats bug me," the chunky Big Bopper explained. In exchange for Waylon's seat on the plane, he would let Jennings use his newly-purchased sleeping bag during the cold, overnight bus ride.

Jennings was not hard to convince; he was young, had never toured before, and enjoyed the companionship of his fellow performers. "It's all right with me, if it's all right with Buddy. You go ask him," Waylon answered.

When Buddy learned that Jennings had relinquished his prized seat on the airplane to the Big Bopper, he jokingly admonished his bass player: "I hope your bus freezes up."

Without thinking, Waylon retorted: "Well, I hope your old plane crashes."

Waylon's last words to Buddy, made in jest, haunted him. "That took me a lot of years to get over. I was just a kid, barely 21. I was about half-way superstitious like all southern people, scared of the Devil and scared of God equally," Jennings wrote years later in his autobiography.

As his fans would later learn, Ritchie Valens had a long-standing fear of flying. On January 31, 1957, when he was a student at Pacoima Junior High School, an F-89 Scorpion fighter jet and a transport plane collided over Van Nuys, California. Wreckage fell on the school's athletic field, killing three students and injuring 78 others. While Ritchie wasn't at school that day (he was attending his grandfather's funeral), the stories he heard about the carnage were haunting.

At the same time, Valens, a warm-blooded Californian, was least prepared for the bitter cold, tired of the freezing buses, and already ill with a head cold. He also wanted to get to Moorhead in time to get his hair cut. Overcoming his fear, Valens approached Tommy Allsup and asked if he could have his seat on the charter flight. At first, Allsup declined, informing Ritchie that he was "starting to freeze every night, too."

"I have never been in a small plane before. Please let me go instead," Valens pleaded.

After saying no, once again, Allsup exited the ballroom with Holly, the Big Bopper, and Carroll Anderson, the latter of whom had agreed to drive the entertainers to the airport in Mason City. Allsup helped the others load dirty clothes and luggage into Anderson's station wagon. Perhaps remembering that Carl Bunch had previously left behind one of his performing outfits, Buddy turned to Allsup: "Tommy, go back in and make sure we got everything loaded."

Inside the ballroom, Valens was surrounded by fans seeking autographs. Eyeing Allsup, Ritchie made his final play: "You going to let me fly guy? Come on—flip."

"Let's flip a coin," Valens repeated

Allsup, who made a split-second, life-saving decision, agreed to a coin toss, "if you want to go that bad." "I don't know why I did it; I'd said no all night," Allsup later reflected.

The pair decided if the coin came up heads, Ritchie would fly. The 50-cent piece landed heads-side up.

Just who flipped the coin? Holly biographer, Ellis Amburn wrote that Valens pulled the half-dollar from his pocket and tossed it in the air. Larry Lehmer, author of *The Day the Music Died: The Last Tour of Buddy Holly, the "Big Bopper," and Ritchie Valens*, along with Philip Norman, who penned *Rave On: The Biography of Buddy Holly*, documented that Tommy Allsup flipped the coin. For the remainder of his life, Tommy Allsup steadfastly maintained that he tossed the coin. A third version comes from Bob Hale, the disc jockey who emceed the Surf Ballroom show. Corresponding with the author in March of 2017, Hale wrote that he was the one who tossed the coin: "I know that I was asked for a coin, because no one else back stage had one." Regardless of who flipped the half-dollar, the result was never in doubt.

"You won the toss," Allsup said.

"What do you know? This is the first time I've ever won," Ritchie smiled.

When the pair went outside to tell Buddy about yet another change in the passenger line-up, Allsup asked Holly to pick up a registered letter that his mother had mailed to the post office in Fargo. Buddy reminded him that he would need some personal identification to claim the letter, and asked for Allsup's driver's license. "Here, take my wallet," Tommy replied; Buddy crammed the billfold inside his pants pocket.

That same night, at the Allison's house in Lubbock, J.I., Joe B., and Sonny Curtis were contemplating their futures. They were puzzled as to why Buddy, Waylon Jennings, Tommy Allsup, and Carl Bunch were touring under the name the Crickets; while *Winter Dance Party* promotional posters read *Buddy Holly and the Crickets,* no one remembered Buddy specifically introducing his new band by that name, while performing on stage.

J.I. and Joe B. were equally concerned that in the weeks since Buddy had left the group, most of Norman Petty's promises to them remained unfulfilled. The two of them, joined by Sonny Curtis and Earl Sinks, the latter of whom Petty recruited as the Crickets' new vocalist, had recorded only two songs, *Love's Made a Fool of You* and *Someone, Someone.* Petty had also failed to book a single live performance for the band.

J.I. and Joe B. attempted to telephone Buddy to discuss the future, including the possibility of keeping Sonny, jettisoning Sinks, and returning Buddy to his lead position with the Crickets. "During that tour (the *Winter Dance Party*), Jerry and I broke up with Norman Petty (not yet officially). And, then we started trying to get in touch with Buddy, because Buddy had said, 'You ever want to get back with me, all you have to do is call.' So, we were trying to call Buddy to say, 'We want to put the group back together,'" Joe B. remembered.

J.I. and Joe B. first called Maria Elena in New York City. She had spoken to Buddy earlier in the evening, and informed them where the *Winter Dance Party* was currently playing. When Buddy's former bandmates telephoned the Surf Ballroom in Clear Lake, they discovered Holly had already departed.

"We called the next place he was going to play, and left a message, and were expecting a call that night or the next day, when he got there. But, we never got to talk to him," Joe B. somberly recalled.

In another part of Lubbock, Larry Holley was listening to the radio before going to bed. When he heard about the abysmal weather in the Midwest, Larry immediately said a short prayer for his youngest brother. "If I knew he was flying, I'd have said a long prayer," Larry sadly remembered.

The *Winter Dance Party's* road manager, Sam Geller, later claimed that he had no idea Holly, Valens, and the Big Bopper were flying to Fargo, until they failed to board the bus, and had already left for the airport. "I would have put my foot down on that," Geller insisted.

Emcee Bob Hale and his wife, Kathy, stood outside the Surf Ballroom and waved good-bye as Carroll Anderson's station wagon pulled out of the parking lot. Since it was snowing "like mad," Hale concluded that no pilot would take off in those weather conditions. He fully expected that Holly, Valens, and the Big Bopper would be forced to spend the night in a local hotel, before flying out the next morning.

Driving home, Hale ominously informed his wife: "This is no night to be flying."

CHAPTER 11

I Think They're All Dead

YEARS LATER, THE *WEATHER CHANNEL* would describe the plane crash outside of Mason City Iowa, on February 3, 1959, as one of its Top 100 biggest weather events in history. Without a doubt, the flight from Iowa to Fargo, North Dakota was doomed from the start.

Immediately after take-off, Roger Peterson ran into snow showers. Choosing to fly below the clouds, he lost the moon and stars as points of reference. When the lights of Mason City and Clear Lake disappeared, Peterson was confronted with an overcast sky above him and snow covered fields below. With only scattered farmhouses, providing scarce and inconsistent light, the pilot could not identify visible landmarks on the horizon. In addition, gusty winds made it difficult to keep the aircraft's wings level, during which time Peterson may also have been distracted by attempts to file his overdue flight plan.

Why did Peterson fail to respond to repeated radio transmissions from the control tower in Mason City? Were he and his passengers already aware that he was losing control of aircraft, and so panicked that Peterson failed to hear the radio? Or, had the plane already crashed by the time the controller radioed him?

Disoriented and non-instrument-rated, the young pilot likely developed vertigo. When the turbulent winds unleveled the plane's wings, Peterson's instinctive response would have been to pull back on the yoke, resulting in the aptly-named "death spiral," propelling the aircraft toward the ground at or near maximum velocity.

In 1981, *The Aviation Consumer Used Aircraft Guide* described how difficult it is to keep a Beechcraft Bonanza airborne during heavy winds: "Once a wing dips a little, it tends to keep going. In instrument weather and turbulence, this low rolling stability can put the pilot into the 'graveyard spiral' very quickly."

Ruth Pickering had spent the entire day and into the night re-painting the walls of her kitchen and cleaning the windows. At approximately 1:00 a.m., as she was rehanging curtains, Pickering saw the lights of a small airplane heading directly toward her house. She quickly switched on the outside lights, hoping to briefly capture the pilot's attention, and then breathed a sigh of relief, when the aircraft missed her two-story house, her barn, and a grove of trees, just north of the farmstead.

Less than a half-mile further north, Reeve Eldridge heard an accelerating airplane passing just over his two-story farmhouse. By habit, Reeve and his wife left a light on in the upstairs hallway, in case their children had to get up during the night. Eldridge detected a change in the sound of the plane's engine as it narrowly missed crashing into his house.

A bit further to the north, Elsie Juhl was experiencing insomnia. As her husband, Albert, lay sound asleep beside her, Elsie was startled by "the worst motor noise I've ever heard." "I knew it was a plane. It was so low, I thought it was going to hit our house," Elsie clearly recalled.

Elsie and Albert's son, Delbert, lived next door in a single-story house. Delbert and his spouse heard an airplane rapidly passing directly overhead. "The wife was up with one of the girls, and she said the plane blew snow on our windows," he recalled. A few hundred yards past the Juhl's homestead, at the end of its unrecoverable spiral, no one outside of the aircraft saw or heard it impact the snow-covered ground at 170-miles-per-hour.

The right wing struck first, plowing a 50-feet-long and six-feet-deep furrow in the dormant, snow and ice-covered farmland, before it separated from the fuselage. Absent a wing, the aircraft bounced and tumbled for 50 feet, then skidded some 500 feet, before the mangled wreckage came to rest against a barbed wire fence.

The plane had crashed 5.2 miles northwest of the Mason City airport. No more than five minutes had elapsed between take-off and the fatal impact.

The county coroner, Dr. Ralph E. Smiley, wrote in his investigative report that the wreckage was located "about ½-mile from the nearest north-south gravel road and the farmhouses of the Albert Juhl's and the Delbert Juhl's..." Smiley also reported that "the shape of the mass of wreckage approximated a ball, with one wing sticking diagonally from one side..."

All three of the passengers were violently ejected from the plane and slammed into the frozen turf. Buddy Holly and Ritchie Valens landed prone, about 17 feet south of the wreckage. The Big Bopper flew 40 feet in the opposite direction, over the barbed wire fence, landing partly prone and on his side. Roger Peterson was trapped, upside down, in the mangled cockpit, with one of his legs pointed skyward. The four occupants of the Beechcraft Bonanza were no doubt killed instantly.

The seams of Buddy Holly's yellow leather jacket were split open, almost to their full length. His injuries were grievous: 1. His skull was fractured and half of his brain was missing; 2. Blood poured out of both of his ears; 3. Deep cuts marred his face; 4. Most of his ribs were crushed; 5. His left forearm and right elbow were fractured; 6. Both of his legs had multiple fractures; 7. His left scrotum was lacerated.

The left leg of Ritchie Valens's black wool pants was ripped open, from ankle to hip. Like Holly, he suffered multiple traumatic injuries: 1. Landing face first, he was no longer recognizable by sight; 2. Parts of his fractured skull and most of his brain were dislocated from his body; 3. His right eye socket was empty; 4. Both arms were fractured.

The Big Bopper's body lay alone in the neighboring field. His injuries were also gruesome: 1. His skull was completely split open; 2. Most of his brain was missing; 3. The right side of his face was completely crushed; 4. He had multiple fractures in his arms, legs, and ribs.

Roger Peterson stayed with the wreckage, until it was stopped by the fence, and the instrument panel was literally wrapped around his upper torso. He, too, suffered numerous traumatic injuries: 1. His brain stem was permanently damaged; 2. His aorta was severed; 3. His heart, lungs, spleen, and liver were lacerated; 4. There were multiple fractures of his skull, sternum, ribs, pelvis, arms, and legs; 5. His right thumb was amputated.

It was after daylight before the crash site was discovered. By then, the bodies were frozen solid by the 18-degree temperature and covered with a dusting of snow.

Having never received any communication from his pilot, Jerry Dwyer instructed the controller to send a teletype to the Fargo Airport, requesting that Mason City be notified when Roger Peterson established radio contact with his ultimate destination. Dwyer also had the teletype sent to three other airports along the route to Fargo—Alexandria, Minneapolis, and Redwood Falls.

At 1:30 a.m., Dwyer left the airport for home. Thirty minutes later, he called the controller and learned that none of the airports along the way had established radio contact with the Beechcraft Bonanza. Fearing the worst, Dwyer could not sleep. At 3:30 a.m., 30 minutes after Peterson's estimated time of arrival, Dwyer telephoned the airport in Fargo. The controller informed him there had been no incoming communication from Peterson, and there likely would be none, because a heavy snow storm was underway in the area.

At 4:10 a.m., Dwyer phoned the controller at the Mason City Airport and instructed him to issue an alert for a missing aircraft. The search for the Bonanza officially became the responsibility of the 10th Air Force Search and Rescue Coordination Center, based out of Minneapolis.

When Dwyer arrived at the airport at 8:00 a.m., there was still no news about his missing aircraft. After waiting for the early morning fog to clear, Dwyer decided to conduct his own search, as he later informed Civil Aeronautics Board investigators: "I decided I just couldn't sit there, and decided I would go fly and try to follow the same course that I thought Roger would have taken…"

After taking off in his two-seat Champ, Dwyer traced Peterson's probable route of departure. He searched from the air with an eagle eye, sometimes flying no more than 25 feet above the frozen farm fields. At 9:35 a.m., roughly eight-and-one-half hours after the crash, Dwyer spotted the wreckage. He immediately radioed the Mason City control tower: "They're all in a pasture…I think they're all dead." Dwyer instructed the controller to contact local law enforcement officials, and remained airborne, circling the crash site until the authorities arrived.

A ham radio operator intercepted Dwyer's message to the tower and immediately relayed the tragic news to a local radio station, even though the pilot had not disclosed the names of the crash victims. Nonetheless, the media learned there had been a fatal plane crash before any of the bodies were identified.

Jerry Allen, the Sheriff of Cerro Gordo County, Iowa, happened to be in St. Louis pursuing a criminal investigation at the time of plane crash. Deputy Sheriff, Duane Mayfield, who was temporarily in command, dispatched Deputies Bill McGill and Lowell Sandquist to the area Dwyer had pinpointed.

When the lawmen reached the gravel road in front of the Juhl's farm, Delbert opened the gate and allowed them to drive past the house, and across his farm land. When Deputy McGill encountered skid marks created by the crashing plane, he drove around them, to avoid contaminating the scene. McGill soon reached what was left of the Beechcraft Bonanza, crumpled against the barbed-wire fence separating the Juhl's farm from their neighbor's. In short order, three Iowa State Patrol officers also arrived at the scene.

Deputy Sheriff Mayfield ordered roadblocks to be erected, hoping to keep civilians from invading the crash site. Mayfield's efforts were mostly in vain. Before long, newspaper reporters, photographers, and at least one television cameraman arrived to document the wreckage and human carnage. Curiosity seekers joined the press, and a few of them tried to carry pieces of the wreckage home as morbid souvenirs, before they were halted by law enforcement officers.

At 11:15 a.m., black Cadillac hearses creaked and groaned as they traversed the frozen field. Carroll Anderson was summoned from the Surf Ballroom to help identify the horribly disfigured bodies. Valens' face was so misshapen that he could only be identified by a tattoo (*RV*) on the underside of his forearm.

Confusion arose when Tommy Allsup's wallet, which Holly had been carrying in his pocket, was found amid the wreckage. Before any of the victims' family members could be notified, *UPI* issued a nationwide bulletin stating that Allsup was among the dead.

Jim Collison, a newly-hired reporter for Mason City's *Globe-Gazette*, was among those present at the crash site. "It was my first assignment and I'd just rather forget the whole ordeal," Collison later recalled.

Authors Note: *As is the case with many tragic events, such as the assassination of John F. Kennedy, there are often discrepancies in the time line. In some of these cases, the passage of time naturally alters a person's memory. Other times, original memories are contaminated by what individuals later read or hear about the mind-numbing event.*

At least two people, both of whom attended Buddy Holly's last performance at the Surf Ballroom in Clear Lake, later recalled hearing about the plane crash in the wee hours of the morning, well before the wreckage was discovered by Jerry Dwyer. In the opinion of the author, the best available evidence supports Dwyer's recollection.

Once he landed, Jerry Dwyer told a friend of his, Bob Booe, about the crash and provided him with the names of the victims. Booe, a television reporter, relayed the information to the *Associated Press* news wire. Booe later rationalized his action, which was justifiably criticized: "These are prominent guys. You don't sit on their names while they notify the next of kin, because this is a very significant story."

Bob Hale, who had emceed the *Winter Dance Party* concert the night before, was hosting his daily show at *KRIB* in Mason City. Mid-morning, he examined a bulletin that came over the radio station's *UPI* ticker. When he learned that a small plane had crashed just outside Mason City,

Hale failed to grasp the significance of the news: "I read that report, and let it go. I didn't even think about it," he remembered.

At 10:10 a.m., Carroll Anderson telephoned the disc jockey: "Bob, they're dead."

"Who's dead?" Hale inquired.

"Their plane went down just north of town. They're all lying out in that cornfield now. They're all dead, Bob," Anderson somberly explained.

When he suddenly realized that Anderson was talking about Holly, Valens, and the Big Bopper, a stunned Hale insisted upon clarification: "Are you sure it's their plane? Are you sure they're all dead?"

"Yes. They're all dead," Anderson repeated.

Hale, who was in a state of shock, interrupted his regular show with the tragic announcement: "I just lifted the needle off the record and told everybody." Teenagers rushed to radio station and stood outside, hoping and praying that it was somehow a mistake. Hale recalled "that the entire day turned into an on-air wake." "I had to have a guy come in—I was just sick to my stomach," Hale later explained.

When twenty-one-year-old DeAnn Peterson awakened at 6:30 a.m., she realized her husband had not returned home. A one-car family, DeAnn had to telephone a fellow employee for a ride to Mason City radio station *KGLO*, where she worked in the accounts department. "We went past the flying service and I looked for Roger's car," DeAnn recalled. When she spotted the Ford in the parking lot, DeAnn was filled with dread: "We got to work, and I had that feeling. I was just waiting for something to happen."

It didn't take long for the news to come over *KGLO's* news wire. DeAnn was crushed, certain that she would "never get over" her husband's death.

When Roger Peterson's mother, Pearl, learned about the crash, she was filled with both grief and anger. She immediately blamed the crash on the dead rock and rollers, who in her opinion, should have departed by bus, along with their fellow entertainers.

At the Mason City Airport, Charles McGlothen was grieving over the loss of his close friend and fellow employee, Roger Peterson, finding it impossible to focus on his regular duties: "Lord, it was terrible. I wanted to go out to the wreck." Deputy Sheriff, Lowell Sandquist, talked him out of it: "You don't want to see."

"I was sitting there, stewing and fretting. I had just rebuilt the airplane and I thought, 'My Lord, what could have gone wrong?'" McGlothen recalled. The aircraft mechanic's physician eventually prescribed him tranquilizers, to help McGlothen cope with the tragedy.

Reporters and editors at the *Clear Lake Mirror-Reporter* were already preparing the newspaper's afternoon edition. The headlines read: DEATHS OF SINGERS HERE SHOCKS NATION. *The* subtitle provided additional details: *Rock 'N' Rollers, Pilot Die in Tragic Plane Crash*. Two wide-angle photographs of the mangled airplane and crash victims' bodies accompanied the front-page article.

It was late in the morning, on February 3rd, before the remaining *Winter Dance Party* tour members arrived at the Comstock Hotel in Moorhead, Minnesota. There are at least two different accounts as to how they first learned about the fatal plane crash.

Waylon Jennings remembered that the tour manager, Sam Geller, entered the hotel, while the others were waking up from their all-night trip. Geller soon re-boarded the bus: "Come outside, I want to talk to you for a while." Waylon refused to exit the bus, fearing something terrible had occurred, and turned to Allsup: "Tommy, you go."

Allsup's account is different; both he and Geller entered the hotel together. Tommy saw the Big Bopper's picture on the lobby television, but could not hear the sound, and assumed it was simply a promotional spot for the upcoming concert. Allsup then asked the desk clerk for Buddy Holly's room.

"Haven't you heard?" the clerk replied, "Those guys got killed in a plane crash."

Allsup immediately returned to the bus and informed the others: "Boys, they didn't make it."

Allsup phoned his mother in Texas to update her on the situation. Luckily, she had not been watching television or listening to the radio.

Over the past two hours, the media had mistakenly reported that her son was dead, based upon the discovery of Allsup's wallet at the crash site.

"My mom hadn't heard a thing about it, yet. But, all the time I was talking to her on the phone, a neighbor of hers, from down the street, was trying to get through to tell her I'd been named as one of the dead..." Allsup recalled.

Waylon Jennings' brother, Tommy, was in Littlefield, Texas when radio station *KVOW* announced that Allsup was among the crash victims. "I went crazy," Tommy recalled, and was infuriated when the media failed to retract the mistaken story for "two or three hours."

At the hotel in Moorhead, Dion DiMucci entered the lobby and heard the television news announcer say: "There were no survivors." Returning to the tour bus, Dion picked up Buddy Holly's Fender Stratocaster and stared at it. "All around me were their belongings," he eerily recalled. "We were on top of the world, one day, and the rug was pulled out from under us. At the age of 19, I wondered why I was here and where I was going and what the meaning of life was," Dion later remembered.

Fred Milano, one of the Belmonts, had been asleep when the bus reached Moorhead, after 10 hours on the road. "The plane had crashed, already, and the whole country knew about it, except us. We heard it last," Milano recalled.

Carl Bunch was recuperating from frostbite in his hospital room, when a nurse wheeled him down the hall to a payphone, to accept a call from his mother. As he neared the telephone, Bunch could not understand why other people were staring at him.

"Honey, what are you going to do now?" Ms. Bunch asked.

"Mom, I'm going to be okay. My feet are just fine," he replied.

"No, honey. I mean, what are you going to do now?" she repeated.

"Well, Mama, just as quickly as I can get thawed out, I'm going to join Buddy out on the road," Bunch answered.

"No, darling. You don't understand," she replied, before informing her son about the fatal plane crash.

After returning to his hospital bed, Bunch was in a state of shock and grief. Looking up, he saw three teenage girls standing in the doorway of his room. One of the girls admitted that the group had skipped school after learning that Buddy Holly's drummer was in the hospital. The teenager's confession took the sting off Bunch's despair, and for a moment, he felt "special."

Buddy Holly's family and closest friends heard about his death in different ways. In each case, it was a cruel shock.

In New York City, Lou Giordano learned about the plane crash from either the radio or television. When he telephoned Maria Elena, Giordano quickly realized that she did not yet know Buddy was dead. After ending the phone call abruptly, Giordano raced to the Holly's apartment, hoping to gently break the terrible news. Her suspicions aroused, Maria Elena turned on the television and learned that her husband had been killed; almost simultaneously, Aunt Provi arrived at the Holly's apartment. Five weeks pregnant, Maria Elena suffered a miscarriage the following day.

At *KLLL* in Lubbock, Sky Corbin was working in place of the absent Waylon Jennings, when he received word of the fatal crash over the radio station's news ticker. Sky pre-empted his brother, Slim, and Hi Pockets Duncan, who were transmitting a remote broadcast: "Boys, I'm sorry to interrupt, but I'm afraid I have some very bad news." When Corbin informed *KLLL's* listening audience that Buddy, Ritchie, and the Big Bopper had been killed, he had no idea that the Holley family had not yet been notified.

Former Cricket, Niki Sullivan, was asleep, when a friend telephoned him with the tragic news. He immediately asked his mother, who was good friends with Ella Holley, to telephone Buddy's mother. When she realized that Ella was unaware of the plane crash, Ms. Sullivan instructed her not to listen to the radio until she arrived at the Holley's house. After Ella and L.O. received other well-meaning, but cryptic telephone calls, they turned on their radio and heard Sky Corbin's report.

When Ella looked out the front window of their house, she saw a group of people approaching the front door, including Ben D. Johnson, the pastor of the Tabernacle Baptist Church, and his associate pastor, Ken Johnson. "Oh, no! It can't be true!" Ella exclaimed, before breaking into sobs.

Later in the day, when the Corbin brothers paid their respects to the Holley family, they were in for a shock. "Sky, you know how we heard about Buddy?" Ella asked.

"I assume your pastor told you," he replied.

"No, we heard you read it on the radio," she explained.

Sky was horrified: "Oh, my God! I'm sorry. It never entered my mind that you wouldn't have been notified before they put that out on the news."

"Don't worry about it. That's all right. We'd just as soon have heard it from you, as anybody else," Ella tried to reassure him.

Travis Holley was taking a coffee break from working on a tiling job, when a waitress at the nearby café approached him: "Shouldn't you go home, as your brother's been killed?" Believing the woman was referring to his older brother, he rushed to Larry's house, and discovered that no one was at home. After he sped to his own home, Travis' wife instructed him to "get out of his work clothes and go to your mother's house."

Larry Holley learned of the tragedy in a more circuitous manner. After taking a lunch break from laying tile, Larry went to the job site where Travis had been working, only to discover his brother's tools scattered about. When he drove home, Larry's wife was not there. After deciding to eat lunch at a local restaurant, Larry overheard a fellow diner comment: "Isn't it terrible about those three boys getting killed?"

Larry immediately sensed that something awful had occurred. "I ran out and drove over to Mother and Daddy's place. I can still feel the sick feeling in my stomach, when I saw all the cars parked outside," he remembered, years later.

Sonny Curtis had spent the night at J.I.'s parents' house and was having coffee with Allison's mother, when a neighbor from who lived across the street, Oleta Hall, notified them about the plane crash. It was close to 10:00 a.m., when Sonny was tasked with the difficult chore of awakening J.I. and informing him of the tragedy.

J.I. was in disbelief: "I thought that there might have been a plane crash, and that Buddy might have been around it, but he couldn't be dead; he couldn't possibly be." After the news sunk in, Peggy Sue remembered that her husband was "paralyzed and devastated."

After J.I. telephoned Norman Petty and informed him of Buddy's death, Peggy Sue recalled that he was livid: "You know what Norman said to me when I was on the phone with him? The first thing out of his mouth was 'God has strange ways of solving problems.'"

Joe B. learned about the tragedy after his sister telephoned him. He refused to believe her, assuming it was a morbid publicity stunt. His sister argued with him: "No, no. Go out and get the newspaper and look at the headlines."

Even then, Joe B. remained in denial about Buddy's death for nearly two years. "One day, he's going to be walking down the street, and I'll see him," he rationalized.

Norman Petty recalled that his reaction was "catastrophic." When Robert Linville, a studio back-up singer, visited Norman and Vi in their apartment on the day of the plane crash, he found both in tears.

The telephone rang repeatedly at the Petty's apartment throughout that long day. When callers insisted, "It's not true," Norman confirmed the tragic reality. What was he truly feeling inside? Whether he acknowledged it, or not, Petty was largely responsible for Holly joining the *Winter Dance Party*.

Holly's long-time friend and former bandmate, Bob Montgomery, along with his new wife, Carol, were driving from his parent's farm in Lampasas, Texas to Clovis, where he was working as a sound engineer for Norman Petty. Bob experienced an eerie feeling as they exchanged positions in the front seat: "When my wife took over, I told her, 'Really be careful how you drive, because I've got this bad feeling in the pit of my stomach, like we could be going to have some kind of accident.'" Stopping briefly in Lubbock, the couple learned that Buddy was dead.

News of the Iowa plane crash rapidly spread throughout the country, and eventually abroad. In Los Angeles, Eddie Cochran, who was one of Buddy's closest friends, was devastated. Cochran's girlfriend, Sharon Steely, recalled the next few days: "The two of them had been like brothers. And, Eddie couldn't get it out of his mind that he'd almost gone on that tour with Buddy, but had dropped out to do the *Ed Sullivan Show*, which was happening that very week. All the Sullivan people were at the airport waiting for Eddie, but he didn't get on the plane. He'd taken his station wagon and gone off into the desert by himself, to mourn."

At *KSYD* in Wichita Falls, Holly's old friend and disc jockey, Snuff Garrett, broadcast live interviews with J.I., Joe B., and Norman Petty. "We often wonder why things like this happen, but there is always bound to be a reason somewhere," Petty opined. When Garrett asked if there were any Holly recordings yet to be released, Petty grew guarded: "It depends." After alluding to potential litigation, Petty ended the conversation.

In New York City, Decca Records' Dick Jacobs was making plans for Buddy Holly's next recording session. Having only glanced at the *New York Daily News*' headlines, Jacobs missed the *AP* report on the inside pages, which read: *3 STARS OF ROCK 'N' ROLL KILLED*. The accompanying article described the plane crash, featured pictures of the three deceased entertainers and included a map, detailing the proposed flight route from Mason City to Fargo.

A colleague soon entered Jacobs' office and told him to sit down: "Did you hear the news?" Jacobs was speechless, before breaking down and crying. He eventually closed his office and went home for the rest of the day. "It wasn't a question of losing an artist. I had lost a friend," Jacobs recalled.

Before going on television to host his *Big Beat Show*, disc jockey and promoter, Alan Freed, noted the sad irony. "Crazy, isn't it, that his new single is called *It Doesn't Matter Anymore?*" Freed thought aloud.

Because of the six-hour time difference between Iowa and London, it was early evening before Brits, who had long-idolized Holly, heard the tragic news from *BBC* television and *ITV* radio bulletins. The following day, the *Daily Mirror* headlined: *TOP "ROCK" STARS DIE IN PLANE CRASH.*

GAC's Tim Gale, who along with Irving Feld, had organized the *Winter Dance Party*, immediately adopted a defensive and business-like tone. "We always fought against the idea of any of them chartering their own planes," Gale announced, before matter-of-factly declaring that the *Winter Dance Party* would continue, absent three of its biggest stars.

The bodies of Buddy Holly, Ritchie Valens, and the Big Bopper were the first to be transported to the morgue. Law enforcement officers were reluctant to remove Roger Peterson's remains from the wreckage until officials from the Civil Aeronautics Board (CAB) or Federal Aviation Administration (FAA) arrived, fearing they might damage the cockpit's instrument panel. After CAB lead investigator, C.E. Stillwagon, and his FAA counterpart, A.J. Prokop, arrived, Deputies McGill and Sandquist used blow torches to free the pilot's body from the crumpled remains of the airplane.

Dr. Smiley, the county coroner, found $193 in Buddy Holly's pockets. From that amount, he deducted $10 for the inquest, 65 cents for mileage (at a rate of seven-cents-per-mile), and one-dollar for the "docket case"—a total of $11.65. He subtracted an identical amount from the cash found on the other crash victims' bodies.

Why wasn't Holly carrying more cash at the time of his death? It is certainly possible that he entrusted the balance of his salary to the road manager, or had earlier arranged for the funds to be wired to his bank account.

When he searched Ritchie Valens' body, Smiley discovered $22.15 in cash, two checks in the amount of $50 drawn on a Hollywood, California bank, several blank checks, a religious medallion, and a bracelet with the name "Donna" on the charm. The Big Bopper's pockets yielded $202 in cash and a guitar pick.

Roger Peterson was the only crash victim to undergo an autopsy. Later that same day, Dr. Smiley, assisted by Dr. George T. Joyce, conducted the post-mortem examination at Mercy Hospital in Mason City. In addition to head trauma and multiple comminuted fractures, the physicians discovered that rib fragments had severely damaged the decedent's internal abdominal organs. Peterson's family was billed $100 for the autopsy.

Holly and Peterson were embalmed later that day at G.W. Wilcox funeral home in Clear Lake. Morticians at the Ward funeral home, also located in Clear Lake, prepared Valens' and the Big Bopper's remains for burial.

Nearly 24 hours after the crash, law enforcement officers arrived at both funeral homes to complete the last of their grim, but necessary tasks. The bodies of each victim were fingerprinted.

On Wednesday, February 4th, Larry Holley, accompanied by his brother-in-law, J.E. Weir, chartered a plane from West Texas Aircraft and flew to Iowa to claim Buddy's body. After landing in Mason City, the pair went directly to the Wilcox funeral home in Clear Lake. When asked to identify his brother's body, Larry admittedly "chickened out." "I just wanted to remember Buddy like he was when he was little…I didn't want to remember him all beat up," Larry remembered.

Larry's brother-in-law agreed to enter the viewing room. When he examined Buddy's remains, J.E. vomited. Afterwards, Weir informed Larry: "He was so tore up. I'm glad you didn't have to see him."

Larry and J.E. eventually visited the crash site, where it was snowing, yet again. FAA investigators, Eugene Anderson and Fred Bechetti, were busily examining the wreckage, while a group of spectators watched. A teenager named Gary Edward Keillor was among those gathered in the frozen field—the young man would later become known to the world as humorist and social commentator, Garrison Keillor.

Larry soon noticed a "very colorful" pile of clothes "stacked real high" on the snowy ground. "Do you want these?" someone, who realized that he was Buddy's brother, asked.

"No, I don't want them," Larry instantly replied.

"These are Buddy's clothes. What do you want us to do with them?" the man protested.

"Get rid of them. Burn them. Give them away—whatever. I don't want to see them again!" Larry informed the stranger.

Larry then experienced a momentary change of heart: "Just as I was leaving, I picked up a little old dop (toiletry) kit, because I had seen Buddy carrying it many times, and knew it was his. It had some tooth powder that had come open and everything was white. There was a prescription or two in there for cold medicine, a razor, a comb, stuff like that."

The zip-up side compartment of the small bag, where Buddy kept his revolver and often stored cash, was missing. While the pistol would later be found, no cash was recovered, other than the money was discovered in the victim's pockets.

Afterwards, Larry and J.E. arranged for Buddy's body to be flown to Lubbock. Having completed their dismal duties in Iowa, the pair returned to Texas.

In Moorhead, Minnesota, Waylon Jennings was grief-stricken: "They took the best people out of that tour and took their lives." "I just wanted to go home," Waylon recalled.

Jennings was making plans to return to Texas for Holly's funeral, when the "people from New York called and begged us to go on for a couple of more days." In exchange for their cooperation, GAC made two promises to Waylon and Tommy Allsup—the promoters would pay them the balance of Holly's performance fees (nearly $4,000) and fly them, first-class, to Lubbock for Buddy's funeral. GAC ultimately refused to honor either commitment.

Buddy Holly's death set into motion the career of an aspiring rock and roller. When fifteen-year-old Bobby Velline, who was a sophomore at Central High School in Fargo, came home for lunch on February 3rd, he learned about the fatal plane crash from his brother. After turning on the radio, Velline heard a disc jockey recruiting local talent to perform at the evening concert, to help fill the void created by the deaths of Holly, Valens, and the Big Bopper.

Diminutive, handsome, and charismatic, Velline had recently formed a garage band. When Bobby's friend and bass player, Jim Stillman, called the radio station and offered the services of their fledgling band, he was instructed to have the group arrive at the Armory in Moorhead for a 7:00 p.m. audition.

Velline and his bandmates hurried to J.C. Penney and bought matching shirts and ties to wear as stage clothes. After passing the audition, the group quickly came up with a group name—the Shadows.

"It was a very bizarre evening. There was no merriment at all," Velline recalled. Frankie Sardo briefly acknowledged the early morning tragedy, before singing some of the deceased stars' hits—his own personal tribute. Many audience members were in tears, and both Jennings and Allsup appeared shell-shocked while performing.

When it came time for the Shadows to perform, Velline recalled that his voice, which sounded like Holly's, started out "a bit unsteady." He quickly regained his focus with a silent mantra: "This is for Buddy." Velline proceeded to sing a series of hits by Little Richard, Jerry Lee Lewis, and the Everly Brothers, which seemed to energize the audience.

Bing Bingstrom, a talent agent who had arranged for the local acts to perform on that February night, concluded that Velline had what it took to become a star. After shortening his name to Bobby Vee, the young performer and his band recorded a series of Top 40 hits, including *Devil or Angel*, *Rubber Ball*, and *Take Care of my Baby*. "Our style was modeled after Buddy's approach. I've never forgotten Buddy Holly and his influence of my singing style," Vee recalled, years later.

Allsup and Jennings, absent Buddy, somehow made it through the show in Moorhead. "Me (sic) and Waylon were in a blue haze for four days; we weren't drunk or anything, but we couldn't figure out what had happened…" Tommy sadly recalled. That first night, Jennings assumed responsibility for Holly's lead vocals, in front of 1,700 audience members.

The show originally called for two performances, emceed by *KFGO's* Charlie Boone, but GAC executives canceled the second show, to lessen the emotional strain on the remaining *Winter Dance Party* performers.

That same night, GAC revoked the first of two promises made to Jennings and Allsup. They received none of Holly's performance fees, which embittered Waylon: "This, after begging us to play—real nice people."

Adding to their misery, immediately after the Morehead show, Waylon remembered the promoter threatened not to pay them anything, since Holly, Valens, and the Big Bopper had not fulfilled their contractual obligations. Near his breaking point, Waylon informed the tour manager: "If they don't give us the money, we'll tear that damn place up to where it will cost them more to fix it than to pay us."

Carl Bunch, who was well enough to be discharged from the hospital, re-joined the *Winter Dance Party* the following night at the Shore Acres Ballroom in Sioux Falls, South Dakota. His feet were still hurting, and Bunch could not play for more than five minutes, before turning the drums over to Carlo Mastrangelo.

GAC flew in additional performers for the Sioux Falls' show—Jimmy Clanton, Ronnie Smith, and Frankie Avalon. Clanton had charted five Top 40 hits in the past six months, including *Just a Dream, A Letter to an Angel, Go, Jimmy, Go!,* and *My Own True Love.* Given his established popularity, no one seemed to mind when Clanton played Holly's Fender Stratocaster, which he discovered in the *Winter Dance Party* tour bus. Clanton recalled that the show was "eerie," and the crowd was "very somber."

Frankie Avalon, an 18-year-old with a full head of dark hair and a radiant smile, was an established star in his own right. Over the past two years, he had recorded several pop hits, including *Dede Dinah, Venus, Just Ask Your Heart,* and *Why.*

For many of the performers, the concert in Sioux City proved even more difficult than the previous night. Carl Bunch remembered the Crickets were "too hurt, too sad, and too sick" to deliver a quality show. "It was horrible. We couldn't get through the music. We'd break down crying..." Bunch recalled. Nonetheless, Waylon Jennings' Holly-substituted vocals generated loud applause from the audience; a harbinger for his future success as a country and western star.

The following night, the tour played the Val Air Ballroom in Des Moines, Iowa. Doug McLeod, a teenager who had attended the *Winter Dance Party* in Fort Dodge on January 30th, when Holly was still alive, offered a unique before and after perspective. "It was hard for Buddy's band, trying to perform his songs on their own, without Buddy. I remember Tommy Allsup standing up there, trying to play and sing, with tears rolling down his cheeks."

On February 6th, the eve of Buddy Holly's funeral, the *Winter Dance Party* was in Grand Rapids, Michigan. After the concert at the Danceland Ballroom, GAC broke their second promise to Jennings and Allsup, refusing to fly them to Lubbock for Buddy's funeral. "I couldn't believe people would act so unfeeling. If that was the way things were, I didn't want any part of the business. I thought, I don't ever want to go out in the world, when there's people like that," Waylon recalled.

Interpersonal conflict developed in the wake of Buddy's death. Waylon and Tommy had never been particularly close, and their relationship grew more distant after Holly was killed. Jennings believed that part of the problem was that Allsup had long been jealous of Waylon's friendship with Buddy.

For the remainder of the *Winter Dance Party*, Waylon assumed that he would remain the lead vocalist for the Crickets, just as he had done in Moorhead and Sioux City. Dion DiMucci was among those who supported Jennings: "Waylon should sing." Jennings believed Tommy thought otherwise, and played a role in recruiting Ronnie Smith to fill in for Holly.

After the *Winter Dance Party* tour ended, Waylon claimed that Allsup spiked his beer with two Benzedrine pills. "It was the first pill I ever took," Waylon recalled; he would, however, consume many more, in the years to come. Jennings vividly recalled his first experience with amphetamines: "I was awake all the way from Chicago to New York, my mind racing, thinking all these terrible things. The bed started moving and shaking. I didn't know what was wrong with myself or the world. Everything I had hoped for was gone."

On February 15, 1959, the ill-fated *Winter Dance Party* concluded in Springfield, Illinois. Jennings and Allsup travelled by bus to Chicago, then took a train to New York City. The pair were intent on visiting GAC's headquarters and collecting the extra money promised to them on the day Holly was killed.

Their meeting with Irving Feld was less than satisfactory. "GAC reimbursed me for the train tickets, but that's all they gave us. They said, 'Well, we had to give Buddy a bunch of money before the tour started, and when he got killed, Maria Elena came over and got some money,'" Waylon remembered. Buddy's widow, however, claimed that she did not have any money from GAC to share with Waylon and Tommy.

GAC verified that it had classified Buddy Holly as an employee, so that his widow could receive an insurance pay out. The promotion company also announced that there would be no further dance party tours. GAC spokesman, Allen Bloom, explained the reason for that decision: "The show really didn't do that much business. In fact, it was a financial failure. We lost money." Buddy Holly, Ritchie Valens, and the Big Bopper, as well as their family and friends, lost much, much more.

A disgusted Waylon Jennings returned to Texas. He was certain that higher-ups in the music industry were nothing but "flesh peddlers." It would be several years before he pursued his dreams of becoming a country music star.

Waylon would never forget his mentor, and years later, told biographer, Serge Denisoff, that "he blamed Norman Petty for Buddy's death.

CHAPTER 12

Good-Byes

ON WEDNESDAY MORNING, FEBRUARY 4, 1959, Ritchie Valens' body was transported home by train. After arriving in California, his casket was taken to Noble Chapel Funeral Home in San Fernando.

Two days later, at 10:00 a.m., nearly 1,000 mourners attended his funeral mass at Saint Ferdinand Church. The only unceremonious incident occurred when Valens' one-time girlfriend, Donna Ludwig, the inspiration for his million-selling hit, *Donna*, angrily knocked a camera out of the hands of a news photographer, who had invaded her personal space.

On a rainy day, a copper-colored hearse transported Valens body from the church to its final resting place. America's first Chicano rock and roll star, only 17-years-old, was buried at San Fernando Mission Cemetery.

On February 4th, J.P. "the Big Bopper" Richardson's body was flown to Beaumont, Texas. His wife, Adrianne, who was nearing the third trimester of her pregnancy, accompanied by the couple's daughter, Deborah, had hurriedly returned to Texas from New Orleans, where they had been visiting family.

The Big Bopper's casket was taken to Beaumont's Broussard Funeral Home. Two days later, he was buried at Forest Lawn Memorial Park.

Roger Peterson had two funeral services. The first was held on February 5th at Redeemer Lutheran Church in Ventura, a small community just west of Clear Lake.

A day later, a separate funeral was conducted in Peterson's hometown of Alta, Iowa. Afterwards, he was buried at Buena Vista Cemetery in Storm Lake, Iowa.

On February 4th, Buddy Holly's casket departed the Mason City airport aboard a plane his brother, Larry, had chartered. The aircraft made it only as far as Des Moines, 100 miles to the south, before it was grounded by severe winter weather.

Larry and his brother-in-law returned to Texas on a separate plane, arriving a day ahead of Buddy's remains. "All the way back, I kept praying, but not for myself. I was saying, 'Please, Lord, let Daddy and Mother find the strength to live through this,'" he remembered.

After landing in Lubbock, Larry drove directly to L.O. and Ella's house. "They had Buddy's music playing; they had his pictures out; I couldn't look at them. I couldn't listen to the music. If I heard half of one of his songs, I'd start crying," Larry recalled.

On February 5th, after arriving in Lubbock, Buddy's body was taken to Sanders Funeral home on Main Street. In west Texas, many teenagers wore black armbands to acknowledge their grief.

Maria Elena and her Aunt Provi flew to Lubbock on February 4th. Still recovering from her miscarriage, a pregnancy that she did not disclose to Buddy's family, Maria Elena secluded herself in the Holley's house.

In death, Buddy received more attention from the local media than when he was alive. On February 3rd, the *Lubbock Evening Journal* headlined: *LUBBOCK ROCK 'N' ROLL STAR KILLED*. The accompanying story, however, was less than effusive, reporting that "friends" described Holly as "probably one the biggest entertainment celebrities ever to hail from Lubbock."

The following day, the *Evening Journal* headlined: *SERVICES PENDING FOR BUDDY HOLLY, VICTIM OF IOWA PLANE CRASH/SINGING STAR'S BODY DUE HERE TODAY*. The newspaper article, however, was carelessly written, identifying Holly's past bandmates, Larry Welborn and Bob Montgomery, as "Larry Willburn" and "Bobby Burgess."

Holly's funeral was held on Saturday, February 7th, a day when mid-winter temperatures were surprisingly mild—the upper fifties. Around 1,500 people attended the service at the Tabernacle Baptist Church; the largest crowd to ever congregate at the church.

The regular organist, Betty Lou Drury, who along with the church pianist, Carolyn Crosby, were scheduled to play at the funeral, nervously asked Ella Holley: "There are going to be so many professional performers in the church, don't you think you should ask one of them?"

"No, I don't. We've brought Buddy home now. I think it should be the way it normally is when Buddy and the family came to church," Ella replied.

The pews filled quickly, and some attendees, many of whom had condemned rock and roll as ungodly, stood in the vestibule and parking lot, where loud speakers were installed.

The pallbearers included the original Crickets (Niki Sullivan, J.I. Allison, and Joe B. Mauldin), Sonny Curtis, and Bob Montgomery. Larry Welborn and two members of the background singing group, the Roses (Dave Bingham and Bob Linville), served as honorary pallbearers.

Maria Elena did not attend Buddy's funeral. She later admitted that her absence was attributable to emotional rather than physical causes: "I was in Lubbock, but I could not attend the funeral. I could not handle that. My reasoning was I didn't want to see Buddy dead. I wanted to keep his memory the way I saw him when he left."

Despite the animosity and the threat of law suits, Norman and Vi Petty attended the funeral. Phil Everly flew to Lubbock, and sat with Buddy's parents. Phil, however, refused to serve as a pallbearer—it was too much for him to see his friend "put down in the ground." Don Everly did not attend the services, explaining that Buddy's death "just freaked me out." "I couldn't go to the funeral. I couldn't go anywhere. I just took to my bed," Don later confided.

Buddy's silver-gray casket remained closed, out of respect for his disfiguring injuries. Instead, a framed 12 x 14-inch photograph was placed atop the coffin.

Reverends Ben D. Johnson and Ken Johnson officiated at the funeral. Many of the mourners shed tears, but Buddy's parents managed to maintain their composure throughout the service. Bill Pickering sang *Beyond the Sunset*, a hymn of praise. The Angelic Gospel Singers performed *I'll Be All Right*, one of Buddy's favorite hymns. A telegram of condolence from Elvis Presley and his manager, Colonel Tom Parker, was read aloud.

Niki Sullivan was disappointed by the pastors' eulogies, likening them to traditional Baptist sermons. Rather that celebrating the life of Buddy Holly, the clergymen seemed more intent on saving lost souls.

After the service, the attendees passed by Buddy's casket in a line led by the Holley family. The pallbearers, caught up in the procession, mistakenly left the casket behind in the sanctuary, before returning to escort Holly's body to the waiting hearse. One of the pallbearers, Joe B. Mauldin, partly blamed the closed casket for his inability "to accept the reality" of Buddy's death.

The funeral procession made its way past the landmarks of Holly's all-too-brief life—radio station, *KDAV*, where his first show filled the airways, Tom Lubbock High School, and the Hi-D-Ho drive-in. The line of vehicles eventually turned into the Lubbock City Cemetery, located about a mile from the house where Buddy was born. After Reverend Ben Johnson delivered brief remarks, the casket was lowered into the grave. L.O. and Ella again remained stoic, as they bid a final goodbye to their youngest child.

Before the day was over, Terry Noland, a singer and musician from Lubbock, gave Holly's parents a letter Buddy had recently sent him. In the missive, Buddy invited Noland to move to New York, where Holly would help him make a record. Noland wanted to remind L.O. and Ella of their son's kindness and generosity, regardless of the church's condemnation of rock and roll music.

Noland recognized that Buddy manifest Christian virtues by the way he treated others, and certainly was not a purveyor of "Satan's Music." Even though he was a member of the Tabernacle Baptist Church, Noland considered Ben Johnson to be hypocrite; while the reverend had repeatedly demonized rock and roll, he still accepted Buddy's sizeable monetary contributions to the church.

Buddy was buried approximately 100 yards north of the cemetery entrance, just a few feet from the road. His gravesite is near two of the scarce trees dotting the west Texas landscape. The first tombstone erected by his family, an upright guitar, was stolen. The replacement is a flat stone marker, engraved with a Fender Stratocaster resting against a pillar, flanked on either side by leaves. Another leaf was engraved on the top left corner. Musical notes appear alongside the inscription: *IN LOVING MEMORY OF OUR OWN BUDDY HOLLEY; SEPTEMBER 7, 1936—FEBRUARY 3, 1959.*

In death, Buddy's correct surname, Holley, was literally etched in stone.

CHAPTER 13

The Investigation

ON WEDNESDAY, FEBRUARY 4, 1959, crash investigators gathered up smaller pieces of the plane wreckage, documented the path followed by the aircraft from the point of impact until its final resting place against the barbed wire fence, and took numerous photographs of the crash site. Later that same day, a winch was used to lift the bulk of the wreckage and place it on a flatbed truck, which was transported to a hangar at the Mason City Airport.

Inside the hanger, the wrecked Beechcraft Bonanza was taken apart, piece-by-piece, to determine the cause of the crash. During its investigation, the CAB used an office in the basement of the airport as its base of operations.

The February 3rd addition of Mason City's *Globe-Gazette* quoted Jerry Dwyer, who said that he did not have the "faintest idea" why his charter airplane crashed. Dwyer told reporters that the aircraft was in good condition, which by all indications, was true. However, Dwyer added two questionable assertions—his pilot was competent and weather conditions at the time of the crash were satisfactory. On February 5th, airport manager, Dick Meltler, who had already met with crash investigators, expressed puzzlement during an interview with a *Globe Gazette* reporter: "How in the world did it happen?"

Buddy Holly's older brother, also a pilot, offered his own opinion as to the cause of the crash: "We went out in the snow and saw the plane wreck," Larry recalled. "They had just installed a Sperry gyroscope on that plane, and they work the opposite of other ones. In one, the little airplane goes up and down in the little window, and in the other, the background changes," Larry explained. Holley believed that Roger Peterson had been "reading the instruments backwards;" an opinion that was taken into consideration by accident investigators.

The official report, File # 2-0001, adopted by the Civil Aeronautics Board (the forerunner of today's National Transportation Safety Board) on September 15, 1959, and released eight days later, cited *pilot error* as the cause of the crash. The investigator's findings included: 1. All dashboard instruments had functioned properly; 2. Air speed at the time of crash was 165 to 170-miles-per-hour; 3. The rate of climb indicator read 3,000-feet-per-minute; 4. The attitude indicator revealed that the airplane was at a 90-degree right bank, in the nose-down position; 5. The aircraft's radio was tuned to the Mason City Airport control frequency; 6. The Lear autopilot was inoperable; 7. The tachometer needle was stuck at 2,200-RPM; 8. The fuel pressure, oil temperature, and oil pressure gauges were "stuck in the normal or green range;" 9. There had been no fire; 10. There was "no evidence of inflight structural failure or failure of the controls;" 11. The landing gear was retracted at the time of impact; 12. "Both blades of the propeller were broken at the hub, giving evidence that the engine was producing power when ground impact occurred;" 13. The airplane's omni selector was positioned at 114.9, which was the same frequency as the Mason City airport.

The CAB report noted that Roger Peterson had passed the written portion of his examination for instrument training, but "failed an instrument flight check on March 21, 1958, nine months prior to the accident." The investigators also revealed that, on November 29, 1958, Peterson had been granted a waiver for a hearing deficiency in his right ear.

The investigators further documented that Peterson's instrument training had been with "the conventional-type artificial horizon," and he had not used a "Sperry Attitude Gyro." The report noted that "these two instruments differ greatly in their pictorial display."

Because the Sperry F-3 Attitude Gyro was caged, investigators documented that "it is possible it was never used during the short flight." If the pilot did employ the Sperry gyroscope, the instrument provided an indication of the bank and pitch attitude of the aircraft, but its pictorial presentation was via "a stabilized sphere, whose free-floating movements behind a miniature aircraft presents pitch information with a sensing exactly opposite from that depicted by the conventional artificial horizon."

The CAB report also closely examined the deteriorating weather conditions at the time of the crash: "There is no evidence to indicate that very important flash advisories regarding adverse weather conditions were drawn to the attention of the pilot. On the contrary, there is evidence that the weather briefing consisted solely of the reading of current weather at in route terminals, and terminal forecasts for the destination. Failure of the communicators to draw these advisories to the attention of the pilot, and to emphasize their importance, could readily lead the pilot to underestimate the severity of the weather situation." At the same time, investigators emphatically stated that the pilot "had a definite responsibility to request and obtain all of the available information and to interpret it correctly."

The investigators reported that when Peterson took off from Mason City, "the ceiling and visibility were lowering, light snow had begun to fall, and the surface winds aloft were so high, one could reasonably have expected to encounter adverse weather..."

Given that weather conditions were deteriorating "along the intended route," and "that the company was certified to fly in accordance with visual flight rules only, both day and night, together with the pilot's unproven ability to fly by instrument," the investigators determined that "the decision to go seems imprudent." The report indicated that "shortly after take-off," Peterson "entered an area of complete darkness and one in which there was no definite horizon," and such conditions "required him to rely solely on flight instruments for aircraft attitude and adjustment." In addition, "the high, gusty winds and attendant turbulence" would have made it difficult for "a pilot as inexperienced as Mr. Peterson" to interpret his instruments "so far as attitude control is concerned."

Near the end of the report, investigators summarized the dilemma that Peterson encountered: "At night, with an overcast sky, snow falling, no definite horizon, and a proposed flight over a sparsely settled area with absence of ground lights, a requirement for control of the aircraft solely by reference to flight instruments can be predicted with virtual certainty."

CAB investigators, James R. Durfee, Chan Gurney, Harmar D. Denny, G. Joseph Minetti, and Louis J. Hector, concluded: "The probable cause of this accident was the pilot's unwise decision to embark on a flight which would necessitate flying solely by instruments when he was not properly certified or qualified to do so." The report further noted that "contributing factors were serious deficiencies in the weather briefing, and the pilot's unfamiliarity with the instrument which determines the attitude of the aircraft."

In years since the release of the CAB report, other experts have reviewed the circumstances surrounding the ill-fated flight. Gary Moore, author of *Hey Buddy*, a pilot, and one-time owner of a flight instructor school and charter aviation company, consulted Dick Rodriguez, an experienced accident investigator. Rodriquez noted that when flying a Beechcraft Bonanza, "once upset with little or no visibility and established into a spiral, you have to be an extremely skilled pilot to recover using instruments only." After reviewing the CAB report, Rodriquez made the following observation: "The rate of climb indicator indicates the plane struck the ground while descending at 3,000-feet-per-minute. This is a very high rate of descent. I don't think it was strictly a matter of misreading the instruments, but more likely that the aircraft became upset by its natural tendency to roll into a bank, which can rapidly develop into a graveyard spiral from which Peterson was too inexperienced to recover using only his instruments." "With no visual reference to assist recovery, the natural reaction of most pilots is to pull back on the yoke to remain airborne, but in this case, it only increases the rate of turn and becomes unrecoverable. Had there been a visual horizon, he could have possibly leveled his wings and recovered," Rodriquez concluded.

Pilot and author, Lam Bastion, has studied and written about fatal celebrity air crashes, including those involving Patsy Cline, John Denver, and John F. Kennedy, Jr. In the crash that claimed the lives of Holly, Valens, the Big Bopper, and Roger Peterson, Bastion reached several conclusions about the pilot's unfortunate conundrum: 1. Visual flight rules (VFR), during darkness, requires the pilot seeing the ground lights to maintain the pilot's equilibrium; 2. Roger Peterson could not see ground, and "when the eye cannot identify an outside horizon, and the mind is left alone to interpret what the inner ear is telling it—one can no longer rely on their sense of balance to know whether they are up, down, sideways, or even upside down;" 3. "What Roger Peterson encountered was a very dark sky exacerbated by 'white out' conditions caused by snow. Visibility may have been two miles, but everything outside the airplane looked the same. No horizon was evident once he left the region of the airport;" 4. "Peterson was only in the air for five minutes. He simply could not see a defined horizon, quickly became disoriented…and then lost the battle in watching his instruments without proper practice and experience. His passengers may have initially distracted him, or this may have happened without distraction at all."

In November of 2016, the author asked Phil Gibson (now Director of Aviation/Operations for Dumont Aviation), an experienced commercial pilot and aviation consultant, to offer his opinion as to the cause of the February 1959 tragedy. After studying the CAB report and reviewing the circumstances surrounding the crash, Gibson agreed with the investigators, citing the pilot's "loss of situational awareness," his "very low instrument flying proficiency," the "gauged directional gyro," and the "confusion of the attitude indicator," all of which "probably led to an unusual attitude, that given the weather conditions, was unrecoverable, give his lack of experience." He also noted the fatigue factor, given that Peterson had been without sleep for 17 consecutive hours.

Gibson agreed that Peterson "did not receive an adequate pre-flight briefing" about deteriorating weather conditions, but reiterated that "the pilot in command is ultimately responsible" for becoming "familiar with all available information concerning the flight." "The cold front, high winds, nighttime flying conditions, along with the possibility of snow and freezing rain, would have loaded up those wings very quickly with clear ice. Ice on the wings is a killer with single-engine aircraft," Gibson concluded.

The lack of necessary communication about the two flash weather advisories is troubling. Were Peterson and Dwyer never informed about these bulletins? Or, did one or both learn of the advisories, and choose to disregard or minimize the deteriorating weather conditions? Since Peterson and Dwyer are both deceased, the answer to that question remains unknown.

As is the case with many widely-publicized tragedies, such as the assassinations of John F. Kennedy, Robert F. Kennedy, and Martin Luther King, in addition to the terrorist attacks on September 11, 2001, conspiracy theories abound concerning the plane crash that killed Buddy Holly and the others. Rumors of potential foul play surfaced within weeks of the crash.

Even though CAB investigators collected as much of the wreckage as possible, many smaller objects were obscured by winter precipitation. In the spring of 1959, after the snow had melted, Albert and Delbert Juhl had to pick up yet-to-be-discovered remnants of the crash, before plowing and planting their farmland. The Juhl family threw most of the debris into tubs. "We picked up bushel after bushel of parts of the plane. All summer, people would stop from all over, wanting to know where the plane crashed, and they were happy to take a piece for a souvenir," Elsie Juhl recalled.

On April 7th, the Juhl family gave the Cerro Gordo County Sheriff's Office several personal items found in the crash zone, including eyeglasses, watches, and cigarette lighters. Buddy Holly's white gold Omega wristwatch, adorned with 44 diamonds, was cleaned by a local jeweler.

Still in working order, the timepiece, estimated to be worth $5,000, was returned to Maria Elena on May 9th.

Delbert Juhl uncovered the most controversial item on April 9th; Holly's six-shot, German-made .22 caliber revolver. After the *Globe-Gazette* reported that two chambers of the revolver had been fired, conspiracy theorists concluded that Roger Peterson must have been deliberately or accidently shot while in flight, leading to the crash.

If Buddy Holly or any of the other passengers had shot Roger Peterson, it would have been an unthinkable act of suicide. Furthermore, no evidence suggests that Holly, Valens, or the Big Bopper were suicidal or homicidal on that February night.

Another theory postulates that the Big Bopper and at least one other occupant of the plane survived the initial crash. Afterwards, when the Big Bopper attempted to seek help, he was shot to death by another crash survivor (most conspiracy-seekers posit Buddy Holly as the Bopper's assassin). Forty years later, the Big Bopper's son asked pathologist, Dr. Bill Blass, to exhume his father's body to determine if he survived the crash and/or suffered a gunshot wound. After performing whole-body x-rays on the Big Bopper's well preserved corpse, Blass determined that the decedent had "probably 200 fractures," which made post-impact survival impossible. Further debunking this bizarre conspiracy theory, the pathologist determined that the Big Bopper's body showed no evidence of bullet wounds.

Twenty years after the plane crash, Cerro Gordo County Sheriff, Jerry Allen, clarified the situation concerning Holly's revolver, reporting that "only one shot had been fired by Albert Juhl." The day that he discovered the revolver, a curious Juhl fired it once into the air, to see if the pistol was still operable.

Another theory suggests that Holly and the Big Bopper were trying to exchange seating positions, which distracted or hampered Peterson, causing him to lose control of the airplane. Given the small confines of the cabin and the post-crash positions of the bodies, it appears that all three passengers remained in their original seats, throughout the brief flight.

Because candy bar wrappers were found at the crash site, some conspiracy seekers concluded that the occupants of the plane were taking illicit substances; the candy serving a means of indulging drug-induced sweet cravings. The bodies of Holly, Valens, and the Big Bopper were never subjected to toxicology studies, but none of them were ever known to be drug users. Holly, in fact, rarely drank alcohol near the end of his life, for fear of aggravating his ulcer. Roger Peterson was the only occupant of the airplane to undergo an autopsy, but the pathologists did not conduct the post-mortem examination until the body was embalmed, rendering any toxicology reports useless. Peterson, however, was never known to drink heavily or use drugs. The candy bars were likely nothing more than a quick source of energy for the fatigued and sleep-deprived entertainers.

More than one person (including the late Waylon Jennings) has suggested that Buddy Holly was piloting the plane at the time of the crash. As impulsive and impatient as he was known to be, Holly had not yet earned his pilot's license, having only taken a few flying lessons. When the crash victims were discovered, Roger Peterson was the sole occupant still strapped in his cabin seat. He was the only one with chest puncture wounds from the instrument panel, and had the yoke embedded in his chest. In addition, Peterson's right thumb was partially amputated, likely the result of his crushing grip on the yoke at the time of impact.

One potential theory centers on the combined weight of the occupants. Critics of the CAB report contend that investigators underestimated the weight of the Big Bopper, which would have pushed the aircraft's center of gravity forward, making it more difficult for the pilot to maintain control of plane. While this theory is not entirely without merit, it does not address the more obvious problems—inclement weather, reduced visibility conditions, and the pilot's lack of instrumentation rating.

Some stories about the crash are purely mythical: 1. The crash occurred in the mountains of North Dakota (this blatantly erroneous account was printed in a book); 2. Another report misidentified the victims, and listed the crash site as Ames, Iowa; 3. The plane was consumed by fire, and all the victims were badly burned.

Nearly four decades after the fatal crash, 81-year-old Al Potter, Chairman of the Aurora, Nebraska Airport Authority, claimed that he had radio contact with the pilot of the doomed Beechcraft Bonanza prior to the crash. In an interview with reporter, John Skipper, of Mason City's *Globe-Gazette*, published on February 18, 1998, Potter stated that in early 1959, he was working as "sort of a flying technician" for Dunbar-Kappel, an Illinois-based grain equipment company. In the early morning hours of February 3, 1959, Potter reported that he was piloting an aircraft in route from Chicago to Colorado.

While flying over Mason City, Iowa, during what he believed to be an "ice storm," Potter informed Skipper that he heard "radio traffic from a pilot who said he was in trouble." The pilot of the aircraft purportedly told Potter "he had taken on ice and was losing power." "I was above the ice and I was above him. I tried to offer suggestions on how he could get rid of ice. It seems like we must have talked for 10 or 15 minutes…" Potter explained.

Potter continued his story: "I know at one point he couldn't hear Mason City and Mason City couldn't hear him, so I was trying to give each of them information, because I could hear them both." Unable to assist the pilot "increase his altitude," Potter proceeded with own his flight, and did not learn about the crash that killed Holly and the other rock and rollers, until he reached Colorado. Potter indicated that he never contacted the CAB: "I was just dumbfounded when I heard about the crash. It never occurred to me to contact anyone about it. I guess I was just so shocked."

Potter, whose story does not match the findings of the CAB crash report, informed Skipper: "I've thought about that night so many times. You feel like, if you could have just reached down and pulled him up, he'd have been all right. It's something that just doesn't go away. I'll never forget it as long as I live."

While Potter's account cannot be absolutely dismissed as fiction, there are many holes in his story. His failure to contact the CAB immediately after learning about a high-profile plane crashing, waiting until February of 1998 (nearly 40 years) to make his story public, the absence of collaboration by anyone else listening to the radio frequency (including the controller at the Mason City Airport), the fact that the plane crashed five minutes after take-off (rather than Potter's "10 or 15 minutes"), severely undermine his credibility.

After the crash, the estates of Holly, Valens, and the Big Bopper filed law suits, ranging from $1,000,000 to $1,500,000, against Dwyer Flying Service. In the largest liability cases ever filed in the Cerro Gordo County District Court, the plaintiffs accused the flying service of negligence, for allowing the plane to take off on "a very stormy and snowy evening."

At that point in time, Iowa state law limited liability payments to $50,000 per claim. On September 11, 1959, the cases settled out of court, and Dwyer's insurance company paid a total of $150,000, which was divided among the three plaintiffs.

For a time, Dwyer was vilified by fans of the deceased rock and rollers. He was even targeted by hate mail, including letters containing death threats.

After the crash, Jerry Dwyer was an enigmatic figure. He refuted the CAB report, which cited pilot error as the cause of the crash. In a 1998 interview, Dwyer opined "that my pilot was incapacitated in some way," perhaps suggesting that Peterson had been shot by one of the passengers. In another of his rare interviews, Dwyer was suspiciously vague: "There was more than what appeared on the report, especially about the head area." "I could tell the *National Enquirer* one hell of a story, but it would hurt a lot of people," he told another source.

Through the years, Dwyer consistently refused to grant most reporters, biographers, and researchers interviews, indicating that he planned to write his own book about the crash. Dwyer did speak on occasion with a member of the local press. John Skipper summarized his exchanges with Dwyer: "...Jerry kept it a secret—and enjoyed keeping it a secret. He once told me it was his kids' inheritance. He told me, another time, he was writing a book about the crash and he didn't want to reveal anything that was going to be in the book. He enjoyed being part of the mystery. But, he was also sensitive to the fact he was the last person to see the singers before their death, and it had an impact on him."

While researching his 2011 book, *Hey Buddy*, which focuses on the different ways Holly shaped others' lives, Gary Moore spoke briefly with Jerry Dwyer's wife, Barb, over the telephone. "Why do you want to talk to us?" We have nothing to add," she curtly greeted Moore.

Ms. Dwyer indicated that her husband was writing his own book about the crash: "You know, the truth has never come about that flight. Jerry will tell the truth, because the truth has never been told." However, she refused to share the Dwyer's version of the "truth" with Moore.

"You want to know how Buddy Holly impacted our lives?" she asked.

"Yes," Moore replied.

"Buddy Holly ruined our lives," she replied, before abruptly hanging up.

Over the years, some of Jerry Dwyer's friends and acquaintances reported that he kept the wreckage and showed them the airplane's cockpit instruments. Was Dwyer simply in a state of denial or consumed with guilt? Was he unwilling to acknowledge that the profit he earned from the charter booking, $108, outweighed the hazards associated with a nighttime flight, plagued by hazardous weather conditions? In 1989, a close friend, Bob Booe, opined that Dwyer "simply doesn't want to admit that Roger was at fault."

Bob Hale, the disc jockey who served as emcee at the Surf Ballroom on the night Holly, Valens, and the Big Bopper performed for the final time, was one of Jerry Dwyer's friends. Hale, however, disagreed with Dwyer about the cause of the crash: "Jerry's got this conspiracy theory going. He still believes that there was a fight on the plane, for whatever reason. He says there's more to this; these guys were not getting along." After spending several hours with the entertainers on the last night of their lives, Hale detected no animosity: "These were good friends. The guys were back-slapping buddies. There wasn't a bit of tension, jealousy, or bitchiness about any of these guys."

Jerry Dwyer died in January of 2016, carrying to the grave his version of the so-called truth about the plane crash that killed Buddy Holly, Ritchie Valens, the Big Bopper, and Roger Peterson.

CHAPTER 14

Early Memories of Buddy

Only 22-years-old at the time of his death, it is not surprising that Buddy Holly had not drafted a will. In 1959, by New York state law, the decedent's spouse was entitled to the first $50,000 of the estate; the remainder was to be equally divided with the deceased individual's parents. Maria Elena, however, designated L.O. and Ella as one-half beneficiaries of the entire estate. At first, the only substantial "estate" was the $50,000 settlement from the Dwyer Flying Service's insurance company.

Maria Elena immediately turned her attention toward Norman Petty. Peggy Sue Gerron (her last name was still Allison at that point in time), remembered an angry Maria Elena left Lubbock for New York City on the same day as Buddy's funeral, which she did not attend.

"I am going back to New York. I am going to get the man who killed Buddy…I will show him he can't push me around. He isn't getting by with killing Buddy," Maria Elena bitterly announced. When Peggy Sue asked about the target of her fury, Maria Elena pinpointed Petty, whose finances she promised to have thoroughly audited.

"The only way I got money was when Buddy died, and I used my lawyers," Maria Elena remembered. When confronted with legal action, Petty reportedly paid the Buddy Holly estate *$40,000* to *$70,000*. It will never be known if that was the entire amount due to Holly, or whether Petty had other monies deposited, possibly in secret accounts. More than once, Petty said that he was going to write a book detailing his representation of Buddy and the Crickets, but no such chronicle was published before or after his death (in the 1980s).

Even though he did not live to see it, Buddy was eventually credited as the sole composer of *Peggy Sue*. The change in song-writing credits gave the Holley family a small amount of emotional and financial solace.

Maria Elena gave many of Buddy's personal possessions, including three guitars to his parents. The widow only kept one of her late husband's guitars—a Gibson J-200 model. In the immediate years after Buddy's death, Maria Elena remained close to the Holley family and addressed Ella and L.O. as "Mother and Daddy." In time, the Holley's relationship with Marina Elena grew strained; neither side has been eager to share those reasons (personal, financial, or perhaps both) with outsiders.

Buttressed by their religious faith, within weeks of Buddy's death, L.O. and Ella could talk about their son and play his records, without breaking into tears. For several years, L.O. occasionally rode Buddy's Triumph Ariel motorcycle, before eventually selling it. More than 20 pairs of Buddy's shoes, too big to fit any other males in the Holley family, were given by L.O. to the family's barber, Jake Goss.

On February 14, 1959, just 11 days after the fatal plane crash, Ella Holley wrote condolence letters to the families of Ritchie Valens and the Big Bopper. Unlike Maria Elena, who bore long-standing animosity toward Roger Peterson, Ella sent a missive to the deceased pilot's family: "We are crushed by this terrible tragedy and the loss of our son, and we know you are suffering the same. We have never known before the grief and suffering from the death of a loved one, but we do know now, and our hearts go out to you, because we know what you are going through. We will keep you in our prayers."

For Larry Holley, coming to terms with his brother's death proved extremely difficult. For years, he would not turn on the radio and listen to music. Buddy's toiletry kit, recovered from the wreckage of the plane, remained unopened for decades, stowed beneath Larry's bed.

Prior to February 3, 1959, Decca executives weren't sure if *It Doesn't Matter Anymore* was going to chart. After Buddy Holly was killed, sales of the record soared. Beginning on March 1st, *It Doesn't Matter Anymore* would remain in *Billboard's* Top 100 for 14 weeks, peaking at Number 13. It was Buddy's first Top 40 hit since *Early in the Morning* (which had been released in August of 1958). On April 6, 1959, when the record's flip side, *Raining in My Heart* peaked at Number 88, it marked the *last time* a Buddy Holly single would chart in *Billboard's* Top 100.

As had always been the case, Buddy's music remained quite popular in the United Kingdom. On May 6th, *It Doesn't Matter Anymore* climbed to Number One on England's *New Musical Express* Top 20. This marked the first time in U.K. history that a deceased performer's record topped the charts. The single also climbed to Number One in Australia.

True Love Ways, another of the string session records has long-been a favorite of Holly fans. Had Coral not waited until 1960 to release this single, it may well have charted on *Billboard's* Top 100. In July of 1960, *True Love Ways* did climb to Number 25 in the U.K.

Early on, American rock and roll and pop music listeners were interested in hearing more of Holly's music. On February 20th, just 17 days after his death, Coral released a four-song extended play album, entitled *The Buddy Holly Story*. In March, of that same year, the record company issued an LP bearing the same name. Essentially a greatest hits' album (including *Peggy Sue, Maybe Baby, Rave On, Heartbeat, Oh Boy, It's So Easy, It Doesn't Matter Anymore, Raining in My Heart*), the cover photo on *The Buddy Holly Story* featured one of the publicity photos taken by Bruno, shortly before Holly's death. The album made it to Number 11 on *Billboard's* chart, higher than any LP released during Holly's lifetime. *The Buddy Holly Story* moved in and out of *Billboard's* Top 100 albums until 1966—*seven* years after his death.

Decca producer, Dick Jacobs, was in possession of the songs Buddy had recorded on the Ampex tape machine in his New York apartment. On June 30, 1959, at Coral Records' studio, Jacobs, assisted by another producer, Jack Hansen, overdubbed six of the songs, using studio musicians (pianist, bassist, and percussionist) and background vocalists (the Ray Charles Singers). In the opinion of many listeners, the overdubbing greatly diminished the purity of the apartment tapes.

In July of 1959, Coral Records released *Peggy Sue Got Married*, with *Crying, Waiting, Hoping* on the flip side. While neither single charted in the U.S., in September of that same year, *Peggy Sue Got Married* climbed to Number 13 in the U.K.

A second Coral LP, *The Buddy Holly Story, Volume 2*, was released in April of 1960. Half of the songs on this album, *That's What They Say*, *What to Do, Learning the Game*, and *That Makes It Tough*, were overdubbed apartment tapes. While this album failed to chart in the U.S., it climbed to Number Seven in the U.K.

The British remained devoted to Buddy Holly. *That'll Be the Day*, an LP collection of Buddy's pre-Crickets' songs, recorded in Nashville in 1956, climbed all the way to Number Five. Long after Holly's singles ceased to be popular in the U.S., the records continued to chart in the U.K., including *Reminiscing* (Number 17 in 1962), *Wishing* (Number 10 in 1963), *Bo Diddley* (Number Four in 1963), and *Love's Made a Fool of You* (Number 39 in 1964).

A handful of tribute songs to Holly, Valens, and the Big Bopper were composed in the early years after their deaths. Disc jockey, Tommy Dee, was working at a San Bernardino, California radio station *KFRM*, on February 3, 1959, when he read the wire service report about the fatal plane crash. "I read it on air, and so many people called up—kids calling, girls crying, everyone upset. It made such an impression on me that when I got off the air, I wrote a song about it, as I was driving home in my car," Dee recalled.

Dee subsequently recorded *Three Stars* for Crest Records, backed by Carol Kay and the Teenairs. The single, released on April 5, 1959 proved popular, selling over 1,000,000 copies and earning a gold record.

Dee asked Holly's close friend and rock and roll star, Eddie Cochran, to also record *Three Stars*. When Cochran reached the portion of the song referencing Buddy, his voice began cracking. Cochran hoped to donate royalties from the record to the dead rock and roller's family members, but was stymied by legal difficulties with his record company. Cochran's over of *Three Stars* was not released until 1966—as a single in the U.K., and on an album in the U.S. By then Cochran, himself, was no longer alive.

Cochran never came to terms with Holly's death. He not only remained depressed, but also experienced disturbing premonitions about his own mortality. On April 16, 1960, Easter Sunday, just over 14 months after Buddy's death, 21-year-old Eddie Cochran was killed in a car crash while being driven to London's Heathrow Airport.

Benny Barnes' single, *Gold Records in the Snow*, was dedicated to the memory of Holly, Valens, and the Big Bopper. In 1961, British singer, Mike Berry, recorded *Tribute to Buddy Holly*, which was a hit in the U.K. Waylon Jennings, who gave up his seat on the plane that claimed Holly's life, recorded two songs about his friend and mentor—*The Stage* and *Old Friend*.

If imitation is truly the sincerest form of flattery, Buddy Holly has been well-remembered. Bobby Vee, whose career was launched on the very day that Holly died, recorded an album of Crickets' songs, as well as an LP of songs previously recorded by Buddy Holly, entitled *I Remember Buddy Holly*.

In 1964, a cover of Buddy Holly and the Crickets' *Not Fade Away* was the Rolling Stones' first American single. The Stones' Keith Richards explained Holly's profound influence on British-born rock and rollers: "He passed it on via the Beatles and us." "This is not bad for a guy from Lubbock, right?" Richards rhetorically questioned.

Another Brit, Eric Clapton, is widely regarded as one of the world's most accomplished rock guitarists. Clapton acknowledged that Holly was "a very big early influence, particularly the way he looked..." "I love the look and sound of his Strats," Clapton added.

In 1965, after the lads from Liverpool were internationally-recognized stars, Holly's *Words of Love* appeared on the *Beatles VI* album. Also during the 1960's, Freddie and the Dreamers recorded *It Doesn't Matter Anymore*, Herman's Hermits covered *Heartbeat*, and Peter & Gordon recorded *Tell Me How* and *True Love Ways*, the latter of which was a Top 10 hit and a million-seller.

Between 1964 and 1972, a group in Ireland, the Dixies, covered Holly songs on the A sides of nine singles. In 1984, the 25th anniversary of Holly's death, the same group released a cover of *I'm Gonna Love You Too*. In 1964, that same song was the only American hit for an English group, the Hullabaloos.

Just one day after Buddy Holly's death, Norman Petty went to work protecting his own business interests. In a letter to Dick Jacobs, Petty made two requests: 1. On behalf of J.I. Allison and Joe B. Mauldin, he wanted Jacobs to ask Brunswick Records to write a new contract for "the group known as the Crickets;" 2. The new contract should specify that future royalties be paid directly to the *Norman Petty Agency* in Clovis, New Mexico.

The Crickets, which now consisted of J.I., Joe B., Sonny Curtis, and Earl Sinks, ultimately fired Petty in the spring of 1959, frustrated by his failure to produce records and promote the band. After breaking with Petty, Joe B. received only $10,000 in royalty payments. "I was sure it ought to have been more than that, but my accountant told me, 'Norman's books are in such a mess, you'd better take what you can,'" Joe B. recalled.

The Crickets ultimately signed with Coral, and recorded eight singles, none of which charted. Perhaps the best known of those songs, *I Fought the Law*, written by Sonny Curtis, later became a smash hit for The Bobby Fuller Four. In the fall of 1959, J.I. and Joe B. provided instrumental background for the Everly Brothers Top Five hit, *Til I Kissed You*.

Failing to produce any hit records, the Crickets soon disbanded. From that point forward, various permutations of the Crickets reunited only on special occasions, such as Buddy Holly tribute shows. New entertainers came and went, with J.I. Allison remaining the only permanent member of the mostly inactive band.

Larry Holley offered his opinion as to why the Crickets ultimately failed: "Did they ever come up with good songs after Buddy died? Anyone with any discernment knows who wrote the songs."

The demand for Buddy Holly's records in the U.S. decreased as the 1960s progressed, and alternative styles of rock and roll became more popular. In the U.K., however, record buyers remained hungry for Holly songs. Decca advised the Holley family to obtain as many of Buddy's unreleased recordings as possible, which could be issued in album form.

Norman Petty was still in possession of most of the tapes Decca had requested. Despite Buddy's past personal and legal difficulties with Petty, the Holley family ultimately decided that the familiar was preferable to the unknown. While their decision troubled many of Buddy's peers, the deceased entertainer's family believed Petty was the best person to coordinate record deals with Decca. In 1962, Petty orchestrated an arrangement whereby all future royalties from Holly releases would be split evenly between himself, the Holley family, and Maria Elena. The royalties, however, were paid directly to Petty, until the Buddy Holly catalogue was sold in 1976.

Ella Holley rationalized that Petty would do the best job of recording Buddy's songs, because Norman was most familiar with her son's likes and dislikes. J.I. Allison, in particular, did not approve, but understood the basis for the Holley family's decision: "I think Buddy would have been terrifically unhappy with the fact that his folks went back to Norman. I can understand why they did it; when you're in Lubbock, Texas, you don't have much choice. They didn't have any choice if they wanted to keep Buddy's name alive and keep records coming out for the fans. They couldn't go flying to New York to keep it going. If they had, they would have just gotten mixed up with some straight biz cat, who just wanted to put out more records..."

When it came time to overdub Holly's unreleased master tapes, Petty refused to welcome the Crickets back into the fold. Instead, he used another band, the Fireballs, whose members lived in Texas and New

Mexico (recording in Clovis, the Fireballs would eventually record their own hit records).

Using Holly's master tapes, backed by the Fireballs, Petty produced an LP entitled *Reminiscing*, which was released in early 1963. In March of that year, the album made it into *Billboard's* Top 40. A month later, the LP entered the U.K.'s Top Five, eventually reaching Number Two.

In early 1964, another Holly LP, *Showcase* was released. While the album did not chart in the U.S., it climbed to Number Three in the U.K.

While they were never top-sellers, two other Holly albums hit the market before the decade ended. *Holly in the Hills*, released in early 1965, contained eight of the early "Buddy and Bob" rockabilly tunes. While the LP failed to chart in the U.S., it climbed to Number 13 in the U.K.

Issued in 1969, *Giant* contained the last of Holly's apartment recordings; by that time, multi-track recording had been developed, which improved the clarity of the background instrumentation and vocals. Like its predecessor, *Giant* did not chart in the U.S., but made it into the U.K.'s Top 20.

Early attempts at memorializing Buddy Holly were relatively short-lived. In 1958, John Beecher, who owned a record and book shop in England, founded the *Buddy Holly Appreciation Society*, which had spread to the United States by 1963. The organization grew to 3,000 members before ceasing operations in the U.S. in 1965. Another Englishman, Ray Needham, formed the *Buddy Holly Society*, which eventually folded.

Holly's own mother set out to write a book about her son, tentatively entitled *The True Story*. She eventually abandoned the manuscript, which she found to be "a lot of work," especially for someone who was already "too busy."

Perhaps Buddy Holly's earliest, most notable legacy was his influence on John Lennon and Paul McCartney. Both freely admitted that the first 40 or 50 of their compositions were inspired by Holly.

In 1958, prior to achieving stardom, the Beatles' (who were then known as the Quarrymen) first record featured Lennon singing lead on Holly's *That'll Be the Day*. Another Beatle, George Harrison, learned to play the guitar listening to Buddy's records: "Buddy Holly was my very first favorite and my inspiration to go into the music business. I still think he is among the very best. He was different, exciting, and inimitable."

Despite his influence on a multitude of 1960s-era musical artists, by the end of the decade, memories of Buddy Holly were beginning to wane.

CHAPTER 15

Buddy's Resurrection

ON NOVEMBER 11, 1971, SINGER and song-writer Don McLean's single, *American Pie*, first appeared on *Billboard's* Hot 100, ranked at Number 69. By January 15, 1972, it had climbed to the Number One position, where it remained for four weeks, and eventually became the best-selling record of the year. In the first six months after its release, *American Pie* sold 3,500,000 copies. Eight-minutes and 27-seconds in duration, the hit single filled both sides of a 45-RPM record.

American Pie recalls a February morning in 1959, when 14-year-old McLean was cutting open a stack of newspapers that he was about to deliver. It was at that moment he first learned about the plane crash that killed Buddy Holly, Ritchie Valens, and the Big Bopper. For McLean, whose own father would die a little over a year later, the headline was "like somebody punched me in the face."

Mclean believes the lyrics of the song "spoke to the loss we had." *American Pie* mourns the loss of innocence of the 1950s and the transformation of that generation's rock and roll into the 1960s' genre, which is symbolically deemed as Godless, if not satanic. McClean's timeless classic is a reminder of "the day the music died."

The LP, also entitled *American Pie*, was dedicated to Buddy Holly. "American Pie became a tool to resurrect the memory of Buddy Holly and get it on track. It's growing all the time," McLean asserted in the early 2000s.

With *American Pie's* immense popularity, Americans once again started buying Buddy Holly's records. For many late-born Baby Boomers (like the author) and members of Generation X, it was our first introduction to Holly's music. Don McLean recalled that radio stations would play *American Pie* and *That'll Be the Day*, back-to-back, "bringing Buddy Holly home." In the 1973 movie, *American Graffiti*, one of the characters declares: "I can't stand that surfing shit. Rock and roll's been going downhill ever since Buddy Holly died."

In the summer of 1957, a young New Englander, Bill Griggs paid 90 cents to attend a touring rock and roll show. Buddy Holly and the Crickets were among the performers.

In 1975, Griggs, who would eventually become the acknowledged master historian of all matters related to Buddy Holly, founded the *Buddy Holly Memorial Society*, which remained active until the early 1990s. "Buddy had been gone for 16 years. I was disgusted that I was hearing nothing about him and could not find his records anywhere..." Griggs recalled.

Griggs was so obsessed with Holly, by 1976, he had moved from the Northeast to Lubbock, Texas. For over ten years, he published a magazine, *Reminiscing*, as well as regular newsletters for Holly fans.

After relocating to Lubbock, Griggs became close to Ella Holley: "I called her my surrogate grandmother." "She never really got over the death of her son. She realized that Buddy was not really appreciated in Lubbock, because of the religious foundation of the community. 'Devil's music,' that's what the paper called it; I think she appreciated my admiration and love for her son, and the fact I was working hard to capture and preserve his history and keep his memory alive..."

For several years, coinciding with Buddy's birthday, Griggs organized a week-long celebration of his life and music. The first annual meeting of the *Buddy Holly Memorial Society* was held in 1978, at the Ramada Inn in Wethersfield, Connecticut. Fans from the U.S., Canada, and the U.K., representing a broad spectrum of educational and socioeconomic classes, gathered to remember Buddy's life and music. Some were older, diehard fans, who owned large Holly record collections, while others had never heard of Buddy until *American Pie* was released. "The trip was a pilgrimage; it was the least I could do," an attendee explained.

Griggs remembered the first convention as an eye-opener: "...People learned that James Taylor didn't write *Everyday*, that Linda Ronstadt wasn't the first to sing *It's So Easy*. I think it really surprised a lot of people that *Not Fade Away* was not by the Rolling Stones, and that *Peggy Sue* was not by the Beach Boys. Buddy began making his come back!"

At the inaugural meeting of the *Buddy Holly Memorial Society*, for the first time in nearly 20 years, the original Crickets, J.I., Joe B., and Nikki, played together. They were joined by Sonny Curtis who had filled in as lead guitarist during the band's brief, active existence, after Holly departed. The Crickets played many of the classics, including *That'll Be the Day*, *Oh Boy*, and *Peggy Sue*, as well as Curtis' own composition, *I Fought the Law*.

In the years to follow, other artists played at the annual event. Buddy Knox, Del Shannon, Bobby Vee, and Don McClean were among those who performed at gatherings of the *Buddy Holly Memorial Society*.

Before the *Buddy Holly Memorial Society* ceased operations in 1991, it boasted approximately 5,200 members from all 50 states and 31 countries around the world. Griggs reported that the decision to close the society in 1991 was based on timing: "Mrs. Holley was gone (Ella Holley died in 1990), and I thought it was the right time for me to move on."

Throughout the 1970s, tributes to Buddy Holly continued. In 1971, the Nitty Gritty Dirt Band, who had covered *Rave On*, played a concert in Lubbock. Surprised that most of the young audience members knew nothing about their town's most famous citizen, the band played a medley of Holly's songs.

Bob Dylan, one of history's greatest song writers and a 2016 Nobel Prize-winner for poetry, was a teenager when he saw Holly perform in Minnesota during the ill-fated, 1959 *Winter Dance Party*. In a 1974 interview with *Newsweek* magazine, Dylan discussed his creative influences: "The music of the late fifties and early sixties, when music was at that root level—that, for me, is meaningful music. The singers and musicians I grew up with transcend nostalgia—Buddy Holly and Johnny Cash are just as valid to me today as then."

In 1976, a sultry, 30-year-old pop music singer, Linda Ronstadt, released a stirring remake of Holly's *That'll Be the Day*, which climbed to Number 11 on *Billboard's* chart. The following year, she recorded *It's So Easy*, which made it all the way to Number Three. Ronstadt's twin hits were the first time a Buddy Holly song had charted in the Top Ten since Peter & Gordon released *True Love Ways* in the 1960s. Interestingly, Peter Asher, formerly of Peter & Gordon, produced both of Ronstadt's singles, which spent a combined six months on the popular music chart.

In 1976, Ronstadt's album, *Hasten Down the Wind*, which included *That'll Be the Day*, reached Number Three on *Billboard's* album chart and earned her a Grammy Award for Best Pop Vocal Performance, Female. A year later, another Ronstadt LP, *Simple Dreams*, which included *It's So Easy*, made it all the way to Number One, selling 3,500,000 albums. The sales of those two albums far exceeded those of Buddy Holly's. In addition, Ronstadt's cover of *It Doesn't Matter Anymore*, performed with an acoustic guitar, rather than strings, charted at Number 47 on the *Billboard* chart.

Country singer, Mickey Gilley, also scored big with a Holly song. His 1980 cover of *True Love Ways* climbed to Number One on the country and western chart.

The astounding success of contemporary remakes of Buddy's songs was a mixed blessing for the Holley family. Royalty money soon began flowing into the Holley estate. Ella, who was overwhelmed with taking care of her sick husband, neglected to pay federal income tax on her family's share of the royalty payments. "Mother had got behind seven years without ever filing (federal income tax). Daddy had his stroke, and all she did was tend to him. Daddy didn't know anything…Mother didn't know anything, and they just let it drift on by, and here comes (the) Internal Revenue Service with about half a million dollars that was owed, and there was no way to get it. We didn't want Mother to lose her house and have the fame of all this coming out that she was an income tax evader," Larry Holley recalled.

At this point, Larry stepped in to keep Buddy's estate financially solvent. To generate money to pay back taxes, the American rights to Holly's songs were sold to Paul McCartney's MPL Company, which was the largest independent music publisher in the world. Larry explained what transpired during a 1992 interview: "I don't hold no grudge against Mr. Eastman (McCartney's then manager, lawyer, and father-in-law). (He) seems like a nice man. We did what we had to do. It's been a long, hard, sordid, tough struggle. I'm the guy that had to tend to it all, because I'm Mother's trustee."

On September 7, 1976, which would have been Holly's 40th birthday, Paul McCartney, who had idolized Buddy since he was a teen, initiated *Buddy Holly Week*. The seven-day celebration remained an annual event for several years, at or around the date of Holly's birthday. Activities during *Buddy Holly Week* included concerts by various artists, as well as assorted competitions, such as the most popular tribute song, the best painting of Holly, the best dancers, and rock and roll trivia challenges.

Norman Petty was among those invited to the first celebration. In later years, Larry Holley, J.I. Allison, Joe B. Mauldin, Sonny Curtis, and Larry Welborn participated in *Buddy Holly Week*.

McCartney has remained a dedicated Buddy Holly fan over the years. In 1979, the Crickets performed with McCartney's post-Beatles band, Wings, during a London concert.

In the 1970s, biography and movie proposals about the life of Buddy Holly took root. An *ABC* television movie (in conjunction with *Universal Studios*) was scrapped before production began, because many of the real-life participants in Buddy's life, including members of the Holley family, Norman Petty, J.I. Allison, and Joe B. Mauldin, would not sign releases.

In 1975, a major motion picture, entitled *The Day the Music Died*, produced by *Innovisions*, was authorized by Maria Elena and Buddy's parents. In September of that same year, another movie, *Not Fade Away*, conceived by J.I. Allison along with screenwriter, Tom Drake, began filming. Scheduled to be released by 20th Century Fox, the film focused on a single month in 1957, when Buddy Holly and the Crickets played their first road tour in three black venues, including Harlem's Apollo Theater, and documented how the boys from Lubbock overcame the racial prejudices of that era. The Holley family and Maria Elena, however, refused to allow themselves to be portrayed in the movie, objecting to the vulgar language and narrowly-focused plot. Maria Elena also contended that both she and the Holley family were entitled to receive more money than the production company offered.

In *Not Fade Away*, actor, Steve Davies, was cast as Buddy Holly, while Gary Busey and Bruce Kirby portrayed J.I. and Joe B., respectively. J.I. Allison was cast as the owner of a music store and Bob Montgomery portrayed a tour promoter. After three weeks of filming, when the movie was one-third complete, 20th Century Fox reviewed the filmed scenes, and concluded that the racially-centered plot line was too serious. When director, Jerry Friedman, refused to consider proposed changes, *Fox* pulled the plug on the movie, at a loss of approximately $1,000,000. The official reason for suspending production of the film was "differences in artistic interpretation" between the studio and the movie's director.

By now, *Innovisions* was committed to producing a full-length motion picture, re-titled *The Buddy Holly Story*. On October 28, 1975, *Innovisions* posted an ad in *Variety* magazine, threatening legal action if any other individual or group attempted to portray Buddy Holly on the big screen.

The Buddy Holly Story began filming in November of 1977 and was completed the following January. Gary Busey, who had been cast in the role of J.I. Allison in the aborted *Not Fade Away*, starred as Buddy Holly.

While entertaining, and at times compelling, *The Buddy Holly Story* is littered with inaccuracies. Filmed in the Los Angeles area, the background scenes feature mountains, topographically opposite from the pancake flatness of Lubbock. The shots featuring Clear Lake as a city with skyscrapers is totally incongruent with the backdrop of the small Iowa town. Busey is also shown playing guitars that were not manufactured until after Buddy's death.

When re-creating Holly's last concert at the Surf Ballroom, the movie mistakenly features Buddy's character playing with a symphony orchestra, rather than two guitarists and a drummer. Buddy's parents are falsely represented as non-supportive tyrants, who try to convince their son to abandon rock and roll. Major figures in Holly's life were renamed or totally omitted from the movie, including Norman Petty, J.I. Allison, Joe B. Mauldin, and Niki Sullivan. J.I. and Joe B. were given the fictional names of *Jesse* and *Ray Bob* (the movie totally ignored Niki Sullivan, one of the four original Crickets, as well as Norman Petty).

Gary Busey is not lacking in musical ability, having once played as a rock and roll drummer, under the stage name of Teddy Jack Eddy. A long-time Buddy Holly fan, he put tremendous energy into the performance. Busey was only 12-years-old when Holly was killed, and during the movie production, he felt Buddy's "spirit was with me," and his songs "made me feel good and strong."

Busey's guitar-playing and vocals partially captured Holly's stage presence, but at age 33, he was more than a decade older than Buddy had been during his brief career. Busey also insisted on singing, rather that lip-synching Holly's original recordings. While not a bad singer, Busey is certainly no Buddy Holly.

On May 18, 1978, the world premiere of *The Buddy Holly Story* debuted at the Medallion Theater in Dallas; not surprisingly, the city of Lubbock made no serious efforts to host the first screening. Most of the stars of the movie attended opening night. The original Crickets, J.I., Joe B., and Nikki Sullivan were also present, even though the movie re-named two of them and failed to acknowledge the third.

Despite its many inaccuracies, the movie has its moments. When Gary Busey sang *True Love Ways*, Maria Elena recalled that "she started seeing Buddy on the screen." Moved by the scene, she began crying, left the theater, and sought privacy in the ladies' room.

After the movie's debut, the Crickets agreed to pose for a photograph with Gary Busey, but were far from pleased with film's content. "The movie just really rubbed me the wrong way," J.I. remembered. Allison later told Bill Griggs: "I've got to be irritated when they say, 'Here's a guy named Jesse, and it's not me.'" Both J.I. and Joe B. were angry that Gary Busey had apparently used information gleaned from them while filming the aborted *Not Fade Away*.

Joe B. did not like "the whole movie, period." He pointed out that Buddy never wore white socks and high water pants. Mauldin was particularly incensed about the scene in which he had a confrontation with his fellow Crickets over smoking a cigar: "J.I. and Buddy didn't get into a fight, and J.I. didn't knock out Buddy's teeth, I did."

J.I. complained that the movie made an "asshole" out of him, and was irate when his fictional character uttered blatantly false sexist and racist comments about Maria Elena. Fifteen years after the movie's debut, J.I.'s disgust had not abated, and he proclaimed that *The Buddy Holly Story* "was all bullshit." "Don't base anything on that movie. (There) wasn't anybody involved in it that knew what went on for real...They spelled Buddy's name right was about the only thing they had right," J.I. added. Considering his contentious role in Buddy Holly's life, perhaps Norman Petty should have been grateful that his character was eliminated from the movie. "I felt like a non-entity, like some very important years of my life had just been wiped out," Petty nonetheless complained.

The movie was slated to open in Lubbock two days after the Dallas premiere. In that short interval, Bill Griggs, John Goldrosen (whose biography of Holly was the basis for the movie), and a few others discovered that 1911 6th Street, where Buddy had lived during his formative years, was an empty lot. The Holley's former house, long since vacated, had been condemned and was about to be razed, before it was moved outside the city limits. Griggs and his cohorts formulated plans to purchase the house, refurbish it, and transform it into a museum dedicated to their icon. Ella Holley, perhaps out of modesty or embarrassment, believed the proposal was not "worthwhile," and convinced them to "drop the idea."

The producers of *The Buddy Holly Story* were chagrined to learn that Lubbock did not have a *single* memorial honoring Holly. In rapid fashion, city officials erected a sign on an undeveloped piece of land beside a lake in northern Lubbock, dedicating it as the *Buddy Holly Memorial Park*. During the hastily-arranged dedication ceremony, both the Mayor, Dick West, and Gary Busey delivered laudatory remarks.

The sound track from the movie, featuring Gary Busey's vocals, failed to crack *Billboard's* Top 40 albums' chart, and fared no better in the U.K. However, a newly-released album by the original artists, *Buddy Holly Lives: Buddy Holly & the Crickets 20 Golden Greats*, climbed all the way to Number One in Great Britain, where it remained for three consecutive weeks. On March 25, 1978, author, John Tobler, wrote about the success of the LP: "Nineteen years after his death, Buddy Holly topped the U.K. album charts for the first time. The compilation album, *20 Golden Greats*, finally achieved this fact; the closest he and his backing group, the Crickets, had been was with 1965's *Reminiscing*." The album earned both gold (500,000 copies sold) and platinum (1,000,000 sales) records.

The Buddy Holly Story opened in Lubbock on May 20, 1978, and for the first time, the entire Holley family saw the movie. When Gary Busey sang *Not Fade Away*, Buddy's aging father stood up, pointed to the screen, and announced to the crowd that the actor was portraying *his* son.

Ever gracious, Ella Holley initially praised the movie as "just great," and proclaimed that Busey had captured her son's "mannerisms" and "attitudes." She only hoped that Buddy's fans in England were not "upset" that the movie failed to document his tour abroad in 1958. Ella later admitted that she saw the film on four separate occasions. Larry Holley, who had reservations about the use of profanity in the movie, stated that he was "real pleased" with the outcome, and Busey "showed Buddy as the go-getter that he was."

Nationwide, *The Buddy Holly Story* was well received. Having cost $2,000,000 to $3,000,000 to film, the movie grossed $26,000,000 at box offices. It was among *Variety's* list of Top 50 money-making movies for five weeks, and climbed as high as Number 10. Gary Busey was nominated by the Academy of Motion Picture Arts and Sciences for an Oscar as 1978's Best Actor. Even though Busey lost out to Jon Voight, who starred in *Coming Home*, *The Buddy Holly Story* won an Oscar for Original Song Score and Its Adaptation or Adaptation Score.

With the passage of time, most of Buddy's family, closest friends, and ardent fans grew increasingly disenchanted with the movie. "We were disappointed that they didn't have more about the Holley family and Buddy's life in and around Lubbock. We felt like we played a big part in his career, but there isn't very much about that in the film," Ella reported.

Larry Holley also voiced his displeasure: "It didn't even seem like Buddy at all in the movie. They didn't ask us anything about Buddy. The only one they asked anybody about was Maria, and she just knew Buddy for five months before he was killed."

Sonny Curtis, lodging his own protest, composed a song, *The Real Buddy Holly Story*. "When I left the movie theater, I thought, 'What a crock.' I thought Gary Busey did a great Chuck Berry, but he missed Buddy Holly all around," Curtis groused.

Even Norman Petty, whose relationship had soured with Buddy near the end of the entertainer's life, criticized the movie. He believed that Holly was portrayed as a "tyrant" and his parents were inaccurately depicted as opposing Buddy's musical career.

John Goldrosen, whose biography of Buddy Holly had been adapted by Robert Gittler for the movie, successfully sued to keep the screenplay from being released as a book. "It really would have bothered me to see that version set down in a book. I really felt like if I let that book go forward, I was contributing to some untruths."

Iowa's *PBS* television network developed its own documentary about Buddy Holly, entitled *Reminiscing*, which was first shown in September of 1979. The one-hour program, which included interviews with the Crickets, was eventually shown nationwide. "For six years, this was the best documentary done about Buddy Holly," Bill Griggs opined.

Paul McCartney was also dissatisfied with the Holly movie, and in conjunction with the *BBC* and *MCA*, developed a 90-minute documentary, entitled *The Real Buddy Holly Story*. It was first aired by *BBC* on the *Arena Show* on September 9, 1985; *Sony* released the videotape in the United States in 1987. *The Real Buddy Holly Story* opens with Sonny Curtis playing and singing his song of the same name. Rather than fictionalized characters, the documentary includes interviews with J.I. Allison, Joe B. Mauldin, Tommy Allsup, Larry and Travis Holley, and Vi Petty, among others. Most Holly fans agree that McCartney's documentary was a much-needed corrective to the big screen movie.

Ella and L.O. Holley sued the producers of *The Buddy Holly Story* in October of 1979. The $300,000 law suit alleged that the movie represented an inaccurate portrayal of their son's life. The case eventually settled out of court for an undisclosed amount.

Rolling Stone magazine joined the bandwagon, questioning the accuracy of the movie. In its September 21, 1978 edition, the magazine featured twin articles—"The Gary Busey Story" and "The Buddy Holly Story." Author, Chet Flippo, wrote: "The movie does not seem (to be) about the real Buddy Holly." Even the film's director, Freddy Bauer, admitted that he was more interested in a "bigger than life" rather than a "true to life" movie.

In 1979, after *The Buddy Holly Story* had focused attention on Lubbock, city officials decided to erect a statue in honor of their hometown rock and roll star. To help raise money for the statue, Waylon Jennings hosted a benefit concert in Lubbock. At that time, Buddy's protégé and former bass player was one of the biggest acts in country music; between 1974 and 1979, alone, Jennings had scored 12 Number One hits. Waylon was so appreciative of Holly's influence on his life, that he named one of his sons Buddy Dean Jennings (his middle name honoring the late actor, James Dean). Former Crickets, J.I. Allison, Joe B. Mauldin, Niki Sullivan, and Sonny Curtis performed on stage with Jennings.

One of Holly's contemporaries, Roy Orbison, rarely played rock and roll revival shows. To help raise funds for Buddy's statue, he made an exception, and along with Bo Diddley, performed at a *Legends of Rock 'n' Roll Show* in Lubbock

On September 5, 1980, a bronze statue of Buddy Holly was unveiled in front of the Lubbock Memorial Civic Center. Sculpted by San Angelo, Texas artist, Grant Speed, using Travis Holley as his living model, the statue stands eight-feet, six-inches- tall. Adjacent to the statue, which was first of its kind to honor a rock and roll star, is the *West Texas Walk of Fame*, with markers honoring singers, song-writers, musicians, and disc jockeys from that area.

The Mayor of Lubbock, Bill McAllister, presided over the unveiling of the statue. The Holley family and members of the *Buddy Holly Memorial Society* were among those in attendance. Bill Griggs, founder of the society, vividly recalled the ceremony: "As all the eyes were on the statue as they pulled the cover off, I was watching Mrs. (Ella) Holley. The smile on her face made all the time and effort in preserving history worth it. Buddy's mom's joy is what kept me going."

On February 3, 1979, exactly 20 years after their deaths, the Surf Ballroom in Clear Lake, Iowa held the first memorial dance honoring Buddy Holly, Ritchie Valens, and the Big Bopper. Approximately 1,700 fans from 35 states paid $17.50 to attend the six-and-one-half-hour-concert, where they were entertained by Del Shannon, the Drifters, and Jimmy Clanton. The concert attendees included one-time Cricket, Niki Sullivan, accompanied by his twin seven-year-old sons.

Even though it was minus-24-degrees during the inaugural event, the memorial celebration was successful enough to warrant continued annual Winter Dance festivals during the first week of February. Future entertainers included Buddy Knox, Don McLean, Bo Diddley, Bobby

Vee, Frankie Avalon, Jerry Lee Lewis, Graham Nash, Peter & Gordon, Wanda Jackson, Ricky Nelson, Carl Perkins, and the Crickets.

Veteran reporter and columnist for Mason City's *Globe-Gazette*, John Skipper, has attended several Winter Dance festivals at the Surf Ballroom. "The events always draw big name entertainment. One of the most interesting aspects is the number of people who come from England every year," Skipper informed the author in February of 2017.

In 1979, Holly fans in Great Britain were rewarded with a new collection of Buddy's songs. A box set, entitled *The Complete Buddy Holly*, included six LP records. Two years later, *MCA* issued the same collection in the United States. The box set also included Buddy's apartment recordings. David McGee, a critic for *Rolling Stone* magazine, wrote that *The Complete Buddy Holly* was symbolic of Holly being "one of the most original musicians this country has ever produced."

On May 31, 1981, the *Los Angeles Times* published the results of a survey involving California teenagers, who were asked to select their favorite singers from the 1950s and 1960s. After being blind-folded, the subjects listened to anonymous records. When the teenagers' selections were tabulated, Buddy Holly finished first, followed, in order, by Elvis Presley, the Rolling Stones, the Doors, Gary U.S. Bonds, Jimi Hendrix, the Drifters, Bob Dylan, Creedence Clearwater Revival, and Ike and Tina Turner. "I only wish Buddy Holly didn't die," a 14-year-old participant proclaimed.

In 1986, the Rock 'n' Roll Hall of Fame opened in Cleveland, Ohio. Buddy Holly was one of the original inductees, along with Elvis Presley, Fats Domino, Jerry Lee Lewis, James Brown, Little Richard, Sam Cooke, Chuck Berry, Ray Charles, and the Everly Brothers.

In June of 1988, a proposal was made to erect a six-feet-high granite monument in front of the Surf Ballroom to honor Holly, Valens, and the Big Bopper. The parents of Roger Peterson immediately expressed their displeasure, believing the deceased pilot should be memorialized alongside the three rock and rollers. Holly's widow, Marina Elena, who was then 55-years-old, objected; nearly three decades later, she still blamed Peterson for choosing to take off during hazardous weather conditions. Ritchie Valens' sister, Connie Alvarez, sided with Mr. and Mrs. Peterson, telling an *AP* reporter that she considered Marina Elena's position to be "selfish and unforgiving." When the marker was ultimately erected, Peterson's name was included.

The unveiling of the marker was Maria Elena's first trip to Clear Lake; she had previously vowed to never visit the venue where her late husband played his last show. When 600 people gathered for the ceremony, Maria Elena's tone softened: "Now that I am here, I am seeing just how much the people here loved Buddy and the others and how they are so sad that this was the last place he ever played."

Jay P. Richardson, born less than 90 days after his father, the Big Bopper, was killed, was present for the dedication of the marker. While he was in Clear Lake, Richardson was given his father's self-winding wristwatch, which had been discovered, still in working order, in an evidence room at the Cerro Gordo County Sheriff's Department. Ritchie Valens' half-brother, Bob Morales, represented the third rock and roller's family at the ceremony.

The marker bears the names of all the individuals who were killed in the tragic plane crash. Beneath the heading, *IN THE MEMORY OF ROCK 'N' ROLL LEGENDS*, the inscription reads: *THE ABOVE LEGENDS PLAYED THEIR LAST CONCERT AT THE SURF BALLROOM, CLEAR LAKE IOWA, ON FEBRUARY 2, 1959. THEIR EARTHLY LIFE TRAGICALLY ENDED IN A PLANE CRASH 5.2 MILES NORTHWEST OF THE MASON CITY AIRPORT, FEBRUARY 3, 1959. THEIR MUSIC LIVES ON.*

In 1986, director, producer, and screen writer, Francis Ford Coppola, debuted his latest film, *Peggy Sue Got Married*, in movie theaters. The film included Holly's un-dubbed apartment recording of the title song.

La Bamba, a big screen movie about the life of Ritchie Valens, featuring Lou Diamond Phillips in the lead role, was released in 1987. In a brief scene, which depicted the rock and rollers boarding the Beechcraft Bonanza at the Mason City Airport, actor, singer, and songwriter, Marshall Crenshaw, portrayed Buddy Holly.

In 1980, the first musical about Buddy Holly, *The Adventures of Buddy Holly*, opened in Dallas, but was short-lived. A far more successful musical, entitled *Buddy*, written by Alan Janes, opened in London in 1989. Paul Hipp, a native of Philadelphia, depicted Buddy Holly, much to the acclaim of audience members. Hipp was delighted to be the star of the show: "I was 24 and I'd been playing rockabilly since I was 12, and I'd always liked Buddy Holly..." The *Sunday Times* entertainment critic wrote that the musical was "an unashamed, rabble rousing fiesta." The *London Telegraph Mirror* lauded "the big cast, big sound, and big entertainment." When Great Britain's Prime Minister, John Major, was asked by a *London Daily Mail* reporter to pick a single record he would choose to listen to, if stranded on a desert island, he selected *Peggy Sue*.

When *Buddy* opened at the Shubert Theater in New York City on November 14, 1990, Paul Hipp mesmerized the audience with his portrayal of Holly. The American debut of the musical coincided with Paul McCartney's *Buddy Holly Week*, also being held in the Big Apple. McCartney hosted a party at Greenwich Village's Lone Star Café, where more than 100 guests were treated to a surprise performance by Hipp and the original Crickets.

The first half of the musical portrays Holly's life, while the remainder re-enacts his last performance at the Surf Ballroom. *Buddy* concludes with *Rave On* abruptly ending in mid-verse, with a spotlight focusing on a chair containing only an acoustic guitar; the instrument's leather strap is embroidered *Buddy Holly*. An entertainment critic for the *New York Post* wrote that "*Buddy* has them dancing in the aisles," before adding, "the audience is elevated to joyful chaos."

From November 1990 through May of 1991, *Buddy* was performed 225 times on Broadway. Hipp was nominated not only for a Tony Award, but also for the Laurence Olivier Award for Outstanding Performance of the Year by an Actor in a Musical.

Beginning in 1991, *Buddy* toured the United States, with different actors, including Joe Warren Davis, Christopher Eudy, and John Mueller, portraying Holly. In 1993, the musical made a tour stop at the Surf Ballroom in Clear Lake, Iowa. On another occasion, *Buddy* was performed in Lubbock, Texas, where members of the Holley family were in attendance. Ultimately, five separate productions of *Buddy* entertained audiences in different countries throughout the world.

Many of Buddy Holly's personal possessions were eventually put up for sale. After keeping Buddy's Triumph Ariel Cyclone for 10 years (Buddy's father occasionally rode motorcycle), the family sold it. In 1979, J.I. Allison, Joe B. Mauldin, and Sonny Curtis purchased the motorcycle, which had low mileage and the original paint job, from its third owner, and gave the two-wheeler to Waylon Jennings as a birthday present. In November of 1988, Paul Kennerly, the husband of singer, Emmy Lou Harris, purchased Holly's Magnatone Custom 280 amplifier.

In the early 1990s, the Holley family decided to sell other memorabilia, which had been held in storage since Buddy's death. Larry Holley recalled that the surviving family members decided to "take everything we've got, inventory it, put it in a pile, and sell it at auction and split the money."

On Saturday, June 22, 1991, Sotheby's, located in Manhattan, held an auction of rock and roll "collectibles." In addition to Holly memorabilia, other sale items included John Lennon's personally autographed acoustic guitar and a cape worn by Elvis Presley.

A Lubbock man purchased the Fender Stratocaster Buddy had played during the *Winter Dance Party* for $110,000. Gary Busey, who portrayed Holly on the big screen, participated in the auction by telephone, and ultimately outbid that same Lubbock resident for Buddy's Gibson J-45 acoustic guitar, paying $242,000. The Lubbock bidder did, however, purchase other items, including articles of Holly's clothing and a notebook, where Buddy had written the initials of *Peggy Sue* and a proposed name for his band (the Scoundrels), ultimately spending $182,000.

Other auction items included: 1. One lot of clothing, including a gray wool stage jacket and French cuff shirt ($5,225); 2. A two-page letter in Buddy's handwriting, dated December 14, 1958 ($4,950); 3. Buddy's birth certificate ($1,100); 4. Buddy's high school diploma ($3,300); 5. Buddy's harmonica, originally purchased in 1956 ($3,850); 6. Buddy's high school class ring ($2,420); 7. A pair of Buddy's eyeglasses (purchased by the Hard Rock Café for $45,100); 8. Buddy's Ampex reel-to-reel tape machine (purchased by Patrick Dinizio, a member of the band, the Smithereens, for $14,300); 9. Buddy's record player and record collection ($5,225). At day's end, the auction of Holly's possessions netted $703,615—double what Sotheby's had predicted.

Beginning in the late 1970's Bill Griggs petitioned the U.S. Postal Service to issue a stamp honoring Buddy Holly. It was not until 1992, when Texas Congressman, Larry Combest, joined the battle that the federal agency agreed to Griggs' proposal. In 1993, both Buddy Holly and Ritchie Valens were among the first rock and rollers depicted in the Legends of American Music stamp series.

On June 16th of that year, Maria Elena and members of the Holley family were introduced to nearly 1,000 Lubbock citizens, who had gathered to purchase stamps. For the first time, Maria Elena, the Holley family, and many of Buddy's closest friends felt like the residents of Lubbock truly appreciated Holly's accomplishments. Travis Holley, "astonished" that Lubbock was taking notice of his younger brother, over 34 years after his untimely death, informed the entertainment editor of the *Avalanche-Journal* that Buddy would be "proud if he were with us today." Larry Holley informed the newspaper that his family had previously "given up on the city doing anything."

J.I. Allison was also surprised that his hometown was "treating us so well." "I guess we've come a-ways from 1956," he surmised.

The postage stamp depicted a smiling Buddy Holly playing his guitar. Maria Elena received the first stamp, personally canceled by Lubbock's Postmaster, John Frisby. After the ceremony concluded, citizens lined up to purchase stamps from a trailer, parked near Holly's statue, which served as a mobile post office. Eventually, 24,571 Buddy Holly stamps were purchased in Lubbock, nearly 10,000 more than those featuring the image of Elvis Presley.

In September of 1994, coinciding with what would have been Buddy Holly's 58th birthday, an American rock and roll band, Weezer, released the single, *Buddy Holly*, from its first album, entitled *Weezer* (also known as *The Blue Album*). The song, written by lead guitarist and lead vocalist, Rivers Cuomo, not only references Holly, but also includes the name of the late actress, Mary Tyler Moore.

Buddy Holly climbed to Number Two on the *Modern Rock Tracks* and charted at Number 34 on the *Mainstream Rock Tracks* chart. The single also reached Number 12 in the U.K.

In 2006, Weezer's *Buddy Holly* was certified as a gold record. In 2010, *Rolling Stone* ranked *Buddy Holly* as Number 499 in the magazine's compilation of the *500 Greatest Songs* of all time. Three years earlier, the television music video channel, *VH1*, ranked the Weezer single as Number 59 among the *100 Greatest Songs of the 90s*.

In the early 1990s, the Lubbock land developer who had purchased Buddy's Fender Stratocaster and other memorabilia during the Sotheby's auction, offered the Holley family $1,000,000 for the right to use Buddy's name on a chain of hotels that he planned to build around the world. The family declined the proposal, fearing potential distasteful commercialization of Holly's name. A second offer, involving construction of a hotel, museum, recreational park, and souvenir shop, failed to materialize; in part, due to financial disagreements among various venue managers.

In July of 1994, the Lubbock City Council voted to purchase the Lubbock land developer's 156-piece collection of Buddy Holly memorabilia. In October of that same year, by a margin of only 600 votes, Lubbock residents voted against a tax increase referendum, which would have funded construction of an arena adjacent to the existing Civic Center, where the Holly collection would be displayed.

Consequently, on September 7, 1995, coinciding with what would have been Holly's 59th birthday, the items were put on public display at the Museum of Texas Tech University. The collection would remain housed there, until future construction of the *Buddy Holly Center*. A year later, Lubbock further recognized its most famous native son, renaming a portion of Avenue H as *Buddy Holly Avenue.*

In 1997, the city of Lubbock purchased the one-time Fort Worth and Denver South Plains railway depot. Designed by Forth Worth architect, Wyatt C. Hedrick, the structure's design is Spanish Renaissance Revival, with a clay tile roof, limestone walls, and a brick-paved platform. Beginning in the early 1950s, after the railroad stopped using the depot, the structure functioned, at various times, as a warehouse, salvage yard, and restaurant. In 1979, the former depot became the first building designated as a historical landmark by the Lubbock City Council. Eleven years later, the structure was listed on the National Register of Historic Places.

On September 3, 1999, the *Buddy Holly Center* was opened in the former depot, located at 1801 Crickets Avenue (the street address is yet another fitting tribute). The center's goals are clearly demarcated: "The *Buddy Holly Center*, a historical site, has dual missions; preserving, collecting, and promoting the legacy of Buddy Holly and the music of Lubbock and west Texas, as well as providing exhibits on contemporary visual arts and music, for the purpose of educating and entertaining the public. The vision of the *Buddy Holly Center* is to discover art through music by celebrating legacy, culture, and community."

A large pair of glasses was erected near the main entrance of the *Buddy Holly Center* in 2002. The converted depot's featured gallery is shaped like a guitar and dedicated to the life of Buddy Holly. The building also contains three other galleries for contemporary visual arts, as well as office space, a gift shop, and a small theater (where visitors can watch a video on Buddy's life).

In the spring of 2017, assistant manager and curator, Jacqueline Bober, informed the author than 35,000 to 40,000 people visit the *Buddy Holly Center* each year. In Bober's opinion, interest in Holly's life and music have grown with the passage of time.

A partial listing of the exhibits from Holly's life, include items from his childhood—Buddy's Cub Scout uniform, marbles, crayons, personal drawings, and a wooden sling shot. Possessions from Holly's later childhood and adolescence are also on display, to include report cards, homework assignments, his *Speak and Write Correctly* workbook, a pair of white, high-top Converse tennis shoes, a baseball mitt, hand-crafted leather items, a leather-working kit, and clay-crafted objects, and his Lubbock High School class ring and diploma. Buddy's bedroom furniture from his parent's house is also on display.

Moving forward into Buddy's adult life, the exhibit features an Ampex tape recorder from *Norman Petty Studios,* the console used at radio station KDAV, an RCA 77DX microphone, single and LP records, photographs of Holly and the Crickets, a small notebook with his hand-written song lyrics, personal clothing items, Buddy's own collection of 45-RPM records, business cards, fan letters, tour itineraries, and Holly's 1958 Triumph Ariel Cyclone motorcyle (the latter of which is on long-term loan from its current owner, George McMahan).

The black, horn-rimmed eyeglasses that Holly was wearing at the time of the fatal plane crash are enclosed in an individual glass case. The glasses, which were found in an evidence room at the Cerro Gordo County Sheriff's Office in 1980, lack the missing lens, but the cracked frame has been repaired.

The gallery includes several of Buddy's guitars—a 1953 Les Paul Gold Top (his first electric guitar, purchased in 1954), the Fender Stratocaster Holly played during the *Winter Dance Party,* a Huffner "President" acoustic guitar purchased in the U.K. (and later given by Buddy to British comedian, Des O'Connor), and the Gibson J-200 acoustic guitar he played when recording his late-in-life apartment tapes.

The *Buddy and Maria Elena Plaza* is located just west of the *Buddy Holly Center,* on the corner of Crickets Avenue and 19th Street. The plaza features the Grant Speed sculpture of Holly and the *West Texas Walk of Fame*, with plaques honoring singers, songwriters, musicians, and disc jockeys from that area, including J.I. Allison, Joe B. Mauldin, Niki Sullivan, Bob Montgomery, the Fireballs, Roy Orbison, Waylon Jennings, Sonny Curtis, Snuff Garrett, Mac Davis, Joe Ely, Mac Davis, and Natalie Means.

The *J.I. Allison House* was added to the grounds of the *Buddy Holly Center* in 2013. The small, two-bedroom, ranch-style house, was restored to appear as it did during Allison's teenage years. Opened to the public on September 7th of that same year, the house tour allows visitors to see the bedroom where Buddy and J.I. composed songs, including the Crickets first hit, *That'll Be the Day*.

"The Day the Music Died," is commemorated each year on February 3rd. "Buddy's Birthday Bash," is celebrated annually on September 7th. Admission to the *Buddy Holly Center* is free to the public on both those dates. In October of 2014, Paul McCartney not only performed a concert adjacent to the *Buddy Holly Center* and the *Buddy and Maria Elena Holly Plaza*, but he also discussed Holly's influence on his musical career.

Five miles north of Clear Lake, Iowa, the site of the plane crash that claimed the lives of Buddy Holly, Ritchie Valens, the Big Bopper, and Roger Peterson is clearly demarcated by a stainless-steel marker, constructed by Porterfield, Wisconsin shipyard builder, Ken Paquette. Standing in the farm field, adjacent to the barb-wired fence where the Beechcraft Bonanza came to rest, the memorial features three 45-RPM records (one for each of the performers), a guitar bearing the names of Holly, Valens, and the Big Bopper, and the date *2-3-59*. A separate stainless-steel marker, shaped in the form of aviator's wings, bears the name of Roger Peterson, a Christian cross, and the date *FEB 3 1959*.

Jeff Nicholas, a native of Clear Lake and President of the Surf Ballroom, owns the farm where the plane crashed. Nicholas, who justifiably prefers the term *memorial site* rather than crash site, noted that hundreds of people visit the marker in his field each year. The day the author visited the crash memorial, April 1, 2017, 10 other people were making the same one-quarter-mile long pilgrimage from the gravel road, alongside the barbed-wire fence.

John Mueller's *Winter Dance Party* continues to perpetuate the memory of Buddy Holly's music. Mueller, a native of Wichita, Kansas, was among the actors/singers who portrayed Holly in the musical, *Buddy*. Beginning in 1999, Mueller organized the *Winter Dance Party* show, which remains widely popular, nearly two decades later.

Mueller, along with Ray Anthony (who portrays Ritchie Valens) and Linwood Sasser (who stars as the Big Bopper), tour the United States and Canada along with a four-piece band; guitar, stand-up bass, drums, and saxophone. Mueller has also played with symphony orchestras, performing the famed string session songs, including *It Doesn't Matter Anymore* and *True Love Ways*.

Prior to his death from heart disease in 2013, at the age of 54, Jay P. Richardson, the Big Bopper's son, portrayed his father during *Winter Dance Party* performances.

The *Winter Dance Party* is the only show endorsed by the estates of Holly, Valens, and the Big Bopper. Mueller's voice, skilled guitar-playing, stage mannerisms, and resemblance to Holly are not only uncanny, but also an entertaining and emotional tribute to the rock and roll icon. Anthony and Sasser are also talented performers, bringing Ritchie Valens and the Big Bopper back to life for concert attendees. At various tour stops, Mueller has invited Holly's past bandmates, including Niki Sullivan, Tommy Allsup, and Carl Bunch to join him on stage.

Mueller's moving, self-composed tribute, *Hey Buddy*, incorporates the titles of 32 songs recorded by Holly. "I don't need to be Buddy. I'm doing this out of love and respect for the artist I admire and have grown to know so well," Mueller explained.

Mueller has also recorded CDs of his own music, while managing to keep up the hectic pace of the *Winter Dance Party* tour. Mueller is engaging, down-to-earth, and possesses a lively sense of humor. In an interview with the author in February of 2017, Mueller indicated that he has maintained a good relationship with Maria Elena and other members of the Holley family over the years.

In like fashion, Ray Anthony has kept in touch with Ritchie Valens' family, while assuming the role of the talented star, whose life was cut short at only age 17: "I love what I do for a living, and portraying Ritchie is a privilege…"

Jay P. Richardson, who was born shortly after his father's death, proudly and joyously brought the Big Bopper back to life, prior to his own passing. Jay spent many hours educating himself about his father, searching out and quizzing people who knew and loved the Big Bopper.

Ironically, John Mueller has played before combined audiences that are much larger than Buddy Holly saw during his 18-month public career. Mueller is most appreciative of the opportunity to perpetuate musical history: "He (Buddy Holly) deserved to know how much of an impact he made."

Other reminders of Buddy Holly's life are permanent fixtures in American culture. On September 7, 2011, a sweltering California day, coinciding with what would have been Holly's 75th birthday, Buddy was inducted into the Hollywood Walk of Stars on Vine Street. Maria Elena, Phil Everly, and the Mayor of Hollywood were among those present for the ceremony.

Some (including the author) believe that the Lubbock rock and roller would be most appreciative of the *Buddy Holly Educational Foundation*, whose stated goal is "extending musical education, including song-writing, production, arranging, orchestration, and performance, to new generations, regardless of income or ethnicity or learning levels." Maria Elena serves as one of the foundations' board members.

The *Buddy Holly Educational Foundation* was founded by Peter Bradley in 2010. He serves as Chairman of the Board of Directors, while his wife, Janet, is the CFO and Treasurer. Peter and Janet regard themselves as "entrepreneurs, philanthropists, but most importantly, Buddy Holly fans to the core!"

The five principles of the *Buddy Holly Educational Foundation* are L.E.A.R.N.: 1. Legacy—promote Holly's music for the generations; 2. Education—Raise funds to promote musical education in youth; 3. Ambassadors—Honor internationally renowned artists from all musical genres, and loaning each of the performers a replica of Buddy's Gibson J-45 acoustic guitar; 4. Recording Studio—To build, in Texas, a teaching studio for students; 5. Next Generation—Honor Holly's legacy and help the next generation to fulfill the "dreams and wishes" of Buddy and Maria Elena Holly.

The title of a posthumous album succinctly describes the iconic performer's enduring legacy: *Buddy Holly Lives.*

CHAPTER 16

People, Places, and Things

BUDDY AND MARIA ELENA HOLLY had been married less than six months at the time of his death. Early on, Maria Elena deliberately avoided any reminders of her deceased husband.

Larry Holley, however, remembered that her attitude markedly changed, once she discovered that there was money to be made from the Holly name. In 1987, Maria Elena testified in front of the Texas State Legislature promoting a bill that would prohibit the unauthorized use of a "personality's" name or image for 50 years after his or her death. The proposed legislation was ultimately passed.

The relationship between Maria Elena and the Holley family has been contentious at times. The Holley's reportedly spent $75,000 in legal fees, before reaching an agreement with Maria Elena on distribution of monies related to the name and likenesses of Buddy Holly. Marina Elena has retained exclusive owner of the rights to her late husband's name, image, trademarks, and intellectual property.

Marina Elena has distanced herself from events surrounding her husband's death, including his gravesite in Lubbock. "In a way, I blame myself. I was not feeling well when he left. I was two weeks pregnant, and I wanted Buddy to stay with me, but he had scheduled that tour. It was the time I wasn't with him. And, I blame myself, because if only I had gone along, Buddy never would have gotten into that airplane," Maria Elena sadly recalled.

Maria Elena's avoidance of certain memories eventually abated. In May of 2008, she visited the Greenwich Village location of the apartment where she and Buddy had once lived. She has also travelled to the Surf Ballroom and attended at least one of the *Winter Dance Party* festivals.

In the 1960s, Maria Elena married Joe Diaz, a Dallas toy manufacturer, who was also of Puerto Rican heritage. She gave birth to three children—two sons and a daughter. She named one of her sons Carlos, the Spanish version of Charles; perhaps in memory of Buddy, who was born Charles Hardin Holley. Maria Elena divorced her second husband during the 1980s.

Since 2010, Maria Elena has served on the Board of Directors of the *Buddy Holly Educational Foundation*, alongside co-founder, Peter Bradley. As of this writing, 85-year-old Maria-Elena Santiago-Holly resides in Dallas, Texas.

Buddy's father, L.O. Holley, suffered a stroke on July 1, 1985, which affected his speech and mobility. A week later, the 83-year-old Holley died, and was buried next to his youngest son in Lubbock City Cemetery.

Ella Holley suffered a heart attack in 1988. After spending five days in the hospital, Buddy's mother returned home, until her death on May 20, 1990, at the age of 87. She was laid to rest in the family plot, with L.O. and Buddy. Holly historian, Bill Griggs, who served as one of Mrs. Holley's pallbearers, described Ella as "one of the sweetest and nicest ladies ever."

After Buddy's death, Larry Holley often assumed the role of family spokesperson. Over the years, he has dreamed about his youngest brother: "I know that Buddy's with the Lord, and that one of these days, I'll see him again and put my arm around his shoulder, just like I used to."

Larry eventually gave Bill Griggs Buddy's brown leather overnight bag, which he recovered from the site of the plane crash in 1959. Years after remaining unopened and stored beneath Larry's bed, Griggs closely examined the luggage, which was missing the attached compartment, where Buddy stored his pistol and a portion of the cash he earned while touring. Inside the bag, Griggs discovered a tube of Colgate toothpaste, a toothbrush, Aspirin tablets, sun tan lotion, a lint brush, a hair brush, and a black plastic comb.

Larry has avoided participating in certain events devoted to Buddy's life and legacy. In a 2008 interview, Larry explained why he had never participated in *Winter Dance Party* commemorations: "...I don't go to that, because it makes me sad..." Larry angrily regrets that Buddy felt compelled to join the *Winter Dance Party*: "All he was seeing was chicken feed and he was having to make it on his tours. Royalty money came in through Petty and Petty was hanging on to it. He (Petty) was going to make him beg for it."

At the time of this writing, Larry Holley, age 92, is still alive. He is the last surviving Holley sibling.

The Holley musical genes have been passed along to another generation. In 1992, Larry's daughter, Sherry, released an album, entitled *Looking Through Buddy's Eyes*. Sherry Holley is not only a talented singer and song-writer, but also an accomplished visual artist; her works include mosaics and pottery, as well as pen and ink drawings on canvas, limestone, ceramic tile, and wood.

In March 2017 correspondence with the author, Sherry shared distant memories of her uncle: "I was just a little girl when Buddy passed away. He used to carry me around and sing to me." She is one of Buddy's five nieces and two nephews (one of whom is deceased), Sherry specifically recalled a significant moment from her childhood: "...He (Buddy) appeared on the *Ed Sullivan Show*, and we stayed home from church to watch that. I thought that was something."

Buddy was a role model for many aspiring musical artists. Sherry Holley is no exception: "He inspired me and I started writing songs and singing at the age of 13."

Larry's younger brother Travis, more reserved by nature, spoke publicly about Buddy on fewer occasions. He was, however, interviewed during Paul McCartney's documentary, *The Real Buddy Holly Story*, and shared fond memories about his little brother. In December of 2016, 89-year-old Travis Holley died from complications of chronic obstructive pulmonary disease.

Buddy's older sister, Patricia Lou Holley Kaiter, died in 2008, at the age of 79. Through her life, the musically talented Patricia Lou remained a fan of different musical genres, including rock and roll, country, and gospel.

Patricia Lou's daughter, Ingrid Holley Kaiter, explained how her mother celebrated Buddy's life: "She remembered him more, not as a musician, but as a little brother." "She would have liked to have had more local things in his name, but we know how that turned out," Patricia Lou informed a local reporter.

The career of famed disc jockey and promoter, Alan "Moondog" Freed, the man who claimed to have invented the term rock and roll, fell into rapid decline in the early years after Buddy Holly died. Payola scandals ruined his job prospects, finances, and health. On January 20, 1965, 43-year-old Alan Freed died of alcoholic cirrhosis and uremia.

Norman Petty, after he was fired by the post-Holly Crickets, continued to work in his Clovis recording studio. In 1959, Petty recorded four records for Lubbock piano player, Don Webb, who Buddy Holly had previously planned to produce.

Petty also composed an instrumental, entitled *Wheels*, which was recorded by the String-a-Lings. In 1961, *Wheels* reached Number Three on *Billboard's* chart, and climbed as high as Number 12 in the U.K.

Petty's greatest success after Buddy Holly and the Crickets came with another rock and roll group, the Fireballs. In 1963, the Fireballs recorded *Sugar Shack*, a Number One hit for five consecutive weeks and the best-selling record of that year. In 1964, *Daisy Petal Picking*, another Fireballs' record, climbed to Number 15 on *Billboard's* chart.

After McCartney's MPL Productions obtained ownership of the Buddy Holly songbook, several composers began receiving heartier royalty checks, which suggests that Petty's self-serving management of Holly-related monies may well have continued for over 15 years after Buddy's death. Nikki Sullivan (who contributed to writing *I'm Gonna Love You Too*) and Sonny West (*Oh Boy* and *Rave On*) are among those who were recipients of larger and more frequent royalty checks. "Ever since 1975 (1976), I've made a lot more money on it than I did before," West attested.

Not surprisingly, Petty never admitted to mismanagement of any of his artists' royalties. Billy Stull, who learned the recording business from Petty and later became manager of the recording studio in Clovis, was one of his rare defenders: "Norman was hurt by all these accusations. I spoke to Norman about it, and he said, 'I'm not the kind of person to go out and try to defend myself. I'm hurt by what people say, but it's not true as far as my owing Buddy money...'"

Petty purportedly began writing a book about his life as a producer and his relationships with different musical artists, but never finished it. For the remainder of his life, Petty never cleared himself of allegations that he had cheated Buddy Holly and the Crickets.

After the success of the Fireballs' *Sugar Shack*, Petty's career as a record producer greatly diminished. His alleged financial improprieties and his vocal criticism of the Beatles' successes repelled many potential recording stars. Unlike other record producers of his era, Petty has yet to be inducted into the Rock 'n' Roll Hall of Fame.

After Buddy Holly's death, Petty continued to spend freely. In 1969, he closed his original studio on West 7th Street and purchased the Mesa Theater, located on Clovis' Main Street. In the much larger building, Petty constructed a technologically advanced control room. Behaving as if money was no object, he highlighted the theater's stage curtains with 14-karat gold strands.

Petty continued to expand his holdings, purchasing two radio stations; one of those, *KTQM*, became Clovis' first FM station. He also opened a retail diamond store. The Citadel, a former church, was among Petty's local real estate acquisitions. He subsequently transformed the church building into living quarters for he and Vi, but rented out the chapel for weddings. Maintaining the appearance of a dutiful Christian, he purchased a pipe organ for his church in Clovis

In 1968, the last hit record was produced at *Norman Petty Studios*. The Fireballs *Bottle of Wine* climbed to Number Nine on *Billboard's* chart.

By the early 1970s, Petty was in dire financial straits. Nonetheless, Petty persisted in promoting himself as a driving force behind Holly's rise to stardom. In 1980, Petty grandiosely misinformed a journalist that he and Buddy wrote songs in a "fifty-fifty partnership."

In the early 1980s, Petty was diagnosed with leukemia—the same blood disorder that killed his older brother, Billy, nearly a half-century earlier. As the illness progressed, Petty was in the process of recording Holly hits utilizing a synthesizer, for a never-to-be released album, entitled *Electric Buddy Holly*.

In June of 1984, Petty enjoyed the final highlight of his controversial career, accepting a gold record for the Buddy Holly album, entitled *20 Golden Hits*. Two months later, on August 15th, 57-year-old Norman Petty died of leukemia. L.O. and Ella Holley were among those who attended his funeral in Clovis. "It's real sad, it really is," a gracious Ella explained.

Petty did not entrust his convoluted estate to his wife. Instead, he named his financial advisor, Lyle Walker, and a former preacher, Kenneth Broad, as trustees. Various reports have indicated that there was little net worth remaining in Petty's numerous small companies and bank accounts.

For many years, the original *Norman Petty Studios* fell into a state of disrepair, and functioned as a storage facility and a home for 36 stray cats Vi Petty had adopted. In 1984, Petty's former business associate, Jerry Fisher, restored the West 7th Street studio to its original state.

During Paul McCartney's 1986 documentary, *The Real Buddy Holly Story*, Vi Petty offered viewers a tour of the renovated studio. She cheerfully discussed the glory days, when Buddy Holly and the Crickets recorded hit records in the building.

Vi survived her husband by nearly eight years. On March 22, 1992, 63-year-old Vi Petty died of liver failure. She was buried in Clovis, next to her husband and the couple's long-time assistant, Norma Jean Berry. All three graves are covered by a single headstone.

Today, *Norman Petty Studios*, located at 1313 West 7th Street, appears as it did in the 1950s. Among the original items on display include the ten-cent-per-bottle Coca-Cola machine (located in the lobby), Petty's famed control board, Western Union clocks, tape recorders, and microphones. The Clovis Chamber of Commerce conducts tours of the studio by appointment, and is proud that "the curators have worked hard to keep the studio as it was, so musical enthusiasts can take a step back in time to the grand old days of rock and roll."

Many of Holly's closest friends and early advisors remained active in the music world after Buddy's death. Hi Pockets Duncan, who was Holly's first manager and had warned Buddy about the pitfalls of associating with Norman Petty, generously relinquished his managerial role when Buddy signed a recording contract with Decca. Even then, he remained a close friend and one of Holly's biggest fans. Duncan finished his career in the radio business, and was serving as the station manager of KRAN in Morton, Texas (located 30 miles northwest of Lubbock) at the time of his death, on December 21, 1981.

Buddy's early bandmate, Bob Montgomery, enjoyed a successful career as a singer, song-writer, music publisher, and producer. Among Montgomery's compositions are Patsy Cline's *Back in Baby's Arms*, and Cliff Richards' *Wind Me Up*. Montgomery died of complications from Parkinson's disease on December 4, 2014, at the age of 77.

Don Guess, who played with Holly during his pre-Cricket days, died of cancer, at the age of 55, on October 21, 1992. Seventy-year-old Dick Jacobs, who befriended Holly and produced his records in New York City, most notably the string session, died on May 20, 1988.

The survivors of the ill-fated *Winter Dance Party* moved forward with their lives, with varying degrees of success. After recovering from frostbite, Holly's drummer, Carl Bunch, enlisted in the U.S. Army for a hitch, and played drums for "Ronnie Smith and the Jitters," Roy Orbison, and Hank Williams, Jr. After waging a successful battle against alcoholism, Bunch worked as a salesman, prison guard, and substance abuse counselor.

After forming New Dove Ministries, Bunch opined that if Holly had lived, Buddy would have led a religious revival in the latter part of the 20th century. "The Devil knew that. That is why the Devil killed him," Bunch proclaimed.

At conventions of Holly's fans, Bunch often signed his autograph as "the frostbitten Cricket." On March 26, 2011, at the age of 71, Carl Bunch died of complications from diabetes.

Tommy Allsup, who relinquished his seat on the doomed Beechcraft Bonanza, after losing a coin toss with Ritchie Valens, returned to Odessa, Texas for a time. He later played guitar for Ronnie Smith, Roy Orbison, and Willie Nelson.

After moving to Nashville in 1968, Allsup worked as a session musician and later produced an album, *24 Hits by Bob Wills and His Texas Playboys*. In 1969, Allsup produced a record by Denny Zager and Rick Evans, entitled *In the Year 2525*, which ultimately sold more than 4,000,000 copies.

In 1979, Allsup opened a club in Dallas, Tommy's Head's Up Saloon; the name was a reference to the coin toss he lost with Ritchie Valens on that fateful night in 1959. Allsup was later inducted into the Oklahoma Music Hall of Fame (his home state) and the Rockabilly Hall of Fame. On January 11, 2017, 85-year-old Tommy Allsup died from complications following hernia surgery.

After completing the *Winter Dance Party*, Waylon Jennings returned to Lubbock and resumed his duties as a disk jockey at *KLLL*. Jennings' first record, *Jolie Blon*, which Buddy Holly produced, was released by Brunswick Records in March of 1959, but never became a hit.

After moving to Nashville in the 1960s, Jennings secured a long-coveted recording contract. While battling and eventually overcoming an addiction to drugs, Jennings became one of the most prolific country and western stars of his generation, winning two Grammy

Awards and three Country Music Association Awards. He was later designated by *Country Music Television* as one of the 40 Greatest Men of Country Music.

Between 1966 and 1995, Jennings recorded 54 albums, 11 of which reached Number One on the country chart. From 1965 to 1981, 96 of his singles charted in the Top 100, with 16 of them climbing to Number One. Jennings hits include *Amanda, Goodhearted Woman, Lonesome On'ry and Mean, Rainy Day Woman, Just to Satisfy You, Are You Sure Hank Done It This Way*, the theme song from the television series *The Dukes of Hazzard* (which he also narrated), and *Bob Wills Is Still the King*.

For the remainder of his life, Waylon would remember Buddy Holly as "the first guy who had confidence in me." Sixty-four-year-old Waylon Jennings died of complications from diabetes on February 13, 2002.

Dion and the Belmonts returned to their native New York City after the *Winter Dance Party*, and later that same year, recorded *A Teenager in Love*, which became the group's first million-selling record. In 1960, Dion and the Belmonts were named by *American Bandstand* as the country's Best Vocal Group.

After the group disbanded in 1960, Dion DiMucci enjoyed a successful solo career, scoring hits with *Runaround Sue, The Wanderer, Ruby*, and *Donna the Prima Donna*. In 1968, after successfully battling a drug problem, Dion released another Top 10 single, *Abraham, Martin, and John*.

In June of 1972, Dion and the Belmonts performed together at a reunion concert, which was recorded as a live LP. In 1989, Dion and the Belmonts were inducted into the Rock 'n' Roll Hall of Fame. As of early-2017, 77-year-old Dion DiMucci is still alive.

Frankie Sardo continued to perform for a few years after the *Winter Dance Party*, but never achieved stardom. On some recordings, he performed as a duo with his brother, under the name "Frankie and Johnny." One of the highlights of Sardo's brief musical career was appearing on *American Bandstand* on September 7, 1960, performing his latest single, *When the Bells Stop Ringing*.

In 1962, Sardo ended his career as a recording artist. After changing his name to Frank Avianca, he subsequently worked as an actor and producer. On February 26, 2014, 71-year-old Frankie Sardo died of cancer.

Bobby Velline, later known to the world as Bobby Vee, launched his highly successful career on the very day that Holly, Valens, and the Big Bopper were killed. Vee ultimately recorded 38 Top 100 hits, 10 of which reached the Top 10, while earning six gold records. On October 24, 2016, 73-year-old Bobby Vee died of complications from Alzheimer's disease.

Ronnie Smith, a young singer from Odessa, Texas, replaced the deceased Buddy Holly as lead vocalist for much of the remainder of *Winter Dance Party*. In 1959, Ronnie Smith and the Jitters recorded *Lookie Lookie Lookie* and *A Tiny Kiss*, neither of which charted.

Smith met an untimely end, as he vainly battled drug addiction and mental illness. On October 25, 1962, he committed suicide while hospitalized in a psychiatric facility.

Sonny Curtis, Buddy's teenage friend, played with him during Holly's 1956 Nashville Decca recording sessions. Curtis' self-composed *Rock Around with Ollie Vee* was later released as a Buddy Holly single.

Curtis joined the Crickets as lead guitarist after Holly's death. Absent Buddy Holly, none of the Crickets' songs were ever hit makers, including a Curtis composition, *I Fought the Law*. In March of 1966, however, *I Fought the Law*, covered by The Bobby Fuller Four, was a huge hit, climbing to Number Nine on *Billboard's* chart.

After Holly's death, Curtis served a two-year hitch in the U.S. Army. In 1964, Sonny's solo record, *A Beatle I Want to be,* failed to become a top-seller. Curtis played intermittently with a revolving cast of Crickets over the years, including the 2004 album, *The Crickets and Their Buddies*; the LP consisted of Buddy Holly's and the Crickets' hits, performed in conjunction with well-known artists of the early 21st century.

Curtis wrote *The Real Buddy Holly Story* in protest to the big screen movie, starring Gary Busey. He performed the song at the inaugural convention of the *Buddy Holly Memorial Society*, and during Paul McCartney's documentary, *The Real Buddy Holly Story*.

Over the years, Curtis has been a prolific song-writer, including *Love is All Around* (the theme song for CBS's 1970s hit television show, *The Mary Tyler Moore Show*), *Walk Right Back* (a hit for the Everly Brothers in 1960 and Anne Murray in 1978), *More Than I Can Say* (co-written with J.I. Allison, and later recorded by Bobby Vee and Leo Sayer), *I'm No Stranger to the Rain* (co-written with Ron Hellard, recorded by the late Keith Whitley, and the 1987 Country Song of the Year), *Straight Life* (recorded by both Glen Campbell and Bobby Goldsboro), and *A Fool Never Learns* (recorded by Andy Williams), as well as *I Like Your Music* and *You Made My Life a Song* (both recorded by Anne Murry on her 1972 album, *Annie*).

As a singer and song-writer, Curtis' discography includes seven albums and more than 20 singles. In 2007, Curtis was inducted into the Musicians Hall of Fame and Museum in Nashville. Five years later, by special committee, he was inducted into the Rock 'n' Roll Hall of Fame, as a member of the Crickets, along with J.I. Allison and Joe B. Mauldin. As of this writing, 79-year-old Sonny Curtis is still alive and performing on stage.

Niki Sullivan, a native of California, was the only original Cricket who was not born in Texas. A third cousin to Buddy Holly, Sullivan has often been referred to as "the other guy in the glasses." Before leaving the Crickets in early 1958, Sullivan had performed on 27 of 32 songs recorded by the group.

Shortly after Sullivan left the Crickets, Dot Records released his solo single, *It's All Over* (which reflected on his break-up with the Crickets) and *Three Steps to Heaven*, on the disc's flip side. The record was a hit in the Southwest, but failed to achieve national acclaim. Norman Petty claimed that Sullivan recorded the single in Clovis, before he (Petty) sold it to Dot Records. Sullivan, however, disputed Petty's version; he remembered recording the single at a studio in Lubbock and giving it to Murray Deutch, who brokered a record deal with Dot.

Sullivan eventually moved to California, where he started his own band, "Soul Incorporated." He also worked for *Sony Electronics*. Sullivan took comfort when Ella Holley told him Buddy had planned to form a publishing company with Paul Anka, and use Niki as a song writer. Two generations removed from his days as a Cricket, Sullivan's granddaughter bears the name Holly.

In 1978, Sullivan played with the two surviving original Crickets during the first *Buddy Holly Memorial Society* festival. While he was totally omitted from the movie, The *Buddy Holly Story*, Sullivan was depicted as a primary character in the acclaimed musical, *Buddy*.

On April 6, 2004, 67-year-old Niki Sullivan died of a heart attack in Sugar Creek, Missouri. His death was unexpected; earlier in the day, Sullivan had completed a round of golf. He was survived by his wife, sister, twin sons, and a granddaughter.

After Buddy Holly's death, Joe Benson Mauldin, Jr. served for two years in the U.S. Army. He later started a trucking company in Texas. Joe B. continued to play during special events with various members of the reconstituted Crickets.

During the 1960s, Joe B. worked as a recording engineer at Gold Star Studios in Los Angeles. The Beach Boys and Phil Spector were among those who recorded at Gold Star.

Mauldin was eventually inducted into the *West Texas Walk of Fame* in Lubbock and the Musician's Hall of Fame and Museum in Nashville. In 2012, Joe B. became a member of the Rock 'n' Roll Hall of Fame—a move to correct the exclusion of the original Crickets, when Buddy Holly became a charter member in 1986.

On February 7, 2015, Joe B. Mauldin died of cancer in Nashville, Tennessee. The former Crickets' bass player was 74-years-old.

Jerry Ivan "J.I." Allison retained legal control of the name the Crickets, which, over the years, included a revolving cast, including Joe B., Nikki, Sonny Curtis, Glen D. Hardin, Earl Sinks, David Box, and Jerry Naylor. Not long after Buddy's death, the Crickets played as back up musicians for the Everly Brothers during a tour to Australia. Absent Buddy Holly, the group never produced a top-selling record, and essentially disbanded, except for special reunions. J.I., the only constant member of the group, has freely acknowledged: "We've pretty well proved in the years since 1958, that the Crickets without Buddy Holly aren't too hot of an item."

J.I. and Peggy Sue's relationship was tumultuous. On April 4, 1962, they renewed their vows in the Catholic Church. In September of that same year, Allison was baptized as a Catholic. Despite the formal sanction of the church, the marriage did not survive, and the couple divorced in 1967.

In the years after Holly's death, Allison played with the "Liberty House Band" and as a back-up musician for Eddie Cochran. J.I.'s percussion was also prominently featured on the Everly Brother's twin hits, *'Til I Kissed You* and *Cathy's Clown*.

After moving to California, J.I. formed a session band, which included Tommy Allsup on guitar and Joe Osburn on bass. During the early 1960's, J.I. also played as drummer for country star, Roger Miller. In the late 1970s, the Crickets toured with Waylon Jennings, who, by then, was an established country music star. The Crickets, in one form or another, collaborated with Nanci Griffith, Paul McCartney, Johnny Rivers, Eric Clapton, Waylon Jennings, and Bobby Vee on record albums.

Forty years after firing Norman Petty, J.I. still believed the Crickets' former manager had taken financial advantage of them. "We were interested in getting out and playing music, and touring and having fun, than we were the money, and assumed that everybody would be fair, especially Norman…but, it wasn't that way," J.I. asserted.

In 2007, Allison was inducted into the Musicians Hall of Fame and Museum in Nashville. He was also inducted in the Rock 'n' Roll Hall of Fame in 2012, as an original member of the Crickets.

As of this writing, 77-year-old J.I. Allison is still alive. He is the only surviving member of the original Buddy Holly and the Crickets.

In January of 2008, J.I. Allison's ex-wife co-authored a memoir, entitled *What Ever Happened to Peggy Sue*. The timing of the book's publication coincided with the year between the 50th anniversaries of Buddy Holly's release of *Peggy Sue* (1957) and his death (1959).

Peggy Sue Gerron used some 150 diary entries, which she started in 1958, as a framework for her publication. "I wanted to give him his voice. It's my book, my memoirs. We were very, very good friends. He was probably one of the best friends I ever had," Gerron spoke about Holly, when promoting her book.

Many of Gerron's recollections were eye-catching, particularly to a displeased Maria Elena Holly. Buddy's widow threatened to sue to keep the book from being published, but Peggy Sue informed the author that no legal action was taken.

Gerron wrote that Buddy expressed his affection for her during the couple's joint honeymoon. While they were sitting at a café table, briefly separated from J.I. and Maria Elena, Peggy Sue recalled that Buddy placed his hand atop hers: "If you belonged to me, I'd give you anything in the world, including the world, if you wanted it."

During the foursome's honeymoon vacation, Gerron recalled that Buddy approached her in private, yet again: "I know I should have said something to you a long time ago, but every time I started to, I decided it wasn't fair to Jerry. The only thing I can say is that he doesn't know what he has. He should be married to someone like Maria; and then, maybe, he'd appreciate how damn lucky he is!"

In December of 1958, just three months or so after Buddy married Maria Elena, Peggy Sue recalled Holly telling her that he had hired two attorneys—one to help him regain his rightful song-writing credits for *Peggy Sue*, and another to file for divorce. During that same conversation, Gerron remembered Buddy accusing J.I. of drunkenness and infidelity during the Crickets' most recent road tour, and urging Peggy Sue to get a divorce, after which time he (Buddy) would take care of her.

After Buddy's death, Gerron recalled Ella Holley telling her that Buddy had written *Peggy Sue Got Married* as a surprise for her (Peggy

Sue), and confided that Buddy planned to divorce Maria Elena. Gerron further remembered that Ella told her Buddy planned to live in New York City for only two years, before returning to Lubbock to operate his newly-constructed studio.

As might have been expected, an angry Maria Elena disputed Gerron's claims. "It is very interesting that this woman makes up all these stories. He (Buddy) never, never considered Peggy Sue a friend," Marina Elena informed a reporter.

Peggy Sue Gerron defended her work: "It's the first book that's ever been written about Buddy Holly by someone that actually knew Buddy Holly and everybody in the book." In March of 2017, Gerron challenged the author's theory that Holly might have been in love with her; an assertion based upon the revelations in Peggy Sue's book, coupled with the themes of heartbreak and longing for a lost lover expressed in Buddy's apartment tapes, recorded only four months after he was married. "I don't know that Buddy was in love with me! I adored Buddy and he was one of my closest friends. I don't know how he really felt, because he didn't discuss it with me, and I didn't discuss it with him," Peggy Sue explained.

Peggy Sue Gerron, now in her 70s, resides in Lubbock. She has actively worked to combat domestic abuse and drug addiction, as well as contributing to the founding of the *Buddy Holly Center* and the *Buddy Holly Festival*. Not surprisingly, *Peggy Sue* is her favorite Holly song. "My second favorite is *Peggy Sue Got Married*," Gerron added.

Buddy's fans owe a tremendous debt to the late William Frederick "Bill" Griggs, who was widely regarded as the foremost authority on Holly's life. Griggs was inducted into the *West Texas Walk of Fame* on September 30, 2010, honoring his four decades of research and assistance to Holly biographers and aficionados, as well as rock and roll historians. "Wow, I have spent 42 years researching and publishing items pertaining to west Texas music and Buddy Holly and the Crickets. To be recognized by the city of Lubbock with a plaque that will be around long after I am gone, is an honor I cannot really describe," Griggs informed well-wishers during his induction ceremony.

In 1978, Griggs produced the first of 11 annual gatherings of the *Buddy Holly Memorial Society* (which he founded). Griggs established a close relationship with the Holley family and served as a pallbearer when Buddy's mother (in 1998) and sister (in 2008) died. Bill Griggs died of cancer in March of 2011, at the age of 69.

Carroll Anderson, the last man to speak to Buddy Holly as the rock and roller was boarding the doomed Beechcraft Bonanza in the wee hours of February 3, 1959, continued to manage the Surf Ballroom until 1967. The deaths of Holly, Valens, and the Big Bopper left Anderson, who helped identify their bodies at the crash site, scarred. "I was hurt badly. It was something I couldn't get over…I'll never get it out of my mind," Anderson explained in a 1995 newspaper interview.

In the 1990s, Anderson met Maria Elena Holly for the first time during the annual *Winter Dance Party* festival at the Surf Ballroom in Clear Lake, Iowa. The two developed an immediate rapport, sharing fond memories of Buddy. Anderson died in 2006, at the age of 86.

The fate of the Beechcraft Bonanza, whose crash claimed the lives of Buddy Holly, Ritchie Valens, the Big Bopper, and Roger Peterson remains the focus of much speculation. The original CAB report indicated the wreckage was sold for scrap. In 1993, however, an employee of the Mason City Airport told Holly biographer, Ellis Amburn: "The plane is out here at the airport. It's locked in a shed down here. Dwyer is going to make key chains out of the pieces. People keep asking him why he doesn't put it in a museum. He just has it locked in a shed."

At one point, Jerry Dwyer's wife, Barb, reported that the bulk of the wreckage was buried under a newly-constructed runway at the airport, but added that her husband had kept certain parts of the plane. Like her late husband, Barb Dwyer has made cryptic statements about the February 3, 1959 crash: "If you knew all the facts about the whole thing, there's a lot that has never come out. There's a lot of things that have never come out, and they never will."

Author, Gary W. Moore, had a brief telephone conversation with Barb Dwyer, but Jerry, who was still alive at that time, never consented to a personal interview. In his 2011 book, *Hey Buddy*, Moore published an open letter:

Jerry,

I will assemble a team of first class aviation experts to examine the wreckage you claim to have in your possession to help you substantiate the reasons for the crash. If the "truth" has never been told, let me help you tell it. If the CAB report is incorrect, let us help verify that fact so we can put all the conspiracies and doubts to rest. But if one of these conspiracies (or something else entirely) turns out to be true, let the truth be told! Jerry, you are the only man in the world who can either help make this happen or forever block the truth from being told. Will you join with me and allow the world to know what happened?

Moore never received any communication from Dwyer, other than the threat of a groundless law suit. In February of 2011, during a book signing for *Hey Buddy*, hosted by Barnes and Noble in Waterloo, Iowa, Moore encountered a gentleman that he estimated to be in his early to mid-70s. During the question and answer portion of the event, the man informed Moore: "If Jerry Dwyer told you that he still has the airplane, he is a damn liar."

The man explained that in 1959, when he was still a teenager, his father owned a dump truck service. At the request of Jerry Dwyer, father and son took the dump truck to the Mason City Airport in July of that year, just over five months after the plane crash. Dwyer, however, insisted that the pair wait until after dark before arriving at the airport.

After sunset, Dwyer took them to a locked hangar, which contained the wreckage of an airplane, including the wings, one of which was badly damaged. The wings were separated from the fuselage, and propped against one of the hangar's walls. The teenager recognized the aircraft as the one in which Holly and the others were killed by its color and identifying tail number.

Dwyer proceeded to assist the pair in loading the wreckage, absent the wings (which remained in the hangar), aboard the dump truck. "I want this out of my life," Dwyer informed the teenager's father.

Dwyer then instructed father and son to transport the wreckage to the nearby landfill (city dump), where an individual would be waiting to admit them after normal working hours. Before departing the airport, Dwyer gave the pair two five-gallon containers of aviation fuel to douse the dumped wreckage, before setting it on fire (presumably to obliterate the tail number, paint job, and other identifying markers). At Dwyer's request, the teenager and his father remained with the burning wreckage until the fire extinguished itself. Dwyer informed them that the charred wreckage would be buried the following day.

Over 52 years after the teenager assisted his father with disposal of the aircraft, he told Moore that he found no fault with Dwyer's decision to rid himself of the wreckage, but grew angry every time he read or heard the charter service operator claim he was still in possession of the airplane. Moore, who found the man's account credible, eventually learned that the site of the 1959 landfill had since been developed into commercial property. The burned wreckage now presumably lies beneath a building or buildings, rendering it inaccessible to excavation. Unless Barb Dwyer or another credible source produces the wrecked Beechcraft Bonanza, it is safe to assume that the bulk of the doomed aircraft will never be examined by researchers and historians (there is the possibility, however remote, that the wings and some instrument panel gauges have been preserved).

The Surf Ballroom in Clear Lake, Iowa, after changing owners several times and having its motif altered, eventually fell into a state of disrepair. In 1994, after being purchased by the Snyder family, the ballroom was restored to its 1959 beach club appearance, and reopened in time for the

1995 *Winter Dance Party*. Each February, since 1979, the Surf Ballroom has hosted a four-day *Winter Dance Party* festival, honoring Buddy Holly, Ritchie Valens, and the Big Bopper.

One block west of the ballroom is an outdoor park, named *Three Stars Plaza*. In 2011, a monument dedicated to Holly, Valens, and the Big Bopper was unveiled in the park; it depicts a record spindle holding three 45-RPM records in the drop position. At night, the monument is illuminated by bright blue lights.

Located at 460 North Shore Drive (aka *Ritchie Valens Drive*), the Surf Ballroom is readily accessible from U.S. Highway 18 via *Buddy Holly Plaza*, which runs east of the building. For concerts and other special events, the Surf can accommodate an audience of 2,100.

The foyer inside the main entrance is designed in art deco style, and leads into the lobby. The lobby wallpaper is decorated with pineapples—the international sign of welcome. Opening directly into the ballroom, the lobby houses the box office, coat check room, the pay phone booth used by Buddy Holly and Ritchie Valens on the night of February 2, 1959 (emcee, Bob Hale, however, argues that Holly used the phone in the manager's office), a gift shop, and office space.

A hall, located to the right of the main entrance, leads from the lobby to the Cypress Room, and marks the beginning of the Wall of Fame, decorated with framed pictures of the entertainers who have performed at the Surf. It is a reminder that the ballroom first hosted stars from the big band and early-jazz eras, including Tommy Dorsey, Glen Miller, Lawrence Welk, Duke Ellington, Count Basie, and Cab Calloway.

The Cypress Room, formerly known as the Surfside 6 Lounge and Café, is a multi-purpose area. It not only contains the refreshment bar, but also serves as a venue for smaller concerts. The Wall of Fame extends into the room, with framed photographs of the rock and roll, rhythm and blues, and country artists who have performed at the Surf over the years.

The Cypress Room also houses a museum displaying numerous artifacts and memorabilia related to rock and roll, including a signed pair of Pat Boone's trademark white buck shoes, a guitar signed by

Bobby Vee, a 24-carat gold-plated record of Don McClean's *American Pie* (accompanied by a portion of the original handwritten lyrics), and an autographed picture of three of the four original Crickets—J.I. Allison, Joe B. Mauldin, and Niki Sullivan.

The deceased members of the *Winter Dance Party* are well remembered in numerous displays, including both a written and map itinerary of the ill-fated concert tour, the Big Bopper's brief case (which survived the plane crash, mostly intact), a composition book belonging to the Big Bopper (along with his hand-written lyrics to a song, entitled *Sweet Lips*), lyrics to *La Bamba* (handwritten by Valens' aunt), one of Valens' bowties, cuff links belonging to Holly, and headphones from the crashed Beechcraft Bonanza.

The ballroom can be entered from the lobby or the Cypress Room, and features a 6,300-square-feet maple wood dance floor. On the periphery of the ballroom are the original green, leather-padded six-person booths. The booths are covered with cabana-like awnings and the interior walls are decorated with murals of ocean waves—enhancing the beach club atmosphere.

Stage right is the Green Room, where the members of the *Winter Dance Party* tour waited prior to performing. In the years since the deaths of Holly, Valens, and the Big Bopper, the walls, ceiling, and doors of the Green Room have been decorated with the signatures of various entertainers who have performed at the Surf, as well as those of a few distinguished visitors. Among the multitude of names are Johnny Rivers, Brian Wilson (of the Beach Boys), Larry Welborn (Buddy Holly's pre-Crickets' bandmate), Don McClean (his signature is accompanied by a portion of the lyrics from *American Pie*), Leonard Skynard, Carlos Santana, ZZ Top, Hootie and the Blowfish, Kevin Costner, and former President, Barack Obama.

The original stage is still intact, though it has been lengthened to accommodate the larger and more sophisticated electronic equipment employed by modern-day bands. Live palm trees flank either side of the stage.

In 1998, the Surf Ballroom was inducted into the Iowa Rock and Roll Hall of Fame. On January 27, 2009, just days before the 50th anniversary of the original *Winter Dance Party*, the ballroom was designated as a historic landmark by the Rock 'n' Roll Hall of Fame and Museum. At that time, a plaque was unveiled: *There are few buildings in existence today that represent a complete shift in our musical history. As the last concert venue for Buddy Holly, Ritchie Valens, and J.P. "the Big Bopper" Richardson, the Surf is the bedrock of where the sound and attitude of rock and roll changed forever.*

Surrounding the plaque, which is mounted on the wall of Surf's lobby, are seven photographs of Buddy Holly and several other performers, taken on February 2, 1959. Those pictures did not surface until 2009; prior to that time, there were thought to be no existing photographs from Holly's last performance.

In January of 2008, the North Iowa Culture Center and Museum was formed to manage the Surf Ballroom. Operating as a 501c3 non-profit corporation, the building is a working museum, an active ballroom, and an educational resource for area schools.

In September of 2011, the Surf Ballroom was officially listed on the National Register of Historic Places by the U.S. Department of the Interior. The Surf, however, is not merely a relic. Jeff Nicholas, President of the Surf Ballroom and a member of the North Iowa Culture Center and Museum Board of Directors, estimates that 8,000 to 10,000 people visit the landmark each year.

In addition to the annual *Winter Dance Party* festival, approximately 40 musical artists perform at the concert venue each year. The historic ballroom also hosts other events, including weddings, Christmas parties, banquets, and high school proms.

When one stands on the stage of the Surf Ballroom, the aura of Buddy Holly is still very much alive, with an enduring and mystical whisper: *LISTEN TO ME.*

EPILOGUE

THERE IS MUCH TO BE admired about Buddy Holly. On a professional level, he was a talented singer, musician, song-writer, performer, burgeoning record producer, and musical innovator. Holly was an inspiration to future recording stars, both in life and death, and many of those performers have freely imitated his style and techniques. Nearly six decades after his death, listeners, old and young alike, appreciate Holly's music. Away from the studio and stage, Buddy was likeable, generous, and remarkably free of prejudice; personality traits that are both admirable and timeless. For lack of more sophisticated prose, Holly was simply a nice guy.

In the early days of rock and roll music, Holly's innovations were both clever and trend-setting. He established the basic line-up for rock and roll bands—a lead guitarist, rhythm guitarist, bass player, and percussionist. After Niki Sullivan left the Crickets, Holly was talented enough to modify his established format by playing both rhythm and lead guitar, while continuing to sing lead vocals. Listeners were impressed that the three-man, Buddy Holly and the Crickets sounded just as good on stage as they did on their records.

Unlike so many early rock and rollers, Holly was both a singer and a composer. Given that his professional career tragically ended after only 18 months and his most prolific song-writing period lasted for just under two years, Holly's is resume is even more impressive.

Even among those who are not rock and roll aficionados, Holly's voice is easily recognizable. Buddy's songs, punctuated with his characteristic hiccups, stutters, and expansive voice range, are both distinctive and unforgettable.

In the studio, Holly was willing to experiment, reproducing an arrangement he had already crafted in his mind. He was among the first to overdub his records, well before multi-tracking technology had been invented. By "layering" his records with vocals and instrumentals, Holly could harmonize with himself, producing melodic songs like *Words of Love* and *Listen to Me*.

He also utilized Norman Petty's now-primitive echo chamber to add a unique flavor to his recordings. The use of percussion paradiddles, played outside of the studio proper and then funneled through the echo chamber, provides a rumbling and repetitive beat, which helps define the unforgettable *Peggy Sue*.

The tap, tap, tapping percussion of J.I. Allison's Levi jeans, coupled with the tinkling of celesta keys, gives *Everyday* an enduring melodic quality. Some of the innovations on Buddy's records were relatively simple, like utilizing an empty cardboard box, rather than a drum set, for percussion on *Not Fade Away*, generating a distinctive, driving beat.

Holly was one of the first rock and rollers to play a Fender Stratocaster electric guitar. Many others would follow his lead, including the late Jimi Hendrix and Eric Clapton.

For someone of such a young age, Buddy Holly was clearly focused on his life's work. Peggy Sue Gerron described him as "hungry," while Niki Sullivan marveled at Buddy's "laser-like focus." "He was ambitious and wanted to push the envelope. He used to say that you don't know if you can do it or not, but if a door opens, walk through it," Gerron recalled.

Rock and roll journalist, magazine editor, and Holly biographer, Bud Scoppe, summarized the impact of Buddy's brief career: "In those two years of feverish activity, Buddy Holly not only wrote a vital early chapter in the history of rock 'n' roll, he made it seem easy, fun, perfectly natural—and that may have been his greatest gift of all..." "Between

February 25, 1957 when the 20-year-old Holly cut the electrifying, utterly unprecedented *That'll Be the Day*, and February 3, 1959, when he died in a plane crash, Holly amassed a remarkable body of work characterized by envelope-pushing innovation as a singer, guitarist, and recording pioneer, while capturing with plainspoken eloquence, the hormonal agony and ecstasy of the young," Scoppe continued.

The late singer and song-writer, Carl Perkins, described the legacy of his contemporary. "Buddy Holly didn't give birth to rock 'n' roll, but sure rocked the cradle," Perkins opined.

Holly's influence on younger artists, particularly Brits, is inarguable. The first song John Lennon learned to play on his banjo was *That'll Be the Day*, which also happened to be the first record cut by Lennon's pre-Beatles' band, the Quarrymen. After they became the most famous band in the world, the Beatles elected to cover Holly's *Words of Love* on an album. Near the end of his 1986 documentary, *The Real Buddy Holly Story*, McCartney sings *Words of Love*, while playing his acoustic guitar; symbolic of his continued appreciation of Holly's music.

The Rolling Stones' first American hit was yet another Holly song, *Not Fade Away*. "Buddy Holly had it all—the lucky devil," the Rolling Stones' Keith Richards proclaimed.

Eric Clapton remembered watching *Sunday Night at the London Palladium* in 1958: "…One night they had Buddy Holly on the show, and I thought I'd died and gone to heaven; that was when I saw my first Fender guitar. It was like seeing an instrument from outer space and I said to myself: 'That's the future; that's what I want…'"

"He looked like the boy next door, and I think that was the secret for a lot of people, because, until then, all the rock 'n' roll idols had looked like Elvis and unreachable. We couldn't look like that, but we could look like Buddy," Paul McCartney remembered in 1988.

The lanky Texan proved to the Brits that performers could also be composers. "John and I started to write because of Buddy Holly," Paul McCartney has freely admitted.

McCartney's enthusiasm and respect for Holly did not diminish with the passage of time. In 1976, McCartney arranged for Denny Laine, a former member of his post-Beatles' band, Wings, to record an album of Buddy's songs.

When Buddy Holly and the Crickets toured the United Kingdom, their influence on aspiring rock and roll singers and song-writers was nothing less than transformative. If not for Holly's 1958 *American Invasion*, would there have been a 1960s British Invasion? If the British Invasion was inevitable, it can be argued that it would have been delayed, absent Holly's earlier influence.

If Buddy had still been alive, would American listeners have found the British Invasion so innovative and mesmerizing? "When Buddy Holly and the Crickets went to England, it was the future," Peggy Sue Gerron succinctly, but profoundly summarized.

Many music historians and performing artists believe the death of Buddy Holly marked the beginning of the end for the first phase of rock and roll. "Rock 'n' roll died in '63, and became rock. In the later 60s, rock 'n' roll splintered. It became surf rock, psychedelic rock, protest rock, (and) drug rock. It wasn't the fun rock 'n' rock roll Buddy created," Holly historian, Bill Griggs, opined.

As indisputably popular as the Beatles and Rolling Stones were, they were not the pioneers of rock and roll music. Don McLean, whose 1971 classic, *American Pie*, resurrected the memory of Buddy Holly, also utilized his song to make a point. "...The English groups were the only ones who are remembered. They came out in the early 60s and everyone thought it was something new, but it wasn't. It was actually music inspired by Buddy's style, and in a few cases, it was actually Buddy's songs they were playing. The British had grasped Buddy's style and made it their own. Americans loved it and acted as if they had not heard it before, but they had. They didn't recognize their own music! When you heard the early Beatles, you were hearing Buddy Holly. How did the Americans not get it?" a perplexed McLean declared.

McLean is not only impressed by Holly's talent, but also his productivity: "...He cut about 60 tracks, then died when he was only 22. His songs were hits. Hits! It's hard to point to anybody who wrote than many songs, all different styles, and had so many hits! That's amazing..."

Holly's horn-rimmed glasses became his most recognizable trademark, and enlarged replicas appear at the entrances to the *Buddy Holly Center* and the path leading to the site of his fatal plane crash. John Lennon, who was nearly as vision-impaired as Holly, concluded that it was acceptable to wear glasses on stage after seeing Buddy do so. Elton John, who had normal vision, started wearing glasses, just to mimic Buddy.

In America, Buddy's fellow Texan, Roy Orbison changed his opinion about eyeglasses after watching Holly perform. Orbison's long-time friend, Orbie Lee Harris, remembered that Buddy's lack of self-consciousness "gave Roy courage," and "made him think, if this guy is going to make it big, maybe I can, too."

Nearly six decades after his death, Buddy Holly has not been forgotten. But, how well has he been *remembered*? In October of 2016, the author undertook a survey, asking 100 people (ranging from ages 21 to 77, representing different sexes, races, occupations, and backgrounds) to select their favorite song Buddy Holly recorded. Through word of mouth, text messaging, and social media, it took less than 48 hours to complete the survey, and only *one* potential respondent, could not recall a single Buddy Holly song. The results by song and number of responses is as follows: *That'll Be the Day* (30), *Peggy Sue* (25), *Oh Boy* (11), *Everyday* (8), *True Love Ways* (8), *Rave On* (6), *Maybe Baby* (3), *Not Fade Away* (2), *Rock Around with Ollie Vee* (2) *Words of Love* (1), *Learning the Game* (1), *I'm Gonna Love You Too* (1), *Heartbeat* (1), and *Bo Diddley* (1). The ability of 100 respondents to recall 14 different songs, over 57 years after Holly's death, is a clear testimony to Buddy's continued relevance.

While Buddy Holly was no saint, he was the small town, boy-next-door, who achieved stardom. While he occasionally drank too much (even then, this indulgence was limited by his peptic ulcers), Holly was never known to take drugs. Like others of his generation, he struggled with the irreconcilable differences between conservative Christianity and his passion for rock and roll music; this paradox was not made easier by a hypocritical church that condemned rock and roll as "Satan's music," yet readily- accepted considerable monetary donations from Buddy.

At a time when it was unpopular, if not dangerous, to deviate from the social mores of one's native environment, Holly rejected racism. He not only toured with black performers, but also made friends with them. Holly invited Little Richard, who offended Texans by being black and flamboyantly gay or bi-sexual, to his parent's house for dinner. In another, less dramatic affront to racial segregation, Buddy named his cat in honor of Booker T. Washington.

It is hard to conceive that Buddy Holly, at any age, would have been as ostentatiously bold as John Lennon, who in the 1960s, opined that the Beatles were more popular than Jesus Christ. Stardom never appeared to go to Holly's head or disrupt his long-standing relationships. "We loved Buddy. He was a good man and we could never detect that success changed him one bit. He was kind, humble, and excessively nice," recording artist and back-up singer, Gary Tollet, acknowledged. Less than two months before his death, Holly was not only willing to play during a *KLLL* remote radio broadcast, but also set in motion plans for a homecoming concert in Lubbock, the following summer.

In correspondence with the author in May of 2017, Sonny Curtis remembered his long-lost bandmate and close friend: "He was very confident, a great singer, guitarist, song-writer, and fun and exciting to pick with, which made him a trailblazer in rock and roll. His talent was extraordinary and he was a good ole boy."

Holly never failed to share his new-found riches. He frequently gave away his possessions and offered loans, knowing that he would have never made it, without financial assistance from family and friends (all of whom he eventually repaid). Gary Tollet's wife, Ramona, summarized Holly's willingness to give, even when the recipient was less than generous toward him: "He bought church pews with his first royalty check."

Buddy's generosity and kind-hearted nature were accompanied by naivete, particularly in the early stages of his brief career. Eager to become a recording star, an impulsive and overly-trusting Holly was ripe for exploitation by Norman Petty. Buddy and his fellow Crickets allowed the far more-worldly producer to talk them into making unwise decisions about song-writing credits, as well as the collection and distribution of their live performance fees and royalty monies.

When Holly became fully aware that he was being financially exploited by Petty, he was nearly broke. In dire financial straits, Buddy embarked on an ill-advised, but necessary, money-making tour that culminated in his premature death.

Who is to blame for the fatal plane crash on February 3, 1959? Was it the pilot, the charter aviation owner, Buddy's impulsive nature, or a combination of all three? Had Holly and Norman Petty reached a financial settlement, would Buddy have even been a part of the doomed *Winter Dance Party*? Why, oh why?

By the end of his brief career, Buddy was an accomplished singer and musician, prolific song-writer, a burgeoning record producer, and an established road manager. Holly's unique voice and mastery of the guitar, however, are timeless gifts, allowing so many to appreciate a simpler, more innocent time. The late Bill Griggs, founder of the *Buddy Holly Memorial Society*, offered a simple, yet profound explanation of Holly's success as a performer: "People came to see Elvis, but they came to hear Buddy."

KRIB disk jockey, Bob Hale, who emceed Holly's last performance at the Surf Ballroom in Clear Lake, Iowa, offered a thought-provoking character perspective: "Buddy Holly was so far ahead of us, not only in entertainment, but in human relations. He traveled in a bus with African Americans, something, that in 1959, caused gasps from the masses.

Buddy, a Baptist Texan, married a Puerto Rican Catholic. Maria Elena is a beautiful and wonderful woman, but in 1958, it was a bold step and an unlikely pairing. Buddy was way out in front of all of us in every part of his life." "He was a pioneer and ahead of his time in so many ways," opined *New York Times* best-selling author, Jim Riordan, whose books include *Break on Through*—a biography of rock and roller, Jim Morrison.

Holly's personal goal was clear and succinct: "Music is my life. I want people to feel wonderful and great when they hear my music." His efforts have proven to be highly successful. "Whenever you mention his name, it always gets the same reaction—everybody smiles," Bill Griggs added. It is, indeed, difficult to feel sad when listening to Buddy Holly play and sing.

The great unanswered question about Holly's life yet lingers. What if? The late Waylon Jennings offered a ready answer: "I'm often asked, if Buddy Holly lived, where would music have taken him? I politely say that they are asking the wrong question. It should be, if Buddy had lived, where would he have taken music?"

Holly's legacy is enduring. In 1999, Peggy Sue Gerron was still receiving letters from "13-year-olds," inquiring about Buddy's music. That same year, former Cricket, Niki Sullivan, estimated that nearly 700 artists had recorded Buddy Holly's and the Crickets' songs. Over the years, *Not Fade Away* and *Peggy Sue* have waged a nip and tuck battle as to which song has most often been covered by other musical artists.

In the *Rock Encyclopedia*, Lillian Roxon summarized Buddy Holly's enduring legacy: "He was one of the giants of early rock and roll, a figure so important in the history of popular music that it is impossible to hear a song on the charts today that does not owe something to the tall, slim, bespectacled boy from Lubbock, Texas…" "Looking back from the twin peaks of psychedelia and electronic gadgetry, he comes through fresher than ever," Roxon added.

In the early stages of researching this biography, the author encountered a young man, who complained that most of Holly's songs seemed to center around love. In today's world, filled with mass shootings, repeated acts of terrorism, and musical genres that not only glorify violence, but also degrade women, the youthful criticism fell on deaf ears. In the words of Henry David Thoreau: "In a world of peace and love, music would be the universal language."

Buddy Holly truly had it all, except for the gift of time.

BUDDY HOLLY'S SINGLES' DISCOGRAPHY

THE DISCOGRAPHY THAT FOLLOWS LISTS singles in both the U.S. and the U.K. Each entry includes the record (and its flip side), artist (Buddy Holly or the Crickets), record label, year of release, and highest ranking (if the record charted) on the *Billboard* Chart (in the U.S.) or the *Guinness Book of British Hit Singles and Albums* (in the U.K.). Whether the single is a recording by the Crickets or a Buddy Holly single, Holly is the lead vocalist in every recording.

The extended play albums, LPs, eight-track tapes, cassette tapes, compact discs, and music downloads containing songs by both Buddy Holly and the Crickets are far too numerous to be included in this brief discography.

U.S. SINGLES' DISCOGRAPHY:
Blue Days, Black Nights/Love Me, Buddy Holly, Decca, 1956

Modern Don Juan/You Are My One Desire, Buddy Holly, Decca, 1956

That'll Be the Day/I'm Lookin' For Someone to Love, Crickets, Brunswick, 1957, #1

Words of Love/Mailman Bring Me No More Blues, Buddy Holly, Coral, 1957

Rock Around with Ollie Vee/That'll Be the Day, Buddy Holly, Decca, 1957

Peggy Sue/Everyday, Buddy Holly, Coral, 1957, #3

Oh Boy/Not Fade Away, Crickets, Brunswick, 1957, #10

Love Me/ You Are My One Desire, Buddy Holly, Decca, 1958

Listen to Me/I'm Gonna Love You Too, Buddy Holly, Coral, 1958, #56

Maybe Baby/Tell Me How, Crickets, Brunswick, 1958, #17

Rave On/Take Your Time, Buddy Holly, Coral, 1958, #37

Think It Over/Fool's Paradise, Crickets, Brunswick, 1959, #27 and #58

Ting-A-Ling/ Girl on My Mind, Buddy Holly, Decca, 1958

Early in the Morning/Now We're One, Buddy Holly, Coral, 1958, #31

It's So Easy/Lonesome Tears, Crickets, Brunswick, 1958

Heartbeat/ Well All Right, Buddy Holly, Coral, 1958, #82

It Doesn't Matter Anymore/Raining in My Heart, Buddy Holly, Coral, 1959, #13

Peggy Sue Got Married/Crying, Waiting, Hoping, Buddy Holly, Coral, 1959

True Love Ways/That Makes It Tough, Buddy Holly, Coral, 1960

Reminiscing/Wait Til the Sun Shines, Nellie, Buddy Holly, Coral, 1962

Bo Diddley/True Love Ways, Buddy Holly, Coral, 1963, #116

Brown-Eyed Handsome Man/Wishing, Buddy Holly, Coral, #113

Rock Around with Ollie Vee/I'm Gonna Love You Too, Buddy Holly, Coral, 1964

Maybe Baby/Not Fade Away, Buddy Holly, Coral, 1964

What to Do/Slippin' and Slidin', Buddy Holly, Coral, 1965

Rave On/Early in the Morning, Buddy Holly, Coral, 1968

Love is Strange/You're the One, Buddy Holly, Coral, 1969, #105

U.K. SINGLES' DISCOGRAPHY:

That'll Be the Day/I'm Looking for Someone to Love, Crickets, Vogue Coral Q, 1957, #1

Peggy Sue/Everyday, Buddy Holly, Vogue Coral Q, 1957, #6

Oh Boy/Not Fade Away, Crickets, Coral Q, 1958, #3

Listen to Me/I'm Gonna Love You Too, Buddy Holly, Coral Q, 1958, #16

Maybe Baby/Tell Me How, Crickets, Coral Q, 1958, #4

Rave On/Take Your Time, Buddy Holly, Coral Q, 1958, #5

Think It Over/Fool's Paradise, Crickets, Coral Q, 1958, #11

Early in the Morning/Now We're One, Buddy Holly, Coral Q, 1958, #17

It's So Easy/Lonesome Tears, Crickets, Coral Q, 1958

Heartbeat/ Well All Right, Buddy Holly, Coral Q, 1958, #30

It Doesn't Matter Anymore/Raining in My Heart, Buddy Holly, Coral Q, 1959, #1

Midnight Shift/Rock Around with Ollie Vee, Crickets, Brunswick, 1959, #26

Peggy Sue Got Married/Crying, Waiting, Hoping, Buddy Holly, Coral Q, 1959, #13

Heartbeat/Everyday, Buddy Holly, Coral Q, 1960, #30

True Love Ways/Moondreams, Buddy Holly, Coral Q, 1960, #25

Learning the Game/That Makes It Tough, Buddy Holly, Coral Q, 1960, #36

What to Do/That's What They Say, Buddy Holly, Coral Q, 1961, #34

Baby I Don't Care/Valley of Tears, Buddy Holly, Coral Q, 1961, #12

Look at Me/Mailman Bring Me No More Blues, Buddy Holly, Coral Q, 1961

Listen to Me/Words of Love, Buddy Holly, Coral Q, 1962, #48

Reminiscing/Wait Til the Sun Shines, Nellie, Buddy Holly, Coral Q, 1962, #17

Brown-Eyed Handsome Man/Slippin' and Slidin', Buddy Holly, Coral Q, 1963, #3

Bo Diddley/It's Not My Fault, Buddy Holly, Coral Q, 1963, #4

Wishing/Because I Love You, Buddy Holly, Coral Q, 1963, #10

What to Do/ Umm Oh Yeah, Buddy Holly, Coral Q, 1963, #27

You've Got Love/An Empty Cup, Buddy Holly, Coral Q, 1964, #40

Love's Made a Fool of You/You're the One, Buddy Holly, Coral Q, 1964, #39

Maybe Baby/That's My Desire, Buddy Holly, Coral Q, 1966

Peggy Sue/Rave On, Buddy Holly, MCA MU, 1968, #32

True Love Ways, Buddy Holly, MCA, 1988, #65

BIBLIOGRAPHY

Books:

Amburn, Ellis. *Dark Star: The Roy Orbison Story.* Carol Publishing Group, 1990.

Amburn, Ellis. *Buddy Holly: A Biography.* St. Martin's Press, 1995.

Bacon, Tony, and Paul Day. *The Fender Book: A Complete History of Fender Electric Guitars.* GPI Books, 1992.

Barsalona, Frank. *Agents: The Making of Superstars.* Doubleday, 1978.

Bastion, Lam. *Four Celebrity Air Crashes That Killed JFK, Jr., Patsy Cline, John Denver, and Buddy Holly.* Self-Published, 2011.

Bayles, Martha. *Hole in Our Soul: The Loss of Beauty and Meaning in American Popular Music.* The Free Press, 1994.

Belz, Carl. *The Story of Rock.* Oxford University Press, 1969.

Berry, Chuck. *The Autobiography.* Simon & Schuster, 1987.

Bree, Marlin. *In the Teeth of the Northeaster.* Clarkson N. Potter, 1998.

Brunson, Fred. *The Billboard Book of Number One Hits.* Billboard Publications, Inc., 1985.

Clayson, Alan. *Only the Lonely: The Life and Artistic Legacy of Roy Orbison.* Sidgwick & Jackson, 1989.

Dannen, Frederic. *Hit Men: Power Brokers and Fast Money Inside the Music Business.* Times Books, 1990.

Deardoff II, Donald. *Bruce Springsteen: American Poet and Prophet.* Scarecrow Press, 2013.

DeCurtis, Anthony, and James Henke, with Holly George-Warren. *The Rolling Stone Album Guide.* Random House, 1992.

Denisoff, R. Serge. *Waylon.* The University of Tennessee Press, 1983.

DiMucci, Dion, with Davin Seay. *The Wanderer: Dion's Story.* Morrow, 1988.

Dodge, Consuelo. *The Everly Brothers: Ladies Love Outlaws.* CIN-DAY, Inc., 1991.

Dodge, Jim. *Not Fade Away.* Atlantic Monthly Press, 1987.

Eisen, Jonathan, Editor. *The Age of Rock: Songs of the American Cultural Revolution.* Random House, 1969.

Fox, Ted. *Showtime at the Apollo.* Holt, Rineheart, and Winston, 1983.

Freelander, Paul. *Rock and Roll: A Social History.* Westview Press, 1996.

Gerron, Peggy Sue and Glenda Cameron. *Whatever Happened to Peggy Sue?* August Words Publishing, 2015.

Gillett, Charlie. *The Rise of Rock and Roll, 2nd Edition.* Da Caro Press, 1996.

Goldrosen, John. *The Buddy Holly Story.* The Bowling Green University Popular Press, 1975.

Gribbin, John. *Not Fade Away: The Life and Music of Buddy Holly.* Icon Books, LTD, 2009.

Guterman, Jimmy. *The Best Rock 'n' Roll Records of All Time*. Citadel, 1992.

Helander, Brock. *The Rock Who's Who*. Schirmer, 1982.

Jackson, John A. *Big Beat Heat: Alan Freed and the Early Years of Rock & Roll*. Schirmer, 1991.

Jennings, Waylon, with Lenny Kayne. *Waylon: An Autobiography*. Warner Books, Inc., 1996.

Leigh, Spencer. *Everyday: Getting Closer to Buddy Holly*. SAF Publishing, 2009.

Knight, Tim. *Chantilly Lace: The Life and Times of J.P. Richardson*. Port Arthur Historical Society, 1989.

Lehmer, Larry. *The Day the Music Died: The Last Tour of Buddy Holly, The "Big Bopper," and Ritchie Valens*. Schirmer Trade Books, 1997.

Miller, Douglas T., and Marion Nowak. *The Fifties: The Way We Really Were*. Doubleday & Doubleday Inc., 1977.

Monnery, Steve, and Gary Herman. *Rock 'n' Roll Chronicles, 1955-1963*. Longmeadow Press, 1991.

Moore, Gary. *Hey Buddy: In Pursuit of Buddy Holly, My New Buddy John, and My Lost Decade of Music*. Savas Beatie, 2010.

Murrells, Joseph. *Million Selling Records*. Arco, 1984.

Nite, Norm N. *Rock On: The Illustrated Encyclopedia of Rock 'n' Roll*. Thomas Y. Crowell Company, 1974.

Norman, Philip. *Rave On: The Biography of Buddy Holly*. Simon & Schuster, 1996.

Pareles, Jon, and Patricia Romanowski. *The Rolling Stone Encyclopedia of Rock*. Summit Books, 1983.

Shannon, Bob, and John Jauna. *Behind the Hits: Inside Stories of Classic Pop and Rock and Roll*. Warner Books, 1986.

Smith, Joe. *Off the Record: An Oral History of Popular Music*. Warner Books, 1986.

Spitz, Bob. *The Beatles: The Biography*. Little Brown and Company, 2005.

Stallings, Penny. *Rock 'n' Roll Confidential*. Little and Brown, 1984.

Stambler, Irwin. *The Encyclopedia of Pop, Rock, and Soul*. St. Martin's Press, 1989.

Whitburn, Joel. *Hot Country Songs: 1994 to 2008*. Record Research, 2008.

Whitcombe, Ian. *The Rockers: The Age of Rock*. Random House, 1970.

White, Charles. *The Life and Times of Little Richard: The Quasar of Rock*. Harmony, 1984.

Williams, Paul. *Rock 'n' Roll: The 100 Best Singles*. Carroll & Graff, 1993.

OFFICIAL DOCUMENTS:
Civil Aeronautics Board. *Aircraft Accident Report: Beech Bonanza, N3794N*. Washington, DC, September 23, 1959.

VIDEO RESOURCES:

McCartney, Paul. *The Real Buddy Holly Story.* *BBC*-TV, 1987.

VH-1. *The Day the Music Died.* 1999.

WEB RESOURCES:

www.buddyhollyarchives.com

www.buddyhollylives.com

www.buddyhollyonline.com

www.musicbrainz.org

www.telegraph.co.uk

www.angelfire.com

www.clovisnm.chambermaster.org

www.winterdanceparty.com

www.globegazette.com

www.buddyhollycenter.org

www.surfballroom.com

www.everythinglubbock.com

www.lubbockavalanche-journal.com

www.mylubbock.us

www.voicesofoklahoma.com

www.digitallibrary.okstate.edu

www.rockabilly.com

www.rockinsos.com

www.yourbuddyjohn.com

www.buddyandthecrickets.com

www.discogs.com

www.imdb.com

www.obitsforlife.com

www.bbc.newsmagazine.com

www.sonnycurtis.com

www.allmusic.com

www.songwriter.co.uk

www.lubbockonline.com

INTERVIEWS AND WRITTEN CORRESPONDENCE:
Gary Moore

John Mueller

John Skipper

Sherry Holley

Peggy Sue Gerron

Jeff Nicholas

Mallory Huffman

Jacqueline Bober

Bill Wobbeking

Scott Harding

Bob Hale

Sonny Curtis

CONSULTANTS:
Brice Kerr

Chris Fulmer

Phil Gibson

ACKNOWLEDGEMENTS

BECAUSE I AM NEITHER A singer nor a musician, I am grateful for the musical education and stylistic feedback provided by two guitar pickers, a couple of generations apart—Brice Kerr and Chris Fulmer. Both helped me better understand the music I have long appreciated.

I received valuable insights from my aviation consultant, Phil Gibson, who is currently the President of Crosswind Consulting. He clarified numerous questions about aerodynamics, aircraft instrumentation, and hazardous flight conditions.

Gary W. Moore, author of *Hey Buddy*, was generous in sharing the knowledge he accumulated before and after the publication of his excellent book. While I had long-harbored aspirations of writing about Buddy Holly, Gary's book inspired me to undertake this biography. *Hey Buddy* and Gary's other books are on my recommended reading list. Gary, you will always be my Buddy buddy.

John Mueller, the talented musician, singer, and actor, who portrays Buddy Holly on *The Winter Dance Party* tour, was most gracious, sharing his experiences and insights. If you've never heard John perform in person, on his website (www.winterdanceparty.com), or on a *You Tube* video, I highly recommend it.

Sherry Holley was generous in sharing childhood memories of her Uncle Buddy and his influence on her own musical career. To learn more about her performing and visual arts, please visit www.sherryholley.com.

Sonny Curtis provided detailed answers to numerous questions in a generous, friendly west Texas manner. Curtis is a gifted singer, musician, and composer, whose song-writing credits and discography are quite impressive.

Jacqueline Bober, the assistant manager and curator of the *Buddy Holly Center*, located in Buddy's hometown of Lubbock, Texas, was an accommodating host. She patiently answered my questions and further educated me about the various exhibits on display. The entire staff at the *Buddy Holly Center* was gracious and welcoming.

Jeff Nicholas, President of the Surf Ballroom, was gracious with his time and vast knowledge. He provided me with valuable information about the legendary venue, where Buddy Holly played his final concert.

Mallory Huffman, the Education Coordinator at the Surf Ballroom was most helpful. She was kind enough to give a portion of her Saturday morning to conduct a personal and detailed tour of the ballroom for me and my wife.

Veteran reporter and columnist, John Skipper, of Mason City's *Globe-Gazette*, generously answered several questions that I posed to him. He also supplied me with the re-print of column he had written years after the fatal plane crash.

Bob Hale, the disc jockey who emceed Buddy Holly's last performance at the Surf Ballroom, freely shared him memories of that night. His stories were both informative and entertaining.

Bill Wobbeking, was among those in the audience at the Surf Ballroom on February 2, 1959. He was kind enough to share his memories of that night.

Scott Harding, who attended the *Winter Dance Party* concert in Montevideo, Minnesota, vividly recalled events surrounding the January 27, 1959 show. Sadly, the Fiesta Ballroom was destroyed in a fire, just a few years after Holly and the other members of the *Winter Dance Party* performed there.

A special thanks to Peggy Sue Gerron, who graciously and thoughtfully answered all my inquiries. How can you write a biography of Buddy Holly, without communicating with *the* Peggy Sue?

As always, I am indebted to the biographers and rock and roll historians, both living and dead, who traveled this same path ahead of me. They are recognized in the Bibliography.

The passage of time extracts a swift toll. In less than a year, while I was researching and writing this book, several key players in the Buddy Holly story passed away, including Bobby Vee, Chuck Berry, Travis Holley, and Jerry Dwyer.

My biggest regret was the inability to interview or exchange correspondence with Maria Elena Santiago-Holly. Neither of my letters to her were acknowledged. Maria Elena, if you happen to read this book, I trust you will discover that I have fairly and accurately depicted a man I have long-admired.

Yet again, Jim Fulmer gave unselfishly of his time to edit this book, helping shape the story's focus and making my words more readable. This is our 13th book together, and I remain grateful to call Jim my friend.

My brother-in-law, Bobby Chestnut, a South Carolinian by lineage, but a Texan by assimilation, coordinated my visit to Lubbock. He also proved to be an able photographer during the sojourn to west Texas.

As always, my wife Anne was patient and understanding while I was focused on the book at hand; she also took abundant photographs, not only at the Surf Ballroom, but also at the crash memorial site (after good-naturedly walking one-quarter mile down a muddy fence row). I love her very much. My sons, Andy and Ben, remain the lights of my life.

I to continue to thank readers for their support. My "Bringing History Alive" books are intended to be both entertaining and educational. I sincerely hope that you enjoyed *LISTEN TO ME: The Brief Life and Enduring Legacy of Buddy Holly.*

ABOUT THE AUTHOR

Jeffrey K. Smith is a physician and a writer. A native of Enterprise, Alabama, he earned his undergraduate and medical degrees from the University of Alabama. After completing his residency at the William S. Hall Psychiatric Institute, Dr. Smith entered private practice in upstate South Carolina. He and his wife, Anne, reside in Greer, South Carolina, and are the proud parents of two sons, Andy and Ben.

OTHER BOOKS BY JEFFREY K. SMITH

NOVELS:
Sudden Despair

Two Down, Two to Go

A Phantom Killer

NON-FICTION ***BRINGING HISTORY ALIVE*** SERIES:
Rendezvous in Dallas: The Assassination of John F. Kennedy (2nd edition)

The Fighting Little Judge: The Life and Times of George C. Wallace

Fire in the Sky: The Story of the Atomic Bomb

Bad Blood: Lyndon B. Johnson, Robert F. Kennedy, and the Tumultuous 1960s (2nd edition)

Dixiecrat: The Life and Times of Strom Thurmond

The Loyalist: The Life and Times of Andrew Johnson

The Eagle Has Landed: The Story of Apollo 11

The Presidential Assassins: John Wilkes Booth, Charles Julius Guiteau, Leon Frank Czolgosz, and Lee Harvey Oswald

The War on Crime: J. Edgar Hoover Versus the John Dillinger Gang

The Wizard of the Saddle: Nathan Bedford Forrest

You Were Right and We Were Wrong: The Life and Times of Judge Frank M. Johnson, Jr.

Grover Cleveland: The Last Conservative Democratic President

Made in the USA
Columbia, SC
10 June 2017